ADVANCES
IN
SELF PSYCHOLOGY

ADVANCES IN SELF PSYCHOLOGY

Edited by
Arnold Goldberg

With Summarizing Reflections by
Heinz Kohut

International Universities Press, Inc.

New York

Third Printing 1983

Library of Congress Cataloging in Publication Data

Main entry under title:

Advances in self psychology.

   Principally based on a conference on self psychology held in Chicago, Oct. 1978.
   Bibliography: p.
   Includes index.
   1. Self — Congresses.   2. Psychoanalysis —
Congresses, 3. Narcissism — Congresses.   4. Psy-
chology, Pathological — Congresses.   I. Goldberg,
Arnold, 1929-   II. Kohut, Heinz. [DNLM:
1. Narcissism — Congresses.   2. Psychoanalysis —
Congresses.   3. EGO — Congresses.   WM460.5.E3
A244   1978]
BR697.A35   155.2   80-13918
ISBN 0-8236-0098-X

Manufactured in the United States of America

Contents

v

Part III

SELF PSYCHOLOGY AND
ITS CLINICAL APPLICATIONS

Part IV

SELF PSYCHOLOGY AND
THE SCIENCES OF MAN

Part V

TWO LETTERS

Part VI

REFLECTIONS ON
ADVANCES IN SELF PSYCHOLOGY

Acknowledgments

Every book owes a debt. Our own indebtedness is to a significantly large number of readers of the previously published books on self psychology, those who have continued to stimulate the contributors to this volume to work toward advancing the field. The challenge provided by the searching questions of these many readers led us to an international conference. For this, we are grateful to Michael Reese Hospital and, in particular, to Dr. Daniel Offer, for sponsorship.

The gratitude of the contributors to this book extends as well to certain individuals whom we are especially fortunate in having had as helpers: Ms. Chris Histed for her secretarial and editorial help, Mrs. Eva Sandberg for her editorial assistance, and Dr. Paul Stepansky, whose personal friendship and tactful editing made the job so easy.

The preparation of the book was financed by funds from the Harry and Hazel Cohen Research Fund.

Contributors

Sheldon Bach, Ph.D. — Faculty, Training Institute, New York Freudian Society; Associate Professor, New York University, Post Doctoral Program in Psychoanalysis; Clinical Assistant Professor of Psychiatry, Albert Einstein College of Medicine.

Bertram J. Cohler, Ph.D. — Associate Professor, Departments of Behavioral Sciences (Human Development) and Education, University of Chicago.

Mark J. Gehrie, Ph.D. — Director, Laboratory of Social Science, Psychosomatic and Psychiatric Institute, Michael Reese Hospital and Medical Center; Research Associate (Assistant Professor) in Psychiatry, University of Chicago; Faculty, Teacher Education Program, Chicago Institute for Psychoanalysis.

Arnold Goldberg, M.D. — Attending Psychiatrist, Michael Reese Hospital and Medical Center; Clinical Professor of Psychiatry, University of Chicago; Faculty, Training and Supervising Analyst, Chicago Institute for Psychoanalysis.

Meyer S. Gunther, M.D. — Faculty, Training and Supervising Analyst, Chicago Institute for Psychoanalysis; Associate Clinical Professor of Psychiatry, Northwestern University School of Medicine.

Kenneth I. Howard, Ph.D. — Senior Research Associate, Department of Psychiatry, Michael Reese Hospital and Medical Center.

Charles Kligerman, M.D. — Faculty, Training and Supervising Analyst, Chicago Institute for Psychoanalysis.

Heinz Kohut, M.D. — Attending Psychiatrist (Hon.), Michael Reese Hospital and Medical Center; Professorial Lecturer,

Department of Psychiatry, University of Chicago; Faculty,
Training and Supervising Analyst, Chicago Institute for
Psychoanalysis.

Nathaniel J. London, M.D. — Geographic Training Analyst and
Faculty, Chicago Institute for Psychoanalysis; Clinical Professor of Psychiatry, University of Minnesota; Director, Minnesota Psychoanalytic Foundation.

Randall C. Mason, Ph.D. — President, Center for Religion and
Psychotherapy of Chicago; Associate in Religion and
Psychological Studies, Divinity School, University of
Chicago; Adjunct Professor, Pastoral Psychotherapy,
Chicago Theological Seminary.

Kenneth Newman, M.D. — Attending Psychiatrist, Michael Reese
Hospital and Medical Center; Training and Supervising
Analyst, Chicago Institute of Psychoanalysis.

Daniel Offer, M.D. — Chairman, Department of Psychiatry,
Michael Reese Hospital and Medical Center; Professor of
Psychiatry, Pritzker School of Medicine, University of
Chicago.

Paul H. Ornstein, M.D. — Professor of Psychiatry, University of
Cincinnati, College of Medicine; Faculty, Supervising and
Training Analyst, Cincinnati Psychoanalytic Institute.

Eric Ostrov, Ph.D. — Research Associate, Psychosomatic and Psy-
chiatric Institute, Michael Reese Hospital and Medical
Center; Lecturer, Department of Psychology, Roosevelt
University.

Jacques M. Palaci, M.D. — French Psychoanalytic Association;
Consultant, Dejerine Center for Psychosomatic Medicine,
Paris; Emeritus Faculty, National Psychological Association
for Psychoanalysis.

Joachim Scharfenberg, Ph.D. — Professor and Psychoanalyst,
University of Kiel; Pastoral Counselor, Psychoanalytic Institute, Heikendorf, Germany.

Evelyne A. Schwaber, M.D. — Faculty, Boston Psychoanalytic
Society and Institute, and Psychoanalytic Institute of New
England East.

Estelle Shane, Ph.D. — Director, Center for Early Education, Los
Angeles.

Morton Shane, M.D. — Assistant Clinical Professor, UCLA; Training Analyst and Supervising Analyst in Adult and Child Analysis, Los Angeles Psychoanalytic Society and Institute.

Miles F. Shore, M.D. — Bullard Professor and Head, Department of Psychiatry, Massachusetts Mental Health Center, Harvard Medical School.

Robert D. Stolorow, Ph.D. — Associate Professor of Psychology, Ferkauf Graduate School of Humanities and Social Sciences, Yeshiva University; Faculty, Institute of the National Psychological Association for Psychoanalysis.

Charles B. Strozier, Ph.D. — Associate Professor of History, Sangamon State University; Lecturer in Psychiatry, Rush Medical College, Chicago.

David M. Terman, M.D. — Attending Psychiatrist, Michael Reese Hospital and Medical Center; Instructor, Chicago Institute for Psychoanalysis.

Marian Tolpin, M.D. — Faculty, Child Therapy Program, Chicago Institute for Psychoanalysis; Faculty, Training and Supervising Analyst, Chicago Institute for Psychoanalysis.

Paul Tolpin, M.D. — Faculty, Training and Supervising Analyst, Chicago Institute for Psychoanalysis.

Ernest S. Wolf, M.D. — Faculty, Training and Supervising Analyst, Chicago Institute for Psychoanalysis; Assistant Professor of Psychiatry, Northwestern University School of Medicine.

Marvin Zonis, Ph.D. — Director, University of Chicago Center for Middle Eastern Studies; Associate Professor of Human Development, University of Chicago.

Introductory Remarks

ARNOLD GOLDBERG

The contents of this book derive in large part from a conference on self psychology held in Chicago in October, 1978. This was a particularly significant time in the history of self psychology.

Although the studies of the disorders of narcissism and the origins of the psychology of the self are clearly the work of Heinz Kohut, during recent years others have written, discussed, argued, and worried over the issues raised by Kohut, to the point that an international meeting was called in order to facilitate ongoing dialogues in the field. More importantly, concern had arisen in 1978 that Kohut's work embodied "dissent" from traditional psychoanalysis.

When Kohut first wrote about the narcissistic personality disorders, the majority of readers were sufficiently impressed by his clinical insights to realize that his study of a small group of special patients could constitute an addition to the corpus of psychoanalytic clinical knowledge. Even such early acknowledgment was accompanied by serious qualifiers. A clear message was sent out that announced: "This is an interesting description of the treatment of some patients, but it is no more than that and most of us have been implicitly incorporating your insights anyway." A second message subsequently followed that warned of the danger of overconsuming Kohut's ideas, ideas that possibly had to do with mere psychotherapy instead of analysis. The imputation was that Kohut was dissenting from the accepted standards of analysis.

Anyone who was impressed by the first reports of Kohut could see that many of his ideas were not congenial to the accepted tenets of psychoanalysis. His writings elevated the self to a position of new importance but withheld from this concept the grace of easy definition. The very concept of "selfobject" was disturbing because we all knew that objects were other people and other people were objects, and this new idea seemed to defy our common-sense perceptions. Above all, Kohut's ideas generated the lurking fear that much of what had been going on for years in psycho-analytic theory and practice was perhaps in error.

As Kohut continued to write and publish, and as more and more analysts enjoyed clinical success with his ideas, opposing ideas likewise gained coherence and strength. The dissent was clear. Self psychology was at odds with classical psychoanalysis. This perceived opposition, however, was not inherently unde-sirable. As Karl Popper (1963) has said: "In order that a new theory should constitute a discovery or a step forward, it should conflict with its predecessor; that is to say, it should lead to at least some conflicting results. But this means, from a logical point of view, that it should contradict its predecessor; it should overthrow it. In this sense, progress in science — or at least striking progress — always is revolutionary."

And there was the problem to be addressed by the 1978 con-ference. Were Kohut's discoveries tantamount to fine adjustments of extant psychoanalytic theory or were they representative of the genuine progress of our science? The conference could not fail to address this issue and could do so only in the form of multiple dia-logues and discussions over a wide range of topics relevant to self psychology. The idea of progress cannot be declared by fiat and the voice of progress cannot be stilled. Especially in psycho-analysis, the status accorded to new ideas is a very personal deci-sion reached after much study and often with much discomfort.

Our hope is that the reader will judge this book in terms of the concept of progress, and understand many of the theses propounded as contrasting significantly with established psychoanalytic assumptions. Each section of the book is relevant to this issue, containing contributions that either attempt to bridge classical concepts with new ideas from self psychology, expand classical psychoanalytic positions, or, finally, insist on the necessity of an entirely new method of conceptualization. Advances in self psychology occur on each of these three fronts.

Initially, as self psychology concentrated on disorders of narcissism, it was seemingly content to work within the framework of the classical theory that treated the self as a content of the psychic apparatus. Eventually, however, the clinical material led to a revision from the narrow viewpoint of self pathology as a problem for some people at some times to the understanding of the self as a concern to everyone on occasions and to some people all the time. The theory, as revised and expanded by Kohut, gave us the option of considering the self in both a broad sense and a narrow sense. Further revisions will undoubtedly refine the definition of the self within psychoanalysis, and at present we offer more of a progress report than a final resolution of the issue. At this juncture, when we speak of advances in self psychology, we are referring to proposed theoretical changes deriving from clinical findings which, in turn, have occasioned the reexamination of traditional theory. We are not only dealing with a different perception of the self of psychoanalysis but, inevitably, we are led to ever-changing perspectives on our clinical practice.

It should be noted that the questions and criticisms of self psychology pertaining to its alleged "deviation" from many of the accepted tenets of psychoanalysis are not always answered in the spirit of this presentation of "advances" in the field. Questions regarding the role ascribed to empathy in psychoanalysis, the ability of psychoanalytic therapy to ameliorate so-called deficiencies in psychic structure, and the central status of the narcissistic transferences are all touched on in the presentations in this volume. Certain theoretical issues are less well represented in the present volume, and no single question seems more germane to these issues than that relating to the theoretical status of the self. Although the self has been repeatedly defined and elaborated by Kohut in his writings (1977), and although a definition more precise than that supplied by Kohut is perhaps not feasible at this stage of the theory, a need still exists to elaborate the way the self of self psychology moves away from the previous comprehensive definitions of leading psychoanalytic scholars. To this end, a very brief overview of theories of the self in psychoanalysis is in order. Such a review will orient the reader to the successive steps that have eventuated in a new theoretical stance.

Although Kohut initially felt it prudent to define self only as "an important content [of] the mental apparatus, i.e., as self-representations (imagoes) of the self located within the ego, the id, and the superego" (1970, p. 588), he soon found it necessary to abandon this restricted definition. The role of the constituents of the self, the development of the cohesive self, and the necessity for the comprehension of total configurations in empathic closures all demanded that a broader and more significant role be ascribed to the self of psychoanalysis. As we shall see, the advancing work of self psychology has thus served to modify our understanding of what the self is, and present formulations are a far cry from the simple concept of a self image first considered by psychoanalysis. A recent working definition that we can utilize as a guide is that of Kohut and Wolf (1978). They state that "the patterns of ambitions, skills, and goals, the tensions between them, the program of action they create, and the activities that strive toward the realization of this program are all experienced as continuous in space and time...they are the self, an independent center of initiative, and independent recipient of impression." Thus we see the scope of the journey that self psychology has taken in its conceptual expansion.

In his "Comments on the Psychoanalytic Theory of the Ego" (1950), Heinz Hartmann made a significant, early attempt to clarify the psychoanalytic meaning of the self. He equated the self with one's own person, and he proceeded to differentiate the self from objects just as the ego, as a psychic system, was differentiated from other substructures of the personality. Hartmann's use of the term "objects," it should be stressed, referred to cathexes of representations and not cathexes of real people, just as Freud himself had originally differentiated between the mental presentations of objects *(Vorstellungen)* and the objects themselves (see

Editor's footnote to Freud, 1905, p. 217, fn. 2). In a subsequent "Contribution to the Metapsychology of Schizophrenia" (1953), Hartmann noted that object relations must proceed from an initial inability to distinguish between objects and activities to a later differentiation between the activity and the object toward which the activity is directed. Ultimately, he pointed out, the self as well is sharply distinguished from objects.

Over the years, a series of difficulties arose from Hartmann's seemingly clear and simple theoretical statement. In the first place, the simple delineation of the self as one's own person has led many philosophers to the exceedingly complex problem of what a person is—a person consists of both mind and body as well as a network of social relationships. When Kohut discovered the clinical prevalence of people using other people as (functional) parts of themselves, he seemed to corroborate what many nonanalysts had been saying for many years, and he likewise underscored the fact that just as the mental self is by no means equivalent to the physical self, so the question of what a "person" is remains problematic. Nowhere was this more clearly demonstrated than in his study of the emergence of selfobject transferences which, by their very existence, demanded a revised definition of the self in psychoanalysis.

The second problem that confounded Hartmann's statement is the realization that development does not seem to proceed to an ultimate eradication of the functional use of objects as selfobjects. In light of this fact, we are confronted with the possibility that the self of psychoanalysis is really the representation of the person in terms of a multitude of functional and lasting relationships with others. If we but take the next step suggested by Roy Schafer (1968, p. 60) and change the word "representation," which often seems confused with a miniaturized replica, to that of "idea," then the self becomes the idea one has of one's relationships with others, with those who continue to sustain and support and satisfy.

The theoretician who has previously dealt most exhaustively with the problems of the self vis-à-vis others is Edith Jacobson, and her major work, *The Self and the Object World* (1964), was the natural successor to Hartmann's initial clarifications. For Jacobson, the self was no more than its representations, both physical and mental, and in much of her book these representations were equated with images or inner pictures of the person (perhaps a loose translation of imago). The self image was initially either fused with object images or otherwise distorted. As development proceeded, one hoped to arrive at a clear and realistic inner picture of a separate self. Jacobson viewed drives as predominant factors in self representations, and she held that clear differentiations from others were the goals achieved by drive regulation and neutralization. She faithfully followed Hartmann's position that the self emerges only vis-à-vis objects, and her work is undoubtedly the basis of many object relations theories that see the self and objects in terms of a multitude of developing relationships. It is a relatively simple matter to transpose external happenings into a framework of internal relationships, and much theory has remained content with this kind of straightforward endeavor. However, as analytic work on the self progressed, it became evident that self images were but temporary printouts or readouts of very complex configurations, much as a computer delivers a reading that is but a minute reflection of the internal network of activity. The metaphor of internal stages and inner images of the self often could not do justice to some (or most) of these complexities. How, for example, does one picture or "image" a self that is dedicated to and idealizes the pursuit of psychoanalytic knowledge? Certainly such "complex configurations" (Kohut, 1959) seem to demand detailed descriptions or different modes of presentation altogether. These complexities further direct our attention to the very developmental processes that are inherent in the process of idealization. The advances that Kohut offered in this area consist of both the delineation and the description of the two major forms of narcissism—the grandiose self and the idealized parental imago—as well as the detailing of the changing maturational steps each form can undergo. Thus representations become, more convincingly than ever, not mere images but "ideas" about the self or, better still, the various meanings attributed to the self.

The other theoretical questions raised by the burgeoning

literature of self psychology concern criticisms that have long troubled psychoanalysis, criticisms that psychoanalytic concepts are scientificially weak and that psychoanalytic theory postulates entities where none exist. Rather than address this broad issue as it relates to the entire analytic field, I will concentrate mainly on the criticism pertaining to the supposed reification of the self. Of course, any science must be granted the use of metaphors and a corresponding construction of hypothetical entities where these facilitate comprehension of its subject matter. We should also realize that the construction of entities often characterizes a later rather than earlier stage of scientific growth (see Moore, 1957). The consideration of the self as an entity is a popular and necessary construction in the pursuit of our science as well as other sciences. The trouble with "the self" is that it is a term shared by many disciplines and therefore easy to misunderstand. It is initially important to concentrate on the self of psychoanalysis and to separate it from the self of sociology and anthropology most closely connected with the work of George Herbert Mead. When we equate the self with the person, we are not referring to the person of Mead's social field. It is equally mistaken, as both Hartmann and Kohut have warned, to equate the self with the ego. The easier equation of the self with the mind or with the sum-total of mental operations is, to the psychoanalyst, equally in error. The self as the concept of the mind, that is, how one conceives of one's mental operations, is a less clear but probably equally faulty definition, inasmuch as large areas of mental operations and contemplation about them seem to exist without self participation. As analysts, we must grasp the comprehensiveness of the person in both his phenomenological and unconscious dimensions, and we must delineate the nature of the matrix of relationships that leads to the emergence of this entity. As Loewald (1978, p. 502) says: "If we use the term object relations for any and all psychic interactions of objectively distinguishable human beings, regardless of whether or not instincts and ego are differentiated from object, then the primary datum for a genetic, psychoanalytic psychology would be object relations. This relatedness is the psychic matrix out of which intrapsychic instincts and ego, and extrapsychic object, differentiate." Self psychology more than any other branch of psychoanalytic inquiry is fundamentally involved with the meaning of these relationships, but self psychology, following Loewald, also insists on an analytic rather than interpersonal understanding of object relationships.

No doubt many psychoanalysts will balk at this growth of the self in the direction of inclusiveness, as well as at the possible tendency of this self to become a social or interpersonal phenomenon rather than an intrapsychic one. Kohut (1968, pp. 471n–472n) was among the first psychoanalysts to insist on the distinction between interpersonal and analytic data when he underscored the difference between the self and identity (Gedo & Goldberg, 1973, p. 64). The latter is a social phenomenon that is not a focus of analytic treatment, while the self of psychoanalysis reveals itself only in the analytic experience. Fortunately, psychoanalysis can turn to its own data to clarify this distinction. In this regard, the crucial clinical question that analysts must address is whether or not any form of selfobject transference does exist and, if so, whether or not this transference is modified by the analytic process. Some analysts seem to accept the first point, but insist that such transferences are either unaffected by analysis or, when effectively handled, lead to a clearer separation of the self from the object. The latter point preserves some distinction between narcissism and object love but, again, one is soon *clinically* confronted with a change or maturation in the selfobject relationship without the accompanying differentiation between self and object that, according to traditional psychoanalysis, is theoretically essential. Here, again, one must wrestle with the clinical evidence in supporting or denying the contention that narcissism has a developmental path of its own. Thus, what Hartmann perceived as an issue of separation between the self and object has, through self psychology, taken on the added dimension of accounting for selfobjects that maintain contact with the self but are subject to a changing relationship with the self.

Other analytic theorists, in their efforts to move away from rigid conceptualizations of psychic structure that suggest space-occupying entities, have argued for a grouping of functions that

place action and activity in the forefront of mental life. As
Loewald (1978, p. 497) has observed, however, such groupings
tend to ignore the fact that we should and do treat psychic structures as organizations rather than as mere collections, and we
thus need to insist that psychic structures have properties that go
beyond their individual and grouped functions. In this spirit, the
self of psychoanalysis, as conceptualized by self psychology, is a
collective noun. It includes a variety of functions having to do
with self-esteem regulation, but it likewise has properties and
features of its own. Though it may suffer the popular fate of being reified or anthropomorphized, it is primarily a generalization
derived from a wide group of observable empirical data. Of
course, an attempt at definition should not lead us to fall prey to
the error of believing that a clarification of our scientific
language alone can remedy the incomplete state of our
knowledge. Only further investigations will enable us to refine
our conceptualizations in order to accommodate better the
clinical data.

Most psychoanalysts would seem to agree that self representations are the changing and varied concepts that are constitutive of
one's person. From the standpoint of self psychology, we can now
reconsider the troublesome question of just what a person (not a
physical body) may be. We are often warned against equating this
person with a tiny homunculus inside our head who will direct as
well as experience life for us. Unfortunately, this latter form of explanation remains prevalent, especially among object relations
theorists, and it has the seductive appeal (mentioned above) of
merely transposing external events into an internal theater.
Through self psychology, however, we have learned to approach
relations not merely as what goes on between people, but in terms
of the significance and meanings that become attached to the "go-
ings on."[1] Our definition of the person will necessarily take the self
as the locus of relationships. Psychoanalysis may well become the

---

[1] In a general sense, self psychology, like Paul Ricoeur, focuses on meaning.
In contrast to Ricoeur's hermeneutic approach, self psychology distinguishes between new meanings and hidden meanings (hermeneutics) and gains its data from
analytic exchange (Goldberg, in Panel, 1979).

basis of a theory of persons that will include both the conscious and the unconscious elements of such a theory. The changes of meanings over time will most likely launch us into an inquiry that allows psychoanalysis to emerge as a psychology of meaning and, therefore, as a discipline that studies the growth and development of this particularly human phenomenon. To justify the analytic quality of our investigations, however, we will always have to insist on the role of unconscious and disavowed meanings in human relations.

The retention of the metaphor of the internal stage or the drama of inner persons in interaction puts psychoanalysis in danger of adopting a form of role theory, albeit an internal one, as its underpinning. Psychoanalysis, however, has never been content to take the position of a role theory that concentrates on overt or manifest roles or behavioral criteria and thereupon ignores the unconscious components of behavior. Although this kind of theory can be enriched by including unconscious roles, it may still inhibit a comprehension of the complexity of human relationships. If, for example, a student speaks to a teacher or a patient questions a doctor, we can usually perceive that these obvious roles may conceal the fact that a child-parent relationship is also set in motion. In fact, this insight of the implicit role(s) of a participant in any sort of meaningful relationship was the first great revelation of psychoanalytic psychology and over the years it has become commonplace. When we add to this very general orientation those particulars of a relationship having to do with development, we take the next great step toward a full analytic comprehension of the hidden roles being enacted, i.e., we learn just what sort of a child lurks in the shadows. Yet, not until we investigate the nature of the exchange do we ever feel that we become truly "psychoanalytic" investigators. Of course, merely watching the person's interactions is never sufficient. Taking into account the components of language, nuance, gesture, etc., serves to enlarge the range of comprehension, but still does not suffice. Ultimately, we must consider the effect one person has on another. What are the feelings involved? How does the one person expect to alter and be altered by the other? In brief, we must consider the nature of the personal experience, the subjective meaning of the interchange. The hidden role of the child talking to a parent simply does not reveal the data in a form that is of analytic interest. Rather, it is merely an aid to orienting oneself in the determination of what this person must feel as both student or patient *plus* child in this interaction. Thus, role theory is notoriously limited for psychoanalysis and to say that the internal drama is the real story behind the external one merely informs us who the real "actors" are, without explaining just what kind of drama is being enacted. One must take the step required by the complexity of the exchange and investigate it via a theory of meaning that is more comprehensive than a theory of inner actors who both replicate and complicate the happenings of the external world.

This is not the place to resolve the many issues inherent in a reconceptualization of the self as a series of relationships with others. Such issues shade into the broader problems of a meaning psychology altogether. Suffice it to say that self psychology seems to offer a clinical approach that solves the dilemma presented by a theory of inner agents directing our life while concentrating on the understanding of personal meanings rather than drive gratifications. Any series of relationships or actions demands some consideration of an agent, but we probably can accomplish this without reifying unduly our conception of the self. This is best achieved by recalling that psychological life as studied by psychoanalysis is always an introspective investigation of complex configurations, and that such configurations are matrices of meanings. We understand the self as a locus of relationships, empirically observed via vicarious introspection and understood via one or another of the analytic models used to approximate reality.

The papers of this symposium do not consider all the theoretical issues posed by self psychology, but they incorporate the recent reconceptualizations that have carried psychoanalysis beyond the earliest, problematic definitions of the self.

A separate section on development begins with a paper by Morton and Estelle Shane. It contrasts the various developmental theories of the self and presents material that may be profitably correlated with Kohut's observations at the end of the book. The

Shanes' presentation elicits the thoughtful discussion of Marian
Tolpin. The centrality of the developmental perspective is also
stressed by Bertram Cohler, and his concerns are echoed in Ernest
Wolf's original survey of development as approached from the
selfobject point of view. The section on health approaches the recurrent question that psychoanalysis has addressed via Freud, Hartmann, and now Kohut: how does one assess matters of sickness, cure,
and health? Paul Ornstein carefully reviews the accepted criteria and
proposes important changes. His presentation elicits the thoughtful
remarks of Robert Stolorow. Meyer Gunther, with equal care, reviews the concept of aggression in relation to health while Daniel
Offer, with Eric Ostrov and Kenneth Howard, introduces a helpful
comparative perspective to the dialogue.

Turning to clinical matters, we begin with a case presentation by
Evelyne Schwaber which is discussed, in turn, by Paul Tolpin (with a
rejoinder from Schwaber), Sheldon Bach, Kenneth Newman, and
Miles Shore. Paul Tolpin next presents an illuminating reassessment
of the borderline concept from the standpoint of self psychology.
This is followed by a more theoretical discussion by Jacques Palaci on
the status of self psychology as psychotherapy. Palaci's paper
prompts Nathaniel London's wide-ranging reflections on psychoanalysis and psychotherapy, and the section concludes with David
Terman's reconsideration of the genesis and status of object love.

The final section of the book deals with applied analysis from the
standpoint of self psychology, and includes papers by Mark Gehrie,
Charles Kligerman, Charles Strozier, Randall Mason, Joachim
Scharfenberg, and Marvin Zonis.

The book concludes with a section of material by Kohut. This includes two clarifying letters written to colleagues along with a summary commentary on the contents of this volume that may be taken as
the current crossroad that the psychology of the self has reached.

It is appropriate at this point to quote at length the remarks of
Alex Kaplan, then President of the American Psychoanalytic
Association, at the conference from which this volume originated:

> In the past 15 years, psychoanalysis as a science, a
> theory, and a clinical practice has faced increasing criticism

both from within the ranks of our own psychoanalytic colleagues as well as from external sources. The overwhelming acceptance of psychoanalysis which followed the success of psychoanalytically oriented psychiatry in World War II resulted in an upward surge in the number of psychoanalytically oriented departments of psychiatry, psychoanalytic institutes, societies, and analysts. However, by the early and mid-sixties, there appeared to be a reduction in the number of applicants applying for psychoanalytic training (more especially true of some institutes). This trend paralleled a similar decrease in the number of graduate analysts applying for membership to the American Psychoanalytic Association. Critical comments concerning the lack of substantial proof of treatment success (outcome studies) in psychoanalysis were coupled with the concern over the inability to prove or disprove the basic theories of psychoanalysis since they were not available for validated research. These last comments often were directed to the metapsychological theories of psychoanalysis (nonexperiential) which up to that time seemed to be in the forefront of psychoanalytic thinking, writing, and teaching, while the clinical psychological theories and observations as regards psychoanalytic practice (experiential) often were neglected. Most often criticisms concerning the metapsychological theories were directed to the structural theory of psychoanalysis, the economic theory with its concept of psychic energy (bound and neutralized), and the instinctual drive theory.

Kohut, in *The Restoration of the Self* (1977), conjectured that the lack of significant empathic parenting in our modern day society might be responsible for the prevailing alterations in personality development and the personality disorders now being referred for psychoanalytic treatment as well as for the reduction of the numbers of classical neurotics being seen. While I accept the viewpoint that social and cultural changes do have an effect on personality development, I am not able to accept the premise that parents 50 years ago or 100 years ago were any more empathic than they are today. What I feel has changed are our psychoanalytic theories of personality from id to ego and now to self psychology which have modified our understanding of personality and psychopathology.

Besides our changed psychoanalytic understanding of the significance of the child's earlier years, there has been a gradual abandonment of some of the older metapsychological theories which no longer seem to be as useful for our understanding of normal and abnormal psychopathology. Indeed, the development of new clinical psychological and "experience-near" metapsychological theories of the mind, of which the psychology of the self is a most significant advance in psychoanalysis today, has forced us to reevaluate our understanding of the prevailing personality structure of our analytic patients and to modify our analytic treatment procedures. But more importantly, these clinical impressions, as regards the reduced numbers or absence of classical neuroses, need to be validated by adequate clinical research.

Obviously giving up old paradigms is not carried out without controversy and much strain. This can be noted in Kohut's description of his proposed metatheories related to the psychology of the self in his first book, *The Analysis of the Self* as compared to the newer theories described in *The Restoration of the Self*. Arnold H. Modell, in his review of several books on the nature of psychoanalytic knowledge, paraphrases Kuhn and Polanyi: "When a discipline in Kuhn's terms shares a paradigm, controversy is essential to its progress. But when the controversy involves the fundamental assumptions of the paradigm, the identity of the group is split so that the opposing parties no longer share a conceptual framework. The same range of experience takes the shape of different facts and different evidence." When this occurs, there is no longer a common language and no longer a possibility for communication. It is quite possible that this kind of splintering polarization is now occurring in psychoanalysis. I am in agreement with these comments but feel that giving up old paradigms, no longer useful in our understanding of psychoanalytic knowledge, will accelerate the acceptance of the centrality of our clinical psychological theories and encourage their development.

I feel we are in the process of developing a more comprehensive clinical psychological theory of the "self" or the "person" with more emphasis on early character development. The continuing flow of articles and books by Kohut, Goldberg, A. Ornstein, P. Ornstein, M. Tolpin, P. Tolpin, Wolf, Settlage, Kernberg, and others, is adding a new dimension to our psychoanalytic understanding of growth and development. Based more strongly on clinical observations, a new frontier in psychoanalysis has been opened up. However, the clinical observations on the psychology of the self have also been related to metatheories. Whether these new metatheories of the self will serve as an adequate explanation for the newly constructed clinical concepts, or again be unnecessary generalizations, remains to be tested.

The essays that await the reader are the inevitable results of a new way of looking at things. For some they will espouse a new point that is simply a revision of classical psychoanalytic theory; for others their approach will indeed be revolutionary. Whichever standpoint the reader adopts, he will have reason to take heart at the continued vitality of psychoanalysis.

References

Freud, S. (1905), Three Essays on the Theory of Sexuality. *Standard Edition,* 7:135–243. London: Hgarth Press, 1953.

Gedo, J. & Goldberg, A. (1973), *Models of the Mind.* Chicago: University of Chicago Press.

Hartmann, H. (1950), Comments on the Psychoanalytic Theory of the Ego. In: *Essays on Ego Psychology.* New York: International Universities Press, 1964, pp. 113–141.

————— (1953), Contribution to the Metapsychology of Schizophrenia. In: *Essays on Ego Psychology.* New York: International Universities Press, 1964, pp. 182–206.

Jacobson, E. (1964), *The Self and the Object World.* New York: International Universities Press.

Kohut, H. (1959), Introspection, Empathy, and Psychoanalysis. In: *The Search for the Self,* vol. 1, ed. P. Ornstein. New York: International Universities Press, 1978, pp. 205–232.

_____ (1968), The Evaluation of Applicants for Psychoanalytic Training. In: *The Search for the Self,* vol. 1, ed. P. Ornstein. New York: International Universities Press, 1978, pp. 461–475.

_____ (1970), Discussion of "The Self: A Contribution to Its Place in Theory and Technique" by D. C. Levin. In: *The Search for the Self,* vol. 2, ed. P. Ornstein. New York: International Universities Press, 1978, pp. 577–588.

_____ (1977), *The Restoration of the Self.* New York: International Universities Press.

_____ & Wolf, E. (1978), The Disorders of the Self and Their Treatment: An Outline. *Internat. J. Psycho-Anal.,* 59:413–426.

Loewald, H. (1978), Instinct Theory, Object Relations, and Psychic-Structure Formation. *J. Amer. Psychoanal. Assn.,* 26:493–506.

Moore, M. S. (1957), Some Myths about "Mental Illness." *Arch. Gen. Psychiat.,* 33:1483–1497.

Panel (1979), Conceptualizing the Nature of the Therapeutic Action of Psychoanalysis, reported by M. Scharfman. *J. Amer. Psychoanal. Assn.,* 27:627–642.

Popper, K. (1963), *Conjectures and Refutations: The Growth of Scientific Knowledge.* New York: Harper & Row.

Schafer, R. (1968), *Aspects of Internalization.* New York: International Universities Press.

Part I

SELF PSYCHOLOGY
AND DEVELOPMENT

Introduction

MORTON SHANE AND ESTELLE SHANE

The following papers on development address the challenge that self psychology poses to other psychoanalytic theories. Two of the papers take opposite positions regarding the feasibility of amalgamating self psychology with more traditional views. The Shanes, consistent with their assignment for the Chicago conference, attempt such an integration. Using data on development of the self drawn from self psychology, from psychoanalytically based infant and child observations, and from cognitive-developmental psychology, they identify three separate categories of data — reconstructive, subjective, and objective data — depending on the mode of observation that is employed. They then construct lines of self development from each of these vantage points. Their thesis is that a single line of self development can profitably be constructed based on points of congruence among these contrasting viewpoints, and that this line represents the psychoanalytic self of the individual patient as it is encompassed in the mind of his analyst.

Bertram Cohler, on the other hand, argues against such an integration. He contrasts Kohut's empathic-introspective method with the more traditional empirical methods utilized in infant and child observation. He stresses the primacy of the patient's subjective experience in the analytic setting as an indispensable feature of

19

self psychology, and he asserts that this very emphasis on subjectivity is not consistently maintained in infant and child observation. Such an empathic-introspective stance in infant and child observation is a prerequisite for the useful incorporation of such observations into a theory of development based on self psychology.

In his summary reflections on this volume, Heinz Kohut takes a position in agreement with Cohler's, while taking issue with the Shanes' attempt at integration. He feels an integration of developmental theories is not possible for one overriding reason: the traditional view of development, as enunciated by Mahler, is not consistent with the self psychological discovery of the individual's lifelong need for selfobjects. A theory of development that posits increasing autonomy and independence from objects as a condition for the fulfillment of self needs cannot be integrated, in Kohut's mind, with a theory of development that views such needs as present and legitimate throughout life, that is, throughout all stages of development.

Marian Tolpin postulates that the concept of the evolving self is a primary configuration. It is her position that the discoveries of self psychology do not form a continuum with earlier psychoanalytic perspectives on the self and cannot be readily integrated with the work of Mahler and others because, in the final analysis, the conclusions of these observers are colored by the Kleinian theoretical framework they bring to their observations—a framework that views infancy as a state to which conflict is basic and assigns to the infant's mind experiential, perceptual, and abstractive functions of which the infant is demonstrably incapable. By implication she also contests the view that self psychology can be integrated with traditional metapsychology, which she sees as a theory of conflict rather than of development.

Completing the section on development is Ernest Wolf's paper adumbrating a developmental line of selfobjects. His contribution represents an elaboration of what both Cohler and Kohut commend: a developmental psychology that expands on the findings of self psychology, derived from the analytic situation with adults. The need for selfobjects throughout life is outlined. The self in the wider sense of a superordinate framework is implied in Wolf's discussion, but this concept is not essential to his thesis.

Far from being disturbed by the differences of opinion expressed in this section, readers should take heart; the differences testify to the health of our scientific approach. Our methods are similar — introspection and empathy guide our approach to the patient. What the discoveries made in this way signify, however, remains open to debate. In any event, the important issues that crystallize for us must, and will, stimulate further discussion.

Psychoanalytic Developmental Theories of the Self: An Integration

MORTON SHANE AND ESTELLE SHANE

The topic of this paper is an integration of developmental theories of the self. We will present the lines of development of three separate categories of self derived from three separate data sources: the self derived from the data of introspection, which for purposes of economy we will term *the subjective self;* the self derived from the data of observation, termed *the objective self;* and the self derived from the data of analytic reconstruction, termed *the reconstructed self.*

We think it important to delineate these three separate selves in order to recognize the limited nature of their respective data bases. Once this is done, it becomes possible to integrate the constructs derived from them and assess their validity in terms of the degree of congruity. Congruence among the developmental lines of the self generates *the psychoanalytic self,* comprised as it is of multiple vantage points and providing as it does an in-depth view, incorporating objectivity, subjectivity, reconstructed personal history, and developmental progression.

We think it is worthwhile to begin by explaining our approach to the material since, as is apparent to anyone familiar with current psychoanalytic thinking, there is an enormous literature on the self and its concomitant theories. Our first task, therefore, is to establish criteria that will aid in determining the comparative usefulness of this abundant material. We accept the following criteria for evaluating theoretical relevance:

1. The psychoanalytic theory adheres to cognitive, biological, neurological, and linguistic limits. This has been a difficult problem for psychoanalysts as much of the conventional wisdom of the field is dated, but nevertheless retained. For example, the infant's capacity for hallucinatory wish fulfillment, a basic tenet of Freud's thinking in 1900, continues to serve as an underlying assumption of some psychoanalytic theories of the self, though it exceeds currently accepted cognitive limits (Basch, 1975; Wolff, 1967).

2. The terms and concepts of psychoanalytic theory should have as referents observable data. High-level abstractions that lose their connections to the phenomena falter in usefulness. For example, theories of drive discharge that do not correlate the introspective sensual experience of children and grownups can be misleading, and fail to facilitate further observation and theory expansion (Klein, 1969).

3. A consistent vantage point in data collection and theoretical explanation must be sought, and discrepancies consciously accounted for. Psychoanalytic data of necessity bridge the two vantage points of introspection and observation. Many psychoanalytic terms obscure this difficult distinction. For example, the sense of self, a highly subjective experience, has been described in objective terms without sufficient account taken for the discrepancy between subjective and objective accounts, as has the concept of drive "tension," which blurs wish and biological needs (Grossman & Simon, 1969).

4. Parsimony, a well-known tenet of theory building, is especially relevant to this discussion of the self, inasmuch as we postulate three separate "selves." Let us restate here that we formulate them only as a heuristic device, aiming toward their integration.

We will turn now to a second problem. To talk about developmental theories of the self implies that there is such a thing as an agreed-upon entity termed *the self*. Unfortunately, this is not the case. The self can be defined as either *within* the psychic apparatus, *superordinate to* the psychic apparatus, *synonymous with* the psychic apparatus, or none of these. It can be defined merely as *an action* of the person, or finally, as *standing for* the person per se. And what about the concept of *identity,* or even worse, *ego identity?* These concepts, even more than the *self,* have been hazily placed *within, above, around,* and *about* the *personality* or the *person,* with even less effort expended at being specific. Some writers have used both concepts, *self* and *identity,* interrelating them in a number of ways. Merely to sort out all of these uses would take a major effort, and in any case is beyond the scope not only of this writing, but also of these writers.

What we will do is define the self as we use it when the objective, the subjective, the reconstructed, and finally the psychoanalytic selves are spoken of. We will also "place" the self within the psychological person.

For the purposes of this paper, the psychoanalytic self is defined as the psychological person (i.e., the person conceptualized in the psychological realm of discourse) as it exists in the mind, conscious and unconscious, of the psychoanalyst. It is conceptualized via complementarity (Gedo & Goldberg, 1973; Kohut, 1977) as roughly coterminous with the psychic apparatus (the tripartite model of the mind) and yet as more easily abstracted from clinical data (Meissner, quoted in Panel, 1976). For example, a sense of continuity within the person is closely linked to what has been abstracted as a cohesive self, and more remotely linked to the abstraction of the synthetic function of the ego. Comparably, the phenomenon of self-approval for a specific action can be abstracted as heightened self-esteem, and more distantly abstracted as the ego ideal aspect of the superego cathecting self representations. Finally the wish to be indiscriminately admired and loved can be conceptualized as grandiose and exhibitionistic experiences of the self with a selfobject, and conceptualized more remotely in terms of drive discharge and the relative distribution of narcissistic and object libido.

One might well question why, given the utility of the self abstraction in describing the data in more experiential terms, one retains the structural model at all. However tempting the prospect, we do not feel it is possible for analysts at this time to escape easily from the structural delineation of id, ego, and superego, and the accompanying perspective on conflicts and defenses. Kohut has retained the tripartite psychic apparatus in his models of the mind via the principle of complementarity, viewing the self in the narrow sense as housed within the psychic apparatus in the form of self representations. And while Kohut has proposed the self in the broad sense as a new, alternative model of the mind, a model that keeps the experiential self in the center of all therapeutic endeavors, one can nevertheless detect the shadow of the tripartite model and the possibility of conflict in the unbroken and nonconflictual continuum of ambitions, skills, and ideals that characterize the new model. Schafer (1976, 1978), too, in his attempt to write a new language for psychoanalysis, shunning all abstractions of the person per se, has these persons active adverbially in superego modes, in id modes, and in primitive ego modes. The abstraction of the tripartite model would seem to be inherent in the activities of Schafer's person.

Second, and more important for the purposes of this paper, we have used self as roughly coterminous with psychic apparatus in order to achieve integration of some useful theories of development of the self, several of which are couched in traditional theoretical formulations.

The tripartite mental apparatus that we accept, however, is one purged for the most part of the deficiencies plaguing it since its inception and incorporating those new insights most useful to an understanding of its nature and function. Were we to quote the myriad of thinkers who have either criticized or contributed to the formulation of this refined and elaborated structure, we would have to include the majority of significant psychoanalytic writers of the past 10 years. This streamlined, clinically grounded psychic apparatus encompasses an id conceptualized in noneconomic terms, made up of peremptory wishes and ambitions categorized broadly as sensual or aggressive, and emerging in relation to significant objects in a predictable epigenetic sequence. It encompasses an ego viewed as a basically nonmechanistic aggregate of functions with defensive and adaptive uses, including skills and talents. Lastly, it includes a superego developed from precursors of idealized parent imagoes, punitive parent imagoes, and projected ideal states of one's person, all of which coalesce around the time of the resolution of the Oedipus complex. The whole mental apparatus is built up over time by internalizations of significant object relationships which coalesce gradually into basic unities of self-cohesiveness and object constancy.

At this point we will address ourselves to the delineation of the developomental lines of the several selves mentioned earlier.

The Objective Self

The objective self is that self derived from the data of systematic, psychoanalytically informed observation. It is interesting to note that despite the burgeoning interest in self psychology and the pathology of the self, little systematic and direct psychoanalytic observation utilizing the self as a serious theoretical formulation has been attempted. Yet the contribution of such observations to our knowledge of the objective self can be very significant for at least two reasons: such observations can begin with the birth of the person, and, as will be seen, they can serve to confirm some conclusions derived from the reconstructed self. Kohut terms a self derived purely from observation of the preverbal child the "virtual self," and Basch, using a cognitive framework, employs the term "sensorimotor self." We suggest "objective self" to clarify vantage point and to encompass more readily development beyond the preverbal level.

Winnicott (1960) has provided an important but, unfortunately, unsystematically collected set of observations on self formation, conceptualized as true and false self. Cognitive-developmental psychologists have also made observations which, though systematic, are basically uninformed by current psychoanalytic thinking. The first sustained and systematic psychoanalytically informed observations of infants and mothers were accomplished by René Spitz (1965). But it is Margaret Mahler and her co-workers (Mahler, 1968; Mahler, Pine, & Bergman, 1975), following the lead of Spitz, who have provided us with the necessary data to construct an objective self through carefully documented, psychologically relevant behavior of infants and toddlers interacting with their parents. These researchers do not use the self as a central theoretical construct. Instead, they use the tripartite model. Their observations and theories of the process of separation and individuation, however, do focus on self formation and subject-object relationships; thus an integration with self theory is feasible, and the charting of a developmental line of the objective self becomes a possible enterprise.

The line of the objective self begins where Mahler begins — with Freud's statement that the ego is first and foremost a body ego, with bodily experiences forming the self's core. Cognitive-developmental theorists confirm this thesis and conceptualize the first 18 months of the infant's life as the prerepresentational, sensorimotor stage. After an autistic phase (0–2 months), during which the infant is postulated as not only unaware of his person, but also as essentially unaware of his environment,[1] a symbiotic phase of dawning awareness is conceptualized. Spitz's social smile, the first organizer of the psyche, heralds its inception (1965, p. 86). During the symbiotic phase, gratifying experiences of closeness to mother are gradually laid down and organized as schemata. The infant's organization of perceptions and actions, his relationship to his mother, the attachment, mirroring, mutual cuing, and progressive assimilation and accommodation of schemata, are all well documented by Mahler and her colleagues, and provide convincing evidence of intra- and interpersonal development. Mahler theorizes that the body ego contains two kinds of self representations through the symbiotic stage: an inner core connected to interoceptive sensation and an outer layer connected to sensoriperceptive sensation. The inner sensations are posited as forming the core of the self; the outer contribute to the self's demarcation from the object world. Thus, to abstract from observable data, a self without subjective awareness is the way the objective self

[1]Harley and Weil (1979, p. xiii) redesignate this phase as "quasi-autistic" in the light of more recent discoveries relating to the infant's capacity to respond to his or her environment.

is best characterized at this stage, as well as during the stage that follows. The latter, however, encompasses an important shift from inner to outer sensation by the beginning of separation-individuation (hatching) at six months.

Aside from Mahler's postulation of discrete representations of self during the first five to six months of life, the above summary constitutes a rather conservative psychoanalytic view of the first half-year of life, well supported by data of cognitive theorists. According to this view, the objective self is in the process of nascent organization. Sensorimotor experiences lead to the refinement of schemata and to the predictability of observable behavior not only in relation to inanimate things, but particularly in relation to gratifying and frustrating objects, perceived by the infant as pre-objects, or, to use the terminology of self psychology, as preself-objects. This enduring sameness and predictability over time is an indication that the objective self is a developing entity.

Cognitive theorists stress the high egocentrism of the infant during this period. The infant occupies the all-powerful center of his universe; people do not exist except as executives of his will; and causality is seen as magically and omnipotently invested in his sensorimotor person. Psychoanalytic observations of both infant and mother confirm these data. Ferenczi (1913) very early described magical gestures, Winnicott (1956) stresses a resonating maternal preoccupation with the infant, and Spitz's and Mahler's observations attest to the infant's essential narcissism. As already indicated, most analysts, including Mahler, find it appropriate to utilize the tripartite model to organize and explain these data. However, it is necessary to twist and strain the tripartite model to bring the person represented as self into the center stage of this system. Conflict more than cohesiveness and development is evoked, or one is left with a static description of self and object representations making up the ego's core, before such self and object representations are even cognitively possible. The self as system, on the other hand, is well designed to maintain the person in the center of its theoretical formulations. Thus, concepts such as the grandiose self and the selfobject fit well with the observational data drawn both from cognitive-developmental and from psychoanalytic sources, and, we believe, provide more useful theoretical constructs to explain the data of early development.

To continue the line of development of the objective self, Spitz's second organizer of the personality, stranger anxiety (1965, p. 160), marks the end of the symbiotic phase and the beginning of the separation-individuation process. Mahler writes that observed stages of separation and individuation of the infant from the mother begin with "hatching," at six to eight months, and proceed to a gradual psychological birth at about 24–36 months, when appreciation of separateness and a subjective awareness begin. Mahler demonstrates through observations of the child's actions and words during this period that the parent is experienced by the child as a very powerful, perhaps all-powerful, person, and as an increasingly separate individual. Transitional objects (Winnicott, 1953) are utilized to master mother's absences.

In discussing the significance of the mother during the separation-individuation process, Mahler remains on a descriptive level, lending a forceful and convincing quality to her material. When she conceptualizes the data using the tripartite model, however, she and her collaborators seem to sacrifice relevant focus. Again, it seems to us the data appear more focused when formulations drawn from self psychology, utilizing concepts such as idealized parent imago and selfobject, are applied. Mahler herself sometimes uses what appears to be a self psychology model, in stating, for example, that "It was characteristic of children at this age (18 months) to use mother as *an extension of the self*—a process in which they somehow denied the painful awareness of separateness" (Mahler, Pine, & Bergman, 1975, p. 95). This compares favorably to descriptions where Mahler uses an economically accented tripartite model in which the "person" loses centrality: "it is the mother's love of the toddler and the acceptance of his ambivalence that enabled the toddler to cathect his self representation with neutralized energy" (1975, p. 77).

To continue the developmental line of the objective self, Mahler conceptualizes a rapprochement crisis at 22 months, during which the child's awareness of, and anxiety and depression about, separateness come to a head. This crisis seems to be resolved at around 24 months through the child's appreciation of his own autonomy, accompanied by a beginning internalization of rules, expectations, and ideals, providing both inner control and reward.

Mahler formulates a fourth subphase of separation-individuation, ending at 24–36 months, and termed "consolidation of individuality and the beginnings of emotional object constancy." She records the following observational data as relevant to this subphase: greater control over affects and bodily actions, more purposeful play, increased relationships to others than mother, increased capacity to endure separation from mother, and new fear of "re-engulfment" by the mother after separation (Mahler et al., 1975, pp. 116, 118). To apply self psychology terminology once more, these observations point to the diminished selfobject quality of the mother and her enhanced anaclitic object quality. An objective self characterized by constancy, cohesiveness, and subjective awareness is revealed.

Mahler's observational data would seem to indicate that the capacity for subjective awareness arises only between the ages of two and a half and three and a half, at which time a subjective self is feasible. The objective self loses its hegemony from this time forward. Even so, much insight about the objective self is derived from observational data after that time, and much can only be learned about the child's self development through this means. For example, the child's affects are only dimly perceived and usually not identified by the child until age four to six and even beyond. Many affects must thus be inferred, via empathy, by the observer. The young child in particular can know, understand, or relate little of his or her own ambivalent feelings, though they are indeed acutely experienced. Moreover, it is interesting to note that the fantasy life of the child remains accessible to observation until the child is eight, and can reveal much about the child's self development. The child's ability to engage in purely private fantasy life is usually not achieved before the advent of Piaget's concrete operational stage. Before then, sensorimotor imaginative play or drawings are generally needed by the child to accompany thought. In addition, egocentric distortion of reality persists well into latency, or even adolescence, supporting the value of objective observation. Finally, cognitive style, choice of defense, and stage of cognitive development are all assessed primarily from the vantage point of an observer; the line of development of the objective self can thus be traced throughout the life cycle. In addition, observation can be used to confirm theoretical formulations; to wit, phases of libidinal and aggressive development are classic examples of the use of observation to confirm reconstruction. Nevertheless, data sources from introspection and analytic experiences become increasingly relevant as the individual matures, and the objective self loses its central position in the formulation of the psychoanalytic self.

The Subjective Self

The subjective self is that self formulated from reported experiences of the individual, exclusive of modifications induced by psychoanalytic intervention. Consequently, this "self" does not encompass a conscious awareness of significant memories or activities currently defended against.

The core data source used in the construction of this self is subjective reports as they are understood by psychologically minded interpreters. This includes, for example, early material from adult and child patients, interviews administered by psychologists, and psychoanalytic investigations of autobiographical or fictional portrayals of developing individuals (e.g., Blos's [1962] use of Mann's character Tonio Kröger to understand and demonstrate adolescence).

While an incipient subjective self can be inferred in the infant at six months via the "dawning self-awareness" referred to above, the subjective self proper is only established at age two and a half to three and a half, when, as Selma Fraiberg (1977) notes, the child reports his perception of himself as an object in a universe of objects through his consistent use of the first-person-singular pronoun, and through his representation of himself in dramatic play. Fraiberg refers to this achievement as the establishment of *the nonsyncretic I*. The child, that is, becomes able to separate himself from his activities and able to reflect on his own actions.

A confirmatory finding regarding the time of attainment of the subjective self comes from those studying the development of gender identity (Stoller, 1968; Money & Ehrhardt, 1972). Sex assignment of the objective self begins with birth, but the subjective self develops its gender tag only gradually at first, and then definitively (though always with relative ambivalence). Two and a half to three years of age is established as the approximate time when core gender identity is consolidated; boys contend that they are boys, girls that they are girls. This relatively immutable psychological attainment is experienced, according to Money, in self-awareness. The establishment of this age range for core gender identity attainment, then, corroborates the time assigned for development of the subjective self.

The subjective self begins as self-centered and remains so for a very long period of time. It is apparently true, however, that the child discovers objects as a prerequisite to discovering himself as an object. Abelin (1977) describes a boy's discovery of himself, including his gender, through observation of his father in relation to his mother. He postulates that the discovery of the father as different from the mother and as having a relationship with her helped the boy to conceptualize himself as also different from his mother and similar to his father, dating this "early triangulation" to the late second year of life. But these first important objects are suffused with subjectivity, and are, in the language of self psychology, selfobjects, just as the transitional object of the early objective self is itself a selfobject (Tolpin, 1971).

Blatt's (1974) findings would tend to confirm this order in which discovery of important others precedes discovery of oneself. He shows that children can draw objects in detail before they can draw themselves in the same detail.

All of this would seem to indicate the existence of early prototypes of empathy and objectivity. But the truth is that accurate empathy, a true perspective on others, is only fully developed during and after adolescence. In fact, the self revealed from the point of view of the subject begins as highly egocentric and presents a world view that is highly subjective. Both the egocentricity and the subjectivity are maintained for a remarkably long period of time. As Kohut tells us, there is a lifelong narcissistic investment in oneself, only the quality of which changes over the course of development.

This persistent egocentricity is best demonstrated by Piaget's early (1923) studies of the decentering process in children and young adolescents. Based upon a clinical method in which each child is interviewed at length about his ideas and thoughts, Piaget's work reveals both the nature of the egocentric thought of the young child and the process by which he develops out of it. In this connection, the language employed by the child in his attempts to express his ideas to others and to the interviewer becomes the principal evidence. Piaget begins by characterizing the different functions of language during children's conversations, and then arranges the various types of conversations into a developmental sequence. He demonstrates that the explanations given by one child to another are egocentric through age eight; the child does not attempt to take another's point of view to make himself understood. Thus, the child behaves as if everyone shares the same knowledge concerning an event as he does. From nine to 11, this egocentric speech gives way to a form of verbal and conceptual syncretism, the function of which is to gain acceptance for his point of view at any cost, often at the expense of logic and clarity. Only with the establishment of formal operations in adolescence is decentering actually accomplished by the individual.

As an analyst sensitive to the work of Piaget, Anne Marie Sandler (1975) also points to the prolonged egocentricity of children. She asks that this be taken into account in assessing narcissistic attitudes and disorders. To discover that a child expects others to know what he or she knows, without having to say it, is to be expected, even at age eight or nine. Were this seen in an adult analytic patient, however, it might be erroneously reconstructed as a developmental arrest stemming from a far earlier period.

Only gradually, too, does the child come to differentiate himself as a person among other persons of importance equal to himself. This process takes place in a spiral fashion throughout the preoperational, concrete operational, and formal operational cognitive stages (Piaget & Inhelder, 1966). Piaget refers to this disparity of concept attainment lost at an earlier developmental level and regained at a later level as vertical décalage, and his observation is confirmed by psychoanalysts, who also note that problems solved at one stage of development are met once more and need to be solved again at the next. Thus the infant's successful separation-individuation experience is echoed and reechoed at various levels (see, e.g., Blos, 1967).

Furthermore, once an advance in subjective observation is achieved at one level of cognitive development, the subjective observations of previous levels are infused with it and the previous concept of oneself all but forgotten. No child and few adults, for example, can conceptualize themselves as incapable of knowing of their own existence. Likewise, it is difficult for an adult to remember a time when his dreams were not distinguished from reality or when large defects in internalization and concomitant mental structures existed in his personality. Freud showed us how repression and other defenses disguise for the adult his picture of himself as a child. Anna Freud (1926, 1936) demonstrated the same phenomenon in children. Piaget (1973), too, points out the limits of the subject in observing and remembering himself throughout childhood and into adult life, although Piaget conceptualizes these limits in cognitive terms.

Psychoanalytic understanding of the development of the subjective self focuses upon the overriding importance of sensual interchanges with significant others experienced during childhood. These sensual interchanges are primarily self-centered and, we believe, must contribute to the prominent egocentricity of the child. The child's capacity to observe and report these experiences increases with age, but is distorted by defenses erected against the developmental hierarchy of anxieties. For example, a child of five is likely to say that he wishes to marry his mother and can see himself currently as his mother's lover. Oedipal anxiety and internalization of parental injunctions make such spontaneous subjective awareness less common once latency is achieved. However, if the child's egocentric productions are not adequately accepted by empathic parents, heightened peremptory wishes may appear as "breakdown products" of a fragmented self, and the child's picture of himself becomes that of a frustrated and fragmented child, with latency not attainable. Successful drive modulation and repression are based upon a sense of underlying acceptance and love from parents, which also leads to the attainment of autonomous self-esteem. Children all along the developmental continuum report states of being good and bad in relation to the attitudes of their parents and significant others toward them, and adults have access to memories of such feeling states from their childhood.

To proceed further along the developmental line of the subjective self, developmental experiences in latency, adolescence, and adult life can improve the subject's ability to observe himself and appreciate his individuality, aside from those areas against which defenses are erected. Forgotten or repressed memories and feelings can be revived in the upheaval of new developmental challenges. For example, the disillusionment with parents in latency can lead to the creation of family romance fantasies and fantasies of exalted birth, expressed, for example, through emulation of television and comic-strip superheroes (Widzer, 1977), to compensate for the repressed lost glory and egocentrism of the oedipal and preoedipal eras. The new experience in adolescence of genital orgasm can threaten defenses against newly revived erotic desires toward parents, and can lead to an increased awareness of a sense of oneself as a highly sexual, even dangerously erotic, person.

Falling in love (Kernberg, 1977), which heightens an individual's capacity for intimacy (Erikson, 1950), provides a new dimension of self-discovery through discovering the uniqueness yet familiarity of an important other, echoing the first experience of discovering oneself through the discovery of selfobjects. Parenthood itself is conceptualized as a developmental process (Benedek, 1959; Panel, 1975) because of the continuous pressure for greater subjective awareness that raising children stimulates.

The line of development of the subjective self continues throughout life. As we have attempted to demonstrate, however, it is severely limited as a data source by certain aspects of its development, including its relatively late attainment, cognitive revisions, intact defenses unaltered by analytic experience, and the discontinuous nature of memory.

The Reconstructed Self

The reconstructed self is the self discovered in the psycho-analytic situation. It is constructed from data supplied by the patient that have been interpreted by the analyst via vicarious introspection and empathy (Kohut, 1959; Greenson, 1967). It includes the full panoply of information that the patient presents or that the analyst infers, but it includes especially information gained through the transference and countertransference experiences in the analysis. In a circular fashion the data are used to bring conviction both to the patient and to the analyst of the accuracy of this reconstructed vision of the self. It is obvious that the reconstructed self is in part influenced by the theoretical choices and personal experiences of the analyst, but, we emphasize, only in part. To the degree that analysts share a common framework, each analyst's reconstructions from his patient's data share commonalities; in other words, different analysts are likely to arrive at a roughly similar reconstructed self for a given patient. Schafer (1978) gives a convincing demonstration of this point.

Sharing this conviction, then, we will outline a reconstructed self developmental line that we think approximates the view of most analysts, crucially modified, of course, by the unique private history of the individual patient to a greater or lesser degree.

An adequately analyzed neurotic patient (in this case male) will discover in the analytic process (though not in any particular order), via transference experiences with his analyst, that his childhood began in a state of helplessness, though he was, as a child, unaware of it for quite some time. His parents were extremely important to him (though they are less so now). In fact, he was very dependent on them for his physical and emotional well-being. He admired them and expected them to admire him. He loved them and resented them and feared their disapproval. He experienced a hierarchical series of anxieties (Freud, 1926), beginning with that of being simply overwhelmed and then of fearing the loss of his self-cohesiveness. Next he feared the loss of his parents as best he could conceive of them at the time (experiencing his parents at first as selfobject extensions of himself and only much later as truly separate from himself). He next feared the loss of their love. He utilized transitional objects to gain mastery over the loss of their soothing and protecting power. He wished them both to approve of his ability to be "good," and not to desert him when he was ragefully "bad."

The patient first saw his mother as good or bad but not good and bad at the same time. Though the analyst assumed that this began as a developmental limitation and later became available as a defensive avoidance of the pain of ambivalence, it is only the latter, defensive use that could be observed in the transference of this (neurotic) patient. As a child he could see himself as either all-good or all-bad but preferred by far the former, unconsciously projecting badness onto others. The oedipal loves, rivalries, and conflicts were lived through in the patient's past, though they were clearly not completely resolved. The internalization of the parents' standards consequent to all of these experiences could be demonstrated through unconscious and preconscious links from his own sense of morality and ideals back to theirs. These internalizations were inferred by the analyst as having begun during the patient's second year and having continued throughout his life, and were variously conceptualized as introjections, identifications, transmuting internalizations, and fantastic and veridical object representations, depending on their degree of integration into this reconstructed self. Depressive feelings and a mourning process over the gradual loss of closeness, both to admiring, mirroring parents and to idealized parents, were fully experienced in the transference before the separation, individuation, and consolidation of the self could be achieved. This mourning process was repeated in each subsequent phase of development experienced in the analysis. The reconstructed self is unavoidably telescoped and distorted under the influence of transference needs in the analysis (for example, the capacity for mourning is limited in terms of the objective and subjective self before adulthood) and because of cognitive limitations to the recovery of past memories. The reconstructed self that emerges, however, is of far greater depth than the subjective self, inasmuch as cognitive discontinuities and the defenses against more complete subjective awareness are removed through the analytic process.

The Psychoanalytic Self

We have just presented the lines of development of three separate selves: the self viewed objectively, the self presented subjectively, and the self reconstructed analytically. Each of these vantage points is in itself relatively limited and to some extent unconfirmed. The construction of a fourth developmental line of the self based upon nodal points of agreement among the other three achieves a stereoscopic view. We have termed this construction the psychoanalytic self and have said that it is more likely to be accurate and to carry conviction because it provides confirmation based upon a confluence of data.

To use a prototypical example, the concept of the Oedipus complex was an interesting hypothesis regarding normal development that Freud based on his own analysis as well as on the transference reactions of his patients. Not until he was able to report direct observations of the phallic, erotic, oedipal activity and fantasy life of Little Hans (1909), however, was he as convinced or as convincing about the universal oedipal experiences of mankind. It seems to us that material from one or two data sources leads to intriguing, even workable hypotheses; a fit among the three examined here, however, would more closely approximate certainty. Such confirmation has been more difficult to achieve in the preoedipal period of normal development. Whereas a Little Hans is able to tell us about his inner life, a younger child is not. We are forced to rely more heavily on the objective self, inevitably distorted by vantage point, and on the reconstructed self, also inevitably distorted, but in this case by preconceptions and adultomorphisms. Reliance upon their combination provides several working hypotheses, making it possible to construct a developmental line of the psychoanalytic self that antedates the oedipal period. These hypotheses should be distinguished from the more certain hypotheses based on the nodal points of confluence that are attainable once the child acquires the capacity for subjective reflection.

During the first year of life and well into the second, one can hypothesize, based on data from the objective and the reconstructed selves, a dawning awareness of oneself as center of the universe. Observations of sensorimotor egocentricity are supported by reconstructions that demonstrate the almost unselfconscious assumption of grandiose centrality of the patient in the analytic situation. In addition, the experience of an unquestioning merger between analyst and patient supports observations of a symbiotic union, transitional experiences, and poor differentiation of subject from object. No data from the subjective self of the infant are available to support these hypotheses, however.

During the second and third year of life, we postulate, on the basis of observation and reconstruction, that the child separates and individuates from his all-powerful mother, conceptualized now on an early symbolic level, because of his gradual disillusionment with her omnipotence. Mahler and her colleagues see the toddler in the middle of the struggle with separation and individuation as unable to function independently of mother, requiring repeated "refueling" from her; Kohut and his colleagues see patients who are poorly differentiated from the idealized analyst as returning to the self-selfobject matrix of toddler times, and therefore requiring from the analyst soothing and approving (refueling) functions. The observed rapprochement period, critical because its resolution leads to a meliorative developmental impact, centers around a disillusionment with the idealized mother. Analytic reconstruction attests to the healing effects of the gradual disillusionment with the omnipotence of the analyst and concomitant transmuting internalizations. This represents a striking confluence of hypotheses based upon data from the reconstructed and objective selves.

During the fourth year of life, Mahler describes the attainment of self and object constancy, indicating that the observed self does not attain cohesiveness until that time. The reconstructed self, on the other hand, is seen as cohesive once the structures of the grandiose self and the idealized parent imago are discernible within the transference. These structures are generally attributed to the earlier toddler period. However, the vulnerability to regression of the grandiose self and the idealized parent imago structures would seem to indicate that further consolidation is required to obtain the degree of stable cohesiveness that can be equated with the relatively immutable self and object constancy postulated by

Mahler. This would tend to situate stable self-cohesiveness and self and object constancy within the same general period, and would suggest that they are different manifestations of the same phenomenon, derived from separate data sources. The flowering of the subjective self during this same time would seem to establish that nodal point of agreement among data sources that we have identified with relative scientific certainty. From this period forward such confluence of data derived from the three selves is available and should be utilized in all psychoanalytic formulations.

The developmental line of the psychoanalytic self through oedipal, latency, adolescence, and subsequent stages of adult life, while inferable from the separate lines we have outlined here, will not be described in this paper. Instead, we will attempt to illustrate the integration of these lines in analytic practice with a few brief clinical vignettes.

The integration of the objective self with the reconstructed self is a commonplace in child analysis. For example, a seven-year-old child beginning an analysis asked his analyst to sit way across the room from him. The boy denied that he was frightened of the analyst, and indeed did not appear to realize that he was; he only seemed aware that he did not like to have the analyst sit too close. The boy's mother had related, with some reluctance, that when the child was two, his father had disciplined him harshly, at times physically. In addition, the two-year-old boy had been left in the care of housekeepers who were strict and coercive. The disciplinary situation had changed since then, but the child was left with symptomatic fears of leaving home, nightmares, and study inhibitions. Integration of the experiences of the objective self, drawn from the mother's report, with aspects of the reconstructed self, based on early transference reactions, afforded the analyst a glimpse of the psychoanalytic self structure of this particular child patient that gradually deepened with the slow unveiling of his subjective self.

Another young patient, a boy of just five, was brought to analysis by his parents for hyperactivity, infantile speech, poor concentration, and angry outbursts directed toward his younger sister. Early in the analysis he would ride the couch pillow, groaning and moaning, and becoming increasingly excited and anxious. He would then exclaim: "All of the air will come out; it will disappear!" Hissing noises coming from the air conditioning would also frighten him. The analyst surmised that the patient had anxieties on a phallic-oedipal level leading to fears of abandonment by his mother for his affectionate and aggressive wishes, and that he feared the concomitant loss of his own cohesiveness. It was only several weeks later that his mother told the analyst that when he was three, the patient had stabbed his beloved plastic clown with a knife and was dismayed when the air whooshed out of it. The child had had a longstanding attachment to the clown, dating from early toddler times, and had utilized it as a transitional object because it was soothing to the touch. He had always liked his mother's nightgown and his own blanket edging. After the child ruined the Bozo, his parents unempathically threw the toy away. They remembered that although the boy had not mentioned the clown again, in retrospect he seemed very disturbed by the loss at the time. When the analyst later confronted the patient with the incident, he did recall it. This recollection helped him to correlate the unexpected result of his affectionately aggressive penetration of the beloved clown with his current distress in the office, manifested in the pillow play and the accompanying exclamations that "All of the air will come out; it will disappear!" Here the unity of the objective, subjective, and reconstructed selves provided a sure understanding of the patient as a child with a shaky sense of himself disguised as phallic aggression.

From adult analytic work, a 32-year-old male demonstrated in the transference profound separation fears with overwhelming anxiety and a sense of disintegration. Friends of the family told him while he was in analysis that as a two- and three-year-old he would "shadow" (to use Mahler's concept) his mother and was terrified if she left him. As might be surmised, his mother was shown to have had her own separation difficulties. The patient was informed that he turned to a brown teddy bear for comfort. None of this was remembered by him, if, in fact, it was rememberable. But once it was told to him, he was able to integrate these outside (objective) observations of himself with his subjective awareness. An echoing of this early shadowing of his mother reappeared later in his development in the area of goals and ideals, when he slavishly followed her directions regarding choice of profession. His tie to her remained unaltered through the oedipal phase, and he remained arrested at this level as well. His subjective awareness was augmented by objective observations made by others, dating not only from his preverbal era, but also from the present. For example, he was unaware of testing his voice to see if it was low enough when talking to someone who he feared might overwhelm him as his father had overwhelmed him. This was observable and required confrontation in the analysis to be made conscious, providing an expansion of self-awareness previously restricted by defenses.

Another example of the relation between the objective self and the reconstructed self concerns a woman in her fifties who remembered being told that her maternal grandmother and her mother literally fought over her when she was an infant, each tugging on her arm to possess her. This experience, augmented by many analogous conflictful tuggings later in childhood between her mother and grandmother, and current internalized conflictful tuggings of all kinds, was observed in the transference and reported to her by others. This added to her subjective self concept of a person with divided loyalties and responsibilities.

A woman patient in her twenties was told that she had had temper tantrums from age four to six following the birth of her brother. She had no memory of them. This objective self datum, however, was useful in formulating the reconstructed self, made evident in her analytic hours, for example, when she kicked a doll house in the corner of the room as she stormed out of the office one day, angry at her current younger "siblings." The interaction between these two selves, leading to a healthier heightened subjective awareness, is obvious.

This presentation has attempted to highlight the need for an ongoing "stereoscopic view" in which observations of infant and child development are correlated with clinical psychoanalytic data. Although analysts are understandably tempted to restrict their purview, we do not hold to the view that the only proper field of data gathering and theory formation is the introspective data gathered from the adult psychoanalytic situation (e.g., Ricoeur, 1977). The psychoanalyst's conception of human development determines in part what he reconstructs for his patients, just as it determines in part what he would discover from infant and child observations. The optimal integration of developmental data with concomitant theories of the self, therefore, must ultimately be a personal integration in the mind of each analyst.

References

Abelin, E. (1977), The Role of the Father in Personality Development. *Psychotherapy Tape Library.* New York: Psychotherapy & Social Science Book Club.

Basch, M. F. (1975), Toward a Theory that Encompasses Depression: A Revision of Existing Causal Hypotheses in Psychoanalysis. In: *Depression and Human Existence,* ed. E. J. Anthony & T. Benedek. Boston: Little, Brown, pp. 485–534.

Benedek, T. (1959), Parenthood as a Developmental Phase. *J. Amer. Psychoanal. Assn.,* 7:389–417.

Blatt, S. (1974), Anaclitic and Introjective Depression. *The Psychoanalytic Study of the Child,* 29:107–157. New Haven: Yale University Press.

Blos, P. (1962), *On Adolescence: A Psychoanalytic Interpretation.* New York: Free Press.

_____ (1967), The Second Individuation Process of Adolescence. *The Psychoanalytic Study of the Child,* 22:162–186. New York: International Universities Press.

Erikson, E. (1950), *Childhood and Society,* rev. ed. New York: Norton, 1963.

Ferenczi, S. (1913), Stages in the Development of the Sense of Reality. In: *Selected Papers of Sandor Ferenczi,* vol. 1. New York: Basic Books, 1950, pp. 213–239.

Fraiberg, S. (1977), *Insights from the Blind.* New York: Basic Books.

Freud, A. (1926), *The Psycho-Analytic Treatment of Children.* New York: International Universities Press, 1959.

_____ (1936), *The Ego and Mechanisms of Defense,* rev. ed. New York: International Universities Press, 1966.

Freud, S. (1909), Analysis of a Phobia in a Five-Year-Old Boy. *Standard Edition,* 10:5–149. London: Hogarth Press, 1955.

_____ (1926), Inhibitions, Symptoms and Anxiety. *Standard Edition,* 20:87–172. London: Hogarth Press, 1959.

Gedo, J. & Goldberg, A. (1973), *Models of the Mind: A Psychoanalytic Theory.* Chicago: University of Chicago Press.

Greenson, R. R. (1967), *The Technique and Practice of Psychoanalysis,* vol. 1. New York: International Universities Press.

Grossman, W. & Simon, B. (1969), Anthropomorphism: Motive, Meaning and

Causality in Psychoanalytic Theory. *The Psychoanalytic Study of the Child,* 24:78–114. New York: International Universities Press.

Harley, M. & Weil, A. P. (1979), Introduction to *The Selected Papers of Margaret S. Mahler,* vol. 1. New York: Aronson.

Kernberg, O. (1977), Boundaries and Structure in Love Relations. *J. Amer. Psychoanal. Assn.,* 25:81–114.

Klein, G. (1969), Freud's Two Theories of Sexuality. In: *Psychology versus Metapsychology,* ed. M. M. Gill and P. S. Holzman. *Psychol. Issues,* Monogr. 36. New York: International Universities Press, 1976, pp. 14–70.

Kohut, H. (1959), Introspection, Empathy and Psychoanalysis. *J. Amer. Psychoanal. Assn.,* 7:459–483.

——— (1977), *The Restoration of the Self.* New York: International Universities Press.

Mahler, M. (1968), *On Human Symbiosis and the Vicissitudes of Individuation,* vol. 1: *Infantile Psychosis.* New York: International Universities Press.

——— Pine, F., & Bergman, A. (1975), *The Psychological Birth of the Human Infant: Symbiosis and Individuation.* New York: Basic Books.

Money, J. & Ehrhardt, A. (1972), *Man and Woman, Boy and Girl.* Baltimore and London: Johns Hopkins University Press.

Panel (1975), Parenthood as a Developmental Phase. Reported by H. Parens. *J. Amer. Psychoanal. Assn.,* 23:154–165.

Panel (1976), New Horizons in Metapsychology: View and Review. Reported by W. Meissner. *J. Amer. Psychoanal. Assn.,* 24:161–180.

Piaget, J. (1923), *The Language and Thought of the Child.* Cleveland and New York: World Publishing Company.

——— (1973), The Affective Unconscious and the Cognitive Unconscious. *J. Amer. Psychoanal. Assn.,* 21:249–261.

——— & Inhelder, B. (1966), *The Psychology of the Child.* New York: Basic Books, 1969.

Ricoeur, P. (1977), The Question of Proof in Freud's Psychoanalytic Writings. *J. Amer. Psychoanal. Assn.,* 25:835–871.

Sandler, A. M. (1975), Comments on the Significance of Piaget's Work for Psychoanalysis. *Internat. Rev. Psycho-Anal.,* 2:365–377.

Schafer, R. (1976), *A New Language for Psychoanalysis.* New Haven and London: Yale University Press.

——— (1978), *Language and Insight.* New Haven and London: Yale University Press.

Spitz, R. A. (1965), *The First Year of Life.* New York: International Universities Press.

Stoller, R. (1968), *Sex and Gender.* New York: Science House.

Tolpin, M. (1971), On the Beginnings of a Cohesive Self: An Application of the Concept of Transmuting Internalization to the Study of the Transitional Object and Signal Anxiety. *The Psychoanalytic Study of the Child,* 26:316–354. New York and Chicago: Quadrangle.

Widzer, M. (1977), The Comic-Book Superhero: A Study of the Family Romance Fantasy. *The Psychoanalytic Study of the Child,* 32:565–604. New Haven: Yale University Press.

Winnicott, D. W. (1953), Transitional Objects and Transitional Phenomena. In:

Collected Papers. New York: Basic Books, 1958, pp. 229–242.

_____ (1956), Primary Maternal Preoccupation. In: *Collected Papers.* New York: Basic Books, 1958, pp. 300–305.

_____ (1960), Ego Distortion in Terms of True and False Self. In: *The Maturational Processes and the Facilitating Environment.* New York: International Universities Press, 1965, pp. 140–152.

Wolff, P. H. (1967), Cognitive Considerations for a Psychoanalytic Theory of Language Acquisition. In: *Motives and Thought: Psychoanalytic Essays in Honor of David Rapaport,* ed. R. R. Holt. *Psychol. Issues,* Monogr. 18/19. New York: International Universities Press, pp. 299–343.

Discussion of
"Psychoanalytic Developmental Theories of the Self: An Integration"
by Morton Shane and Estelle Shane

MARIAN TOLPIN

At least a score of psychoanalytic theories of early childhood development and analytic treatment, like the theory of separation-individuation and of a rapprochement conflict, are derived from Freud's theory of neurosis. Regardless of their not insignificant manifest differences, the multiplicity of theories of a self split by conflict referred to by the Shanes, and the even greater number of theories of psychic splitting in which a self organization is merely taken for granted, are based on one and the same premise. This common premise is that the infant and small child are endangered and split from within both by their own impulses and their "early objects," and by the archaic defenses which are instituted against both impulses and objects.

Kohut's theory is based on an entirely different premise. Consistent with a tremendous amount of observational data on the very early beginnings of the reciprocal child-parent relationship (cf. Lozoff et al., 1977, for an excellent summary and bibliography), certain concepts of psychoanalytic developmental

psychology which do not fit conventional theories of early objects
of love and hate, and certain penetrating psychological insights of
Freud (1905)[1] and Ferenczi (1913) which do not fit into conflict
theory (cf. below, pp. 57–63), Kohut arrives at the following
premise: The normal infant, toddler, or young child experiences
himself as a reasonably cohesive unit, an independent center of initiative with continuity in space and time, with (in-phase) urges to
achieve and accomplish his own purposes, with (in-phase) feelings
of competence, effectiveness, and power by virtue — and only by
virtue — of an ongoing, expectable (mutual) tie with his expectable
selfobjects (cf. Tolpin, 1971, 1978, and Tolpin & Kohut, 1979, for
a discussion of the crucial developmental distinction between objects of infantile love and hate and selfobjects needed as precursors of the normal workings of a cohesive body-mind-self). Until, or unless, a cohesive-enough self is firmly established, the
primary psychological danger is psychic helplessness, which is invariably accompanied by threatened (signal) or actual (overwhelming, traumatic) "disintegration" or "fragmentation" anxiety,
mental "pain" of any kind (Freud, 1926), depression-depletion,
and rage. Differences in terminology notwithstanding, it can be
reasonably argued that this thesis is at least implicit in Freud's
(1926) genetic series of dangers, beginning with psychic helplessness and the traumatic state, and that it is the basis for most
analytic theories of development and treatment. However, my
point is that Kohut's theory is an exception to the rule of assuming
that infantile rage over helplessness of necessity leads to conflict
psychopathology.

Transient helplessness and signal disintegration reactions, for
Kohut, are inevitable, and these psychological states immediately
give rise to a normal baby's or toddler's assertive demands and appeals to his selfobject. (It is part and parcel of normal development

[1]It should be noted that Freud (1905) did not systematically investigate what
I would term his "affectionate mother" hypothesis (p. 223) or his hypothesis concerning the "signal function" of "upbringing" (p. 162). Likewise, he did not consider the possibility that transferences reactivated the psychological configurations that are involved in these phenomena. I discuss these unexplored
"paradigms" in a paper now in preparation.

for the small child to expect the selfobject to respond as a matter of course, and it is part and parcel of the pathology of self-cohesion that once normal demands which were traumatically frustrated persist as out-of-phase demands, they also become abnormally intensified and split off from expectable transformations.) Reasonably attuned selfobject responses *preserve* the feeling of expectation which is already present in the child (it is inherent in a normal infant born into a normal human environment), and these responses fit together with an inherent tendency in the child gradually to take over functions for the self (via transmuting internalizations) where the selfobjects' functions normally leave off. Prolonged, unrelieved psychic helplessness and "disintegration products" (anxiety, depression, rage, withdrawal, etc.) originate first and foremost in faults and failures in the "workings" (Tolpin, 1971) of the original self-selfobject unit of childhood, and in the workings of the core self in later life. The crucial corollary of Kohut's basic premise is that the goal of children's normal development, and of psychoanalytic treatment for the group of patients with analyzable, nonneurotic, primary disorders of the self (Kohut, 1971, 1977; Tolpin, 1979), is the acquisition and/or strengthening and consolidation of insufficiently established self-maintaining and restoring capacities and functions.[2]

The implication of Kohut's basic premise is that the developmental task of early childhood is the establishment of a cohesive self, that disorders of the first years of life are primarily disorders of self-cohesion, and that typical (neurotic) conflict develops when, and only when, self-cohesion is reasonably well established. Therefore, in reply to the Shanes' stimulating and challenging contribution I will highlight the fundamental and far-reaching differences between Kohut's theory and theories of psychic conflict — in particular, the theory of Margaret Mahler. I will discuss the

---

[2]The *developmental writings* of Mahler and other ego psychologists who are also adherents of object relations theory recognize the importance of the formation of psychic structure. However, failures of cohesion, integration, etc., are nonetheless attributed to conflict (cf., for example, Mahler et al., 1975, pp. 214, 222). Their *clinical theories*, on the other hand, disregard the problem of structure formation and continue the emphasis on the primacy of conflict.

concept of the "prestructural" selfobject as an invaluable theoretical bridge which closes the longstanding gap between psychoanalytic developmental psychology and clinical theory and practice, thereby opening the way to overcoming the major difficulty in
the present-day path of psychoanalysis: fragmentation of the field
by the extraordinary number of theories of psychic conflict that
proliferated in an unsuccessful attempt to fill this gap (Munroe,
1955; A. Freud, 1969; for discussion of this gap, cf. Greenacre,
1971; Murphy, 1973).

The starting point of my reply is a fact already alluded to
above, which is entirely overlooked in the psychoanalytic literature
in spite of its great relevance to the issue of theoretical integration.
The fact is that almost every analytic theory of development and
treatment is a derivative ("earlier") version of Freud's theory of a
nuclear oedipal conflict and of Freud's theory of the treatment of a
classical transference neurosis. To restate this fact differently,
many analysts continue to ignore the explanatory limits of the
conflict hypothesis (Freud, 1937, pp. 220–221), and continue to insist that psychic conflict is the basis for all forms of
psychopathology. It is equally true that Mahler, Spitz, and many
other analysts have attempted to derive a new theory from the
hypothesis of intersystemic (structural) conflict, although this
hypothesis can only account for neurosis in terms of the conflict
between psychic agencies that are already established.

Hard-won psychoanalytic knowledge is obscured by continuing "intrasystemic" and "intersystemic" controversies between
analysts who are proponents of the various conflict theories (cf.,
for example, Schwartz, 1978; Levine, 1978; Stein, 1979. In this
connection cf. also the late George Klein's [1976] important
writings on the limits of conflict theory). This knowledge, which
Anna Freud has emphasized and reemphasized in her writings, includes several basic insights: First, structural deficits go unrecognized while analysts of otherwise widely divergent opinions hold
that conflict in the first and second years of life accounts for
bedrock psychopathology, and that such early conflict is accessible
to psychoanalytic treatment. Second, the psychoanalytic theory of
psychic conflict which has actually proved its usefulness applies

exclusively to the normality and pathology of oedipal development if and when a "normal ego" is actually established (on this point cf. Freud, 1937; Eissler, 1953; A. Freud, 1968, 1969, 1970; Greenacre, 1971; Kohut, 1971, 1977). Third, the problem of massive anxiety, depression, rage, psychic pain, etc. (Freud, 1937), associated with "ego abnormality" is beyond the explanatory limits of any and all theories of psychic conflict.

In short, the long-investigated developmental problem of structural insufficiencies and disintegration reactions, coupled with the longstanding clinical problem of faults in the structure of the ego and need for a theory and technique which can overcome the obstacles to cure posed by these faults, is a compelling motive force for psychoanalysis as a whole to make a reintegrating shift — a shift from id psychology, ego psychology, and theories of an ego or self split by conflict, to the psychology of a cohesive self and its prestructural selfobjects.

Mahler's Baby and Kohut's Baby — Crucial Developmental-Clinical Differences

Like the baby originally postulated by Karl Abraham (e.g., 1924) and Melanie Klein, Mahler's baby is endangered from within by its own libidinal and hostile-aggressive drives and their "early objects," by introjective, projective, and splitting mechanisms of defense against the dangers from drives and drive objects, and by resultant archaic psychic conflict. Mahler's baby is regarded as autistic at birth and for the first few weeks of life, and as merged or fused with a hallucinated representation of an omnipotent (maternal) symbiotic object or part-object for the next five to six months (Mahler et al., 1975). Moreover, with its maternal object split up into good-satisfying and bad-frustrating part-objects and introjects, this baby differentiates and develops into a toddler who is further endangered by normal physical and mental growth and maturation. In Mahler's view, that is, the toddler is endangered psychologically because motoric maturation leads him away from his mother to hypercathexis of his autonomous equipment and premature psychological separation, and he is endangered psychologically because normal cognitive maturation exposes him to traumatic deflation and disillusionment.

Mahler specifically postulates that the prematurely separated junior toddler is so in love with his autonomous equipment and what he can do with it that he is relatively oblivious to his mother, and that he matures cognitively around 15–16 months only to discover suddenly that he is small and his mother is not all-powerful. This discovery destines him for sudden, traumatic deflation of his grandiosity, and for sudden, traumatic disillusionment in his belief in the omnipotence of the maternal object. In Mahler's theory, then, an injury inflicted by cognitive growth, rather than by injurious (traumatically deflating and disappointing) interactions with the parents, inevitably leads to a developmental "position" of serious anxiety and depression. (As in Melanie Klein's theory, a "normal depressive position" follows an earlier "paranoid-like position" when the infant's hostility is projected onto a body part-object or "bad object.") At this point in development the toddler is required to resolve a primitive psychic conflict between an all good-loved-omnipotent-idealized maternal imago and an all bad-hated-impotent-depreciated maternal imago. How is this accomplished? Here Mahler's developmental-clinical theory (in contrast to her general developmental writings) invokes the real mother. If the real mother, as opposed to the split-up good and bad internal imagoes, can counteract the pathogenetic effect of the introjects by her "continuing libidinal availability," the toddler can resolve his intrapsychic conflict by fusing the split introjects into a whole live object. (The effects of the maternal availability on the toddler, or lack thereof, are observable. However, Mahler's developmental-clinical *theory* that a split-up object in the form of good and bad introjects undergoes fusion provided there is maternal availability is another matter. The latter proposition is a metapsychological proposition derived from preexisting theory for which there is no evidence.)

Clinical work based on Mahler's theory of separation-individuation, as on other conflict theories, starts with the assumption that normal early childhood development, including the growth and development of a "normal ego" (Freud, 1937), depends on conflict resolution; and that psychopathology originating in the first years of life involves faulty conflict resolution, fixation on archaic defenses, and failure to construct a whole internal object representation out of split-up parts. Like other conflict theories, the theory of separation-individuation does not account for the growth and development of "the normal workings of the mind" (Freud, 1926; Tolpin, 1971) which keep mental pain, distress, anxiety, depression, and rage to an expedient signal; for the "central regulations" provided by a nonconflict sphere of the mind (Hartmann, 1939); or for the "regulator systems" (Glover, 1945) which must eventually replace "auxiliary ego" functions of an expectable environment (Spitz, 1965; Hartmann, 1939). And like other theories which emphasize the centrality of infantile sadism and aggression as a primary response to frustration and the defenses against rage which "split" the psyche, Mahler's theory overlooks psychoanalytic knowledge of the fact that there is inevitable frustration from birth on (Ferenczi, 1913; Winnicott, 1965), along with the fact that the idea of sudden overwhelming frustration from cognitive maturation does not square with the reality of everyday small-scale frustrations.

Glover (1945) was the first to recognize that developmental theories of psychopathology built on the "mental disintegration products" encountered in later psychopathology (for example, autism, hallucinated merging, paranoid projection, disintegrated "objects" and "drives") are mistaken — the child's normal psychology and the adult's mental disintegration products are not the same, as early object relations theory would have it. (See in this connection Erikson's [1950] overlooked discussion of the notion that the infant's and small child's drives are "naive.") Mahler's theory that the baby is closed off in an autistic orbit of its own for several weeks, symbiotically merged or fused with a hallucinated object, preobject, or part-object for the next months, dangerously split by drives and defenses which make objects good and bad, prematurely separated, and traumatically deflated and disillusioned, because of normal physical and mental growth, is based on assumptions borrowed from the theory of neurosis and adapted to fit infantile psychology. The theory of a decisive conflict which comes to a head in the second year of life fails to consider psychic reality. Mahler's theory agrees neither with the psychology of everyday life of parents and young children, with Freud's (1905) and Ferenczi's (1913) important nonsystematic observations and pioneering insights into the psychology of healthy infants and young children who receive normal care, with Spitz's (1963, 1964) evocative descriptions of a normal "dialogue" and "derailment of the dialogue" between mother and child, nor with the vast body of observational data obtained from the studies of analytic and non-analytic developmental psychologists alike.[3]

The theory of a reasonably cohesive self-selfobject unit, of the formation of a cohesive self via optimal frustration and bit-by-bit (transmuting) internalization along with the lasting danger of disintegration anxiety, depression, and rage resulting from traumatic faults in self-cohesion, finally offers psychoanalysis a tenable alternative to Mahler's theory, and, indeed, to all of the other psychoanalytic theories of danger from the aggressive impulse, "early objects," and splitting defenses. Kohut's baby, like Freud's baby in the *Three Essays* (1905) and Ferenczi's baby in "Stages in the Development of the Sense of Reality" (1913), is a baby which "every mother knows" although heretofore this baby has not been integrated into a tenable clinical theory. Fitted together with its human environment from the start, this is an active, vigorous baby with vigorous in-phase developmental needs and urges, with inborn capacities actively to "signal" (Freud, 1926) and actively to make its needs known to its "retinue" (Ferenczi, 1913), and with an inherent "feeling of obviousness and sure expectation" that it has the "power" to succeed in reaching and getting what it goes after. Moreover, this is a baby whose normal "feelings of obvious-

---

[3]Erikson's (1950) emphasis on "mutuality" as a regulating principle, for example, is far from the notion of normal infantile autism and symbiosis; and traumatic deflation and disillusionment, in his view, would belong clearly to "disordered mutuality." For an overview of findings of nonanalytic developmental psychologists on reciprocal interactions between parenting adult and infant as effector, see Lozoff et al. (1977). These reciprocal interactions as the basis for ego development are encompassed in Hartmann's (1939) developmental concept of "fitting together"; and, ultimately, in Kohut's developmental-clinical concept of a structure-building self-selfobject unit and of selfobject transferences.

ness and sure expectation" (Ferenczi, 1913, p. 217), or normal "entitlement" or "primary confidence" (Kohut, 1978) if you will, are not extinguished by the inevitable frustrations of everyday life, and by the inevitable small-scale anxieties, depressions, and rages accompanying frustration which are the lot of the human child, and of all human beings, throughout life. Reasonably well equipped with the cohesion-maintaining and restoring care of its selfobjects, the care which Freud and Ferenczi simply took for granted as "affectionate care" and "normal care," this baby is reasonably well equipped to use and to enjoy its own autonomous equipment. In other words, in-phase autonomous equipment, like the selfobject, is there for the baby simply to use and enjoy "on his own" as it were, from the very beginning. The baby's capacities to root, suck, swallow, refuse and push away the nipple, grasp, touch, cry, scream, kick, struggle, propel himself with swimming movements, look, listen, move in synchrony with the human voice, etc., are in-phase autonomous capacities. Their exercise is as significant for the baby's rudimentary feeling of "competence," "efficacy" (White, 1963), pleasure, satisfaction, "self-esteem," and "self-fulfillment" as the capacities to crawl, walk, talk, exercise sphincter control, and exhibit himself and all of his proud achievement are for the toddler (cf. also Broucek, 1979; Kagan, 1979).

Normally equipped with expectable endowment and an expectable selfobject environment, Kohut's baby experiences itself and is experienced as a strong, effective, independent center of initiative, capable of achieving and accomplishing its own (in-phase) purposes and goals (cf. Erikson, 1950; White, 1963). When reasonably attuned selfobject responses meet the baby's active initiative and his normal expectations part way, his inherent vitality is simply preserved; and when this is the case, he automatically continues to exercise to the hilt all of his progressively growing and unfolding capacities and all of the expanding signals and signs at his disposal in order to continue to assert himself and to announce his legitimate developmental needs.

Kohut's baby grows into a toddler and an older child who can respond to frustration with the normal tendency gradually to take over for himself where his selfobjects' functions leave off.

With his own capacities as heir to his selfobjects' functions, he manages to preserve a nucleus of health: the nuclear "feeling of obviousness and sure expectation" (Ferenczi, 1913) with which he began life that he and everything that belongs to him are perfectly fine. He grows into a toddler, an older child, and finally an adult with psychological capacities that enable him to preserve a vital remnant of the original feeling of his own perfection, and a vital remnant of the original feeling of his own and others' power and effectiveness. In other words, given reasonable care, humans are so constituted that they preserve a "piece of the old grandiose delusion" (Ferenczi, 1913) and the old (infantile) delusion of others' omnipotence, in spite of the fact, and even because of the fact, that from the beginning of life a countless number of inevitable in-phase ("optimal") frustrations and injuries begin to modulate and transform these delusions by teaching us the limits of our own and others' power.

Kohut's baby, if you will, grows up with "the incurable megalomania of mankind" (Freud) intact. This baby may grow up and need psychoanalytic treatment to correct an "inadequate decision" made in regard to fantasied dangers from oedipal impulses and their parental objects (Freud, 1937, p. 220). When the cohesiveness of the self can be taken for granted, that is, the theory of a nuclear oedipal conflict and of unconscious compromise formations between the mature, coherent, organized part of the mind and repressed oedipal impulses may indeed become relevant. Anna Freud (1968, 1969, 1970), however, has pointed to the fact that most children in psychoanalytic treatment do not suffer from either neurotic conflict or from other postulated forms of conflict, and that structural deficits are the basis for their psychopathology. Leo Stone (1961), moreover, has observed that neurosis and neurotic conflict are in fact rare, and that a "basic transference" remains to be understood and distinguished from the classical "transference neurosis." Instead, the "selfobject transferences" of many children and adults reactivate persisting, pathologically intensified needs and expectations toward the analyst as a reinstated childhood selfobject, along with defenses against these needs. In particular, the selfobject transferences reactivate the faults and failures in the original self-selfobject unit, the disintegration anxiety associated with these failures, and most of all, the persisting underlying needs to augment the insufficiently established capacities of the cohesive self. It is the establishment of these capacities which is at issue in a tenable theory of early development and analytic treatment for developmental disorders beyond infantile neurosis and the classical transference neurosis. In other words, it is the issue of structural deficit pathology which makes it necessary for psychoanalysis to go beyond the conflict hypothesis to the hypothesis of prestructural selfobjects and the formation of a cohesive self.

The Explanatory Limits of Conflict Theories

In 1937 Freud confronted the negative results of his own and other colleagues' analytic work, i.e., the therapeutic failures, including interminable analysis, with a group of patients who, as it turned out, did not suffer from a typical infantile (oedipal) neurosis (1937, p. 220). Freud's quiet, sober discussion of negative results and the reasons for negative results has been ignored, while his insistence that his investigations had reached psychological bedrock is well known and frequently cited (1937, p. 252). Freud reluctantly and ambivalently admitted that he and other analysts were mistaken:

> One is tempted to make strength of the instinct and early defensive struggle against instinct responsible for unfavorable alteration of the ego. . . in the sense of its being dislocated and restricted. But it seems that the latter too has an aetiology of its own. And, indeed, it must be admitted that our knowledge of these matters is as yet insufficient. They are only now becoming the subject of analytic study. *In this field the interest of analysts seems to me to be wrongly directed. Instead of an inquiry into how a cure by analysis comes about (a matter which I think has been sufficiently elucidated) the question should be asked of what are the obstacles that stand in the way of such a cure* [1937, p. 221, italics added].

In fact, analytic study of psychopathology which could be explained neither by the theory of oedipal conflict nor by theories of defensive struggles against earlier impulses and their early objects had been going on for more than three decades at the time Freud wrote that the continued interest of analysts in early defensive struggles against instinct seemed misplaced. In his thinking over the years (1915, 1926, 1937) on the psychopathology which is now fruitfully regarded as structural deficit pathology, Freud enjoined analysts to pinpoint a factor which could explain why, on the one hand, patients with typical neuroses could subject their anxieties to the normal workings of the mind following analysis of the unconscious components of their nuclear conflicts, while, on the other hand, analysts and the patients with ego modification continued to come to grief over the problems of anxiety, depression, rage, injury, mortification, failure, "splintered-up" and compulsive infantile sexuality and sexual acts (1918, pp. 43–44), severe phobias, etc.

Negative analytic results like those Freud obtained and faithfully reported from 1915 on led to his and many other analysts' important efforts to pursue new directions in clinical theory and technique. Diligent attempts to discover the psychic reality of the parents of infancy and early childhood marked all of these efforts. Although maternal transferences which previously had been entirely overlooked were discovered by Freud and female colleagues (Fliess, 1948), the significance of the mother in early development and these transferences continued to be explained with the preexisting conflict hypothesis. No further new discoveries were made, and variations on Freud's and Abraham's own derivative "earlier" versions of the theory of psychic conflict and of earlier defensive struggles against impulses and early objects began to proliferate in earnest.[4] Analysts with very divergent viewpoints

[4]By positing the absence of *new* discoveries, I mean that the maternal transference was immediately fitted into the preexisting theory, and the preexisting theory was adapted to the early years of life. In terms of developmental-clinical theory, this meant that the early maternal imago was phallic. The little boy's task was to master "preoedipal" anxieties vis-à-vis the phallic mother; the little girl's task was to master deprivation (of a penis) at the phallic mother's hands by turning to the father, and then to master further deprivation (of a penis-baby) at the father's hands. Subsequent theory building on the role of the mother in

continued to retain the basic premise that psychic conflict is central to normal and pathological development and that psychoanalytic treatment and technique aim at conflict resolution. Thus, for example, Melanie Klein's *Love, Hate and Reparation* (1937), Horney's *New Ways in Psychoanalysis* (1939), and Sullivan's *Interpersonal Theory of Psychiatry* (1953), all share an emphasis on early splitting defenses, infantile impulses and their "good" and "bad" objects, and decisive psychic conflict.

Two years after Freud's discussion of undiscovered obstacles to analytic cure and the limits of conflict theory, Hartmann made a theoretical attempt to continue the discussion from where the psychology of neurosis left off. His new approach to the problems recognized by Freud may well represent the point at which Kohut's self psychology begins. Distancing himself from the clinical realities (negative analytic results) that provided the impetus for *Ego Psychology and the Problem of Adaptation* (1939), Hartmann tried to tell analysts that drive and conflict theory left out the genetic factor at issue. More specifically, the thrust of his monograph pointed to the fact that theory based on the conflict hypothesis left the actuality of the child's parents out of the etiological equation. Erikson (1950, 1959) and Rapaport (1959), following Hartmann, realized that parental care constitutes a series of average expectable environments, and that an "environment" with sufficient "nutriment" is a necessary condition for maturation and development of the "central regulations" of a conflict-free sphere of the mind. Normal workings of the mind, central regulations of a conflict-free sphere, etc., are part and parcel of the workings, regulations, and regulatory systems (Glover, 1945) of a cohesive self — an independent center of initiative which is capable, within human limits, of using its own functions for regulating itself. Although present-day ego psychology and psychoanalytic developmental psychology are rooted in Hartmann's concept of parents as an expectable environment, and in Spitz's (1965) concept of the "auxiliary ego," neither concept fits into theories of early

---

early development has retained the central emphasis of conflict and conflict resolution contained in Freud's and Abraham's original constructions.

objects, and neither concept bridges the gap between developmental theory and psychoanalytic practice (Greenacre, 1971; Murphy, 1973). Paradoxically, the very analysts who study "fitting together" of the young child and the human environment or the "auxiliary ego" (self), and who attempt to encompass faulty fitting together in a widened clinical theory and technique, remain tied to the earliest psychoanalytic propositions—propositions which are limited to explaining conflict in children and adults with an already established "normal ego," i.e., cohesive self. In all of the conflict theories, an environment which is actually deficient in essential psychological supplies or a deficient auxiliary ego simply leads to more serious splitting of the psyche and more severe psychic conflict than would otherwise be the case.

Twelve years after Freud's reluctant admission that conflict theory cannot explain "ego alteration," and 15 years after fruitless "controversial discussions" over early object relations theory further split an already divided profession, Glover (1945) also took issue with the overextension of the conflict hypothesis. The points he made very explicit have been overlooked. He noted that theories of conflict with internal objects leave out the critical factor we need to explain—how psychic structure and "regulatory systems" are actually established. He noted further that these theories are constructed from the *mental disintegration products* of patients with serious disorders, i.e., patients whose entire development was abnormal and whose regulatory capacities were never normally established in the first place. Although Glover's critique, like Rapaport's (1959) reference to "id mythology," was specifically directed at Melanie Klein's theory, the critique of object relations theory applies equally well to the multiplicity of theories of an infantile self split by conflict, and the multiplicity of theories of preoedipal and phallic-oedipal conflict on the present-day analytic scene. (The theory of separation-individuation no less than other theories of early objects explains psychological life by starting out with the disintegration products—"splintered-up" impulses and objects—which are the hallmark of failed or failing self-cohesion.)

Three decades after Freud's realization that he had been wrong about the causal role of early defensive struggles against drives and the objects of the drives when it came to the patients in question, Phyllis Greenacre (1971) singled out the same patients and addressed precisely the same clinical-theoretical issues in her article in *Separation-Individuation: Essays in Honor of Margaret S. Mahler* (McDevitt & Settlage, 1971). Although the volume honored Mahler's work, Greenacre described the unbridged gap between Mahler's, Spitz's, and other analysts' observational studies of infants and young children, and the mothers or mother substitutes who cared for them, and the theory and practice of psychoanalysis. In effect, Greenacre said that psychoanalysis needed a new hypothesis to fill this gap, one that could accommodate observational data on environmental failures and failed development and correlate these data with new principles and/or technical procedures which are valid and clinically effective for a subgroup of apparently analyzable patients. The subgroup Greenacre herself delineated is now familiar from Kohut's contributions; it consists of patients who are neither neurotic, borderline, nor psychotic, and whose "basic transference" she had tried to fathom for many years.

Greenacre's clinical observations led to her highly important descriptions of the serious human failures in these patients' childhood parental "environments"; of the patients' considerable successes, strengths, and talents; of their sufferings from deficiencies in normal self-esteem, self-sufficiency, and object constancy, as well as from anxiety, depression, rage, envy, and devaluation of their ideals; of their complex defenses which had been confused with neurotic defenses, etc. Most of all, Greenacre's clinical observations led to her entirely overlooked description of a "necessary bulwark" in the patients' personality which they rightly tried to protect — a bulwark, according to Greenacre, which was assaulted instead of strengthened in analytic treatment addressed to unconscious preoedipal and oedipal wishes and their "objects," to unconscious resistance (defense), and to psychic conflict. Her clinical descriptions, including her description of the "bulwark," and her attempts to understand such patients' basic transferences, leave no doubt that Greenacre came on the same psychological phenomena Kohut conceptualized as the nuclear, core, or central self and the selfobject transferences of patients with self pathology. The fact that Greenacre "stumbled on" (cf. Freud, 1914, p. 17; 1925, p. 35) a previously unrecognized transference and that it was "discovered" and subsequently "forgotten" is not surprising. Freud first stumbled on the Oedipus complex, and discovered, forgot, and finally rediscovered it over many years. (In this connection, cf. Tolpin [in Panel, 1974], for a discussion of "optimal failure" and psychoanalytic discovery.) In other words, selfobject transferences, like oedipal transferences, were discovered, forgotten, rediscovered, and finally conceptualized after many years during which Kohut, along with the rest of us, continued to insist mistakenly that one or another self conflict, preoedipal conflict, and/or phallic-oedipal conflict provided the structural basis for "ego abnormality."

In her contribution to the volume of essays honoring Margaret Mahler, then, Greenacre made some extremely candid and cogent points concerning Mahler's and others' observational studies and the conflict hypothesis. Their observational studies, she said, failed to generate a new psychoanalytic hypothesis despite the vast amount of empirical data that had accumulated over several decades. As a consequence, she continued, the results of psychoanalytic treatment with Mahler's and others' developmental and clinical theories of fateful psychic conflict during babyhood continued to disappoint analysts and patients alike. Some patients, she acknowledged, derived benefits from their still unexplained basic transferences and from *active nonanalytic efforts* on the part of the analyst to establish and reestablish rapport. In Greenacre's experience, however, interpretations and genetic reconstructions of wishes, longings, loves, hates, rage, defenses, psychic conflicts, etc., held to originate in the second year of life or later, left patients with supposed insights into their babyhood which, at the very best, were merely interesting encumbrances. At their worst, such interpretations and reconstructions not only fail to promote conflict resolution and expanded self-awareness, but are experienced by the patient as assaults on a bulwark of the personality which has to be protected. Like Freud in 1937, Greenacre in 1971 also made the point that the fault lay with conflict theory and with insufficient

understanding of the patients, the obstacles to cure, and the transferences in question.

Finally, like Freud in 1937, Greenacre pointed out that the
conflict hypothesis satisfactorily explained no more than psycho-
neurosis and its treatment. And like Anna Freud in her extensive
writings (1968, 1969, 1970), Greenacre pointed out that the use of
this hypothesis to explain early childhood development and
analytic treatment of disorders beyond the infantile neurosis involved an unwarranted extension of a valid theory into a realm of
childhood mental life which drive and conflict theory simply could
not explain. In the ego psychological framework within which psychoanalytic investigations of the past have been carried out, the
realm which the conflict hypothesis cannot explain is the realm of
the functions of an "auxiliary ego" and the formation of psychic
structure necessary for the establishment of the functions of a
"normal ego." In the self psychological framework of the present
era, this is the realm of the cohesion-promoting self-selfobject
unit, and a new edition of the unit in which further maturation and
development of the very psychological capacities patients with self
pathology need most can take place.

The Shift to the Concept of Selfobjects

It is a fundamental tenet that the emotional valence of the
care a normally endowed child receives must be taken into account
in every etiological equation. The course of normal maturation
and development of psychic "structure" undergoes alteration unless a series of average expectable maturation- and growth-
facilitating environments automatically fit together, or cogwheel
through mutual empathy, with the child's legitimate developmental needs.[5]

With the discovery of the psychic reality of a selfobject en-

[5]Anyone familiar with the psychoanalytic literature will recognize references
in the foregoing to the developmental contributions of Freud, Hartmann,
Erikson, Winnicott, and Anna Freud. Again, my main point is that the conflict
hypothesis does not do justice to these contributions. It is precisely on this point,
moreover, that there are decisive differences between Kohut's theory and those of
Winnicott, Fairbairn, and Guntrip.

vironment which normally acts almost automatically to preserve and promote the child's normal illusion ("delusion") of independence and his nuclear initiative, psychoanalysis has reached another crossroad. Like Freud's early seduction theory, the theories of psychic conflict that attribute primary psychological danger to infantile impulses and their early objects no longer do justice to clinical psychoanalytic discoveries. Of his "mistaken idea" that his hysterical patients had suffered literal seductions in early childhood, Freud would observe that the theory "broke down under the weight of its own improbability and contradiction. . . . Analysis had led back to these infantile sexual traumas by the right path, and yet they were not true. . . at last came the reflection that, after all, one had no right to despair because one has been deceived in one's expectations; *one must revise those expectations"* (1914, p. 17, italics added). If we follow Freud's example and revise our expectations concerning the explanatory range of theories of psychic conflict, it will no longer be necessary to turn away from our own field and our own methods of research in the hope that the research methods of cognitive psychologists and other nonanalytic developmental psychologists can replace mistaken psychoanalytic theories with better ones. And further, with our expectations revised, it will no longer be necessary to fill the theoretical gap between principles of psychoanalytic developmental psychology and the psychoanalytic situation by postulating that a real alliance or a real relationship with an ally, a real person, or new object must be fostered so that conflicts and fantasied dangers from impulses and their early objects can be analyzed. Patients who develop selfobject transferences do so because of persisting developmental needs for the multiple psychological functions of an "ally"–selfobject, and persisting needs to acquire adequately these functions themselves.

When we revise our expectations of finding and analyzing conflicts in instances where selfobject failures, "mental disintegration products," and structural deficits are present, it becomes apparent that the path to further psychoanalytic research into the psychological life of children will lie open to us once again; and it becomes equally apparent that the path to the second line of advance in psychoanalytic treatment — the line pertaining to structural deficit disorders — will also lie ahead. (The discoveries which led to the second line of advance for disorders of the self are unthinkable without those which led to the establishment of the first line of advance for the psychoneuroses. By the same token, however, continuing progress in the understanding and treatment of the neuroses is unthinkable without continuing progress in the understanding and treatment of self pathology.)

Freud's discovery of the psychic reality of parents as oedipal objects cleared up the "mistaken idea" of seduction that had proved near-fatal to the young science of psychoanalysis (see Freud, 1914, 1925). Similarly, Kohut's discovery of the childhood psychic reality of selfobjects clears up the "mistaken idea" of early objects and archaic conflict. By revising our expectations in precisely the way Freud revised his when he realized the seduction theory was mistaken, and by shifting our point of view to the self as a primary psychological configuration, we can apply the theory of selfobjects and the formation of a cohesive self to psychoanalytic treatment; to psychotherapy for structural deficit disorders which are not analyzable; to preventive work with the many parents and children who fail to thrive because of persisting deficits in the parents and persisting needs of the children for selfobjects; and to continuing psychoanalytic research both inside and outside the clinical situation.

In brief, at this stage in our developmental dialogue the concept of the prestructural selfobject links fundamental insights of developmental psychology concerning mutuality and the consequences of disordered mutuality with clinical psychoanalysis. In doing so the selfobject concept constitutes a necessary theoretical bridge between structural deficit pathology, which is heir to failures of an average expectable environment, and the theory and technique of psychoanalytic treatment of the selfobject transferences, which give analyzable children and adults with disorders of the self a second chance to take over for themselves the psychological functions of their reinstated selfobjects.

As the link enabling analysts to put developmental theory into practice, the concept of the selfobject also constitutes a theoretical bridge which enables psychoanalysis to continue to use the psychology of the self from the point where Freud, Hartmann, Glover, Anna Freud, Greenacre, and Kohut realized that the psychology of neurosis and the psychology of conflict leave off. As such, the concept serves as a unifying path for a field which has been split and divided by the multiplicity of theories — earlier self theories, preoedipal and phallic-oedipal theories — that have mistaken psychological disintegration products for components of unconscious conflict. In this respect, the developmental-clinical concept of selfobjects overcomes the major difficulty in the present-day path of psychoanalysis (A. Freud, 1969), and opens the way to reintegration and restoration of the field as a whole.

References

Abraham, K. (1924), A Short Study of the Development of the Libido, Viewed in the Light of Mental Disorders. *Selected Papers on Psycho-Analysis.* London: Hogarth Press, 1927.

Broucek, F. (1979), Efficacy in Infancy: A Review of Some Experimental Studies and Their Possible Implications for Clinical Theory. *Internat. J. Psycho-Anal.,* 60:311–316.

Eissler, K. R. (1953), The Effect of the Structure of the Ego on Psychoanalytic Technique. *J. Amer. Psychoanal. Assn.,* 1:104–143.

Erikson, E. H. (1950), *Childhood and Society.* New York: Norton.

_____ (1959), *Identity and the Life Cycle. Psychol. Issues,* Monogr. 1. New York: International Universities Press.

Ferenczi, S. (1913), Stages in the Development of the Sense of Reality. In: *Sex in Psychoanalysis: The Selected Papers of Sandor Ferenczi,* vol. 1. New York: Basic Books, 1950.

Fliess, R. (1948), *The Psychoanalytic Reader.* New York: International Universities Press.

Freud, A. (1968), Indications and Contraindications for Child Analysis. *The Writings of Anna Freud,* 7:110–123. New York: International Universities Press, 1971.

_____ (1969), Difficulties in the Path of Psychoanalysis. *The Writings of Anna Freud,* 7:124–156. New York: International Universities Press, 1971.

_____ (1970), The Infantile Neurosis. *The Writings of Anna Freud,* 7:189–203. New York: International Universities Press, 1971.

Freud, S. (1905), Three Essays on the Theory of Sexuality. *Standard Edition,* 7:135–243. London: Hogarth Press, 1953.

_____ (1914), On the History of the Psycho-Analytic Movement. *Standard Edition,* 14:3–66. London: Hogarth Press, 1957.

_____ (1915), Observations on Transference-Love. *Standard Edition,* 12:157–171. London: Hogarth Press, 1958.

_____ (1918), From the History of an Infantile Neurosis. *Standard Edition,* 17:3–122. London: Hogarth Press, 1955.

_____ (1925), An Autobiographical Study. *Standard Edition,* 20:3–76. London: Hogarth Press, 1959.

_____ (1926), Inhibitions, Symptoms and Anxiety. *Standard Edition,* 20:77–175. London: Hogarth Press, 1959.

_____ (1937), Analysis Terminable and Interminable. *Standard Edition,* 23: 209–253. London: Hogarth Press, 1964.

Glover, E. (1945), Examination of the Klein System of Child Psychology. *The Psychoanalytic Study of the Child,* 1:75–118. New York: International Universities Press.

Greenacre, P. (1971), Notes on the Influence and Contribution of Ego Psychology to the Practice of Psychoanalysis. In: *Separation and Individuation,* ed. J. B. McDevitt & C. F. Settlage. New York: International Universities Press, pp. 171–200.

Hartmann, H. (1939), *Ego Psychology and the Problem of Adaptation.* New York: International Universities Press, 1958.

Horney, K. (1939), *New Ways in Psychoanalysis.* New York: Norton.

Kagan, J. (1979), The Form of Early Development: Continuity and Discontinuity in Emergent Competences. *Arch. Gen. Psychiat.,* 36:1047–1054.

Klein, G. (1976), *Psychoanalytic Theory: An Exploration of Essentials.* New York: International Universities Press.

Klein, M. (1937), *Love, Hate and Reparation.* London: Institute of Psycho-Analysis & Hogarth Press.

Kohut, H. (1971), *The Analysis of the Self.* New York: International Universities Press.

_____ (1977), *The Restoration of the Self.* New York: International Universities Press.

_____ (1978), Remarks About the Formation of the Self—Letter to a Student Regarding Some Principles of Psychoanalytic Research. In: *The Search for the Self,* vol. 2, ed. P. H. Ornstein. New York: International Universities Press, pp. 737–770.

Levine, F. G. (1978), Book Review of *The Restoration of the Self* by Heinz Kohut. *Bull. Phila. Psychoanal. Assn.,* 4:238–247.

Lozoff, B., Brittenham, G. M., Trause, M. A., Kennel, J. H., & Klaus, M. H. (1977), The Mother-Newborn Relationship: Limits of Adaptability. *J. Pediat.,* 91:1–12.

Mahler, M. S., Pine, F., & Bergman, A. (1975), *The Psychological Birth of the Human Infant.* New York: Basic Books.

McDevitt, J. B. & Settlage, C. F., eds. (1971), *Separation-Individuation: Essays in Honor of Margaret S. Mahler.* New York: International Universities Press.

Munroe, R. L. (1955), *Schools of Psychoanalytic Thought: An Exposition, Critique, and Attempt at Integration.* New York: Holt, Rinehart, & Winston.

Murphy, L. B. (1973), Some Mutual Contributions of Psychoanalysis and Child Development. In: *Psychoanalysis and Contemporary Science,* vol. 2, ed. B. Rubinstein. New York: Macmillan, pp. 99–123.

Panel (1974), The Analyst's Emotional Life During Work. Reported by R. Aaron.

J. Amer. Psychoanal. Assn., 22:160–169.

Rapaport, D. (1959), A Historical Survey of Psychoanalytic Ego Psychology. In: *Identity and the Life Cycle,* by E. Erikson. *Psychol. Issues,* Monogr. 1. New York: International Universities Press, pp. 5–17.

Schwartz, L. (1978), Book Review of *The Restoration of the Self* by Heinz Kohut. *Psychoanal. Quart.,* 47:436–443.

Spitz, R. A. (1963), Life and the Dialogue. In: *Counterpoint,* ed. H. Gaskill. New York: International Universities Press.

_____ (1964), The Derailment of Dialogue: Stimulus Overload, Action Cycles, and the Completion Gradient. *J. Amer. Psychoanal. Assn.,* 12:752–775.

_____ (1965), *The First Year of Life.* New York: International Universities Press.

Stein, M. H. (1979), Book Review of *The Restoration of the Self* by Heinz Kohut. *J. Amer. Psychoanal. Assn.,* 27:665–680.

Stone, L. (1961), *The Psychoanalytic Situation.* New York: International Universities Press, 1977.

Sullivan, H. S. (1953), *The Interpersonal Theory of Psychiatry.* New York: Norton.

Tolpin, M. (1971), On the Beginnings of a Cohesive Self. *The Psychoanalytic Study of the Child,* 26:316–352. New York: Quadrangle.

_____ (1978), Self-Objects and Oedipal Objects: A Crucial Developmental Distinction. *The Psychoanalytic Study of the Child,* 33:167–184. New Haven: Yale University Press.

_____ (1979), Discussion of "The Sustaining Object Relationship" by H. B. Levine. *The Annual of Psychoanalysis,* 7:219–225. New York: International Universities Press.

_____ & Kohut, H. (1979), The Psychopathology of the First Years of Life: Disorders of the Self. In: *The Course of Life,* ed. S. Greenspan & G. Pollock. Washington, D.C.: U. S. Government Printing Office.

White, R. W. (1963), *Ego and Reality in Psychoanalytic Theory. Psychol. Issues,* Monogr. 3. New York: International Universities Press.

Winnicott, D. W. (1965), *The Maturational Processes and the Facilitating Environment.* New York: International Universities Press.

Developmental Perspectives on the Psychology of the Self in Early Childhood

Bertram J. Cohler

Concern with the course of personality development, particularly across the childhood years, is of particular significance for psychoanalysis, both as a framework for understanding actions and intents and as a specific form of psychotherapy. This developmental perspective has been based on two very different forms of observation, retrospective accounts regarding childhood experiences obtained from the analysis of adults, and more or less systematic observational study of young children, including those children participating directly in child analysis.

To date, most observational and retrospective developmental data have been viewed within the context of the object-libidinal line of development, which is concerned with the experience, over time, of increasingly reciprocal and need-satisfying relationships with others based on the nature and extent of satisfaction of very

The present paper was assisted by grants from the National Institute of Mental Health (ST 32 MH 14668-03) and National Institute on Aging (PHS 5 Pol AG00123-03). The work of Drs. Marian Tolpin and Bernice Neugarten has been of particular help in understanding the course of personality development across the life cycle.

early needs, particularly the need for nurturance itself. With the emergence of psychology of the self, attention has focused on the development of the child's increasing capacity for regulating inner tensions associated with acceptance of important ambitions and, somewhat later, central values, and on the integration of these aspects of self in order to provide for the experience of cohesiveness and continuity over time. Correspondingly, important questions have been raised regarding the adequacy of the object-libidinal line as the only line of development to be considered in understanding the course of human development. At the same time, because psychology of the self has emerged largely as a result of findings from the study of "transferencelike" phenomena reenacted by adults in analysis, it is important to consider the self developmental line from the prospective perspective as well, and to examine the benefits to be derived not only from these retrospective data, but from data obtained directly from the study of young children.

The Developmental Perspective in Psychoanalysis

Genetic propositions in psychoanalysis concern both statements of the origins or ground plan out of which later behavior arises, and the later vicissitudes of these origins. As Hartmann and Kris (1945) note in their discussion of the genetic approach:

> The genetic approach in psychoanalysis does not deal only with anamnestic data, nor does it intend to show only "how the past is contained in the present." Genetic propositions describe why, in past situations of conflict, a specific solution was adopted; why the one was retained and the other dropped, and what causal relation exists between these solutions and later developments [p. 14].

Consistent with this view, Rapaport and Gill (1959), in describing the defining characteristics of the genetic perspective as a metapsychological point of view, note that genetic propositions do not merely address themselves to issues of origin and development. In addition, they concern maturation according to an epigenetic ground plan in which earlier modes of mental functioning, although superseded by later forms, remain potentially active, with the totality of the person's earlier experiences codetermining later outcomes.

Early Psychoanalytic Developmental Formulations

Freud (1913a) notes that the developmental perspective has always been central to psychoanalytic study of the person. As he comments:

> Not every analysis of psychological phenomena deserves the name of psycho-analysis. The latter implies more than the mere analysis of composite phenomena into simpler ones. It consists in tracing back one psychical structure to another which preceded it in time and out of which it developed. . . . from the very first psycho-analysis was directed towards tracing developmental processes. It began by discovering the genesis of neurotic symptoms, and was led, as time went on, to turn its attention to other psychical structures and to construct a genetic psychology which would apply to them too [pp. 182–183].

As Freud notes, psychoanalysis has had to "take seriously the old saying that the child is father to the man" (p. 183). Explicit discussion of this developmental perspective is rarely found within Freud's own writings, however, and then typically in discussions either of predisposition to particular forms of psychopathology or of the process of reconstruction (Cohler, 1980). In addition to the *Three Essays on the Theory of Sexuality* (1905b), which Freud continued to revise through 1924, reference to genetic propositions is made in several of the early letters to Fliess (1887–1902), the paper on the "neuro-psychoses of defence" (1896b), the Clark lectures (1910a), the paper on the disposition to obsessional neurosis (1913b), and in a brief discussion of the phallic phase of development (1923), which was included in a somewhat abbreviated manner in the 1924 revision of the *Three Essays*.

Much of this earlier discussion of the process of development and regression is also summarized in Lectures 22 and 23 of the *Introductory Lectures* (1916-1917) in 1917. The revised formulation of instinctual development, as described in the 1924 revision of the *Three Essays*, is also contained in Lecture 31 of the *New Introductory Lectures* (1933) and as Chapter 3 of the *Outline of Psycho-Analysis* (1940).[1]

Beyond these discussions of the development of libido, offered principally in relation to the etiology of the neuroses, the paper on the "Two Principles of Mental Functioning" (1911) and the discussion of the case of Little Hans (1909) refer more generally to the process of development in childhood. On the other hand, the monograph on *Psychopathology of Everyday Life* (1901), the psychobiographical study of Leonardo (1910b), the Wolf Man case (1918, 1919), together with the very late paper on "Constructions in Analysis" (1937), deal with developmental issues from the perspective of reconstruction.

It is significant that, in work spanning more than 50 years and 23 published volumes, there is so little explicit reference by Freud to the genetic point of view except in reference to the problem of choice of neurosis. Indeed, it was first Ferenczi (1913) and later Abraham (1916, 1921a, 1921b, 1924a, 1924b, 1925) who really developed the epigenetic concept and explicated the concept of development. As Abraham comments:

> Observation has taught us that no developmental stage, each of which has an organic basis of its own, is ever entirely surmounted or completely obliterated. On the contrary, each

[1]Of particular relevance in the present context, little consideration was given to development of the self, as contrasted with the object-libidinal line of development in Freud's work. Although the basis of superego (ego ideal) development is outlined in the work on group psychology (1920c), continued in *The Ego and the Id* (1923), and summarized in the *New Introductory Lectures* (1933), it has remained a problem within psychoanalysis, with significant contributions made by Jacobson (1964); Sandler, Holder, and Meers (1963); Schafer (1960); and more recently, Kohut (1971, 1977).

new product of development possesses characteristics derived from its earlier history...even after childhood, the character of the individual is subject to processes of evolution and involution [1925, pp. 416–417].

This statement, which predates Erikson's more detailed formulation of the epigenetic process by more than 25 years, contains much of what we understand today as the genetic perspective in psychoanalysis.

It is of considerable importance for the fate of the genetic perspective in psychoanalysis that Freud's first appreciation of the importance of childhood in determining later outcomes was as a result not of empirical observation but, rather, of his own introspective investigation. As Jones (1953) and Sadow et al. (1968) both have noted, Freud's discovery of infantile sexuality emerged as a result of his self-analysis, although he was interested in obtaining independent confirmation through observational study like that provided by the material from Little Hans (1909). This case study, and the brief paper on sexual enlightenment that appeared two years earlier in 1907, together with the recounting of childhood dreams as wish fulfillments in the *Interpretation of Dreams* (1900), a review of anecdotes told by friends about children in *Totem and Taboo* (1913c), a brief but beautiful account of a one-and-a-half-year-old child's reaction to the temporary departure of his mother in *Beyond the Pleasure Principle* (1920b), and a comment (1920a) on a letter received from the American mother of a four-year-old regarding her daughter's associations to overheard conversations among adults, represent the major references made by Freud in his work to actual observations of children or interpretations based on observations provided by associates.

Reconstruction and the Genetic Perspective

Freud's introspective method for retrospectively discovering infantile sexuality was critical for the future of psychoanalysis as a clinical technique, a set of hypotheses regarding human behavior, and a mode of observation of normative developmental processes.

From the perspective of clinical psychoanalysis, it led to the development of one of the most essential interventions of the psychoanalytic process. Understood as the attempt by the analyst to correlate conflictual experiences repressed by the analysand with present forms of actions such as dreams, transferences, and free association (Moore & Fine, 1968), reconstruction is based very much on a topographic model of the mind (Rapaport & Gill, 1959; Gill, 1963; Kohut & Seitz, 1963) emphasizing the problem of the access of contents of the mind to consciousness, together with the associated problems of unraveling the distortions required by the censor in order to make the unconscious contents acceptable as aspects of the preconscious.

Reconstruction in Clinical Psychoanalysis

There has been much discussion in the psychoanalytic literature about reconstruction as a clinical technique. Greenacre (1971, 1975) has noted that reconstruction is less often employed than in past years as a central aspect of the analyst's activity, and others have questioned the significance of such reconstructive activity (Kris, 1956; Fine, Joseph, & Waldhorn, 1959). Too often, reconstruction becomes an activity isolated from the reality of the transference itself, thereby losing immediacy of experience for the analysand. When the transference is correctly interpreted, the analysand is able to move from the transference interpretation to the relevant genetic experiences associatively linked with the transference in a way that renders explicit genetic reconstructions relatively insignificant in the psychoanalytic process (Kanzer, 1953; Novey, 1968). Increased attention to the interpretation of the transference itself, as advocated by Gill and Muslin (1976), may provide a more successful and emotionally powerful link between present and past than that achieved by reconstruction alone. As Schimek (1975) has noted, drawing upon Erikson's (1962) discussion of actuality in the life history, the most effective interpretations are those based on the analysand's own perceptions rather than on "objective" constructions of reality.

As a means for understanding human behavior, hypotheses

generated by the reconstructive approach have proven problematic in the development of a truly psychoanalytic understanding of development across the course of the life cycle. Freud struggled with this problem throughout his work, addressing it in his early collaboration with Breuer (1893–1895) and correspondence with Fliess (1887–1902) and in papers written near the end of his life, like the one on the use of constructions in analysis (1937).

Much of this early discussion of the role of the past was contained in Freud's consideration of the seduction hypothesis, by which Freud referred to the apparent power of remembered incidents from childhood to elicit symptoms in adults (1895, 1896a). On the basis of the first hysterical patients with whom he worked, Freud concluded that a specific traumatic event was derived from childhood sexual stimulation that was too great to be regulated, and was represented in awareness only through associations or symbols standing for it.

As a result of an intense intellectual and personal struggle, Freud came increasingly to realize that the important factor was not the actual event but, rather, the child's developmentally determined fantasy of the event (Freud, 1896a & b). By the time of the Dora case (1905a), Freud had come to realize that such neurotic fantasies were based not on memories of the actual occurrence of an event, but rather on the child's fantasy of an event. Indeed, in the *Three Essays on the Theory of Sexuality* (1905b) Freud suggested that children learn sexual repression not through a model, either child or adult, but as a result of "spontaneous internal causes" (p. 191). This same position was adopted a year later in the paper on sexuality in the neuroses (1906) where Freud also noted that the factors accounting for such childhood fantasies were not intrinsically different in neurotic and "normal" persons.

Reconstruction and the Development of Memory

With the abandonment of the seduction hypothesis, and the discovery of the Oedipus complex, psychoanalysis took a fateful step away from reliance on external events in understanding the course of psychological development, although Freud, as we have observed, continued to struggle with this issue. Indeed, it is this reliance on "internal events" or fantasies rather than "external or actual events" that distinguishes psychoanalytic from other formulations of human development. Memory, rather than being viewed as a repository of earlier, actually perceived events, becomes a source of displacement for childhood wishes and fantasies. What is remembered is the wish, and not the event itself. As Freud observed, "A man's conscious memory of the events of his maturity is in every way comparable to the first kind of historical writing (which was a chronicle of current events); while the memories that he has of his childhood correspond, as far as their origins and reliability are concerned, to the history of a nation's earliest days, which was compiled later and for tendentious reasons" (1910b, p. 84).

Memories such as those concerning childhood observation of parental sexual relations, seductions by adults, or threats of castration are understood as reflections of wishes transposed onto events connected in time and space with the appearance of the wish (the so-called screen memory or screen experience). As early as 1899, Freud makes it quite clear that these so-called screen memories reported by adults in analysis are not mere reproductions of childhood memories, but successive transformations, across childhood and adulthood, of earlier wishes that were unacceptable when admitted to mind and, now disguised, appear in adulthood as transferences (Freud, 1899). Freud cautions us against assuming that adult memories have a direct correspondence with the memories of earliest childhood:

> It may indeed be questioned whether we have any memories at all *from* our childhood: memories *relating to* our childhood may be all that we possess. Our childhood memories show us our earliest years not as they were, but as they appeared at the later periods when the memories were aroused. In these periods of arousal, the childhood memories did not, as people are accustomed to say, *emerge;* they were *formed* at that time. And a number of motives, with no concern for historical accuracy, had a part in forming them, as well as in the selection of the memories themselves [1899, p. 322].

So-called childhood memories which appear in adulthood, such as those referring to the primal scene, are based on developmentally determined wishes, together with developmentally appropriate defenses against the emergence of such wishes into consciousness, and are later transformed by successive experiences across childhood and adulthood (A. Freud, 1951; Cohler, 1980).

As a result of changes in the very organization of memory itself, together with accompanying changes in our sense of time, earlier experiences are successively reordered across the life cycle in such a way as to meet not only the demands of a psychic censor, but also to meet the changing developmental needs of the organism. Across the life cycle, there is a constant process of revision of previous memories of both recent and older experiences (Pollock, 1971; Loewald, 1976, 1978). Such changes appear to be carried out in the service of maintaining a consistent life history, which in turn leads to increased feelings of well-being or inner cohesion (Schachtel, 1947; Vaillant & McArthur, 1972).

Reconstruction and the Study of Child Development

From the perspective of psychoanalytic observation of the course of child development, concern has been expressed that reconstructions have led to assumptions about childhood mental development that are based on adult frames of reference (Masterson & Rinsley, 1975), or that generate methods and findings regarding child development that are so narrow in scope and so mechanistic as to be psychoanalytic in name only.

Freud makes few references to direct observation of young children in his own work, other than to note, both in the *Three Essays* (1905b) and the case of Little Hans (1909), that such observations, together with reconstruction, can provide increased certainty for the findings of psychoanalysis. His discussion of the developmental process did inform the first generation of child observers and analysts, however, many of whom came to psychoanalysis through education. Early contributions by Hug-Hellmuth (1919), Bernfeld (1925), and Anna Freud (1927, 1930), falling directly in the mainstream of psychoanalysis, were further enriched by the writings of the British school, including both Melanie Klein (1928) and Susan Isaacs (1930, 1933). Whereas the theoretical contributions of the British school have been questioned, along with their emphasis on direct analysis of the transference early in the process of child analysis, there can be little question of the wealth of detailed observational material it contributed regarding the psychological development of young children.

It was only following World War II that these early clinical studies became a part of the mainstream of child development research. In part, this research was stimulated by the war nursery project of Anna Freud and Dorothy Burlingham (1943, 1944) that focused systematically on the issue of separation and its role in the child's development. Spitz's well-documented study of the effects of hospitalization (1945, 1946) and the later Yale longitudinal study on the course of development across the first three years of life (Kris, 1951; Escalona, 1953; K. Wolf, 1953, 1954; Senn & Hartford, 1968) were among the first American studies demonstrating the significance of psychoanalytic perspectives for studying the course of child development. These pioneering studies have been followed by more recent, detailed cross-sectional studies such as those regarding the development of cognition (Wolff, 1966) and emotional expressiveness (Stechler & Carpenter, 1967; Emde, Gaensbauer, & Harmon, 1976).

Although it is claimed that much of this basic developmental research was informed by psychoanalytic concepts (Rapaport, 1960; Murphy, 1973), G. Klein had pointed to a tendency to claim, as a part of psychoanalytic ego psychology, research that actually falls within the tradition of general experimental and developmental psychology. Further, since this developmental research has generally relied upon data collected outside the empathic mode, which is an important defining characteristic of the psychoanalytic approach, there is some question about what can be learned about the course of psychic development from such empirical research.

Within psychoanalysis itself, there has been some attempt to use the results of empirical investigations, such as those concerning perceptual learning in early childhood, to provide proof for psychoanalytic propositions regarding aspects of development which, to date, have not received support using the traditional modes of inquiry within psychoanalysis. To the extent that the findings of developmental research have had an impact on either the theory or practice of psychoanalysis, they have served primarily to provide what is believed to be scientific verification of particular assumptions (such as the significance of critical periods in infancy) that are derived from genetic psychoanalytic propositions regarding the origins of behavior in early childhood. This use of findings from developmental research, and the confusion that results from combining findings based on empirical and empathic modes of observation, may make it even more difficult to establish a psychoanalytic developmental psychology.

The Developmental Perspective and the Critical Period Hypothesis

Far too often, psychoanalytic studies of child development have focused on childhood events solely in terms of their possible impact on adult development alone, without sufficient concern for developmental processes across childhood itself. Many of these developmental studies have been concerned with the demonstration of some "critical period" in development. Such studies presume that there is some psychobiologically determined "moving window" in development that is open only for a brief period of time, after which, if particular events do not occur, subsequent impairment ensues. This critical period concept has been applied in developmental psychology primarily regarding the development of the mother-child bond. As a result primarily of Bowlby's (1958) paper, a great deal of study was devoted to the consequences of earlier deprivation for the child's later socioemotional and cognitive development (Khan, 1963). The critical period hypothesis has figured prominently in formulations of libidinal development as well as in explanations of character traits associated with fixation at particular nodal points in development.

The problem with the critical period concept is that recent evaluations of the course of development have shown that even when serious cognitive and socioemotional pathology is present,

there is a greater degree of reversibility than was previously realized (Clarke & Clarke, 1976; Schaffer, 1977). Indeed, even those
working within the ethological paradigm itself have begun to question the basic assumption of this critical period hypothesis.
Harlow and his colleagues now report that the impact of social
isolation on infrahuman groups may not be as great as previously
believed, and in many instances can be reversed or corrected
(Novak & Harlow, 1975). Such findings are consistent with Connolly's (1972) review of the current literature on the critical period
hypothesis, which suggests that, even if true for other species including primates, the critical period concept may not be gene-
ralizable to human behavior.

The critical period concept is of interest to psychoanalysis
precisely because it seems to provide support for the reconstructive
efforts of psychoanalytic therapy, including the effort to postdict
from adult outcomes to childhood development. Freud, however,
questioned the fruitfulness of attempting postdiction, observing
that:

> So long as we trace the development from its final outcome
> backwards, the chain of events appears continuous, and we
> feel we have gained an insight which is completely satisfactory
> or even exhaustive. But if we proceed the reverse way, if we
> start from the premises inferred from the analysis and try to
> follow these up to the final result, then we no longer get the
> impression of an inevitable sequence of events which could
> not have been otherwise determined. . . . The synthesis is thus
> not so satisfactory as the analysis; in other words, from a
> knowledge of the premises we could not have foretold the
> nature of the result. . . . Hence the chain of causation can
> always be recognized with certainty if we follow the line of
> analysis, whereas to predict it along the line of synthesis is im-
> possible [1920d, pp. 167–168].

Developmental Perspectives and the Psychology of the Self

On the basis of this brief review of methods of study in

psychoanalytic developmental psychology, it appears that a fresh start may be necessary to advance our understanding of the development of patterns of meaning and intent. Such a new beginning must be based on a truly psychoanalytic frame of reference, rather than relying on the methods of developmental psychology. Such a frame of reference posits (1) that the method of study is empathic observation rather than the tabulation based on measurable data, and (2) that the issues of proof and validity rest in the consistency of interpretations and are unrelated to external forms of validity, including the creation of general laws and inferences from sets of observations.

The Method of Empathic Observation

Reliance on the analyst's own introspective processes, including the analyst's affective response to the other, is the basis of the empathic method of observation and a major element of the psychoanalytic process. As Kohut (1959) has observed: "We designate phenomena as mental, psychic or psychological if our mode of observation includes introspection and empathy *as an essential constituent*. The term 'essential' in this context expresses (a) the fact that introspection or empathy can never be absent from psychological observation and (b) that it can be present alone" (p. 463).

This is in keeping with Freud's (1912) recommendation that the analyst maintain "evenly hovering attention" when listening to the analysand. This attitude was first termed the empathic mode by Reik (1937), who observed that the analyst shares the experience of another as if it were his own. Murray (1938) has referred to this process as "recipathy" (reciprocal empathy), and Schafer (1959) as "generative empathy." It represents what Fliess (1942) has described as a kind of "trial identification" in which the analyst affectively reacts to the analysand's material by "tasting" or introjecting this material.[2]

[2]Cohler (1977) has noted that, at least in working with seriously disturbed patients, this empathic response is itself therapeutic, for it is experienced by the patient as the therapist's willingness to bear the burden of the bad and

   This empathic mode of observation is contrasted with empirical modes of observation characteristic of the natural sciences. Such empirical modes have been adopted by developmental psychology and applied to such areas as the study of the mother-child relationship by classifying and coding a discrete number of behaviors reliably agreed upon by observers as "equidistant from the interacting parties, occupy[ing] an imaginary point *outside* the experiencing individual" (Kohut, 1971, p. 219). It does not matter whether the theoretical framework has been informed by psychoanalytic theories of development (Mahler, Pine, & Bergman, 1975). What is critically important is the method used to collect the observations. The external frame of reference is to be contrasted with that so well described by Kohut as one in which "the observer ...occupies an imaginary point *inside* the psychic organization of the individual with whose introspection he empathically identifies" (1971, p. 219).

   Too often, particularly when there is a dual emphasis on understanding both the child's subjective perspective of his world and the relationship of parent and child, it becomes all too easy to move outside the empathic framework and to describe qualities of the actual relationship in contrast to the inner experiences of mother and child. While the study of the real relationship between mother and child is of value in describing the qualities of the child's social development (Clarke-Stewart, 1973), this is a different enterprise from that included within psychoanalytic forms of observation.[3]

---

unacceptable wishes and fears until the patient is once more able to integrate them with the rest of the personality. From the perspective of Kohut's (1977) work, the therapist's willingness and empathic understanding have a soothing quality, promoting a sense of increased psychic cohesion.

   [3]There is little to be gained in the attempt to rewrite either developmental psychology or psychoanalysis in the terms of the other discipline (Décarie, 1965). For example, as Mahler, Pine, and Bergman (1975) suggest, attempts to reconcile the use of the term "object" as defined by Piaget and by psychoanalysis may have obscured rather than clarified the understanding of the use of this term in either discipline. The methods used by positivistic psychology and empathic psychoanalysis are too disparate to be joined, and there is little to be gained by transforming psychoanalysis from the study of conflict into a "general psychology." These two quite different forms of scholarship aim at quite different kinds of

The role of empathic processes in the analytic study of adults can perhaps be appreciated more easily than the use of such empathy in the study of childhood, particularly the preverbal infant period. As Kohut (1959) has noted in his discussion of empathy, the use of this empathic method in the period of childhood presents a particular challenge. It is perhaps for this reason that it is difficult to find persons skillful in infant and child observation, for many adults find it too difficult to use their own "child-self" in responding to the child's state. (Freud's impressive discussion of the issue of separation and loss in a toddler [1920b] and Winnicott's work are examples of what can be done with the empathic method.) Such difficulty, of course, should not deter us from attempting to study infant and child development from this truly psychoanalytic perspective.

The psychology of the self, with its focus on the empathic method and its concern with the development of meanings and subjective intents rather than with functions and mechanisms, may be of particular help in furthering our understanding of personality development. Enriched by an understanding of the object-libidinal line of development, while adding yet another dimension to our understanding of the person, it may provide renewed inspiration for clinical-observational study of the developmental process across childhood, from infancy through adolescence. Such studies would complement the classic studies reported in the child analytic literature, such as those found in the special 1935 issue of *The Psychoanalytic Quarterly,* or in the early volumes of *The Psychoanalytic Study of the Child.*[4]

---

knowledge. While each may be fascinating in its own right, neither discipline will be advanced by efforts at integration. Recognizing such problems, Basch (1977) has made a fresh start in dealing with the integration of Freud and Piaget at the level of clinical theory rather than at the level of metapsychology.

[4]Little distinction has been made in the present discussion between those empathic observations collected during analytic treatment and those collected in naturalistic settings for the purpose of inquiry. The empathic mode of observing is equally applicable in treatment and more formal research settings, as K. Wolf (1953, 1954) has so sensitively demonstrated.

Interpretation and the Problem of Proof

From the outset, psychoanalysis was faced with the issue of validity or proof of its basic constructs. Working within the natural science model prevalent in Western European science at the turn of the century, it is not surprising that Freud simply adopted the philosophy of science that typified the intellectual milieu in which he worked. This positivist framework was later adopted by American social sciences as well, and has dominated much of the thinking about the significance of psychoanalytic contributions within developmental psychology (Rapaport, 1960), leading to contributions which are difficult to characterize as psychoanalytic. Elsewhere, I have discussed in greater detail the concept of validity in psychoanalytic research (Cohler, 1980). Following recent discussions of the issue of validity in psychoanalytic research (Sherwood, 1969; Ricoeur, 1977; Schafer, 1978; Kovel, 1978), it may be questioned whether the natural science model, which is concerned with generalization on the basis of observations, is the most useful one for psychoanalysis. The method of the historical sciences, concerned with the nature of the interpretations linking facts into a narrative, might be a more appropriate model, particularly when dealing with the genetic perspective (Collingwood, 1946; Gardiner, 1959; Wyatt, 1962, 1963; Novey, 1968; McGuire, 1971). Sherwood (1969) notes that much of what is considered to be explanation and generalization within psychoanalysis is, upon reflection, another form of descriptive narrative, ordering the material of a life history into a coherent account. The criterion for an acceptable account is one of narrative intelligibility, including whether the account can be followed clearly so that it is "self-explanatory" (Ricoeur, 1977). As Ricoeur notes:

> narrative intelligibility...comes to terms with the general condition of acceptability that we apply when we read any story, be it historical or fictional....Psychoanalytic reports are kinds of biographies and autobiographies whose literary history is a part of the long [oral epic] tradition...of

storytelling that provides a relative autonomy to the criterion of narrative intelligibility as regards...the consistency of the interpretative procedures [p. 869].

It is perhaps to this narrative intelligibility that Freud appeals when, in discussing the adequacy of a construction in analysis (1937), he suggests that the successful construction leads to a "sense of conviction" in the analysand regarding its adequacy.

This new approach to the solution of the problem of validity and proof places psychoanalysis within the realm of humanistic studies, and replaces the natural science approach with the historical approach, surely the most appropriate for a developmental psychoanalysis. It also resolves many of the problems associated with reconstruction in psychoanalysis, for it recognizes that just as history is successively rewritten by different epochs, so personal history is successively rewritten across the life cycle. Earlier experiences are interpreted in quite different ways as one's perspective on these experiences changes. Every analyst is familiar with patients who, on beginning analysis, view their parents in a particular manner, but shift their views during the course of the analysis. Generally, when the analytic outcome is favorable, the analysand acquires increased tolerance for his parents' own foibles, and sees that memories of earlier experiences, previously experienced as particularly malignant, may have additional significance beyond that first realized.

Just as we need to change our method of study of psychic development from a natural science model based on the frame of reference of the external observer to that of the empathic observer attempting to understand the person's subjective world, and just as we need to shift from a concern with validity to a concern with adequacy of interpretation in the study of psychoanalytic "proof," so we need to shift our theoretical frame of reference. To date, most research in developmental psychology that is informed by the concepts and findings of psychoanalysis has been concerned with the vicissitudes of the object-libidinal line of development. Beginning with Freud's *Three Essays,* and continuing with the work of Ferenczi and Abraham to the present-day conceptualizations of

Anna Freud and Erikson, development has been understood large-ly in terms of the vicissitudes of instinctual drives. Even Erikson's concept of identity is based on the epigenetic formulation first pro-posed by Freud and by Abraham of fixation points and regression in drive development. His resulting view of identity is very different from the concept of a sense of inner cohesion and con-sistency as described by Kohut (1977) in his presentation of the psychology of the self.

What is required is a study of the line of development of the self that covers the life span. With the exception of earlier papers by Wolf, Gedo, and Terman (1972) and Goldberg (1978b), both of which concern development of the self during adolescence, this ap-proach has been concerned thus far with the consequences of earlier psychopathology of the self on *adult* personality. What is needed is more detailed prospective study of the development of the self, using those methods of study and forms of "proof" that are unique to psychoanalysis.

Psychology of the Self and the Course of Development in Childhood

Considering the magnitude of the problems associated with formulations of development based on the object-libidinal line, it is striking that the line of development of the self was neglected for so long in psychoanalytic developmental psychology. In part, as Gedo and Goldberg (1973) have suggested, the problem may lie in the very confusion that exists regarding the model to be used in understanding personality development. Whereas Freud's very early model of the tension arc may have had greater sig-nificance for understanding the developmental process than was earlier realized, he became increasingly concerned with the ques-tion of how we gain access to the contents of consciousness and, later, with the problems created by this topographic model of the mind.

The creation of the tripartite model, with its emphasis on so-called "functions" of the ego, appeared to deal adequately with the problem of development; it became relatively easy to translate psychoanalytic observations regarding functions such as memory and attention into the apparently equivalent language of experimental psychology, leading to the equation of ego psychology with a general experimental psychology. In addition to the serious problems of method already noted as a result of this invocation of an external frame of reference for psychic development, a serious logical mistake was also made. As Gedo and Goldberg (1973) note so well in their discussion, the very basis of the tripartite structural model is the existence of three structures of the mind that develop as a result of the resolution of the Oedipus complex. By definition, this structural model is not applicable to the preoedipal period of development and cannot include consideration of psychic development across the first three years of life. Further, at least for ego psychology, since the ego itself is said to develop out of the id, the concept of intersystemic conflict is built into the tripartite model. Such conflict pertains not only to the relation of the ego to the id, but to the relation between the different stages in the development of the libido itself.

Such consideration of development solely in terms of an object-libidinal framework is reflected in the attempts of object relations theories to deal with the prestructural period of early childhood development with essentially structural concepts. It is interesting that, in spite of this serious conceptual problem, and the associated attempt to explicate development only in terms of the object-libidinal line of development, a number of child analysts perceived another aspect of development which, often mistakenly, was understood in object-libidinal terms. The formulations of Melanie Klein and, somewhat later, of Edward Glover, René Spitz, and D. W. Winnicott are important in this regard.

Melanie Klein and the Emergence of an Intrapsychic Perspective

Klein's description of the developmental process is posed solely in the psychological (rather than social-psychological) terms characteristically used to describe the impact of the mother-child relationship on the child's development. Her timetable for early development appears to be somewhat compressed within the first two years of life (the youngest child she actually worked with was two and three-quarters years of age), but her method of study is an empathic-observational one, and she provides detailed observations and complete case reports to document her conclusions. Her method of proof, like her method of observation, is a truly psychoanalytic one.

One of the most controversial aspects of Klein's formulations, particularly those based on the early observations that culminated in her classic study, *The Psychoanalysis of Children* (1928), concerns the early onset of the Oedipus complex and the experience of anxiety associated with this process (Klein, 1932). In the light of Gedo and Goldberg's criticism of structural theories of development, it is possible that Klein too became aware of the inconsistency of applying the structural model to the preoedipal period, but resolved it by placing the development of structure earlier in the developmental process than had previously been recognized.

From the perspective of later formulations of the psychology of the self, Klein's concern with the regulation of anxiety and tension states is apparent. She suggests that the child experiences tension as anxiety, initially related to possible annihilation in retaliation for envy and the aggressive wishes to which it leads and, later, related to the sadness evoked by the realization of the loss of support engendered by these aggressive acts. Clearly, in her concept of early superego formation, Klein recognizes that internalization of the mother's own attitudes toward the modulation of aggression is important in the child's developing capacity for regulation of his or her own inner tensions, but this internalization only becomes possible after the child has been able to withstand the ravages of the paranoid-schizoid phase. As Klein notes:

> In the early stages the projection of his terrifying imagos into the external world turns that world into a place of danger and his objects into enemies; while the simultaneous introjection of real objects who are in fact well-disposed to him works in the opposite direction and lessens the force of his fear of the terrifying imagos. Viewed in this light, super-ego formation, object-relations, and adaptation to reality are the result of an

interaction between the projection of the individual's sadistic impulses and the introjection of his objects [1928, p. 148].

The paranoid-schizoid and depressive phases in early development are viewed as normative, reflecting more or less auspicious outcomes for subsequent development.

Whereas the roles of figures in the time/space world are important as a part of the developmental process, it is not the actual relationship with these persons but, rather, the child's subjective interpretation that is significant. Temperamental or constitutional factors must be taken into account, together with external factors, in understanding the child's perception of the world. The important factor is the child's perception of the quality of the care received, rather than particular observed characteristics of the parents or other significant persons: internalizations do not have a point-for-point correspondence with events in the time/space world.

Edward Glover, René Spitz, and the Concept of Developmental Organizers

Both Glover and Spitz have been concerned with the regulation of tension, except that they clearly postulate the development of means of tension regulation in terms of the structural theory, which is not really appropriate in discussing the preoedipal period of development. Glover views the ego as developing out of autonomous "nuclei" or "organizers" which can be traced to general processes of neural development and not necessarily to energy borrowed from the id. These ego nuclei are concerned with such different aspects of the adaptation to reality as perception, cognition, motility, and relationships with others (Glover, 1932; Spitz, 1959). Glover, speaking of these ego nuclei, notes that:

it is obvious that not only the adult ego but the ego of a child of five, however well organized, is essentially a composite... viz. that any psychic system which (a) represents a positive libidinal relation to objects or part objects, (b) can discharge reactive tension... and (c) in one or other of these ways reduces anxiety, is entitled to be called an ego system or *ego-nucleus* [1932, pp. 168–169].

Spitz (1957, 1959, 1965) seems to arrive at a similar conclusion after having taken a different route: rather than approaching the study of ego functions from clinical studies of adults, he approaches it from the systematic observational study of child development. Spitz speaks of "psychic organizers," and regards the major developmental organizers as the capacity for responding to others (smiling response), the capacity for making both spatial and interpersonal differentiations (eight-month anxiety), and the capacity for speech (particularly "yes" and "no" as symbols). In speaking of these developmental organizers or nuclei, Spitz comments that:

> the organizer is a theoretical construct. It designates a state of coordination and integration of a number of functions, both somatic and psychological. The result of this integration is a new level of organization which actually changes the properties of the elements from which it originates. [If a disturbance in development results], the ego's integrative tendency will compensate the resulting retardation of specific ego nuclei through a deviant integration. . . . Such luxuriating and consequently abnormal ego nuclei may then become the constituents of a "fragmented ego" [which] will inevitably come into conflict with the normal demands of the environment at a much later stage. . . [1959, pp. 83, 86–87].

Winnicott and the Object Relations Approach to the Study of Inner Regulation

More recent formulations of the development of inner regulation have moved away from consideration only of the development of mental functions to include the context of the child's first relations with his parents as well, together with the impact of the parent-child relationship on the child's subsequent development. This consideration of the parent-child relationship, however, has raised once more the problem of applying the structural model to the prestructural period, along with the problem of the role of reality factors in the child's psychological development.

The "object relations" approach (Guntrip, 1969) assumes that the first bond formed between child and parent is based on the mother's ability to satisfy basic biological needs, particularly provision of nurturance. Winnicott's (1960) paper on the theory of the parent-infant relationship portrays quite well this more recent change in understanding the impact of the parent-child relationship on psychic development. Reviewing psychoanalytic discussions of infancy, Winnicott emphasizes the fact that, since the infant is dependent upon the mother, inherited potential cannot be realized except as linked to actual maternal care, particularly as realized through maternal holding. It is as a result of holding that the infant is able to emerge from his merger with the mother and become a separate person. Winnicott is less clear about the mechanism involved in fostering the development of a sense of separateness, but he suggests that the process of "living with" can satisfy basic tensions so that the child can gradually build a sense of self separate from others. Winnicott views this process as one of emergence from the holding relationship to a relationship in which the mother lives with the child as a separate being. As Winnicott observes, in discussing holding and the transition to "living with,"

A further development is the capacity for object relationships. Here the infant changes from a relationship to a subjectively conceived object to a relationship to an object objectively perceived. This change is closely bound up with the infant's change from being merged with the mother to being separate from her, or to relating to her as separate and "not me." This development is not specifically related to the holding, but is related to the phase of "living with". . . [1960, p. 589].

Elsewhere, in discussing this later developmental phase of "living with," Winnicott notes that "the term 'living with' implies object relationships, and the emergence of the infant from the state of being merged with the mother, or his perception of objects as external to the self" (1960, p. 588).

As a result of this process, the child develops stable and satisfying object relations. The mother's empathy is crucial in this process of the development of a sense of personal continuity in a manner similar in many respects to Kohut's formulation of the role of empathy in the development of the self. However, his perspective is still informed primarily by the object-libidinal line of development. Winnicott's primary concern is with the development of satisfying relationships with others, rather than with the development of a capacity for regulation of tensions associated with the ambitions stimulated by the experience of nuclear grandiosity. For Winnicott (1945, 1951, 1960), as for Mahler and her associates, the mother is viewed as a need-fulfilling object rather than a source of soothing in the presence of tensions so intense that they can lead, if not regulated, to feelings of fragmentation of the child's fragile self.

Mahler and the Developmental Line of Individuality

Mahler has attempted to study the development of inner regulation from the perspective of the mother-child relationship itself. Her formulation of the child's developing sense of self as a separate person, from the phase of "normal autism" through the periods of differentiation and hatching, to the practicing and rapprochement subphases, and finally, to the consolidation of individuality (Mahler, 1968; Mahler, Pine, & Bergman, 1975) is too well known to warrant further discussion.

It is less well recognized that Mahler's discussion of the development of individuality is not just a description of the formation of object constancy and the capacity for satisfying relationships with others, but equally important, a description of the process by which the child learns regulation of inner tension. As the child develops a sense of individuality, he also learns inner regulation that was formerly provided by the mother as soothing caretaker. Perhaps the best example of this process is found in the shadowing and darting of the rapprochement phase (18–24 months). In the process of moving away and coming back toward his mother, the child develops the ability to provide optimal dosage of inner tensions, seeking the mother's aid and comfort when these tensions become too intense, and moving away for exploration once again after appropriate soothing. Finally, the child discovers an optimal distance from mother that permits the opportunity for exploration without an intolerable increase in anxiety. As Mahler and her associates note, the development of this sense of optimal distance is an indication of the process of internalization and the development of self-regulation (1975, p. 101). They observe that "The 'internal mother,' the inner image or intrapsychic representation of the mother, in the course of the third year should become more or less available in order to supply comfort to the child in [the] mother's physical absence" (1975, p. 118).

Earlier, they noted that:

> the narcissistically fused object was felt to be "good" — that is, in harmony with the symbiotic self — so that primary identification took place under a positive valence of love. The less gradually, the more abruptly, intrapsychic awareness of separateness occurs, or the more intrusive and/or unpredictable the parents are, the less does the modulating, negotiating function of the ego gain ascendancy. . . . the less predictably reliable or the more intrusive the love object's emotional attitude in the outside world has been, the greater the extent to which the object *remains* or *becomes* an unassimilated foreign body — a "bad" introject, in the intrapsychic emotional economy. . . . In short, great ambivalence may ensue which continues to mar smooth development toward emotional object constancy. . . the consequences for those children in whom the too sudden and too painful realization of their helplessness has resulted in a too sudden deflation of their previous sense of their own omnipotence, as well as of the shared magical omnipotence of the parents. . . [p. 117].

If the parental function of tension regulation is withdrawn too suddenly or prematurely, before this function has been successfully internalized, it can lead to a sense of inner turmoil which is later experienced as feelings of fragmentation (Kohut 1971, 1977; Gedo & Goldberg, 1973) or, in the language of the older object relations theory, to splitting (Guntrip, 1969).

The Emergence of Psychology of the Self

Natural Science and Empathic Modes of Observation in Psychoanalytic Formulations of Development

In contrast with the earlier work of Freud and Glover, the contributions of Klein, Winnicott, Spitz, and of Mahler and her colleagues are informed by observation of the course of psychological development among young children. However, the introduction of observational data, itself, raises problems of method. In the case of Klein and, particularly, Winnicott, the observer is empathically concerned with understanding the child's subjective perception of the world. On the other hand, for Spitz and particularly for Mahler and her colleagues, the observer is essentially the "objective" and detached observer operating from a natural science framework, i.e., concerned with the collection of comparable observations that will permit generalizations regarding developmental processes beyond the realm of meanings and intents. These observers appear at times to step outside the psychoanalytic method of studying the developmental process.

There is no particular reason why observation of the child, including his interaction with his mother, cannot be carried out by means of the empathic modality, rather than in terms of the concepts and methods of social psychology. Kohut (1977) believes that all observational study, and also all formulations regarding the child's relationship with the parents, are necessarily outside of the psychoanalytic framework (relying, instead, on a so-called sociobiological perspective). The important issue here is not the basis of the observations that are made, however, but rather the method used in making the observations, together with the model of proof employed in integrating these observations. It is possible, as Winnicott's work has shown, to observe the child in his family, and yet to do so from an empathic rather than a social-psychological perspective.

Object Relations and Selfobjects

Finally, it should be noted that each of these formulations of the developmental process focuses on development in terms of the object-libidinal line of development. Even the discussions of Winnicott and Mahler and her colleagues regarding the role of the mother in the development of the internal world presume that the importance of the mother for the child's development is principally in terms of her ability to satisfy basic bodily needs; it is the regularity and constancy with which she is able to meet these needs which is the principal element in the process of internalization, as described by Schafer (1968) and Modell (1968). According to Winnicott and Mahler et al., adequate maternal attention to these bodily needs fosters the development of the capacity for loving and for mature relatedness in an object relations sense. These formulations fail to emphasize adequately the importance for the child's development of the manner in which the maternal provision of care is carried out. Whereas Winnicott does speak of the "good enough" mother who is empathic with the child's needs (1960, p. 591), he does not discuss in sufficient detail exactly what it is that makes the mother "good enough," or precisely why the mother's empathy is so significant for the child's development.

Kohut (1971, 1977) suggests that an important aspect of this quality of being "good enough" is not simply the mother's dependability, but the very soothing quality of these actions, not as judged from an external frame of reference, but as perceived subjectively by the child: the mother is a selfobject for the child. With little self-other differentiation possible during the first months of life, the child perceives caretaking not as something performed from without, but as part of the emerging self. Unlike Winnicott, Kohut recognizes that maternal comforting is not merely useful in promoting the infant's capacity for loving relatedness, but in facilitating the capacity for tension regulation associated with early grandiosity. The mother's ability to soothe her child by providing for successful regulation of tension is not just gradually internalized by the child from without, but begins by being perceived, originally, as residing within, as a part of the self. Child and mother, that is, are perceived by the child as merged into one self-object unit. Only later, after the period of the transitional object, is the mother's ability to soothe realized by the child as an internal capability rather than something residing in the mother. This results in the feeling of individuality or individuation. As Tolpin (1971) describes this process:

> This view of the infant's capacity to create for himself an aux-iliary soother which ultimately becomes part of an inner reg-ulatory structure suggests that despite the human infant's prolonged dependence his mental equipment includes innate factors which, sufficiently supported by mothering, potential-ly guarantee development into a self-regulating separate psychic entity with partial independence.... When the soothing functions of the mother and [later] the blanket are effectively internalized, a normal phase of relative structural insufficiency has passed [pp. 332–333].

Tolpin notes that the mother assists in this tension regulation by assisting the child in developing signal anxiety that leads to the recognition of increased tension and, thus, to the ability to take measures to regulate this tension. Gradually, the mother is relin-quished as a selfobject and the capacity for tension regulation is increasingly experienced by the child as a part of the self. In later life, under circumstances of life stress, in areas where the function of tension regulation was earlier not permitted to develop optimal-ly, persons rely on others once again to serve as selfobjects, pro-viding the same soothing and signal anxiety function previously ex-perienced with the mother as selfobject. Finally, it is important to note that this inner regulation is effected as a result of a series of transmuting internalizations which have been recognized as a part of the treatment process (Kohut, 1971, 1977) but which may be regarded as equally important in the course of development prior to the oedipal period. In providing for optimal dosing of frustra-tion, it is important neither to prevent the child's own developing sense of inner regulation nor to permit levels of tension to increase too greatly. As a result of transmuting internalizations, the child takes on regulating functions performed earlier by the mother, and is able to develop a sense of the upper and lower limits of tolerable tensions with respect to both early ambitions and also, to a more limited extent, ideals (Kohut, 1977).

The Development of the Bipolar Nuclear Self

The process of development, as suggested by Kohut (1971, 1977) and Tolpin (1971), should be understood entirely from the perspective of the child's subjective experiences, using the empathic method uniquely characteristic of psychoanalytic observation. From this perspective, the important aspect of the mother-child relationship is the use which the child makes of this relationship in his struggle to achieve that successful regulation of tensions that leads to a feeling of continuity over time.

This totally psychological focus is in contrast to the interpersonal formulations on the child's developing sense of self, as presented by such social-psychological theorists as Cooley (1902), Mead (1934), and Sullivan (1953). It also marks a departure from the developmental formulations of Anna Freud (1965) and, particularly, Erikson (1950), who views identity, presumably a concept similar to continuity as discussed by Kohut and his colleagues, as rooted in the development of a sense of trust in the ability to realize satisfaction of libidinal needs consistent with Abraham's (1925) epigenetic formulation of object-libidinal development. Rather than emphasizing such interpersonal determinants, or simply the extent to which the child obtains success in the satisfaction of basic needs for nurturance that foster the later capacity for satisfying relationships, the psychology of the self, while recognizing the importance of object-libidinal development, emphasizes that the important factor in development is the increased capacity for self-soothing that is possible only as a result of what Winnicott (1960) has termed "good enough" mothering.

This "good enough" mothering is good enough not from the standpoint of an outside observer, but as subjectively experienced by the child, regardless of the actual mother-child relationship, and taking into account the child's perception of the mother's ability to provide the necessary soothing in an optimal manner over time. The child's developing identification with the parents' own empathic, developmentally timed, and appropriate care-taking, as well as with the increased regulatory capacity resulting from "dosed" caretaking, becomes itself a part of the child's inner regulatory apparatus. As Kohut (1977) notes:

> The child that is to survive psychologically is born into an empathic-responsive human milieu (of self-objects). . . . When the child's psychological balance is disturbed, the child's tensions are, under normal circumstances, empathically perceived and responded to by the self-object. . . that can realistically assess the child's need and what is to be done about it, will include the child into its own psychological organization and will remedy the child's homeostatic imbalance through actions [p. 85].

Kohut notes that the first of these measures, the empathic perception of the child's needs, is particularly important in constructing a nuclear self that becomes the supraordinate psychic organization concerned with the integration and continuing realignment of ambitions and ideals, that leads to a sense of continuity over time, including the continuity of memory itself. Later experiences of fragmentation and disintegration are a result of initial difficulty in developing a cohesive nuclear self.

The child experiences disappointment when his needs are not attended to in ways subjectively experienced as soothing; tensions arise which the child, and later, the adult, cannot regulate because there is no previous history of the experience of such soothing as first experienced with the mother; there is no internalized regulatory process. Tensions are later felt as a restlessness or sense of vague anxiety, and even as hypochondriacal symptoms as the process of fragmentation continues. In a last-ditch attempt to contain these tensions, the person may experience a sense of apathy, lack of responsiveness, or even complain of a feeling of inner deadness.

Parenting and the Development of the Self

Much of this theory of psychic development in the pre-structural period has been derived by Kohut and his associates from the analysis of adults showing disturbances of self-regulation. Using the empathic mode, which figures importantly both in the development of the self and in the reconstruction and restoration of the self in treatment, Kohut has attempted to reconstruct the child's original experiences within the family and, through such reconstruction, to locate the problems in the original parent-child relationship that led to the disturbance of the self. The problem with this approach is to be found precisely in the assumption that the adult's report of earlier events has an exact correspondence with these events as the child previously experienced them. For example, nearly all patients report that their parents were not empathically responsive to their needs. They evidence their sensitivity to lack of empathy through the reenactment of the early relationship within the context of treatment itself, which then serves as the basis for the formulation of earlier development failures.

On the basis of this material which emerges in the treatment process, it is difficult to speculate about the conditions leading to the original disturbance of the self. Certainly, it is clear that parental ability to perceive and meet the child's needs, specifically as experienced by the child, is central to the development of the child's own ability to regulate inner tensions. Observations by a number of different research groups within the field of psychoanalytic child psychology have supported this emphasis on the parents' ability to meet the child's needs as central to fostering the child's development in an optimal manner. They have also provided additional evidence of the critical importance of a reciprocal relationship between mother and child for the child's later development (Sander, 1962, 1964, 1969; Erikson, 1950; Bettelheim, 1967). What has not been understood to date is the variety of factors accounting for a more or less successful meshing of the needs of mother and child, together with the fact that such factors are to be appraised entirely in terms of the child's own perspective.

From the perspective of adult analysis, using the empathic method and "tasting" the analysand's material, it would appear that parental care had not been in synchrony with the child's needs, presumably as a result of parental psychopathology. Kohut makes it quite clear that minor failures or breaks in empathy are a "natural" part of the process of parenting and, indeed, are essential to helping the child achieve the development of inner regulation. He is also quite clear that such minor empathic failures, along with specific traumatic factors in the course of development, are less central for the child's later development than aspects of the personality of the parents:

> I believe that psychoanalysis will move away from its preoccupation with the gross events in the child's early life. There is no doubt that gross events...can play an important role in the web of genetic factors that lead to later psychological illness. But clinical experience tells us that in the great majority of cases it is the specific pathogenic personality of the parent(s) and specific pathogenic features of the atmosphere in which the child grows up that account for the maldevelopments, fixations, and unsolvable inner conflicts characterizing the adult personality. Stated in the obverse: the gross events of childhood that appear to be the cause of the later disturbances will often turn out to be no more than crystallization points for intermediate memory systems, which, if pursued further, lead to truly basic insights about the genesis of the disturbance [1977, p. 187].

Kohut (1977) notes that the basis of the self pathology in the offspring is the parent's own lack of empathy, not just occasionally, but pervasively in the parent-child relationship. He adds that this failure is not simply one of overstimulating the child, or even of failing to provide necessary stimulation, but of providing tasks for the child that are not appropriate to the child's needs at that level of development. The important element, in this formulation, is the parental empathic deficiency that results in an asynchrony between what the parent can provide and what is optimal for the child at a given point in development.

The problem with this formulation is that Kohut appears to be concerned with parental responses which are grossly and not subtly or occasionally disruptive of the child's developing inner regulation, whereas more recent discussions (Goldberg, 1978a; Tolpin & Kohut, 1978) attempt to relate less significant deficits in parental empathy to quite serious psychopathology of the self among offspring, suggesting that such occasional problems in empathy may be magnified in the child's subsequent development in ways not generally realized.

Reconstructive and Prospective Study of the Development of the Self

In his discussion of the psychopathology of the self, Kohut repeatedly stresses the fact that his formulations derive from reconstructions from the analysis of adults. Indeed, since Freud's own pioneering discovery of the Oedipus complex as a result of his self-analysis, psychoanalytic formulations of development have been informed principally by such reconstructive efforts. It remains for those concerned with prospective studies, particularly those working within the tradition of child analysis and psychoanalytic child psychology, to apply the important findings of the psychology of the self to the study of the development of the self during childhood and adolescence, and to clarify further findings obtained by means of the retrospective reports of adult analysands.

It is clear that adults, whose disorders of the self include feelings of inner depletion and "unmirrored ambitions" (Kohut, 1977, p. 243), do reenact this psychopathology of the self in their relationship with the therapist, and do make connections between these present feelings and childhood experiences. As one of Winnicott's patients observed, "An interpretation given at the right time *is* a good feed" (1960, p. 591). It is important to keep in mind, however, that every adult retrospectively develops a picture of what his or her parents were like. This picture of one's parents fluctuates across the life cycle: adolescents necessarily view their parents in terms of competition and struggle, whereas older persons view their parents in highly idealized terms (Lieberman & Falk, 1971; Prosen, Martin, & Prosen, 1972).

Although there is no "true" past, but only that which is remembered at any point in the life cycle, reconstruction and reminiscence *can* provide clues regarding important aspects of personality to be considered in prospective investigations. Kohut cautions us that such prospective investigations may lead to a misplaced concern with the reality of the child's experiences, including the quality of the mother-child relationship as it appears to an "objective" observer outside the subjective frame of reference. While recognizing the importance of this caution, it may still be possible to complement the retrospective approach so often followed in psychoanalytic discussions of development with a psychoanalytically informed prospective approach relying upon the same empathic method employed in the analysis of adults. Certainly, this is an approach that has been shown to be possible time and again in the classic child analytic literature. This approach emphasizes not how the mother actually cares for her child, but how the child comes to interpret this maternal care.

The Child and His Caretakers

It is important to recognize that, even in the earlier responses to maternal care, such as the gusto with which the infant sucks or the clarity with which he makes his needs known to his mother (Sander, 1962, 1964, 1969), temperament enters into the subjective response to maternal caretaking efforts (Thomas et al., 1963; Thomas & Chess, 1977; Freedman, 1974). This is but another way of restating Freud's concept of the "complemental series" in psychic development (Freud, 1905b [1915/1920] pp. 239–240).

The child's response to caretaking is always a complex combination of such constitutional factors, together with the child's reaction to important aspects of the mother's personality, including her own developmentally determined response to parenthood (Behrens, 1954; Benedek, 1959, 1973).

It is clear that the factors impinging upon the parent-child relationship are reciprocal and complex and not just unidirectional;

the child influences the parent to nearly the same extent that the parent influences the child. As Bell (1964) has shown, the child sets upper and lower limits on his parents' behavior, and thereby shapes the quality of parental responses. A variety of careful observational studies reported in the volume edited by Lewis and Rosenblum (1974), together with the detailed review of earlier studies reported by Bell (1977), suggest that, both in the normative developmental process and where there is some problem in the development of the parent-child relationship, characteristics of the child must be taken into account together with those of the parent. Children may overtax the resources of their parents, or be particularly sensitive, irritable, and unable to quiet. Further, it should be noted that, in social-psychological research on the parent-child relationship, correlations should not be regarded as implying causation.

Even parental psychopathology does not necessarily interfere with the development of an empathic relationship between parent and child. In the first place, studies of offspring at risk for mental illness on the basis of parental psychosis have not been found to show greater rates of incidence for serious psychopathology than would be expected simply on the basis of genetic factors alone (Hanson, Gottesman, & Heston, 1976; Hanson, Gottesman, & Meehl, 1977). In the second place, detailed observational study of mentally ill mothers and their very young children, at least partially informed by the empathic method, has not found higher incidences of psychopathology among these children. In a study carried out under the influence of the object-libidinal formulation of development, chronically ill schizophrenic mothers have been observed to care for their children in a tender and wholly appropriate manner, and to be more sensitive than well mothers in the community to the baby's cues of his needs (Grunebaum et al., 1974).

Careful psychiatric interviews of somewhat older children in this research, carried out by a board-certified child psychiatrist and graduate child analyst, revealed no greater psychopathology or problems of adjustment among the children of mentally ill mothers than among the children of well mothers. More recent study of the social and personal adjustment of the 10-year-old sons and daughters of groups of schizophrenic, depressed, and well mothers revealed an incidence of adjustment problems no greater among either group of children of mentally ill mothers than among the group of children of well mothers (Grunebaum et al., 1978).

Whereas much of this research pertaining to the offspring of mothers with serious psychopathology only partially lies within the psychoanalytic method of empathic observation, the results of this research suggest that we need to understand much better than we do at present the impact of the mother's disturbance on the child's own development. An initial attempt to approach this problem from a psychoanalytic perspective has been reported by Anthony (1971) using the object-libidinal framework. More recently, Bemesderfer and Cohler (1980) have attempted to apply the concepts of the psychology of the self to the observational study of two children of psychotic depressed mothers. The role of the mother's psychopathology in the development of the child's self-selfobject relationships has important implications for our understanding of the self and the factors associated with more or less successful development of inner regulation of psychic tensions.

Future research in psychoanalytic developmental psychology should avoid the mistake of much past research that has employed psychoanalytic concepts in an essentially social-psychological format, operating outside the empathic method and relying on natural science rather than historical modes of proof. Otherwise, psychoanalysis will endlessly repeat the error of the seduction hypothesis, assuming that specific aspects of the child's environment such as parental psychopathology or particular socialization practices must be responsible for present and later outcomes. The nature of the mother-child relationship must be appreciated, but principally from the standpoint of the child's subjective response rather than from actual characteristics of the relationship which stand outside the subjective frame of reference and present themselves as measurable data. Such data are reduced from more complex patterns of interaction between mother and child, or presumed on the basis of the older reductionist framework to account for later outcomes.

Most important of all, informed by the perspective provided by the psychology of the self, it will be necessary to study in detail the development of the bipolar self during childhood, both among children showing disturbances of the self and among their well-functioning counterparts. This involves more than the reanalysis of existing findings, such as those obtained by Mahler and her colleagues. It means a reorientation of our very framework for viewing the child's development, with particular respect to the child's search for competence and realization of ambitions, together with the nature of the means used for modulating tensions arising in the course of the developing self.

The earlier work of Murphy on *The Widening World of Childhood* (1962) points to a new direction in child study, but Murphy's work was informed primarily by a view of mastery derived from the structural model of development, including emphasis on the development of autonomous ego functions. Further study is required of the concepts of ambitions and ideals as formulated within the psychology of the self. Such study should address itself to the nature and extent to which each of these aspects of the bipolar self is important in the development of a sense of self, and to the relative degree of independence of these two aspects of self over the course of childhood, both from each other and from the object-libidinal developmental line.[5]

Conclusion

Kohut's (1959) discussion of the empathic method represents

---

[5]Whereas developmental psychologists have come to appreciate concepts like competence (White, 1963) and mastery, the basic framework for studying the child's development of a sense of effectance remains the structural theory. Although the postulation of "independent ego-energies" made possible by Hartmann's work (1939) represents an important step away from the more narrow libidinal model of development, the concepts of mastery and competence in this model of the mind are very different from the concept of ambition based on the grandiose self as discussed in the psychology of the self. While ambitions, in Kohut's sense, refer to very early strivings toward a sense of wholeness that appear during the first 18 months of life, competence as a motive has been understood in terms of ego psychology and the structural model that pertains to the period between the third and fifth years involved in the formation of psychic structure (Gedo & Goldberg, 1973).

a major contribution in the attempt to develop a psychoanalytic perspective free of the constraints imposed by the older natural science approach, with its emphasis on observation from outside the vantage point of the experiencing person. In more recent contributions (1971, 1977), Kohut has applied this empathic mode of observation to the study of the parent-child relationship itself, particularly to fluctuations in parental empathy as subjectively experienced by the child, and has considered the role of empathy in the development of the child's capacity to regulate inner tensions.

Contributions to the psychology of the self have relied principally on retrospective accounts based on the analysis of adults. Such reconstructions can be understood as part of the continuing collaboration between analyst and analysand in writing a history of the analysand's life that changes across the course of the analysis. With increasing capacity for tension regulation, achieved through transmuting internalizations and the resolution of the mirroring and idealizing transferences, such reconstructions are more usefully understood as part of the changing history of the course of the analytic relationship itself than as an accurate record of the analysand's past. Indeed, the very goal of a single "best" or most accurate history independent of the context in which this record is written is, itself, impossible to realize (Collingwood, 1946; Novey, 1968; McGuire, 1971; Schafer, 1979). The history constructed by a particular person at a particular phase of his or her analysis, is very different from that constructed either very much earlier or very much later. Reconstructions themselves may be understood as attempts at creating the sense of inner cohesion and continuity which, as Kohut (1977) notes, is so essential for inner well-being. Just as there is no one most accurate history, so there is no single most complete reconstruction outside of the context — and this includes both the phase of the life cycle and the phase of the analysis — in which the reconstruction is made.

From this perspective, the reconstruction of the early mother-child relationship as determined from the analysis of adults with psychopathology of the self should be regarded as providing an interesting perspective on psychic development to be further investigated through the psychoanalytically informed observation of children and their parents. Psychology of the self offers an important means for understanding the course of developmental psychic development. It permits us to attend to phenomena previously overlooked, using the empathic method which, itself, has been discredited in recent years as the most appropriate means for studying this developmental process. Too great a reliance on natural science methods and concepts and too great a concentration on object-libidinal development have prevented psychoanalytic developmental psychology from moving in directions which might lead to increased understanding of the person, and have too often rendered the study of psychic development little more than one aspect of experimental developmental psychology.

In the *Three Essays on the Theory of Sexuality* (1905b), Freud observed that:

> Psychoanalytic investigation, reaching back into childhood from a later time, and contemporary observation of children combine to indicate to us still other regularly active sources of sexual excitation. The direct observation of children has the disadvantage of working upon data which are easily misunderstandable; psycho-analysis is made difficult by the fact that it can only reach its data, as well as its conclusions, after long detours. But by cooperation the two methods can attain a satisfactory degree of certainty in their findings [p. 201].

If we replace the "sexual excitation" referring to the object-libidinal line of development by another term, such as "tensions created by unregulated ambitions in the development of the nuclear self," the paradox that Freud described is equally true today. By relying on an empathic method in studying the "easily misunderstandable" actions and intents of young children, however, we may be in a position to realize the goal that Freud held out: that of achieving increased certainty regarding the course of psychic development not just across childhood, but, it is hoped, across the entire life cycle.

References

Abraham, K. (1916), The First Pregenital Stage of the Libido. In: *Selected Papers on Psychoanalysis.* New York: Basic Books, 1960, pp. 248–279.
_____ (1921a), Contributions to a Discussion on Tic. In: *Selected Papers on Psychoanalysis.* New York: Basic Books, 1960, pp. 322–235.
_____ (1921b), Contributions to the Theory of the Anal Character. In: *Selected Papers on Psychoanalysis.* New York: Basic Books, 1960, pp. 370–393.
_____ (1924a), The Influence of Oral Eroticism on Character Formation. In: *Selected Papers on Psychoanalysis.* New York: Basic Books, 1960, pp. 393–406.
_____ (1924b), A Short Study of the Development of the Libido, Viewed in the Light of the Mental Disorders. In: *Selected Papers on Psychoanalysis.* New York: Basic Books, 1960, pp. 418–479.
_____ (1925), Character Formation on the Genital Level of the Libido. In: *Selected Papers on Psychoanalysis.* New York: Basic Books, 1960, pp. 407–417.
Anthony, E. J. (1971), Folie-à-Deux: A Developmental Failure in the Process of Separation-Individuation. In: *Separation-Individuation: Essays in Honor of Margaret S. Mahler,* ed. J. McDevitt & C. Settlage. New York: International Universities Press, pp. 253–273.
Basch, M. (1977), Developmental Psychology and Explanatory Theory in Psychoanalysis. *The Annual of Psychoanalysis,* 5:229–266. New York: International Universities Press.
Behrens, M. (1954), Childrearing and the Character Structure of the Mother. *Child. Develop.,* 25:225–238.
Bell, R. Q. (1964), The Effect on the Family of a Limitation in Coping Ability in the Child: A Research Approach and a Finding. *Merrill-Palmer Quart.,* 10:129–142.
_____ (1977), Socialization Findings Reexamined. In: *Child Effects on Adults,* ed. R. Q. Bell & L. V. Harper. New York: Erlbaum-Halstead-Wiley, pp. 53–84.
Bemesderfer, S. & Cohler, B. (1980), Depressive Reactions during the Period of Separation: Individuation and Self among the Children of Psychotic Depressed Mothers. In: *Children of Depressed Parents,* ed. H. Morrison. New York: Grune & Stratton (in press).
Benedek, T. (1959), Parenthood as a Developmental Phase. *J. Amer. Psychoanal. Assn.,* 7:389–417.
_____ (1973), Discussion of "Parenthood as a Developmental Phase." In: *Psychoanalytic Investigations.* New York: Quadrangle, pp. 401–407.
Bernfeld, S. (1925), *Sisyphus or the Limts of Education,* trans. F. Lilge. Berkeley: University of California Press, 1973.
Bettelheim, B. (1967), *The Empty Fortress.* New York: Free Press-Macmillan.
Bowlby, J. (1958), The Nature of the Child's Tie to His Mother. *Internat. J. Psycho-Anal.,* 39:350–373.
Breuer, J. & Freud, S. (1893–1895), Studies on Hysteria. *Standard Edition,* 2. London: Hogarth Press, 1955.
Clarke, A. & Clarke, A. D. B., eds. (1976), *Early Experience: Myth and Evi-*

dence. New York: Free Press-Macmillan.

Clarke-Stewart, K. A. (1973), Interactions between Mothers and Their Young Children: Characteristics and Consequences. *Monographs of the Society for Research in Child Development.* 38: Whole Number 153.

Cohler, B. (1977), The Significance of the Therapist's Feelings in the Residential Treatment of Anorexia Nervosa. In: *Adolescent Psychiatry,* vol. 5, ed. S. Feinstein & P. Giovacchini. New York: Aronson, pp. 352–386.

_____ (1980), Adult Developmental Psychology and Reconstruction in Psychoanalysis. In: *The Course of Life,* ed. S. Greenspan & G. Pollock. Washington, D.C.: U.S. Government Printing Office.

Collingwood, R. G. (1946), *The Idea of History.* New York: Oxford University Press, 1976.

Connolly, K. (1972), Learning and the Concept of Critical Periods in Infancy. *Develop. Med. Child Neurol.,* 14:705–714.

Cooley, C. H. (1902), *Human Nature and the Social Order.* New York: Shocken, 1964.

Décarie, T. G. (1965), *Intelligence and Affectivity in Early Childhood: An Experimental Study of Jean Piaget and Object Relations.* New York: International Universities Press.

Emde, R., Gaensbauer, T., & Harmon, R. (1976), *Emotional Expression in Infancy: A Behavioral Study. Psychol. Issues,* Monogr. 37. New York: International Universities Press.

Erikson, E. (1950), *Childhood and Society,* rev. ed. New York: Norton, 1963.

_____ (1962), Psychological Reality and Historical Actuality. In: *Insight and Responsibility.* New York: Norton, 1964, pp. 159–256.

Escalona, S. (1953), Emotional Development in the First Year of Life. In: *Conference on Infancy and Early Childhood.* Transactions of the Josiah Macy Foundation, pp. 11–91.

Ferenczi, S. (1913), Stages in the Development of a Sense of Reality. In: *Sex in Psychoanalysis.* New York: Dover, 1956, pp. 181–203.

Fine, B., Joseph, E., & Waldhorn, H. (1959), *Recollection and Reconstruction/ Reconstruction in Psychoanalysis.* New York: International Universities Press, 1971.

Fliess, R. (1942), The Metapsychology of the Analyst. *Psychoanal. Quart.,* 11: 211–227.

Freedman, D. (1974), *Human Infancy: An Evolutionary Approach.* New York: Halstead.

Freud, A. (1927), Four Lectures on Child Analysis. *The Writings of Anna Freud,* 1:3–69. New York: International Universities Press, 1964.

_____ (1930), Four Lectures on Psychoanalysis for Teachers and Parents. *The Writings of Anna Freud,* 1:73–133. New York: International Universities Press, 1964.

_____ (1951), Observations on Child Development. *The Psychoanalytic Study of the Child,* 6:18–30. New York: International Universities Press.

_____ (1965), *Normality and Pathology in Childhood: Assessments of Development.* New York: International Universities Press.

_____ & Burlingham, D. (1943), *War and Children.* New York: International Universities Press.

_____ _____ (1944), *Infants Without Families.* New York: International Universities Press.

Freud, S. (1887-1902), *The Origins of Psycho-Analysis: Letters to Wilhelm Fliess, Drafts, and Notes.* New York: Basic Books, 1954.

_____ (1895), Project for a Scientific Psychology. *Standard Edition,* 1:295-387. London: Hogarth Press, 1966.

_____ (1896a), The Aetiology of Hysteria. *Standard Edition,* 3:191-221. London: Hogarth Press, 1962.

_____ (1896b), Further Remarks on the Neuro-Psychoses of Defence. *Standard Edition,* 3:159-188. London: Hogarth Press, 1962.

_____ (1899), Screen Memories. *Standard Edition,* 3:299-322. London: Hogarth Press, 1962.

_____ (1900), The Interpretation of Dreams. *Standard Edition,* 4 & 5. London: Hogarth Press, 1953.

_____ (1901), The Psychopathology of Everyday Life. *Standard Edition,* 6. London: Hogarth Press, 1960.

_____ (1905a), Fragment of an Analysis of a Case of Hysteria. *Standard Edition,* 7:7-122. London: Hogarth Press, 1953.

_____ (1905b), Three Essays on the Theory of Sexuality. *Standard Edition,* 7:130-243. London: Hogarth Press, 1953.

_____ (1906), My Views on the Part Played by Sexuality in the Aetiology of the Neuroses. *Standard Edition,* 7:271-282. London: Hogarth Press, 1953.

_____ (1907), The Sexual Enlightenment of Children. *Standard Edition,* 9:129-140. London: Hogarth Press, 1959.

_____ (1909), Analysis of a Phobia in a Five-Year-Old Boy. *Standard Edition,* 10:5-152. London: Hogarth Press, 1955.

_____ (1910a), Five Lectures on Psycho-Analysis. *Standard Edition,* 11:3-55. London: Hogarth Press, 1957.

_____ (1910b), Leonardo da Vinci and a Memory of His Childhood. *Standard Edition,* 11:63-138. London: Hogarth Press, 1957.

_____ (1911), Formulations on the Two Principles of Mental Functioning. *Standard Edition,* 12:213-226. London: Hogarth Press, 1958.

_____ (1912), Recommendations to Physicians Practising Psycho-Analysis. *Standard Edition,* 12:109-120. London: Hogarth Press, 1958.

_____ (1913a), The Claims of Psycho-Analysis to Scientific Interest. *Standard Edition,* 13:165-192. London: Hogarth Press, 1958.

_____ (1913b), The Disposition to Obsessional Neurosis. *Standard Edition,* 12:311-326. London: Hogarth Press, 1958.

_____ (1913c), Totem and Taboo. *Standard Edition,* 13:1-164. London: Hogarth Press, 1958.

_____ (1916-1917), Introductory Lectures on Psycho-Analysis. *Standard Edition,* 15 & 16. London: Hogarth Press, 1963.

_____ (1918), From the History of an Infantile Neurosis. *Standard Edition,* 17:1-122. London: Hogarth Press, 1955.

_____ (1919), "A Child Is Being Beaten": A Contribution to the Study of the Origins of Sexual Perversions. *Standard Edition,* 17:175-204. London: Hogarth Press, 1955.

_____ (1920a), Associations of a Four-Year-Old Child. *Standard Edition,* 18:266. London: Hogarth Press, 1955.

_____ (1920b), Beyond the Pleasure Principle. *Standard Edition,* 18:1-64.

London: Hogarth Press, 1955.

———— (1920c), Group Psychology and the Analysis of the Ego. *Standard Edition*, 18:65–144. London: Hogarth Press, 1955.

———— (1920d), The Psychogenesis of a Case of Homosexuality in a Woman. *Standard Edition*, 18:145–172. London: Hogarth Press, 1955.

———— (1923), The Ego and the Id. *Standard Edition*, 19:3–68. London: Hogarth Press, 1961.

———— (1931), Female Sexuality. *Standard Edition*, 21:221–246. London: Hogarth Press, 1961.

———— (1933), New Introductory Lectures on Psycho-Analysis. *Standard Edition*, 22:5–184. London: Hogarth Press, 1964.

———— (1937), Constructions in Analysis. *Standard Edition*, 23:255–270. London: Hogarth Press, 1964.

———— (1940), An Outline of Psycho-Analysis. *Standard Edition*, 23:141–208. London: Hogarth Press, 1964.

Gardiner, P. (1959), *Theories of History*. New York: Macmillan-Free Press.

Gedo, J. & Goldberg, A. (1973), *Models of the Mind*. Chicago: University of Chicago Press.

Gill, M. (1963), *Topography and Systems in Psychoanalytic Theory. Psychol. Issues,* Monogr. 10. New York: International Universities Press.

———— & Muslin, H. (1976), Early Interpretation of the Transference. *J. Amer. Psychoanal. Assn.,* 24:779–794.

Glover, E. (1930), Grades of Ego-Differentiation. In: *On the Early Development of Mind,* vol. 1. New York: International Universities Press, 1956, pp. 112–122.

———— (1932), A Psycho-Analytic Approach to the Classification of Mental Disorders. In: *On the Early Development of Mind,* vol. 1. New York: International Universities Press, 1956, pp. 161–186.

———— (1943), The Concept of Dissociation. In: *On the Early Development of Mind,* vol. 1. New York: International Universities Press, 1956, pp. 307–324.

———— (1950), Functional Aspects of the Mental Apparatus. In: *On the Early Development of Mind,* vol. 1. New York: International Universities Press, 1956, pp. 364–378.

Goldberg, A., ed. (1978a), *The Psychology of the Self: A Casebook*. New York: International Universities Press.

———— (1978b), A Shift in Emphasis: Adolescent Psychotherapy and the Psychology of the Self. *J. Youth Adoles.,* 7:119–132.

Greenacre, P. (1971), Notes on the Influence and Contribution of Ego Psychology to the Practice of Psychoanalysis. In: *Separation-Individuation: Essays in Honor of Margaret S. Mahler,* ed. J. McDevitt & C. Settlage. New York: International Universities Press, pp. 171–200.

———— (1975), On Reconstruction. *J. Amer. Psychoanal. Assn.,* 23:693–712.

Grunebaum, H., Cohler, B., Kauffman, C., et al. (1978), Children of Depressed and Schizophrenic Mothers. *Child Psychiat. Human Develop.,* 8:219–228.

————, Weiss, J., Cohler, B., et al. (1974), *Mentally Ill Mothers and Their Children*. Chicago: University of Chicago Press.

Guntrip, H. (1969), *Schizoid Phenomena, Object Relations and the Self*. New

York: International Universities Press.

Hanson, D., Gottesman, I., & Heston, L. (1976), Some Possible Indicators of Adult Schizophrenia Inferred from Children of Schizophrenics. *Brit. J. Psychiat.*, 129:142–154.

———, ———, & Meehl, P. (1977), Genetic Theories and the Validation of Psychiatric Diagnoses: Implications for the Study of Children of Schizophrenics. *J. Abnormal Psychol.*, 86:575–588.

Hartmann, H. (1939), *Ego Psychology and the Problem of Adaptation.* New York: International Universities Press, 1958.

——— & Kris, E. (1945), The Genetic Approach in Psychoanalysis. In: *Papers on Psychoanalytic Psychology,* ed. H. Hartmann, E. Kris, & R. Loewenstein. *Psychol. Issues,* Monogr. 14. New York: International Universities Press, 1964, pp. 7–26.

———, ———, & Loewenstein, R. (1946), Comments on the Formation of Psychic Structure. In: *Papers on Psychoanalytic Psychology. Psychol. Issues,* Monogr. 14. New York: International Universities Press, 1964, pp. 27–55.

Hug-Hellmuth, H. (1919), *A Study of the Mental Life of the Child.* Washington, D.C.: Nervous and Mental Diseases Publishing Company.

Isaacs, S. (1930), *Intellectual Growth in Young Children.* New York: Shocken, 1966.

——— (1933), *Social Development in Young Children.* London: Routledge & Kegan Paul, 1967.

Jacobson, E. (1964), *The Self and the Object World.* New York: International Universities Press.

Jones, E. (1953), *The Life and Work of Sigmund Freud,* vol. 1. New York: Basic Books.

Kanzer, M. (1953), Past and Present in the Transference. *J. Amer. Psychoanal. Assn.,* 1:144–154.

Khan, M. (1963), The Concept of Cumulative Trauma. In: *The Privacy of the Self.* New York: International Universities Press, 1974, pp. 42–58.

Klein, G. (1976), *Psychoanalytic Theory: An Exploration of Essentials.* New York: International Universities Press.

Klein, M. (1928), *The Psychoanalysis of Children.* New York: Delacorte, 1976.

——— (1932), Notes on Some Schizoid Mechanisms. In: *Developments in Psychoanalysis,* ed. M. Klein, P. Heiman, S. Isaacs, et al. London: Hogarth Press, 1952, pp. 292–320.

Kohut, H. (1959), Introspection, Empathy and Psychoanalysis. *J. Amer. Psychoanal. Assn.,* 7:459–483.

——— (1971), *The Analysis of the Self.* New York: International Universities Press.

——— (1977), *The Restoration of the Self.* New York: International Universities Press.

——— & Seitz, P. (1963), Concepts and Theories of Psychoanalysis. In: *Concepts of Personality,* ed. J. Wepman & R. Heine. Chicago: Aldine, pp. 113–141.

Kovel, J. (1978), Things and Words: Metapsychology and the Historical Point of View. *Psychoanal. Contemp. Thought,* 1:21–88.

Kris, E. (1951), Opening Remarks on Psychoanalytic Child Psychology. *The Psychoanalytic Study of the Child,* 6:9–17. New York: International Universities Press.

———— (1956), The Recovery of Childhood Memories in Psychoanalysis. *The Psychoanalytic Study of the Child,* 11:54–88. New York: International Universities Press.

Lewis, M. & Rosenblum, L. (1974), *The Effect of the Infant on Its Caregiver.* New York: Wiley-Interscience.

Lieberman, M. & Falk, J. (1971), The Remembered Past as a Source of Data for Research on the Life-Cycle. *Human Develop.,* 14:132–141.

Loewald, H. (1976), Perspective on Memory. In: *Psychology versus Metapsychology: Psychoanalytic Essays in Memory of George Klein,* ed. M. Gill & P. Holzman. *Psychol. Issues,* Monogr. 36. New York: International Universities Press, pp. 298–325.

———— (1978), *Psychoanalysis and the History of the Individual.* New Haven: Yale University Press.

Mahler, M. (1968), *On Human Symbiosis and the Vicissitudes of Individuation.* New York: International Universities Press.

————, Pine, F., & Bergman, A. (1975), *The Psychological Birth of the Human Infant.* New York: Basic Books.

Masterson, J. & Rinsley, D. (1975), The Borderline Syndrome: The Role of the Mother in the Genesis and Psychic Structure of the Borderline Personality. *Internat. J. Psycho-Anal.,* 56:163–177.

McGuire, M. (1971), *Reconstructions in Psychoanalysis.* New York: Appleton-Century Crofts.

Mead, G. H. (1934), Self. In: *George Herbert Mead on Social Psychology,* ed. A. Strauss. Chicago: University of Chicago Press, 1964, pp. 199–243.

Modell, A. (1968), *Object Love and Reality.* New York: International Universities Press.

Moore, B., & Fine, B., eds. (1968), *A Glossary of Psychoanalytic Terms and Concepts.* New York: American Psychoanalytic Association.

Murphy, L. (1962), *The Widening World of Childhood.* New York: Basic Books.

———— (1973), Some Mutual Contributions of Psychoanalysis and Child Development. In: *Psychoanalysis and Contemporary Science,* vol. 2, ed. B. Rubinstein. New York: Macmillan, pp. 99–123.

Murray, H. (1938), *Explorations in Personality.* New York: Oxford University Press.

Novak, M. & Harlow, H. (1975), Social Recovery of Monkeys Isolated for the First Year of Life: I. Rehabilitation and Therapy. *Develop. Psychol.,* 11:453–465.

Novey, S. (1968), *The Second Look: The Reconstruction of Personal History in Psychiatry and Psychoanalysis.* Baltimore: Johns Hopkins University Press.

Pollock, G. (1971), On Time, Death and Immortality. *Psychoanal. Quart.,* 40:435–446.

Prosen, H., Martin, R., & Prosen, M. (1972), The Remembered Mother and the Fantasized Mother: A Crisis of Middle Age. *Arch. Gen. Psychiat.,* 27:791–794.

Psychoanalytic Quarterly (1935), *Child Analysis Number,* 4 (Number 1).

Rapaport, D. (1960), Psychoanalysis as a Developmental Psychology. In: *The Collected Papers of David Rapaport,* ed. M. Gill. New York: Basic Books, 1967, pp. 820–852.
_____ & Gill, M. (1959), The Points of View and Assumptions of Metapsychology. In: *The Collected Papers of David Rapaport,* ed. M. Gill. New York: Basic Books, 1967, pp. 795–811.
Reik, T. (1937), *Surprise and the Psychoanalyst.* New York: Dutton.
Ricoeur, P. (1977), The Question of Proof in Freud's Psychoanalytic Writings. *J. Amer. Psychoanal. Assn.,* 25:835–872.
Sadow, L., Gedo, J., Miller, J., et al. (1968), The Process of Hypothesis Change in Three Early Psychoanalytic Concepts. In: *Freud: The Fusion of Science and Humanism,* ed. J. Gedo & G. Pollock. *Psychol. Issues,* Monogr. 35/36. New York: International Universities Press, 1976, pp. 257–285.
Sander, L. (1962), Issues in Early Mother-Child Interaction. *J. Amer. Acad. Child Psychiat.,* 2:141–166.
_____ (1964), Adaptive Relationships in Early Mother-Child Interaction. *J. Amer. Acad. Child Psychiat.,* 3:221–263.
_____ (1969), The Longitudinal Course of Early Mother-Child Interaction: Cross-Case Comparison in a Sample of Mother-Child Pairs. In: *Determinants of Infant Behaviour,* ed. B. Foss. London: Methuen, pp. 189–228.
Sandler, J., Holder, A., & Meers, D. (1963), The Ego Ideal and the Ideal Self. *The Psychoanalytic Study of the Child,* 18:139–158. New York: International Universities Press.
Schachtel, E. (1947), Memory and Childhood Amnesia. *Psychiat.,* 10:1–26.
Schafer, R. (1959), Generative Empathy and the Treatment Situation. *Psychoanal. Quart.,* 28:342–373.
_____ (1960), The Loving and Beloved Superego in Freud's Structural Theory. *The Psychoanalytic Study of the Child,* 15:163–188. New York: International Universities Press.
_____ (1968), *Aspects of Internalization.* New York: International Universities Press.
_____ (1978), *Language and Insight.* New Haven: Yale University Press.
_____ (1979), The Appreciative Analytic Attitude and the Construction of Multiple Histories. *Psychoanal. Contemp. Thought,* 2:3–24.
Schaffer, R. (1977), *Mothering.* Cambridge, Mass.: Harvard University Press.
Schimek, J. (1975), The Interpretation of the Past: Childhood Trauma, Psychical Reality and Historical Truth. *J. Amer. Psychoanal. Assn.,* 23:845–865.
Senn, M. & Hartford, D. (1968), *The Firstborn.* Cambridge, Mass.: Harvard University Press.
Sherwood, M. (1969), *The Logic of Explanation in Psychoanalysis.* New York: Academic Press.
Spitz, R. (1945), Hospitalism: An Inquiry into the Genesis of Psychiatric Conditions in Early Childhood. *The Psychoanalytic Study of the Child,* 1:53–72. New York: International Universities Press.
_____ (1946), Hospitalism: A Follow-Up Report. *The Psychoanalytic Study of the Child,* 2:113–117. New York: International Universities Press.
_____ (1957), *No and Yes: On the Genesis of Human Communication.* New

York: International Universities Press.

_____ (1959), *A Genetic Field Theory of Ego Formation.* New York: International Universities Press.

_____ (1965), *The First Year of Life.* New York: International Universities Press.

Stechler, G. & Carpenter, G. (1967), A Viewpoint on Early Affective Development. In: *The Exceptional Infant,* vol. 1, ed. J. Hellmuth. New York: Brunner/Mazel, pp. 165–189.

Sullivan, H. S. (1953), *The Interpersonal Theory of Psychiatry.* New York: Norton.

Thomas, A., Birch, H., Chess, S., et al. (1963), *Behavioral Individuality in Early Childhood.* New York: New York University Press.

_____ & Chess, S. (1977), *Temperament and Development.* New York: Brunner/Mazel.

Tolpin, M. (1971), On the Beginnings of a Cohesive Self. *The Psychoanalytic Study of the Child,* 26:316–352. New York: Quadrangle

_____ & Kohut, H. (1978), The Disorders of the Self: The Psychopathology of the First Years of Life. Unpublished manuscript. The Institute for Psychoanalysis, Chicago.

Vaillant, G. & McArthur, C. (1972), Natural History of Male Psychologic Health: I. The Adult Life-Cycle from 18–50. *Seminars in Psychiatry,* 4:415–427.

White, R. W. (1963), *Ego and Reality in Psychoanalytic Theory. Psychol. Issues,* Monogr. 11. New York: International Universities Press.

Winnicott, D. W. (1945), Primitive Emotional Development. In: *Collected Papers.* New York: Basic Books, 1958, pp. 145–156.

_____ (1951), Transitional Objects and Transitional Phenomena. In: *Collected Papers.* New York: Basic Books, 1958, pp. 229–242.

_____ (1960), The Theory of the Parent-Infant Relationship. *Internat. J. Psycho-Anal.,* 41:585–595.

Wolf, E., Gedo, J., & Terman, D. (1972), On the Adolescent Process as a Transformation of the Self. *J. Youth Adoles.,* 1:257–272.

Wolf, K. (1953), Observation of Individual Tendencies in the First Year of Life. In: *Conference on Infancy and Early Childhood.* Transactions of the Josiah Macy Foundation, pp. 97–139.

_____ (1954), Observation of Individual Tendencies in the Second Year of Life. In: *Conference on Infancy and Early Childhood.* Transactions of the Josiah Macy Foundation, pp. 121–134.

Wolff, P. (1966), *The Causes, Controls and Organization of Behavior in the Neonate. Psychol. Issues,* Monogr. 17. New York: International Universities Press.

Wyatt, F. (1962), A Psychologist Looks at History. *J. Soc. Issues,* 26:66–77.

_____ (1963), The Reconstruction of the Individual and Collective Past. In: *The Study of Lives: Essays in Honor of Henry Murray,* ed. R. W. White. New York: Atherton, pp. 305–320.

On the Developmental Line of Selfobject Relations

ERNEST S. WOLF

The concept of developmental lines was introduced by Anna Freud (1965) with the practical aim of aiding in treatment decisions and with the theoretical aim of formulating clearer pictures of the mental disorders, and, in general, of increasing insight into the developmental processes themselves. She observed that "While drive and ego development are viewed separately for purposes of dissection, their action is seen as combined in the *lines of development* which lead from the individual's state of infantile immaturity and dependence to the gradual mastery of his own body and its functions, to adaptation to the object world, reality and the social community, as well as to the building up of an inner structure." External and internal factors influence the separate but parallel lines of development. Thus, she continued, "Whatever level has been reached by any given child in any of these respects represents the result of interaction between drive and ego-superego development and their reaction to environmental influences, i.e., between maturation, adaptation and structuralization" (Anna Freud, 1965, p. 64). As a prototype of a developmental line, the progression from the newborn's utter dependency on maternal care to the young adult's emotional and material self-reliance was outlined in

117

some detail (Anna Freud, 1965, pp. 64–68). Other developmental lines have been charted, though perhaps not as completely. Among these are lines from relative lack of body control toward body independence, from egocentricity to companionship, from body to toy and from play to work. Normal endowment lays down the interaction sequences in the development of libido and aggression on the one hand, and the progression toward organization, defense, and structuralization on the other. Accidental environmental influences may promote or inhibit individual lines of development. These are embodied mainly in parents' personalities, their actions and ideals, the family atmosphere, and the impact of the cultural setting as a whole.

Clearly, Anna Freud's concept of developmental lines recognizes that development is a process which involves an interaction between innately given sequences and accidentally impinging environmental events. Little is said explicitly about the mechanisms by which environmental events influence the innately given, sequential maturation. In accord with classical drive and defense theory, however, one may assume that excessive or insufficient stimulation of libido and aggression by either a discrepancy in parallel ego development or by accidental environmental impact results in regression and anxiety against which the ego defends by all defensive means at its disposal, particularly, by denial, repression, reaction formation, and identificatory mechanisms.

The concept of developmental lines has proved to be very useful in the clinical assessment of children and in presenting clear theoretical formulations. The augmentation of classical formulations by a psychoanalytic psychology of the bipolar self has added a further dimension to psychoanalytic theory and practice. Therefore, it will be useful to examine how the insights and tenets of self psychology are reflected in the concept of developmental lines and vice versa.

Self psychology represents a shift in emphasis toward the explicit acknowledgment of the empathic-experiential base of psychoanalytic data — introspective data had always been implicit in Freud's theorizing — concomitant with a shift in conceptualization from a natural science model of the psychic apparatus to an experiential self-selfobject model. Furthermore, the self psychological focus on interactions of the self with selfobjects results in a more balanced view of the influence of the environment on the subject. These environmental influences are not seen as mere accidents impinging on drive and ego development that is relatively innate and autonomous. Rather, in self psychology the interactions between self and selfobjects are conceptualized in terms of continuous and reciprocal influences. The feedback processes between the self and its selfobject milieu result in the continuous modification of both. The relationship, therefore, is gradually changed over time. In this way, the self-selfobject model makes it possible to construct a developmental line of selfobject relations (a more euphonious term than self-selfobject relations).

Information about the details of the developmental line of selfobject relations is still relatively scanty. In the following, therefore, I will examine the selfobject relations at various nodal points from which a continuous developmental line may be visualized, even though it is not yet possible to construct it in great detail.

At birth, strictly speaking, the neonate cannot be assumed to have an organized psychic structure that is experienced as continuous over time and space, i.e., as a self. From the perspective of the neonate, therefore, it cannot be said that a self or a selfobject exists in a definitive form at birth. However, the caretakers (usually the parents and particularly the mother) as a rule imagine the neonate to be a person, a self, and address him in a way (e.g., by name) that acknowledges his selfhood. Careful observation reveals that the infant responds to these communications, almost imperceptibly at first, but within a few weeks with a smile or even an energetic total body response.

Recent studies of the earliest neonate-caretaker interactions have given convincing demonstrations of the subtle yet wide scope of these responses. The psychoanalytic observer cannot but be impressed by the potential significance these research findings hold for psychoanalytic theory and practice. I would like to emphasize two observations in particular because they bear on the topic of a developmental line of selfobject relations.

The first of these observations is the reciprocal nature of the child-caretaker interactions. By reciprocity, I refer to the presence of two active participants, each of whom may initiate interaction, and each of whom responds to the other, not passively via a predetermined reflex, but actively in a complex pattern that is shaped partly by the evoking stimuli and partly by the inherent predispositions of the responder. Responses are neither totally preprogrammed and evoked nor totally dependent on the characteristics of the particular evoking stimulus. Furthermore, it seems to me, the participants in the reciprocal interaction are slightly *changed* by their participation: they have learned something and their future interactions will be ever so subtly different by virtue of their having been changed through previous interactions.

I am sure there is nothing very new in my emphasis on reciprocity. Still, it bears repeating, if only to avoid getting trapped in the nature versus nurture controversy. The biologistic bias that sees babies (and mothers) behaving in predetermined patterns is as much an oversimplification as the sociologistic bias that sees behavior as primarily determined by the environment. When self psychologists speak of the "faulty interactions between the child and his selfobject [that] result in a damaged self" (Kohut & Wolf, 1978, p. 414) they place blame neither on the child nor on the caretaker who provides the selfobject responses needed by the child. Our experience demonstrates, indeed, that in most cases the caretaker's own damaged self (for which responsibility obviously cannot be assigned to the damaged victim) prevents full responsiveness to the child's selfobject needs. Yet, the particular way in which the baby attempts and fails to evoke the needed selfobject responses — e.g., via an innately high sensory threshold masquerading as apathy — may itself be the greatest obstacle to a smoothly functioning selfobject relationship.

No two babies are alike even at birth. One cannot rule out the possibility (I believe that fortunately this happens only rarely) that a relatively healthy set of parents may have a healthy child and yet the resulting selfobject ambience will not be even minimally adequate to the selfobject needs of child or parents; in other words, there may be a misfitting that has tragic consequences for parents and children alike. While we know a great deal about the failures of caretakers in providing adequate selfobject responses, we know very little about the infant's failures to trigger properly the needed responses or to respond properly to selfobject initiatives, i.e., to become the infantile participant in the mother-child-selfobject unit. Information about such failures is not likely to come from psychoanalytic reconstructions but from sophisticated, psychoanalytically informed infant-mother observations.

There is another observation of neonate-caretaker interaction that is relevant to our developing selfobject theory. It is difficult not to notice the heightened joy of both mother and child when the mother's approach has become associated with a sequence of reciprocal responses involving both as participants. Indeed, we know by their affective reactions whether or not there has been mutual and effective responsiveness. It must be obvious to even the minimally empathic observer, moreover, that the subjective experience which underlies the joyful affect is one of feeling blissful, good, whole, together—any number of words will do to describe the experience which, conceptually, we designate as a firm, vigorous, cohesive self. The empathic observer sees two selves, mother and child, actively evoking responses in each other that are experienced by both as satisfying states of the self. It is these satisfying experiences of a cohesive self that we conceptualize as deriving from the inclusion of the selfobject in the experience of the self.

In summary, a reciprocal relationship exists, from the beginning between what Kohut has called a virtual self and what we may here designate as its *virtual selfobjects*. What justification exists in calling this a virtual selfobject relation even though, strictly speaking, there is neither self nor selfobject? I think the justification lies in the reality of a relationship which (1) is reciprocal, (2) is experienced as if it were a selfobject relation, and (3) normally eventuates in a selfobject relation. Clearly, neither infant nor parent act indifferently to each other. They respond to each other, and, characteristically, they respond to each other's responses. As I have already indicated, it further appears, to the empathic observer, that this existing, reciprocally responsive relationship is experienced by both infant and parent with a heightened feeling of well-being. Although it would be an adultomorphic distortion to talk about anything as differentiated as the infant's fantasies or thoughts, still, there can be no doubt in the eyes of the observer that the child affectively experiences itself as more pleasantly alive during and subsequent to such interaction. (I am of course assuming a healthy, normal interaction.) The same observation can be made of the normal healthy parent who participates in such a relationship with an infant, though, of course, the parent's self experience will be at least partially differentiated into conscious and unconscious thoughts, affects, and fantasies.

Conversely, the parent's failure to address the infant as a virtual self will over time be experienced by the infant as a lack, a deficiency that is destined to interfere with feelings of well-being and eventually with normal psychic development. The parent will, therefore, not be rewarded with the joyful responsiveness that he feels he has the right to expect. Parental self-esteem consequently also suffers. In extreme cases, infantile marasmus and death or parental depression may ensue.

A further possibility of misfitting that I mentioned earlier concerns some inborn or acquired inability on the part of the infant that interferes with either experiencing or responding to an appropriately attuned parental virtual selfobject. The consequences are similar to those that occur in the wake of an absent virtual selfobject: instead of reciprocal relationships that mutually enrich the self experiences, a vicious cycle of mutual deprivation, disappointment, and psychological illness may be engendered. Reciprocal virtual selfobject relations, therefore, appear to be an indispensable aspect of normal, healthy psychic development. Absent or faulty selfobject relations are associated with the experience of discomfort and eventually of illness. In other words, the infant experiences the parent and the parent experiences the infant as an essential aspect of the well-being of the self—as selfobject. Finally, the unhindered development of virtual selfobject relations eventuates in the emergence of a cohesive infantile self existing within a selfobject matrix. A relation between virtual structures thereby becomes actual.

What more can be said about virtual selfobject relations beyond the fact that they normally come into existence shortly after birth?[1] Since there is no actual infant self but only the virtual self imprinted on the infant by the parent, one would expect the virtual selfobject relation to be relatively diffuse, *nonspecific,* and displaceable. In fact, this is what can be observed. Seen from the perspective of the neonate, almost any good parenting will do, and the experience of selfobject qualities shifts easily from person to person: any competent and empathic caretaker is acceptable to facilitate psychic development. Similarly, caretakers find that they are able to shift easily from one infant to another without significant loss of the capacity to form adequate relations. Successful wet nurses and adoptive mothers experience this early plasticity in virtual selfobject relations. Psychodynamically, this is best conceptualized as a merger in which the virtual outlines of the infant's potential self become part of the caretaker's self organization. One can further conceptualize how certain qualities or aspects of the virtual selfobject-caretaker merge with these earliest precursors of the infant's self organization. Via a process that Kohut has designated *transmuting internalization,* the merged aspect of the virtual selfobject is incorporated into the infant's virtual proto-self, which is thus given added psychic organization and structure. More could be said about the optimal conditions for transmuting internalization, but in keeping with the focus of this paper, I shall return to the topic of developmental lines.

At some time during the second year of life, perhaps, but probably even earlier, the precursors of the infant's self, under the benignly facilitating influence of an empathically attuned caretaker, consolidate into a cohesive self. Such consolidation is fleeting at first, but becomes more permanent with additional increments of psychic structure. If average good mothering is available, a discernible self will have emerged before the end of the second

---

[1]The observations about postnatal virtual selfobject relations do not, of course, contradict the fact that the parents, and especially the mother, have a relation to the growing fetus in which the fetus is experienced as part of the parental self, i.e., as a selfobject for the parent. Such a relation is not reciprocal, however, and cannot become reciprocal until after birth.

year of life. With the emergence of a self it becomes possible to talk about *actual selfobject relations.*

It is difficult to compare quantitatively the need of the emerging self for selfobjects with the need of the neonate for virtual selfobjects. However, it is useful and instructive to make qualitative comparisons. The emerging self's needs are observed to demand a specific, concrete individual; much of the easy displaceability of the earliest weeks and months of life is thereby lost. In fact, this state of needing the concrete presence of a *specific,* familiar selfobject becomes manifest even during the first year of life when separation anxiety and stranger anxiety make their appearance, that is, even before the emergence of a self.

Separation anxiety is conceptualized from the point of view of the psychology of the self as disintegration anxiety that is felt by the infant when the absence of the selfobject-caretaker threatens to disintegrate the beginning organization of the precursors of the self. For it is the selfobject qualities of the caretaker that lend organization and structure to the potentialities out of which the self emerges. To speak metaphorically, the selfobjects are like the glue that holds the self cohesively together.

Stranger anxiety demonstrates very clearly that the normal selfobject relation is based on more than a mere satisfying of average expectable needs. Both infant and mother—the well-attuned mother is as loath to the intruding presence of a stranger as the baby—sense, perhaps mainly unconsciously, that they have a unique and special relationship that has grown out of a history of finely attuned reciprocal responses which have gradually transformed baby and mother into custom-fitted parts of a unique mother-child unit. Both experience themselves as part of this unit that imparts strength to their individual selves through a kind of merger. A threat to this mother-child unit is, therefore, also experienced as a threat to the individual baby and individual mother, or more precisely speaking, as a threat to the cohesion of baby's and mother's self: stranger anxiety is the expected outcome, at least in Western culture.[2]

[2]Roland (1980) has recently demonstrated that self development in India seems to aim toward the emergence of selves that experience themselves more as

Shortly after the emergence of the self, the child feels the need to establish and test his mastery over his own body by confronting the control exerted by the selfobject without losing the selfobject's continued availability for mirroring and idealization in the process. In our culture this confrontation becomes a nodal point on the developmental line of selfobject relations as the battle is joined between infant and selfobject over the issue of sphincter control. The healthy, attuned mother will appropriately confirm her child's self by acknowledging the child's success in achieving mastery, e.g., in placing his feces into the proper place at the proper time.[3] It must be added that the struggle to master one's sphincter is just one example of the progressive moves to make the self stronger, more cohesive, and more sharply demarcated from the environment. Other behaviors that are not as intimately related to self-control over the child's body can also serve as battle grounds. Mothers who have lived through a period of negativism, when "no, no, no" is asserted without apparent rhyme or reason, might have been helped by recognizing that such negativism is also a necessary expression of the boundaries of the self in the context of a selfobject milieu.

Viewed from the point of view of a developmental line of self-object relations, the basic issues can be conceptualized as follows: from birth to the emergence of the self the primary need is for self-object relations that lend organization to the emerging self. Once the self has emerged the most prominent issue becomes strengthening and securing the self's boundaries. The boundaries are strengthened within the context of the selfobject relationships by drawing on the aid of the confirming selfobject as an ally while

---

the "we" of the group than the "I" of our Western individualism. It seems reasonable that cultural influence may modify the developmental line of selfobject relations and I wonder, for example, whether stranger anxiety is less prominent or managed differently in the East.

[3]The properly empathic mother will avoid either neglectful or over-stimulating responses that might fragment the child's vulnerable self. Such a fragmented child would be left with a disposition toward warding off feelings of emptiness or deadness by seeking the phase-appropriate erotic pleasures of the anal mucosa and by reconstructing a new but impoverished and distorted self around the pleasures of anal sexuality to make up for the lost joy of a whole self.

simultaneously confronting the selfobject as an antagonist against whom self-assertion mobilizes healthy aggression that promotes the cohesive strength of the self. These contradictory needs for an ally-antagonist selfobject account for the inevitable ambivalence of this phase of development. These contradictions color all subsequent relations and, in general, impart a dialectical element to the human enterprise.[4]

Ambivalence and contradiction are not easily compatible with self-control. As part of the maturing child's growing self-awareness and cognition of the world around him, the circle of possible selfobjects widens. Eventually both parents are recognized as separate individuals and infantile sexuality progresses to the oedipal phase of development. At this time, an amelioration of the ambivalence toward the ally-antagonist selfobject becomes possible by a differentiation of this contradictory need into specifically different demands on the individual parents. First one parent is needed as the selfobject that confirms the maturing self and is idealized by the child, while the other parent becomes the needed selfobject-antagonist against whom the aggression that strengthens the self can be mobilized. These roles often are switched back and forth among the parental selfobjects. During

[4]Tension between divergent constituent trends of the self becomes an integral part of the organization of the self from the very beginning. Kohut (1977) has discussed the bipolar nature of the self in great detail. The tension arc from the pole which harbors the nuclear ambitions to the pole which is the carrier of the nuclear ideals makes internal contradiction and tension part of the very constitution of the self. The program of action of a specific self is a product of the field of tension in which it is embedded, i.e., it "is determined by the specific intrinsic pattern of its constituent ambitions, goals, skills and talents and by the tensions that arise between these constituents" (Kohut & Wolf, 1978, p. 414). The bipolar organization of the self may well be an expression of the fundamental dialectic of all life precariously balanced between the entropic direction of matter and the negentropic direction inherent in biological organizations. Thus the self is also forever precariously balanced between the entropic yearning for union (or merger) on the one hand, and the negentropic striving for differentiation, separateness, and boundaries on the other. Freud correctly recognized the inevitability of intrapsychic conflict, in terms of pleasure (i.e., drive versus defense) and beyond pleasure (i.e., Eros versus Thanatos). Like Freud's life and death instincts, the dialectic of the self is beyond the pleasure principle, but unlike these instincts the dialectics of the self are experience-near and graspable by empathic perceptions rather than experience-distant and biologically inferred.

this time the dialectic of contradictory needs may continue to fuel the tensions of triadic relationships until, through the gradual strengthening of the self via transmuting internalization, a strong, stable, and relatively irreversible cohesive self is achieved within the context of a stable and empathic selfobject ambience.[5]

It should be noted that during the oedipal phase a decisive advance is made in selfobject relations, namely the ability to split and distribute the formerly one-person dyadic needs over both parents. This achievement is rooted in the even earlier capacity to substitute temporarily a sibling for the parental carrier of the selfobject quality. During the oedipal phase, the gradually broadening selfobject need can be increasingly satisfied by the intrafamilial selfobject ambience, i.e., several family members may become the source of confirming selfobject responses at the same time as others may be available for idealizing needs. At the same time, with increasing socialization, siblings and peers may also meet various selfobject needs. This is the beginning of a trend which lasts until the end of life: selfobject needs are met by increasing numbers of persons who are substitutable for each other and thus decrease dependence on any one of the selfobjects.

Selfobject needs and relations do not disappear with maturation and development; they become more diffuse and less intense. During adolescence the need for selfobject relations usually is met to a large extent, if not totally, by the peer group. The group at that time often becomes much more important for the maintenance of self-esteem than the parents because the latter empathically lose touch with, and may even feel alienated from, the younger generation. An adolescent may derive from the selfobject peer group the confirmation for his phase-appropriate grandiosity; equally important, he may develop an idealizing selfobject relation with a peer group idol. When internalized, the latter

[5]A healthy oedipal phase would be characterized by parents who are empathically in tune with the child's erotically tinged needs and who, through appropriately controlling and soothing responses, aid the youngster in the task of integrating his uncomfortable tension. Unempathic responses on the part of the selfobject milieu will tend to facilitate the fragmentation of the child's self in accord with the well-studied neurotic sequelae that are associated with overstimulated oedipal conflicts.

relation strengthens the pole of values and ideals of the bipolar self and may well set the direction for choice of vocation and of mate (Wolf, Gedo, & Terman, 1972). It is characteristic of the progressive changes in the developmental line of selfobjects that symbols as well are increasingly substituted for persons as selfobjects. This process probably begins already during latency. In adolescence it becomes noteworthy. The adolescent, for example, by merging with powerful musical symbols as selfobjects, e.g., with the powerful rhythms of jazz and rock, may infuse his own self with a sense of power. Identification with a larger group, the state or the nation, may become a similar source of self-esteem through internalization of the symbols of patriotism. Such symbols may also serve as idealized selfobjects that enrich the young adult with the values of the larger community. The heroes of history and of culture may serve as selfobject conduits for internalizing the ideals of a cultural tradition.

Setting aside, for the moment, any particular age-appropriate form of the selfobject need, one may compare the need for the continuous presence of a psychologically nourishing selfobject milieu with the continuing physiological need for an environment containing oxygen. It is a relatively silent need of which one becomes aware sharply only when it is not being met, when a harsh world compels one to draw the breath in pain. And so it goes also with selfobject needs. As long as a person is securely embedded in a social matrix that provides him with a field in which he can find the needed mirroring responses and the needed availability of idealizable values, he will feel comfortably affirmed in his total self with its ambitions and goals. In short, he will feel himself strong and, paradoxically, relatively self-reliant, self-sufficient, and autonomous. But if by some adversity of events this person should find himself transported into a strange environment, it will be experienced as alien and even hostile, no matter how friendly it might be disposed toward him. Even strong selves tend to fragment under such circumstances. One can feel loneliest in a crowd. Solitude, psychological solitude, is the mother of anxiety. Emigrants to a new country are familiar with the discontinuity of their sense of self which, disconcertingly, is often accompanied by

symptoms that we have learned to recognize as evidence of fragmenting selves: depression, hypochondriasis, even paranoia.
When after the end of World War II the soldiers of the Polish army who had been fighting on the Allied side were not allowed to
return to their homeland but were dispersed as individuals to live
and work on friendly English farms, an astonishing number began
to show the signs of severe paranoid psychotic reactions, which
only gradually disappeared concomitant with integration into a
familiar and supportive social matrix.

Closer to home, introspective consideration will reveal to the
self-aware reader how dependent he is on the particular social
matrix within which he feels himself functioning well. Do we not
feel it in the very core of our being when the neighbor whom we see
but a couple of times a year suddenly does not recognize us and
fails to return our casual greeting? It is always astonishing to
become aware of the importance of an almost unnoticed relationship when the sudden absence of it announces itself with a painful
jolt.

We are similarly dependent on the invulnerability of the symbols and rituals that have become, as internalized selfobjects,
aspects of ourselves. People fight for the symbolic tokens of their
values and ideals as if their very lives depended on it — which, in a
psychological sense, they do.

"Shoot, if you must, this old gray head,
But spare your country's flag," she said.

This may sound old-fashioned in an age of burned draft cards, until one notices that the need for selfobjects, namely in this case the
devotion to the former symbols of patriotism, has not disappeared
into self-sufficient detachment. Nor has it turned into the disavowal of the need for idealized selfobjects that we recognize as the
pretentiousness of cynicism. Rather, we see a continuing need for
the expression of the country's idealized values that serve a selfobject function in giving cohesion to the selves of its citizens. As
evidence for this I would point to a new devotion to the ideals that
are symbolized in the image of *America,* like the ideal of

equality that comes to the fore, for example, in the fight for the rights of minorities.

Substitution of persons, depersonal diffusion, and symbolization create for the adult a whole matrix of selfobject relations that take over much of the function of the originally highly personal, concrete, and focused relation to the archaic selfobjects of childhood. Of course, many important personal and individual selfobjects remain, in particular, spouses, children, and intimate friends. Kohut (1977, pp. 187n–188n) has observed: "The psychologically healthy adult continues to need the mirroring of the self by the selfobject (to be exact: by the selfobject aspect of his love object) and he continues to need targets for his idealization. No implication of immaturity or psychopathology must, therefore, be derived from the fact that another person is used as a selfobject — selfobject relations occur on all developmental levels and in psychological health as well as psychological illness." The progression of the developmental process also continues so that by the time the adult has reached old age, he may often have achieved a selfobject relation with the wider world of mankind and beyond. Mature selflessness is really the expansion of the self and its selfobjects to take in the whole world. It is in this furthest development of the line of selfobject relations that we can discern those noble goals that are rooted in the transformations of infantile narcissism — the goals of wisdom and the acceptance of transience.

References

Freud, A. (1965), *Normality and Pathology in Childhood*. New York: International Universities Press.

Kohut, H. (1977), *The Restoration of the Self*. New York: International Universities Press.

_____ & Wolf, E. (1978), The Disorders of the Self and Their Treatment: An Outline. *Internat. J. Psycho-Anal.,* 59:413–426.

Roland, A. (1980), Psychoanalytic Perspectives on Personality Development in India. *Internat. Rev. Psycho-Anal.,* vol. 7 (in press).

Wolf, E., Gedo, J., & Terman, D. (1972), On the Adolescent Process as a Transformation of the Self. *J. Youth Adoles.,* 1:257–272.

Part II

SELF PSYCHOLOGY
AND THE
CONCEPT OF HEALTH

Introduction

Ernest S. Wolf

Few ideas are as difficult to reduce to a definition as the concept of health. Most everyone, at some time, has experienced a state of well-being, but the conceptualization of health remains elusive. An old proverb tells us that sickness is felt, whereas health is not. This is doubly true of mental health, with the result that the line between mental "health" and mental "sickness" has become blurred. Expanded conceptions of mental sickness now subsume most, if not all, of the territory of health. In fact, the ubiquity of intrapsychic conflict has promoted the fashionable distortion of labeling everyone at least "normally neurotic." In this manner of thinking the designation "neurotic" has almost become an oxymoron, as witnessed by Lionel Trilling who, in "Art and Neurosis" (1945), says, "We are all ill: but even a universal sickness implies an idea of health."

The understanding of health as the ideal state that no one ever quite achieves is the confused legacy of a reductionism to which even Heinz Hartmann fell victim in observing that in the analytic process "health clearly includes pathological reactions as a means toward its attainment" and, further, that "successful adaptation can lead to maladaptation" (1939, p. 7).

Hartmann ended his incisive discussion of psychoanalysis and the concept of health with the injunction to develop a new analytic

133

theory of health, since psychoanalysis was at present unable to formulate a concept of mental health in simple, unequivocal, definitive terms. Still, Hartmann insisted, the concepts of "health" and "illness" necessarily exerted a "latent" influence, so to speak, on analytic habits of thought, and it could not but serve a useful purpose to clarify the implications of these terms. There can be no doubt that the emergent psychology of the self already has had a major impact on the concept of health, at least for those analysts who are familiar with Kohut's thinking. Perhaps this impact might have been foreseen, for the very word "health" is derived from the old English root "hāl" that means whole, complete, sound. The word "health" therefore points toward the description of a totality rather than a description of parts. A healer is one who makes whole.

Paul Ornstein's paper details the shift in psychoanalytic perspective in the wake of self psychology away from the narrower focus on parts and functions of a mental apparatus gone wrong to a wider perspective on the self as it strives for health through firming and expansion. Classical psychoanalysis, as Robert Stolorow points out, has produced only a pallid and underdeveloped concept of health in comparison with its richly detailed formulation of the pathological alterations of mental functioning. To be sure, psychoanalysis has approached a holistic definition of mental functioning in describing the various metapsychological points of view. Stolorow notes, however, that these definitions, in effect, reduced health to the absence of pathology, and resulted in the incomplete definition of health by default that was also criticized by Hartmann. One might add that no living dynamic whole can be defined by the sum of its parts, and even if one were to double or triple the metapsychological points of view, the positive definition of the concept of health requested by Hartmann would remain elusive.

Can the psychology of the self do better? Can the psychoanalytic self psychologist provide a positive definition of health against which deviations from the norm can be delineated? We believe he can and we believe, indeed, that such a concept of health already informs the theory and practice of psychoanalytic self psychology. The healthy self is one that age- and phase-appropriately is in the process of realizing its life plan as this was constituted during the nuclear self's emergence. Such a life plan derives from that self's specific, individual pattern of ambitions and ideals mediated by its skills and talents. Health, in this sense, is clearly not a steady state but a process moving in a direction. "How fares my lord?" Shakespeare's characters inquire, again and again. Psychoanalysis is beginning to ask the same question, and, for us, this is evidence that psychoanalysis is faring quite well.

References

Hartmann, H. (1939), Psychoanalysis and the Concept of Health. In: *Essays on Ego Psychology.* New York: International Universities Press, 1964, pp. 3–18.

Trilling, L. (1945), Art and Neurosis. In: *The Liberal Imagination.* New York: Viking, 1950.

Self Psychology and the Concept of Health

PAUL H. ORNSTEIN

My topic in this presentation is the concept of health as it has evolved thus far in self psychology.[1] It is perhaps unusual for psychoanalysts to focus on health, normality, and adaptation before defining the nature of the psychopathology against which the former concepts are to be delineated. In the context of self psychology, however, it is a logical reflection of the decisive shift of emphasis away from a preoccupation with the pathological and toward a focus on the potentially healthy or more adaptive aspects of the personality.

This decisive shift of emphasis, its clinical and theoretical consequences, and its ever-clearer and more precise articulation

---

[1] I have clearly delimited the range of exploration of the concept of health. I am aware of the fact that a comprehensive survey, even if only limited to psychoanalytic contributions, would have served as a necessary backdrop against which the contributions of self psychology could be more appropriately assessed. But my primary aim is not a comparative evaluation, nor an integration of various psychoanalytic points of view, but only an explication of the contributions of self psychology. For the broadest and most comprehensive critical survey and integration of the medical-psychiatric, psychological, psychoanalytic, sociocultural, and anthropological concepts of health and normality, see Offer and Sabshin (1966) and Offer (1975).

with each step in the evolution of self psychology are the main themes of my presentation. I shall begin with a brief overview and some general remarks about self psychology as a new paradigm and as the context for a new conception of health and illness. I shall then show the subsequent expansion and refinements of the definition of health and adaptation and conclude with a discussion of the clinical, theoretical, and sociocultural implications of a self psychological concept of health.

Toward a New Concept of Health and Illness

Kohut's clinical-empirical approach to the study of narcissism and the theories that emerged from it immediately aimed at correcting a widespread "negatively toned evaluation" of narcissism (Kohut, 1966). By stressing its adaptive value and by assigning it a developmental position different from that of classical metapsychology, it was no longer necessary to view narcissism as exclusively or predominantly pathological. Instead, in order to effect a shift in our prejudicial attitude toward a more scientifically based neutrality, Kohut focused from the outset on the contributions of narcissism to "health, adaptation and achievement" (Kohut, 1966). His early recognition of narcissism as a *developmental driving force* — or a developmental tendency or potential, as he later put it — has therefore not only enriched our understanding of the nature of psychopathology in the narcissistic disorders, but has pointed the way toward a new concept of health and adaptation.

The remobilization of this developmental drive through the reactivation of the archaic, but more or less phase-appropriate (i.e., healthy and adaptive) "grandiose self," or the archaic, but more or less phase-appropriate (i.e., healthy and adaptive) "idealized parent imago" is the core experience of the selfobject transference that occurs during psychoanalysis. Such transference offers the only means by which belated maturation and development can take place within the psychoanalytic process. This is how Kohut put it: "This transference is based on the therapeutic regression to precisely that point where the *normal development* of the psychic structures of the self was interrupted or where the consolidation of those structures of the self which so far had only been precariously established was not carried further towards completion. The analytic situation, then, brings about a reactivation of that developmental point in time at which the basic disorder began. Thus, the interrupted psychological growth process is given the opportunity to continue beyond the point of its arrest" (1970a, pp. 554–555, italics added). The emphasis on belated maturation and development and on the acquisition of new psychic structures points to the fact that psychoanalysis aims — as it always has — at more than mere symptom removal and the absence of psychopathology. In stressing the completion of the structuralization in the self, the striving for the achievement of wholeness, psychoanalysis is able to aim more precisely at establishing the preconditions for the attainment of health, adaptation, and higher achievements.

It follows from these clinical observations that narcissism can contribute either to health or to illness depending on the degree to which the two major archaic narcissistic constellations can be transformed and thereby serve the strengthening of existing self structures or the formation of new ones, via transmuting internalizations.

The concepts of the *selfobject* and of structure building through *transmuting internalization* have thus become central to our understanding and explanation of health and illness in self psychology. The pivotal role of these two new concepts derives from the fact that they refer at once to the empirical data of the psychoanalytic process and to the developmental-genetic precursors of health and illness. Furthermore, it is the broad concept of the "selfobject environment" and its role and function in structure building and in psychoanalytic cure that relates the impact of "external reality" (i.e., the sociocultural context) to the development of health and illness in a more meaningful and encompassing way than had previously been possible. To put it differently, the concept of the selfobject serves as a bridge across which the intrapsychic, developmental-genetic determinants of health and illness can be integrated with their psychosocial determinants. The new integration also permits the notion of mere *adjustment* to external reality to be clearly differentiated from a metapsychologically sophisticated conception of *adaptation* to reality. Ultimately, the concept of the selfobject enables us to replace even this ego psychological concept of adaptation with a higher-order concept of adaptation that places at its center the unfolding of the intrinsic patterns for creative action laid down in the nuclear self.

The relativistic, value-laden concepts of individual health and illness can thus be brought, both in their clinical and theoretical dimensions, into a more value-neutral scientific view. This may be illustrated by an early statement describing specific changes in the self in health and illness with reference to the mutual relation between self and ego:

> A person's secure feeling of being a well-delimited unit — i.e.,
> his clear concept of who he is, which rests on the deep yet
> nameless sense of nuclear cohesiveness that is acquired in ear-
> ly life — is one of the preconditions for the ego's reliable ability
> to perform its functions. . . the self may serve as an *organizer*
> *of the ego's activities.* If, on the other hand, the self is poorly
> cathected, temporarily or chronically, then ego functions may
> also suffer, may be performed without zest, be disconnected
> one from the other and be lacking in firmness of purpose and
> integrated cohesion [Kohut, 1970b, p. 587, italics in the
> original].

Before concluding this account of the evolution of the concept of health in self psychology in the narrower sense and turning to a description of its further, systematic expansion by Kohut in the psychology of the self in the broader sense (1977), I wish to return once more to the decisive shift of emphasis away from the pathological toward the potentially more healthy and adaptive. I will illustrate this shift by commenting on the changed role and meaning of narcissistic resistances and narcissistic rage.

In presenting his new approach to the treatment of narcissistic personality disorders, Kohut clearly stated (1966, 1968, 1970a, 1972) that there are more or less powerful and prolonged resistances to the development of the selfobject transferences that require intensive working through in many instances.[2] Patients who fall into this category cannot make use of the analyst's empathy for the reinstatement of their archaic selfobject transferences until considerable working through of their resistances has been achieved (A. Ornstein, 1974). There are other patients, however — perhaps the majority of those with analyzable narcissistic disorders — in whom an initial, tentative, and often short-lived reinstatement of the patient's archaic needs, wishes, and demands signals both capacity and readiness for the therapeutic remobilization of the developmental drive to complete the traumatically interrupted growth and development in the bipolar self. Kohut's presentations have elaborated the nature of these early, easily thwarted attempts of patients to reinstate one of the archaic selfobject transferences, referring to the patient's "germinally displayed exhibitionism...or the cautiously offered tendrils of his idealization" (Kohut, 1977, p. 259). These attempts have frequently been misunderstood simply as manifestations of the basic psychopathology, rather than as prognostic signs of the accessibility of the patient's ultimate potential for attaining health and the capacity for adaptation through the psychoanalytic treatment process. Thus, the recognition of the earliest manifestations of the remobilization of one of the selfobject transferences and the analyst's empathic responsiveness to them, while undoubtedly of invaluable tactical advantage in the treatment process, are of considerable clinical-theoretical significance for our concept of cure and, therefore, for our concepts of health and adaptation in general. This view does not disregard resistances, nor does it fail to take the manifold symptoms of the specific forms of self pathology into consideration, but it evaluates them from a different perspective, alongside the greater emphasis upon the processes

---

[2]Kohut did not dwell on these resistances extensively in his early published writings. He acknowledged their ubiquitous existence and stated that they were well known to psychoanalysts and did not need further elaboration. To many of his critics, however, he appeared to give short shrift to these resistances. For a broader perspective on "defensive narcissism" and the specific and unspecific narcissistic resistances, see Kohut (1970a).

mobilized for the completion of the structuralization of the self.[3]

Again, in his early writings Kohut clearly indicated his view of the significance of the role of aggression and rage in narcissistic disorders, although he presented his extensive clinical findings and theoretical formulations on this subject more systematically in a separate essay at a later date (Kohut, 1972). He proposed a radically new clinical and theoretical position for narcissistic rage. By considering narcissistic rage apart from the study of the "libidinal investment of the self," Kohut underlined the fact that he viewed the appearance of narcissistic rage, as it usually emerged in response to narcissistic injuries in the enfeebled or fragmented self, as a secondary manifestation: as a breakdown product of healthy aggression rather than as an untamed, primitive drive regularly investing the self along with the libido. Aside from the far-reaching consequences of this proposition for the subsequent formulation of the relation of the drives to the self (Kohut, 1974, 1977), the message was directly relevant to the evolving concept of health. The appearance of destructive aggression, hitherto viewed as a primary drive and as a significant pathogenic element in symptom formation, always drew our attention first to the pathological, i.e., to the form and content of the rage. But now such narcissistic rage could more appropriately be considered a secondary phenomenon: not a cause, but a consequence of self pathology. The aggressive drive as healthy self-assertiveness, however, was now more appropriately viewed as a constituent of the self — a constituent of the primary unit of psychological experience.

These altered conceptions of resistances and of aggression are outstanding examples of the various way stations leading to further changes in the concept of health within self psychology in the broader sense.

[3]From the vantage point of the appropriate function of the analyst in the psychoanalytic treatment process, the empathic response (e.g., recognition and silent acceptance, rather than conscious, deliberate, or inadvertent rebuff) to such early manifestations of the remobilization of the developmental drive leads to a very different view of the nature and content of the resistances and to a very different analytic atmosphere. For "resistance as a healthy force" and for the differentiation of resistance in narcissistic disorders and in structural neuroses, see Kohut (1977, pp. 149-151, 136). For a change in the analytic ambience, see Kohut (1977, pp. 249-266) and Wolf (1976).

Further Expansion and Refinements: The Bipolar Self

By raising the bipolar self to a supraordinate position vis-à-vis the mental apparatus and the drives, and thus introducing his new scientific paradigm, Kohut has also expanded and refined the concept of health and illness. The concept of the bipolar self had been implicit in the psychology of the self in the narrower sense from the outset. Its developmental-genetic origins, its structure and basic constituents, and its aims and functions and their fate in health and disease, however, were spelled out in great detail as they emerged from the empirical foundation provided by the study of the bipolar selfobject transferences (Kohut, 1966, 1968, 1970a, 1971, 1972). At this stage of Kohut's work, however, the implicit bipolarity of the self was still embedded in the structural theory and the tripartite model of the mind. What transformed and broadened the bipolar self into the core concept of a new paradigm was the further understanding of its origins and the discovery of the new relationship of its structures to the mental apparatus, the three psychic agencies, and the drives (Kohut, 1975, 1977).

This new relationship, reflected in the ascription of a "supraordinate position" to the bipolar self, had empirical roots (like the assumption of separate lines of development for narcissism and object love) in observations related to the outcome of selfobject transferences and the reconstructions of their developmental-genetic antecedents. The development and maturation of the grandiose-exhibitionistic self in the original, empathic (usually maternal) selfobject relationship were found to promote healthy self-assertiveness and ambition at one end of the pole. Conversely, development and maturation of the idealized parent imago in the original, empathic (usually paternal) selfobject relationship were found to promote health-sustaining capacities to regulate inner tension at one pole, along with internalized values and ideals at the other. The inevitable tension between ambitions and ideals was found to activate innate talents and skills and to put them into action to fulfill the intrinsic patterns for creative expression laid down in the structures of the bipolar self.

To the extent that the developmental unfolding at both poles

of the nuclear self led to the further maturation and structuralization of these capacities for health, self psychology found itself to
be dealing with *primary structures.* To the extent that the unfolding of the grandiose self met with traumatic dysfunctions of
empathy in the mirroring selfobject relationship, the resulting
defects in the self were found to be covered over with *defensive
structures.* Such defects prevented the further unfolding and structuralization of the capacities for health associated with that pole of
the self. To the extent that later mirroring or turning to the idealized selfobject meets with success and affords a further chance for
structure building at either of the two poles of the bipolar self, self
psychology found itself dealing with *compensatory structures.* The
shape of the self, then, ultimately depends on the particular mixture of primary, defensive, and compensatory structures. The
completeness of the structuralization of sectors of the primary
and/or compensatory structures, the firmness, strength, and the
unity or coherence they acquire during development or, belatedly,
in analysis, are the preconditions for the healthy or the
rehabilitated self to attain its functional freedom "in which ambitions, skills and ideals form an unbroken continuum that [then]
permits joyful creative activity" (Kohut, 1977, p. 63) — one of the
hallmarks of health from the vantage point of self psychology.[4]

[4]For the sake of simplicity, and because this presentation focuses exclusively
on some of the contributions of self psychology to the concept of health, I have
omitted references to the idea that a comprehensive "depth-psychological explanation of psychological phenomena in health and disease requires two complementary approaches: that of a conflict psychology and that of a psychology of
the self" (Kohut, 1977, p. 78). Although it is not central to the theme of this
paper, a brief examination of the complementarity of conflict psychology and self
psychology is in order. It is fully in keeping with Kohut's use of theory and with
his repeated emphasis that psychoanalysis is an empirical science par excellence
that he retained conflict psychology where it stood us in good stead, i.e., where it
still had explanatory power and retained its therapeutic leverage. He has undoubtedly narrowed the range of its applicability to the neuroses and neurotic
character disorders — the original empirical soil from which conflict psychology
emerged — by introducing his self psychology, with its greater explanatory power
and increased psychoanalytic-therapeutic (rather than psychotherapeutic)
leverage for the disorders of the self. Kohut himself expressed this unambiguously
when he stated that "the classical theory is limited by its focus on structural
conflicts and the structural neuroses. Psychoanalytic theory will come closer to

It should be stressed, however, that this "joyful creative activity" need not be unusual, socially valuable, or broadly acknowledged,

---

claiming its legitimate aspirations of becoming an encompassing general psychology if it now expands its border and places the classical findings and explanations within the supraordinate framework of a psychology of the self" (1977, pp. 229–230). He also stressed that the structural theory in this more restricted sense is not necessarily in error. I do believe, however, that structural theory has lost its heuristic potential, both in terms of generating new knowledge and in terms of further increasing the therapeutic leverage of psychoanalysis. We may, therefore, justifiably ask whether we should retain conflict psychology—modified and expanded though it may be by self psychology in the narrower sense—and self psychology in the broader sense, side by side, using the principle of complementarity as Kohut suggests. Is not the main defining characteristic of a new scientific paradigm that it supersedes the previous one and integrates within its own structure the valid and significant clinical findings and theories of the previous paradigm? After all, numerous clinical examples have demonstrated (Kohut, 1977) that conflict psychology, as expanded by the psychology of the self in the narrower sense, offers a more encompassing and more relevant understanding and explanation of the clinical data than had heretofore been possible. Furthermore, a recent study of an analysis conducted by Kohut prior to the advent of self psychology and a reanalysis several years later guided by his new ideas (Kohut, 1979) illustrated both the heuristic and the therapeutic advantages of an approach based on the psychology of the self in the broader sense. Do these additional clinical observations, therefore, not suggest that an integration of conflict psychology within the new paradigm of self psychology is the logical next step in psychoanalysis? The answer to this question is a decisive no. This demand for integration misses a very important methodological point Kohut has repeatedly made. By not forcing the integration of theories that grow out of differing clinical experiences, the door is left open to new discoveries based on the accumulation of fresh empirical data within the new paradigm.

I want to illustrate this point by referring to an earlier, similar juncture in the evolution of self psychology, when D. C. Levin (1969) suggested that the self be viewed as a fourth agency of the mind. Kohut preferred at that time to retain the concept of the self as a content of the mind, since he saw no compelling clinical evidence of a need to elevate the self into the position of a fourth agency. His research tactic and mode of theorizing did, indeed, lead Kohut several years later to the unanticipated result that he could assign the bipolar self—based on new and now compelling clinical data—a supraordinate position vis-à-vis the three agencies of the mental apparatus (Kohut, 1977; P. H. Ornstein, 1978).

Similarly, it is my perception at present that the complementary use of conflict psychology and self psychology is closer to the available clinical data. Leaving them unintegrated—and maintaining thereby the duality of "Guilty Man" and "Tragic Man"—we are opening the way to new discoveries in relation to the neuroses and neurotic character disorders from the vantage point of the paradigm of self psychology. That this is indeed the case is already amply attested to by Kohut's new formulations regarding the etiology, pathogenesis, and but rather an activity that is deeply rooted in the structure of the nuclear self. Furthermore, the cure we speak of does *not* generally relate to the "total self" but only to a sector of it — often a narrow sector of it, where an unbroken line between ambitions, talents, and ideals may be securely established.

We need not trace the development and maturation of the self in its entirety here, but should refer only briefly to one of its earliest phases and to the contribution of the Oedipus complex to its further consolidation.

Kohut reconstructed the developmental-genetic processes that lead to the healthy self in great detail in his earlier work, but he has recently amplified his reconstructions by describing the two crucial steps in early maternal responsiveness to the rudimentary self of the newborn. These two steps are the prerequisites for the development and consolidation of the nuclear self (Kohut, 1977, pp. 85–90). The early development and consolidation of internalized psychological structures (in the nuclear bipolar self) depend on wholesome maternal responses to the infant's mounting anxiety and rage and to his drive needs. The mother's response to the total child (by touching, holding, carrying, and talking to it) establishes the needed merger with the omnipotent selfobject. This response ensures that the child's mounting anxiety and rage will be limited to a "signal," rather than reaching panic proportions. This allows the child to participate in the mother's calmness and composure. Subsequent to this merger, the mother ministers to the child's bodily and drive needs. Kohut has stressed the importance of this two-step sequence in which empathic merger with the selfobject is followed by need-satisfying actions performed by the selfobject. He notes that "*if optimally experienced during childhood, it [this sequence] remains one of the pillars of mental health throughout life* and, in the reverse, if the selfobjects of childhood

---

psychopathology of the neuroses and neurotic character disorders in his as yet unpublished writings since *The Restoration of the Self* (1977). Thus, instead of attempting to integrate the *theories* of conflict psychology and self psychology, we should continue to focus our attention on the further collection of clinical data in relation to the structural neuroses with the approach suggested by our new paradigm (see Kohut, 1977). A premature and forced integration would have precluded the new discoveries and discoveries that are yet to be made.

fail, then the resulting psychological deficits or distortions will remain a burden that will have to be carried throughout life" (1977, pp. 87–88, italics added).

With these "pillars of mental health" acquired early, the nuclear self can continue its consolidation and enter the oedipal phase with relative firmness, strength, and cohesiveness and with its shape delineated fairly sharply. Kohut's recent assessment of the form and content of the Oedipus complex and its broad significance for the development of the self is, therefore, also central to the expanded concept of health in self psychology (Kohut, 1977). Contrary to the expectations of those who view narcissism as a defense against the Oedipus complex and ultimately expect it to be reactivated in the form of a classical transference neurosis in every case, Kohut found that "...despite some simultaneous anxiety, the brief oedipal phase [at the end of an analysis] is accompanied by a warm glow of joy—a joy that has all the earmarks of an emotionality that accompanies a maturational or a developmental achievement" (1977, p. 229). From such clinical observations, he concluded that these oedipal issues arose *de novo,* as a result of the functional rehabilitation of the self, and did not represent a remobilized Oedipus complex. Significantly, these observations drew attention to the essentially healthy and adaptive aspects of the oedipal period. This contrasted with the viewpoint of classical theory in which the positive qualities acquired by the psychic apparatus during the oedipal period were seen as the *result* of the oedipal experience and not as a *primary intrinsic aspect of the experience itself* (Kohut, 1977, p. 229). The contrast between the two theories is evident: "Seen from the point of view of classical analysis the oedipal phase is par excellence the nucleus of neurosis; seen from the point of view of the psychology of the self in the broader sense of the term, the Oedipus complex...is a matrix in which an important contribution to the firming of the independent self takes place, enabling it to follow its own pattern with greater security than before" (pp. 238–239).

This recognition of the positive aspects of the oedipal period[5] —

[5]Consider, for instance, an astute observation regarding children's play by Peller (1954, p. 189): "The mood pervading oedipal play is usually one of happiness, even of triumph, of naive invincibility."

the idea that it is a developmental achievement — is quite compatible with conflict psychology, but the focus there has undoubtedly been on the "pathogenic nucleus" of the experience. As long as normal development was reconstructed on the basis of the revival of the infantile (oedipal) neurosis in the form of the therapeutically revived transference neurosis, emphasis upon the pathogenic elements seemed almost inevitable. The concept of the infantile neurosis has had a twofold significance in conflict psychology (although in recent years the nature of its form and content has often been questioned): (1) Adult neurosis is always based on a preceding infantile neurosis. (2) The infantile neurosis is universal and ubiquitous; it is thought to have been present in infancy even where no overt or clinical neurosis followed it in adulthood. Thus, if the Oedipus complex was a regularly occurring ("normal") pathological and pathogenic development to begin with, conflict psychology could only conceive of health and the capacity for adaptation emerging out of pathology, i.e., out of the resolution of infantile oedipal conflicts. In self psychology, conversely, the potential for health and adaptation is seen as present *a priori* in any given empathic self-selfobject relationship. We may therefore look upon the relationship between the rudimentary self and its archaic selfobjects as the earliest embodiment of that wholeness which the self strives to attain to ensure its potential for adaptation and health. In this context, the vicissitudes of the Oedipus complex are not roadblocks to be overcome, but opportunities for the further development of a "creative-productive-active self" (1977, p. 76) that can both fulfill its basic program of action and simultaneously meet the demands of its particular sociocultural context. In other words, the oedipal, triangular relationship to mother and father is a phase-appropriate opportunity for the more or less firmly cohesive self to experience love, hate, rivalry, competitiveness, and jealousy and thereby further consolidate and strengthen its cohesiveness and enrich its content. In the context of an empathic oedipal-selfobject milieu these strivings will remain well contained as constituents of the bipolar self.[6] Only when the nuclear self cannot

---

[6]"Well contained as constituents of the bipolar self" is meant here to convey what was described in the language of structural theory as "ego dominance" or

maintain its firmness or cohesiveness will these oedipal strivings appear in isolated, intensified form as breakdown products expressing the underlying self pathology.

In this connection it should be stressed that it is quite likely that the customary view of the infantile Oedipus complex as highly conflict-laden and ubiquitously pathological is an artifact of erroneous reconstructions from the transference neurosis. What is revived in the transference neurosis is the Oedipus complex that already in childhood developed its pathological form, content, and intensity rather than its so-called "normal" infantile precursor. This is quite analogous to the revival of the more or less pathological grandiose self and the more or less pathological idealized parental imago. In these instances only the proper analytic ambience, characterized by the analyst's empathic responsiveness, will allow a further spontaneous pathognomonic regression that ultimately leads to the revival of ". . . that point where normal development. . . was interrupted. . . and. . . at which the basic disorder began" (Kohut, 1970a, p. 554). As a consequence of this further therapeutic regression, the healthy grandiose self and the healthy idealized parental imago will be revived in the transference. It should be considered whether the particular analytic ambience (the so-called "neutrality") and the technique that focuses upon the pathological conflicts, with an attempt to correct the patient's "transference distortions" rather directly, prevent this further pathognomonic regression and the remobilization of the healthy oedipal strivings in the analytic situation. This is an empirical question which, if answered affirmatively, will deepen our understanding of the impact of the oedipal experiences upon our concept of health and adaptation.

A very brief clinical vignette should highlight the intensification of the patient's resistances which will preclude the necessary further regression and which will then be erroneously interpreted as the remobilization of the infantile oedipal struggles in the transference.

"mastery over the instincts." Under "ego dominance" the ego remains in contact with drive needs in depth and exerts control over them, rather than severing its ties with the deeper layers of the psyche as in "ego autonomy" (see Kohut, 1972, pp. 620–621).

A young psychiatrist, as he was about to apply to a psycho-analytic institute, repeatedly voiced his concerns that he might not be accepted. His apparently muted feelings of enthusiasm at the prospect of becoming a candidate alternated with hints of fear of retaliation and punishment, both in his dreams and in his associations. To the analyst these feelings signaled the mobilization of a fierce, unconscious oedipal-competitiveness and superego response that he proceeded to interpret. He focused on the patient's unconscious intent to surpass the father-analyst and on the idea that his aspirations to become an analyst were now the expression of his hostile-competitive struggle in the transference. In response to these interpretations the patient became sulky at first, more openly furious later on, and in his dreams he expressed murderous rage at father-analyst figures. The analyst was convinced that he had tapped his patient's infantile Oedipus complex with his interpretations. He then embarked on helping his patient tame and sublimate his competitive rage by recognizing that his rage at the analyst had infantile roots in his competitive rage at his father.

The possibility did not occur to the analyst that the patient's intense reaction was in fact triggered by his own response to the patient's self-assertiveness. The analyst did not realize, in other words, that his interpretation repeated the original trauma: the oedipal father's lack of empathic acceptance of his son's emerging self-assertiveness. This oversight precluded the reconstruction that this sequence in the analysis might otherwise have permitted.

The psychoanalyst approaching this clinical problem from the viewpoint of self psychology would most likely have considered that the patient's muted enthusiasm about the prospects of his applying for psychoanalytic training might have represented the first tentative forward steps in his self-assertiveness and ambition, via identification with the father-analyst in his attempt to reach for higher-level professional goals. Empathic acknowledgment of this budding self-assertiveness, as initially expressed in the patient's short-lived enthusiasm, could have been followed by recognition of the internal, conflictual obstacles in its path (fear of retaliation, punishment, ridicule, or fear of failure — whatever the case may have been). This approach would most likely have allowed the patient himself to turn his attention to the interfering conflicts and compromises on his own.

The point is that our usual interpretive focus on the compromise formations made necessary by the unresolved conflicts now has to be extended to a consideration of how such conflicts hamper the expression of ambitions, talents, and values as conceptualized from the standpoint of the bipolar self. Thus, in this case, the isolated focus on the "competitive drive" prevented the early recognition of the emergence of the patients' potential for healthy self-assertiveness.

To conclude our survey, I will summarize the essential points about cure and health in Kohut's own words. In keeping with the complementary use of structural theory and self psychology, Kohut has formulated a dual definition of *cure:*

> Because psychological health was formerly established through the solution of inner conflicts, cure, whether in a narrow or in a broad sense, was then seen exclusively in terms of conflict solution through the expansion of consciousness. But because psychological health is now achieved with ever-increasing frequency through the healing of a formerly fragmented self, cure, whether in a narrow or broad sense, must now also be evaluated in terms of achieving self-cohesion, particularly in terms of the restitution of the self with the aid of a re-established empathic closeness to responsive selfobjects [1977, p. 281].

In a similar vein, Kohut has offered a broad dual definition of *mental health:* "Within the framework of the psychology of the self, we define mental health not only as freedom from the neurotic symptoms and inhibitions that interfere with the functions of a 'mental apparatus' involved in loving and working, but also as the capacity of a firm self to avail itself of the talents and skills at an individual's disposal, enabling him to love and work successfully" (1977, p. 284).

With these clarifying definitions in mind, we may now briefly turn to the clinical, theoretical, and sociocultural implications of the self psychological concept of health.

Clinical, Theoretical, and Sociocultural Implications

One of Heinz Hartmann's conclusions in his landmark contribution to the concept of health provides us with a proper context for our reflections: "It is clearly essential," Hartmann said, *"to proceed on purely empirical lines,* i.e., to examine from the point of view of their structure and development the personalities of those who are actually considered healthy instead of allowing our theoretical speculations to dictate to us what we 'ought' to regard as healthy" (1939, p. 312, italics added). He added that the "theoretical standards of health are usually too narrow in so far as they underestimate the great diversity of types which in practice pass as healthy." For Hartmann, moreover, psychoanalysis did in fact possess "criteria intended to serve as a purely practical guide, such as tests so frequently applied of a capacity for *achievement* or *enjoyment"* (1939, p. 312, italics added).

Offer and Sabshin (1966), at the end of their extensive analysis of the concept of health, also called for further *empirical research* on health and normality in order to deal, among other issues, with the "difficulty in generalizing from studies in psychopathology to normal behavior" (p. 155). They have endorsed the need to arrive at a clinical-theoretical concept of health from a direct study of the healthy.

Psychoanalysis cannot approach the study of the "healthy" or the "normal" *directly.*[7] Nevertheless, the new empirical data derived from the analysis of narcissistic personality and behavior disorders, presented by Kohut in his writings since 1966 and, recently, in his discussion of the termination phase of the analyses of patients suffering from such disorders (especially Mr. M.; see Kohut, 1977, pp. 33ff.), have yielded new knowledge about health, adaptation, and maturity. The validity of these insights can now

[7]The observations generated within the psychoanalytic treatment process, however, and the hypotheses derived from them, can be used to study the healthy or the normal with a variety of other methods. For the description of such studies using psychoanalytic observations and theories, see Offer and Sabshin (1966).

also be examined with other methods.

In psychoanalysis, it has always been the process of cure along with the developmental-genetic reconstructions that promote cure which has informed us about health and normality. This kind of evidence has led to the notion of a fluidity between health and illness rather than to a reliably sharp dichotomy between them. The limitations involved in approaching the concept of health from a study of psychopathology and maladaptation have been progressively tempered by more accurate reconstructions[8] of the psychogenetic factors leading to the various forms of psychopathology and of the normal phases of personality development.

From observations that clarify what is missing in the bipolar self *structurally* and what interferes with the expression of its creative-productive activity *dynamically,* we have gained new knowledge about the necessary ingredients of the self-selfobject relationship for normal growth and maturation. Kohut's clinical observations of specific failures in the analyst's empathy toward his patient's archaic needs and his reconstructions of analogous failures in the selfobject's empathy toward the phase-appropriate needs of the growing infant and child, have led to new ideas regarding those aspects of the selfobject's empathic responsiveness that create an optimal environment for the attainment of health. The psychoanalyst's clinical-empirical view of cure, traditionally tied to his view regarding the nature of the presenting psychopathology, can now be expanded by fusing his knowledge of both self pathology and normal development of the self into a broader concept of health.

In general, the psychoanalytic clinician is more directly concerned with the concept of cure than with the broader concept of health. He defines cure pragmatically as the disappearance of the presenting psychopathology, which may then lead to an increased capacity for adaptation. The question often arises whether this

[8]These reconstructions may be checked for their validity against both the patient's recall of childhood memories during analysis and the direct, systematic observation of children by psychoanalytically trained observers. For a detailed discussion of the methodological issues involved, see Kohut (1975).

concept of cure is adequate to avoid or at least minimize the intrusion of cultural values and biases into the definitions of health and illness. Hartmann (1939) expressed the hope that the development of a psychoanalytic "normal psychology" would ultimately lead to a definition of health that did not merely contrast it with the neuroses. Such a new definition, based on a "normal psychology" that, for Hartmann, was still "very largely non-existent" (p. 317), might also be a more scientific and therefore less value-laden definition. Hartmann associated this hope with his belief that the concepts of the "adaptation to reality" and the "synthetic function of the ego" led to a more biologically rooted (hence for him more scientific) evolutionary concept of health (p. 320). He observed, however, that such an evolutionary concept "does not as yet enable us to formulate a concept of mental health in simple, unequivocal, definitive terms" (p. 321).

Offer (1975) has firmly stated that "normality and health cannot be understood in the abstract. Rather, they depend on the cultural norms, societies' expectations and values, professional biases, individual differences, and the political climate of the time, which sets the tolerance for deviance" (p. 463).

This is undoubtedly still true to some extent. But by expanding the definition of health and bringing the clinical-empirical and theoretical definitions into a much closer relationship to each other, self psychology has not only broadened the concept of health considerably (without biologizing it), but has also lessened the intrusion of some of the hitherto unavoidable cultural and professional biases. With the discoveries of self psychology, post-oedipal genitality and postambivalent object love are no longer the sole criteria of maturity and mental health. This shift has left considerably more room for the inclusion of a greater diversity of types or of socially marked "deviance" under the rubric of *varieties of health*. The nature of the various forms of health can be spelled out more precisely on the basis of a study of the structural-dynamic considerations of the specific features and combinations of the primary and compensatory structures in the bipolar self, which determine each particular constellation of health.

To reemphasize once more, the central contributions of self psychology to the clinical-theoretical concept of cure rest on the empirical observations in the working through of the selfobject transferences. The clinical-theoretical definitions of health and maturity rest on the reconstruction of normal development from our new understanding of the process of cure. The concepts of selfobject and transmuting internalization are relevant both to the processes of cure and to normal development. They serve as the new and improved bridges from the observable events in the analysis to the reconstructed events of infantile and childhood development.

To be sure, health and our various conceptions of it will continue to depend on sociocultural influences. The concepts of selfobject and of structure building through transmuting internalization, however, serve, in this connection, too, as improved bridges toward a better understanding of the relationship of the intrapsychic and sociocultural determinants of health. I refer here to the fact that the acquisition of self-assertive ambitions on the one hand, and of internalized values and ideals on the other, is mediated through transmuting internalization of the functions of the selfobjects. The successful internalization of the functions of these selfobjects (as the embodiments of the early sociocultural environment) provides the bipolar self with those structures and contents that will ensure its "functional freedom" and thus its capacity for health. This is the point at which the role of the sociocultural environment and the process of adaptation to it can be further illuminated for the concept of health in self psychology.

Kohut once observed that the psychoanalyst's "vision of man tends to be restricted by the fact that he observes people in a specific therapeutic context and in a specific setting—the psychoanalytic situation" (1975, p. 704). This restricted vision led to a "medicotherapeutic conceptualization of psychic disequilibrium ...which...is too confining." Kohut called for a broader outlook by proposing that "psychological disturbance should not be looked upon as a disease—or at any rate not exclusively so—but *as a way station on the road to man's search for a new psychic equilibrium*" (1973, pp. 538–539, italics added).

In the highly imaginative and often poetic essay on "Psycho-analysis in a Troubled World" from which I have just quoted, Kohut exemplified the meaning of this proposition. He spelled out the possible drastic changes in the external environment that might occur with the advent of a mass society and an overcrowding on earth under the shadow of the atom bomb. The details of this presentation are of interest, but here I can only refer in passing to the adaptive solution that he envisaged as possibly necessary to en-sure the survival of the human race under such changed circum-stances. He saw the intrapsychic adaptive response in the "intensi-fication and, above all, the elaboration and expansion of man's inner life" (1973, p. 540). This effort at adaptation, at building new psychological structures to cope with the new psychological tasks, often leads to psychological disturbances. But the latter, Kohut stated, "should in certain respects be understood as man's groping toward the enlargement and intensification of his inner life...and should be seen as *attempts that have come to grief.*" Kohut pro-ceeded with the strong assertion "that these miscarried attempts should be evaluated as more courageous and potentially more creative, then some of the forms of psychic equilibrium that make up the area of emotional maturity or health" (1973, p. 541).

Is this assignment of creativeness to the highest level in the hierarchy of values a personal bias of the creator of self psychology? I am sure it is. But beyond that, is this creativeness not also a central phenomenon that derives from the empirically based, structural-dynamic constellation of the bipolar self, once it has attained its "structural completion" and "functional freedom"? This is the role Kohut ascribed to creativeness in the cure of the individual:

> A well-conducted analysis...which has been brought to a proper conclusion, provides the analysand with more than a diminution or disappearance of his painful and disturbing symptoms — existing in him now is a certain psychological openness, perhaps even a spark of that playful creativeness which turns toward new situations with joyful interest and responds to them with life-affirming initiative. Such a person

may yet continue to be more traumatized than one who has learned to maintain a reliable yet restricting psychic equilibrium. But he will also be more perceptive and responsive than the rigidly normal [1973, p. 545].

In *The Restoration of the Self* (1977), Kohut returns from his vision of the future to "The Changing World" (pp. 267–280) of the present and recent past in order to put his clinical discoveries into the broader sociocultural context of our time. He identifies as the *"psychotropic social factors"* those sociocultural changes that have ultimately, albeit indirectly, created the leading personality patterns and the leading forms of psychopathology of our time. In this large sociohistorical sense, it is one of Kohut's most significant contributions to have extended his purview beyond the understanding of the nature of this leading psychopathology, its etiology and pathogenesis, and beyond the development of a psychoanalytic method for its treatment. Beyond these contributions, he has restored to psychoanalysis its original responsiveness to the broader sociocultural milieu. Just as Freud grasped profoundly the leading individual and social psychopathology and the nature of individual and societal health of the Victorian era, so Kohut has captured the essence of the leading individual and social psychopathology and the nature of individual and societal health in our time. In so doing, he has brought external and internal reality into a more broadly meaningful relationship to one other.

In this endeavor, Kohut has freed psychoanalysis from the constraints of ego psychology. He has put self psychology side by side with ego psychology in a complementary relationship and demonstrated that the new paradigm of self psychology can encompass certain aspects of mental health and illness that could not be adequately accounted for within the previous paradigm. Through self psychology, it has become possible to obtain a new understanding of healthy pride, healthy self-assertiveness, healthy admiration for the idealized selfobject, the capacity for enthusiasm, and certain aspects of the "creative-productive-active self." With the introduction of the bipolar self as a supraordinate constellation and especially with the differentiation of primary,

defensive, and compensatory structures within it, it now becomes
our task to evaluate whether the nature of pathology, cure, and
health in the realm of the self has attained a new precision and
become more clinically relevant in both structural and dynamic
terms than preexisting models.

References

Hartmann, H. (1939), Psychoanalysis and the Concept of Health. *Internat. J.
    Psycho-Anal.*, 20:308–321.
Kohut, H. (1966), Forms and Transformations of Narcissism. In: *The Search
    for the Self,* vol. 1, ed. P. Ornstein. New York: International Universities
    Press, 1978, pp. 427–460.
_____ (1968), The Psychoanalytic Treatment of Narcissistic Personality Dis-
    orders. In: *The Search for the Self,* vol. 1, ed. P. Ornstein. New York: Inter-
    national Universities Press, 1978, pp. 477–509.
_____ (1970a), Narcissism as a Resistance and as a Driving Force in Psycho-
    analysis. In: *The Search for the Self,* vol. 2, ed. P. Ornstein. New York:
    International Universities Press, 1978, pp. 547–561.
_____ (1970b), Discussion of "The Self: A Contribution to Its Place in Theory
    and Technique" by D. C. Levin. In: *The Search for the Self,* vol. 2. New
    York: International Universities Press, 1978, pp. 577–588.
_____ (1971), *The Analysis of the Self.* New York: International Universities
    Press.
_____ (1972), Thoughts on Narcissism and Narcissistic Rage. In: *The Search for
    the Self,* vol. 2, ed. P. Ornstein. New York: International Universities Press,
    1978, pp. 615–658.
_____ (1973), Psychoanalysis in a Troubled World. In: *The Search for the Self,*
    vol. 2, ed. P. Ornstein. New York: International Universities Press, 1978,
    pp. 511–546.
_____ (1974), Remarks about the Formation of the Self. In: *The Search for the
    Self,* vol. 2, ed. P. Ornstein. New York: International Universities Press,
    1978, pp. 737–770.
_____ (1975), The Psychoanalyst in the Community of Scholars. In: *The Search
    for the Self,* vol. 2, ed. P. Ornstein. New York: International Universities
    Press, 1978, pp. 685–724.
_____ (1977), *The Restoration of the Self.* New York: International Universities
    Press.
_____ (1978), *The Search for the Self,* 2 vols., ed. P. Ornstein. New York:
    International Universities Press.
_____ (1979), The Two Analyses of Mr. Z. *Internat. J. Psycho-Anal.,* 60:3–27.
Levin, D. C. (1969), The Self: A Contribution to Its Place in Theory and
    Technique. *Internat. J. Psycho-Anal.,* 50:41–51.
Offer, D. (1975), Normality. In: *Comprehensive Textbook of Psychiatry/II,* ed.
    A. M. Freedman, H. I. Kaplan, & B. J. Sadock. Baltimore: Williams &
    Wilkins, pp. 459–464.

_____ & Sabshin, M. (1966), *Normality: Theoretical and Clinical Concepts of Mental Health.* New York: Basic Books.
Ornstein, A. (1974), The Dread to Repeat and the New Beginning: A Contribution to the Psychoanalysis of the Narcissistic Personality Disorders. *The Annual of Psychoanalysis,* 2:231–248. New York: International Universities Press.
Ornstein, P. H. (1978), The Evolution of Heinz Kohut's Psychoanalytic Psychology of the Self. In: *The Search for the Self,* vol. 1, ed. P. Ornstein. New York: International Universities Press, pp. 1–106.
Peller, L. E. (1954), Libidinal Phases, Ego Development, and Play. *The Psychoanalytic Study of the Child,* 9:178–198. New York: International Universities Press.
Stolorow, R. D. (1978), The Restoration of Psychoanalysis (Book Review of Heinz Kohut's *The Restoration of the Self*). *Contemporary Psychology,* 23:229–230.
Wolf, E. (1976), Ambience and Abstinence. *The Annual of Psychoanalysis,* 4:101–115. New York: International Universities Press.

Discussion of *"Self Psychology and the Concept of Health" by Paul H. Ornstein*

ROBERT D. STOLOROW

Paul Ornstein has provided us with an illuminating and exceptionally cogent exposition of the new concept of psychological health that has developed in concert with the evolution of psychoanalytic self psychology. With scholarly precision, he has drawn out this singularly important thread from the rich fabric of Kohut's thought, has traced its historical unfolding from the initial studies of narcissism to the recent conceptualization of the supraordinate bipolar self, and has explored its major theoretical and clinical implications. Since I find nothing in this splendid paper to criticize or with which to disagree, my discussion will take the form of underscoring and expanding certain points made by Dr. Ornstein that seem to me to be particularly significant and compelling.

Dr. Ornstein has referred to self psychology as a "new scientific paradigm" for psychoanalysis — a designation with which I entirely agree. This new paradigm, which places the experience of self and its motivational primacy at the center of psychoanalytic inquiry, has enabled us to comprehend a wide variety of pathological states from the standpoint of a person struggling to maintain a sense of self-cohesion in the face of threats of self-disintegration, rather than solely from the standpoint of a mental apparatus processing drive energies and dealing with instinctual conflicts (Kohut, 1977b). But, as Dr. Ornstein has shown, this shift in paradigm has not only changed and enhanced our understanding of pathology; it has profound implications for our concept of psychological health as well. In this new paradigm, health is *redefined* in terms of the consolidation of a bipolar self, with its individualized array of primary ambitions and idealized goals, and in terms of the degree of cohesiveness, firmness, and vitality attained by this nuclear self.

What are the features of this new concept of health which distinguish it from those features implicit in earlier psychoanalytic models rooted in the "mental apparatus," "drive discharge" paradigm?

First, the self psychological concept of health is essentially *phenomenological*—it is formulated in terms of a person's self experience. As such, it approaches the understanding of health from a personalistic, rather than a mechanistic, perspective. It thus derives from a realm of discourse that is entirely different from that of traditional metapsychology.

Second, the self psychological concept of health is fundamentally *developmental*—it is formulated in terms of the epigenesis of self experience, the progressive transformation of archaic selfobject constellations as they evolve throughout the formative years through the requisite empathic responsiveness of caretakers to the child's changing psychological requirements. The implication here is that the form and content of psychological health are phase-specific and that the experience of health is distinctly different at different phases of self development. Furthermore, these phase-appropriate varieties of health should be discernible as they make their appearance in a properly conducted psychoanalysis.

Third, the self psychological concept of health is basically a *structuralist* one—it is formulated in terms of the structuralization of self experience and, hence, in terms of the development of the person's capacity to organize and represent his subjective universe. In this connection, it is of more than passing interest that Kohut (1977a) recently wrote a charming tribute to Piaget on the occasion of the latter's eightieth birthday, since both of these men have devoted themselves, albeit from different vantage points, to the study of the growth of psychological structure and the structuralization of human subjectivity.

Dr. Ornstein has noted that it is "unusual for psychoanalysts to focus on health...before defining the nature of the psychopathology against which the former [is] to be delineated." He refers to the "decisive shift of emphasis away from a preoccupation with the pathological and toward a focus on the potentially healthy...aspects of the personality" that typifies self psychology. To these accurate observations I would add that, in comparison with the richly detailed, in-depth understanding of psychopathology that has been provided by classical psychoanalysis, the psychoanalytic conception of psychological health has heretofore seemed pallid and underdeveloped. To be sure, the various metapsychological points of view do contain explicit and implicit concepts of health. One could speak, for example, of psychic energies available for loving and working once they are no longer dammed-up, of the prevalence of sublimatory over countercathectic solutions to instinctual conflict, of the dominance of the conscious, rational, and volitional ego over the unconscious superego and id, and so forth. Yet, on close scrutiny, formulations such as these are more indicative of the absence of pathology than the presence of health. None of these formulations, for example, encompasses the "warm glow of joy" that accompanies the successful pursuit of nuclear ambitions and guiding ideals and which, as Dr. Ornstein has noted, is one of the hallmarks of the healthy personality.

In truth, "mental apparatus" psychology could never adequately describe health. A mental apparatus can be functional or operational, but only a *person* can experience psychological health, and it is this experience that requires a psychology of the self for its comprehension and description. Hartmann's monumental contributions notwithstanding, mental apparatus psychology could never succeed in becoming a general psychology because it could only describe the presence or absence of malfunctions in the apparatus. Thus, until now, classical psychoanalysis has remained principally a theory of psychopathology, providing an exhaustive description of the multitude of "disintegration products" that can issue from a fragmenting self structure, but telling us little about the developing person's growth toward health. The latter can be encompassed only by a theoretical paradigm which brings to focus the epigenesis and structuralization of self experience, and which recognizes in the consolidation of a cohesive nuclear self structure a central constituent of the healthy personality.

Dr. Ornstein's theoretical discussion pertaining to the altered conceptions of resistance, aggression, and the oedipal period which self psychology has made possible alerts us to some extremely important technical implications of the self psychological concept of health. This new perspective can help us to recognize in a patient's archaic states, not only the manifestations of his pathological fixations, conflicts, and defenses, but also the "indicators" of his emerging potential for health — his efforts to reinstate previously aborted developmental thrusts and to complete formerly abandoned developmental tasks, to heal old wounds, and to fill the voids in his self experience. It can help us to avoid those catastrophic interpretive errors and to prevent those transference artifacts, iatrogenic impasses, and so-called "negative therapeutic reactions" that ensue when we fail to comprehend and acknowledge the significance of a developmental step, of a tentative groping toward greater self-cohesion and, hence, toward health, by dismissing it solely as an aspect of the patient's psychopathology (Stolorow & Lachmann, 1980).

At this point I would like to introduce a minor caveat concerning the concept of complementarity between the mental apparatus and self psychological paradigms. This concept has great theoretical appeal, particularly insofar as it averts an irreconcilable rift between self psychology and classical conflict theory. Yet, at any given clinical moment, the analyst must make a distinctive choice as to which paradigm will take precedence in guiding his empathic listening and his interpretive activity. At any one moment in the transference, the patient cannot experience the therapist *both* as a separate and whole object, a target for classical transference displacements, *and* as a selfobject. If I may be permitted an unforgivable paraphrase, the patient cannot both have the analyst and be him too.

Gedo and Pollock (1976) recently edited a monograph with the felicitous title, *Freud: The Fusion of Science and Humanism.* There can be no doubt that self psychology, anchored as it is in clinically derived human developmental principles rather than in remnants of 19th-century physiology, has added greatly to the scientific precision of both our theoretical understanding and our therapeutic interventions. At the same time, the self psychological concept of health, so lucidly outlined and summarized by Dr. Ornstein, may be seen as a definitive and revitalizing triumph for the humanistic trend in Freudian thought. Hence, self psychology continues and refines that unique, evolving amalgamation of science and humanism that has characterized the psychoanalytic enterprise from its inception, and in which psychoanalytic patients have always found their cures.

References

Gedo, J. & Pollock, G., eds. (1976), *Freud: The Fusion of Science and Humanism. Psychol. Issues,* Monogr. 34/35. New York: International Universities Press.

Kohut, H. (1977a), Reflections on the Occasion of Jean Piaget's Eightieth Birthday. *The Annual of Psychoanalysis,* 5:373–375. New York: International Universities Press.

_____ (1977b), *The Restoration of the Self.* New York: International Universities Press.

Stolorow, R. & Lachmann, F. (1980), *Psychoanalysis of Developmental Arrests: Theory and Treatment.* New York: International Universities Press.

Aggression, Self Psychology, and the Concept of Health

Meyer S. Gunther

General Considerations

Introduction

Health has always been a difficult concept to formulate mean-ingfully in psychoanalytic metapsychological terms. It is partic-ularly difficult to do so with respect to the role of aggression. At its simplest, aggression is defined as "attack or hostile action" (Moore & Fine, 1967, p. 5). However, complications develop when we con-sider activities—wishes, fantasies, overt acts, holistic exper-iences—where aggression is present as a *quality of meaning,* that is, as *aggressiveness.* Definitions now become broad and multiple, ranging from "attacking" through "self-assertive" to "enterprising" or "pushy" (*Webster's*). How, then, shall we judge *which* quality determines the overriding *meaning* of a particular act, that is, its "sense or significance" or the "body of habitually associated ideas" (*Webster's*)? First, the manner in which an observer participates in the experience of the act and the stance he takes toward the doer will influence the specific meaning he assigns to the quality of ag-gressiveness of the act. Here Kohut's work on the introspective-

167

empathic orientation of the analytic observer, that is, the orientation that operates *from within the experiencing self of the patient,* constitutes a unique contribution to the problem of determining meaning. Two other relevant considerations should be kept in mind. Concepts of health are often strongly influenced by relativistic sociocultural norms, often unrecognized. Second, undertaking a psychoanalytic value judgment of an act — determining whether it is healthy or unhealthy, mature or infantile — has been troubled by the problem of whole context versus dichotomized components. Without question, the meaning of certain acts speaks for itself because of some incontrovertible quality or effect of the act, as indicated, for instance, in murder, incest, or cannibalism. Shall we therefore conclude that an act carries indelible meaning based on either the presence of singular, circumscribed motivating forces or on particular purposes served? Or shall we consider that an act derives its meaning from a balanced, integrative judgment that includes the situation in which it occurs, the history of the development and the current dynamic context of the person performing the act, as well as an in-depth understanding of the fantasies that the person is experiencing while involved in the act? Clearly, acts of moral ambiguity or contradictory outcome may be better evaluated in relationship to these multiple criteria.

The Problem of Aggression

The presence — and persistence — of diverse theories of aggression throughout the development of psychoanalytic theory suggests that a single, fully satisfactory explanation for aggression has never been devised. Modeled on Freud's libidinal theory, the various psychoanalytic theories of aggression have all been founded on the assumption that behavior as seen by the outside observer is derived from complex modifications or transformations of elemental motivational forces lying at some depth from consciousness within the individual. Considerable distance and considerable "work" separate resultant behavior from the instinctual wishes that are taken to be its primitive bedrock of origin. Thus, psychoanalytic theories have seen aggressive behavior as an end product derived from the taming of primitive psychobiological forces. As with the libidinal instincts, the ultimate aim in these theories — pleasure via tension reduction — is modeled on 19th-century physics and physiology, in particular on Fechner's Constancy principle or Cannon's Homeostasis principle.

Several problems immediately arise. (1) What is the relationship between the motivating force and the modifying structures? (2) How is the motivating force modified and how is the guidance of the modifiers accomplished? (3) How do we account for the vast array of aggressive aims and behavior seen in clinical practice? Disconcertingly, much of the psychoanalytic theory of aggression may be one vast tautology. Following certain behavioral observations, that is, assumptions are made regarding the meaning of those observations. Then, presumptive hypotheses regarding underlying forces are offered to account for the origin of those inferred meanings. Then the original observational data are simply turned around and utilized to prove the validity of hypotheses of assumed underlying forces.

In this paper I shall outline a brief history of psychoanalytic concepts of aggression, emphasizing the elements of origin, aim, modification, and outcome. Then I shall summarize in some detail Kohut's ideas regarding the relation of aggression to pathology, health, and development.

The History of Basic Concepts of Aggression

Some Generalizations

In utilizing Table 1, several questions should be kept in mind.

1. Where is the emphasis in the explanation — on the origin, on the mechanisms of modification, or on the aims and outcome of aggression?

2. What is the level of complexity of the explanation in terms of the interconnections and sophistication of the principles involved?

3. At what point does Freud's basic model (motivational forces plus modifying process produce discharge behavior)

TABLE 1
THE HISTORY OF BASIC CONCEPTS OF AGGRESSION

Author (Date)	Origin	Modification	Aim or Outcome	Comments
Freud (1896)	Mastery wish component of sexual wishes "learned from childhood experience.	"Defense" (= repression) instigated by parental/societal expectation.	Subservient; to "subdue the object," facilitating sexual pleasure, via tension discharge.	Experience is vital. Functions poorly delineated; goals clear, specific, and limited.
Freud (1905)	Sadomasochistic component of libidinal instinct	Instinctual vicissitudes (plus topographic transference).	Subservient; similar to above; relationship to sexual aims more complex and integrated with them.	Postseduction model; now "complete" as biological-like system.
Freud (1915)	Ego instincts	Unclear; by ego itself, especially ego ideal.	Unrelated to sexual aims. Self-preservation of the individual; tension reduction issue unclear.	Freud was not happy with this explanation; problem of Constancy principle.
Freud (1920)	Death instinct (Thanatos)	Somewhat by defenses of the ego, more by admixture with Eros.	Return to original, quiescent inorganic state of matter (= death) by gradual or sudden discharge of all tension into the soma.	Freud satisfied; the consistency of system restored, despite vagueness of clinical utility, especially regarding the aims or outcomes.
Freud (1923)	Death instinct (Thanatos)	Defense by the ego is primary; role of Eros secondary.	As above; addition of discharge outward via musculature onto objects.	Outcomes less of a problem but still troublesome.
Hartmann, Kris, & Loewenstein (1949)	Aggressive instinct	As above, but several complex ego functions in service of defense.	Vast array of specific aims, all tension-reduction-related, but distant from it.	Clinical focus restored, especially through attention to aims and outcomes.
Hendrick (1942)	Mastery instinct	As above, but less total modification necessary.	Mastery of ego functions; by active practice of them; destructive only with regression.	
Kohut (1972–1977)	Biological predisposition to activity.	Whole self, via its nuclear goals and values.	Self-preservative, self-assertive or self-fulfilling influence (?) on the object world. If regression, then depression or narcissistic rage; both are secondary or subservient to "whole self" aims.	Separateness of motivations, modifiers, and outcomes is diminished again. Instinct theory is "buried."

begin to appear inadequate as an explanation?

4. How have successive thinkers attempted to solve the apparent inadequacies which Freud, even through the use of a series of emendations and alterations, was ultimately not able to solve in a generally satisfactory way?

Freud's Pre-1900 Explanation

The origin of aggression is unclear, but it is apparently a loose component of an experientially stimulated, normally present but latent sexual wish; it is the hypothesized mastery component that exists to facilitate the consummation of sexual pleasure. In concert with the dominant sexual wish, modification is accomplished in an "all or none" manner through defense, that is, repression, instigated by the incompatibility between such wishes and other consciously learned ideas that arc in the service of ethical standards derived from social or parental precepts. The aim, if one can speak of the aim of such an unclear aggressive component, is subservient to the achievement of explicitly sexual goals. Note that basically there are no separately conceptualized theories to account for the separate functions of origin, modification process, or aim. Note also the extensive role of experience in explaining all aspects of behavior (see Freud, 1896a & b).

Freud's 1905 Model

This is the basic version of the topographic model developed after the abandonment of the seduction theory and the publication of *The Interpretation of Dreams* (1900). The conceptual ideas of aggression contained in this model are best expressed in *Three Essays on the Theory of Sexuality* (1905). Aggressive acts are seen to originate from the sadomasochistic component of the libidinal instinct, not from environmentally stimulated "normal" wishes. This component-instinct is now seen as an integral but subordinate part of the libido. Modification of this part instinct is minimal and is accomplished by the intrinsic processes of the libido or by the process of topographic transference. Aim and outcome are subordinated to guarantee through mastery the achievement of the sexual goals. These in turn are defined as end pleasure and equated with the experience of tension reduction. This explanation is fully compatible with the Constancy principle, which is seen as a reliable and useful construct for explaining the overall workings of the mind.

Freud's 1914–1917 Model

This is the period of Freud's papers on metapsychology and his *Introductory Lectures* (1916-1917). By this time, many problems had arisen from clinical experience — unconscious defenses, structural regression, etc. — which suggested limits to the utility of the libido as an explanation for both self-preservative and self-destructive behavior. Freud felt that a new theoretical addition was needed to equip the ego with energies with which to meet its more complex tasks. Aggression is therefore reconceptualized as originating from the ego's self-preservative instincts. Modification of aggression is not only effected by ego defenses but also by the activities of a dominant portion of the ego specially set aside for this purpose — the ego ideal. Aim and outcome are no longer limited simply to end pleasure and tension reduction but now influence self-preservative strategies that point to the conservation of energy rather than its discharge. This theory represents a departure in a number of ways from Freud's previous guiding principles (see Freud, 1915).

Freud's 1920 Model Based on Beyond the Pleasure Principle

In 1920, with *Beyond the Pleasure Principle,* Freud attempted to resolve a number of contradictions with which his theories were beset: antipathy between the ego instincts and the libidinal instincts, and contradictions between clinical phenomena like guilt, depression, and the negative therapeutic reaction and the presumed hypothetical goal of all human behavior — the reestablishment of a pleasure state through tension discharge. The repetition of unpleasure as a well-ordered, consistent aim seemed unexplainable and incompatible with the then current theory. At this point, therefore, Freud proposed a basic revision of the existing dual instinct theory. According to the new theory, the death instinct, or Thanatos, operated to provide aggressive cathexis now assigned to the id. This cathexis was subject to modification by the ego's defenses as well as through admixture with Eros, the libidinal cathexis of which provided for some forms of sublimation and neutralization. The postulation of the death instinct, together with its structural relationships, made Freud's system compatible once more with Fechner's Constancy principle, which was now revised to include both the Nirvana principle and the repetition compulsion. Specifically, the aim or outcome of the death instinct was the return of the individual to some primary inorganic state. This was effected via gradual tension reduction through discharge inward, ultimately producing a total cessation of all life activities, that is, death. Thus the repetition compulsion, an intermediate clinically based abstraction, was seen as explaining self-destructive behavior. But the repetition compulsion itself was seen as the ultimate expression of the death instinct, and so the death instinct itself, in turn, became a mechanism guaranteeing the Constancy principle. These theoretical contributions achieved importance by tying together — although somewhat abstractly — the questions of origin, aim, modification, and governing principle. Many clinically oriented psychoanalysts, however, found that the all-or-nothing quality of this web of explanations presented endless trouble in their thinking, especially with respect to everyday clinical phenomena.

Freud's 1923 Model Based on The Ego and the Id

In 1923, the origin of aggression is still assigned to the death instinct, but the defenses of the ego account for increasingly complex modifications of the instinct's original aims. Additional alteration of the instinct's primary aim is provided through what Freud termed a "tendency" of the death instinct to discharge itself outward via the musculature, thereby achieving end pleasure through outwardly directed (destructive) activity. Nevertheless, the instinct could still discharge itself internally into the soma, producing self-injury, psychosomatic illness, and conceivably suicide. To meet its expanded transformational tasks, the ego appears to have new energy assigned to it through the neutralization of some portion of aggressive cathexes. Thus, Freud returns to a consistent view of aim and outcome as a reduction of tension, restoring his older forms of order once more within a closed theoretical system.

Ego Psychology and the Problem of Aggression

In 1949, Hartmann, Kris, and Loewenstein coauthored "Notes on the Theory of Aggression," the apogee of psychoanalytic ego psychology with regard to the problem of aggression. The origin of aggressive acts is attributed to an innate propensity or constant driving force explicitly likened to an instinct, but now associated with aggression per se rather than death. Their second unique addition was to link aggression with the functions of an ego now viewed as an extremely complex organizing, modifying, and managing structure. The aims of aggression are broadened to include not only harm or destruction but also mastery and transformations of the object world through work, creativity, and the like. The problem of the repetition compulsion is largely ignored. Instead, several interesting new theoretical constructions are offered: (1) The authors suggest that splitting of the ego's identifications occurs with respect to the objects of aggression. (2) They note that an aggressive instinct alone is insufficient to explain aggressive acts of social magnitude. (3) They offer a potentially tautological explanation based on their attribution to the ego of the vast array of functions accounting for the presence of the wide variety of "aggressive" behaviors seen in clinical practice—all apparently the result of extensive modification of the aggressive instinct. (4) With Freud, they feel aggression is more clearly related to the ego's aims and functions than is the libido. (5) The authors remain unsatisfied with their own efforts at explaining the role of the pleasure aim in aggressive discharge. For instance, active mastery is viewed as not biological enough, fight or flight as not psychological enough, and the deprivation/regression thesis apparently as not instinctual enough. Whereas deprivation is seen to be an important component in mobilizing aggression, they feel there is something irreducibly instinctual-like in the intrinsic curve of recurrent arousal and discharge of aggression as well as in the apparently universally present human need for normal, safe discharge pathways for aggression following its arousal. (6) Perhaps most important of all, the authors are concerned with attempting to clarify on a higher theoretical level the relationship of self and object rather than ego and object, especially in terms of the vicissitudes of aggression. However, they do not explore this vital area extensively.

Hendrick's "Instinct and Ego during Infancy" (1942)

In this interesting, odd paper, Hendrick suggested that it is not necessary to postulate a death instinct or even an aggressive instinct. Instead, he suggested that we focus on a mastery instinct which, as a constant driving force arising at the borderline of biology and psychology, meets Freud's technical criterion of instinctuality. The modifications of the mastery instinct are accomplished by, and interwoven with, all of the functions of the ego. The pleasure aim is experienced incrementally through the modest transformations that result from the mastery of new independent ego functions, as these are interwoven with behavioral activity and practice on the object world. Thus, although the aims of the mastery instinct appear plastic or even fuzzy, their incremental realization produces a predictable lowering of aggressive tension. Being so interwoven in an intrinsic developmental process, many elements are modified in the mastery experience — the energies, the incipient new ego functions, the specific behavioral forms in which mastery activity occurs, and possibly even the aims of the instinct themselves. (More recently, Robert White [1963] elaborated similar views about the relation between mastery and pleasure.)

Hendrick's paper is important because it suggests that the primary motivating forces should be viewed neither as primitive nor as requiring nearly as much modification as had been previously thought. Furthermore, questions of motivating forces, modifying elements, aim, and outcome seem to be much more closely interwoven with one another in a patterned manner than they were at the height of ego psychology.

An Overview of Heinz Kohut's
Ideas on Aggression (1971, 1972, 1977)

Kohut holds that the origin of aggressive behavior is a biological predisposition of the human personality toward self-assertive activity that is contentless with respect to intrinsic aims and specific goals. Thus assertiveness, as a quality, is a nonspecific, fundamental building block of the human psyche. Consequently, any focused aggressive activity is an integrated function of the whole psyche with all its component structures rather than the expression of a narrowly delineated part of it. Parenthetically, it can be a function of a disintegrated as well as an integrated psyche. The transformation and organization of assertiveness into some overt form of aggression occur through the activity of the whole psyche under the guidance of one's nuclear values and ambitions. A new supraordinate principle is proposed: the lawful development, maintenance, and expression of the nuclear self. Normal, healthy self-assertive behavior expresses the basic nuclear pattern of the self, its guiding ideals, etc. Alternatively, in the face of stress, disappointment, loss, or overstimulation (ultimately related to inadequacy of idealization of basic ideals and values) there ensues a threat to the cohesion of the self or to the sustaining qualities of its ideals. At this point, a state of rage, fragmentation, or depression may supervene, signifying the presence of a significant tension imbalance that must be dealt with through symptom formation.

Some Generalizations about Kohut's Ideas
of Aggression and Psychoanalytic Theory

Introduction

Kohut's psychology is a self psychology of the "whole," one

that considers the meaning of acts within the context of the whole more than classical ego psychological thinking. It focuses on the meaning of experience — especially complex affect states — and only secondarily on forces, process, and conflict. Over the past 10 years, its fundamental concepts have changed somewhat, as have some of its definitions. Troublesome issues remain, especially regarding the definition of self and the ultimate relationship among the major structural configurations, that is, among the bipolar nuclei of the self, the two major transferences and their transformations, etc. Biology is assigned a less circumscribed, less clear role, particularly with respect to the issue of the biological determinants of the pattern of self development.

In summary, the following may be the most enduring features of Kohut's contributions for purposes of the theory of aggression: (1) Psychoanalytic theory is no longer considered a finished product. Rather, it is a permanently evolving process, inexorably interrelated with its observational-empathic-introspective methodology. (2) The lawful development, maintenance, and expression of a cohesive nuclear self is an overriding principle of depth psychology. (3) The meaning of individual acts can best be understood in relationship to an entire self context, both developmentally and dynamically. In viewing aggressive behavior, the origins of motivating forces cannot be separated from the process and product of such acts or from current personality status and relationships. (4) The determination of psychological meaning is influenced in part by the position of the observer. By taking an empathic, introspective stand one may sample the full range of experience from within the self of the patient as well as one's own array of inner responses. One may thereby become privy to more complex levels of intuitive "knowing" that can supplement cognitive understanding in determining the meaning of a patient's experience. (5) Some immediate clinical consequences follow from the centrality of empathy and introspection: The making of correct interpretations becomes more difficult. Comprehensive, individualized understanding of the patient's complex experiential states becomes necessary. The citing of orthodox precepts is no longer sufficient to answer questions regarding meaning and motivation. Meaning is no longer to be equated with the discovery of universal unconscious forces and the tracing of their transformational processes. A more sophisticated level of knowing and understanding is now demanded in the analyst's daily work.

Pathology

There are three broad divisions of symptomatic pathology involving aggression, all related, but all involving somewhat different vulnerabilities in self structure and self function. The following description explicates the particular role of aggression in each category of pathology.

Narcissistic Rage. This condition manifests itself in a spectrum ranging from mild annoyance to catatonic furor. Its occurrence follows disappointment or failure regarding one's expectations toward an object that is viewed unconsciously in primitive, infantile, self-selfobject terms.[1] Narcissistic rage is characterized by the persistence of the goal of physical destruction of the object beyond the goal of simple competitive victory or the elicitation of an apology or some other form of redress. Feelings of humiliation, overt or concealed, usually accompany such an outrage. Such outrage and humiliation express the overt regression from an adult to an infantile level of relating, i.e., to an openly archaic and primitive self-selfobject relationship that follows a failure of the normally hidden grandiose expectations toward the object. Four specific qualities usually accompany narcissistic rage: (1) an expectation of absolute control over the object's behavior; (2) an expectation of perfection of response from the object; (3) an utter incapacity for empathy with the object, the object's behavior, or the object's motives; (4) an incapacity to distinguish the issue or problem from the object as a separate entity. In addition to its acute form, narcissistic rage may occur as a chronic state of spitefulness, bitterness, suspiciousness, or preparanoid grudge-collecting in which no

---

[1]See Wolf (this volume) for an elaborate description of self and selfobject transferences.

quantity of discharge behavior, no degree of restitution, and no apology by the offender can ever make up for the injury. In either form of narcissistic rage, a hidden fixation on archaic infantile grandiosity is always present. At a more basic but broad level, the inadequacy of basic healthy idealization of the nuclear self is revealed, especially with respect to resilient reliability, integrity, and capacity to influence the world.

Typically, the vulnerable fixation of the self and its expression in the aim of grandiose, adultlike performance are not represented. Rather, they may exist in a dissociated state, split off from the central controlling sectors of the personality. Under threat, they become reactivated, even to the point of controlling the central executive sectors of the personality in consequence of the previously described sequence of disappointment, regression, and reawakening. This inadequately idealized nuclear core of an impaired psyche reveals its underlying helplessness and anguish indirectly, through rage and retribution. Thus, narcissistic rage may serve as a compensatory compromise between several goals: (1) At one and the same time, it signals helplessness and vulnerability together with a pretended denial of that vulnerability. (2) It constitutes a shrill demand that the offending object responsible for this unwelcome self-discovery be erased from its existence. (3) It may constitute an omnipotent, implicitly magical attempt to carry out that insistent demand—as if the logic of the primary process were ultimately superior!

Let me cite an example. A bright, young adult patient suffering from a disguised phobic attachment to his mother was, following the successful completion of a graduate program, quite literally unable to go to work. He had always been a firm believer in the inherent goodness and selflessness of his parents with respect to his and his siblings' well-being and overall needs. He believed that his own role in the world was necessarily guided by similar selfless, angelic but grandiose principles. When, after several years of analytic work, significant progress had been made with the phobia and he had begun to acquire insight in the form of self-doubt and self-curiosity regarding the relationships among his peculiar ideals, his parents' behavior, and his neurotic attachment to them, he was finally able to leave the house and obtain a reliable, intermediate-level, professional job.

At this stage of the analysis, his analyst decided to raise the fee from the modest level at which it had initially been set. When this modest fee raise was announced, the patient sat up and feigned utter disbelief. After a few minutes of simplistic questions and answers to reassure himself that he had heard correctly, he unleashed an uncontrolled stream of verbal fury culminating in a threat to punch the analyst in the nose. Getting up from the couch, he paced the room and finally rushed from the office in an effort to manage his intense rage by simply removing himself from the offending stimulus. Over the next few months, several focal elements emerged, following this traumatic deidealization experience. It was utterly unbelievable to the patient that the analyst was not as selflessly devoted to his well-being as he had believed all along, and actually made his living from his work with patients. This realization shook his conviction in the concepts of goodness and selflessness as universal motivations. Secondly, and possibly more basically, the possibility that he had chosen such a flawed analyst began to impinge on the patient's confidence in his judgmental capacities and to undermine his conviction that, in this as in all things, his ability to understand a situation and take correct action was absolutely perfect, as his parents had endlessly reassured him. This paralleled his dawning awareness of his repressed rage at his own pseudophobic helplessness. Thirdly, after many uncomfortable attempts to avoid the issue, the patient revealed that in the past his sublimely ethical standards for himself had been imperfectly realized. He had a tendency, when under the stress of disappointment over his inability to carry out certain goal-directed behavior as perfectly, or as easily, as he wished, to revert to a particular form of mild, but utterly unacceptable, delinquent behavior over which he felt considerable shame and humiliation: the stealing of petty items from stores. This seemed to express a split-off, angry, acquisitive "my wants come first" self. The similiarity to what he believed he had detected in the analyst became the unbearable stimulus for his attack of narcissistic rage.

Depression, Self-Destruction, and Suicide. Depressive episodes are part of every human being's experience. They may express themselves in emotions ranging from mild self-annoyance or irritation with one's self to overtly suicidal acts, from simple disappointment in one's performance efforts to the deliberate destruction of all or part of the mind-body self no longer felt to be of any positive use or meaning. Whatever the specific experiences of these affects or their ultimate consequences, three things are characteristic of patients in such conditions. First, their feeling quality is that of a sad, dead, desertlike world, devoid of human warmth, human responsiveness, or a sense of aliveness. It is the world of the empty self, so pervasive and so unmistakable to the empathic observer. Patients complain of feeling insubstantial, of fearing that they will vanish into others or simply melt away, becoming ghostlike or invisible figures on an empty, cold landscape. Secondly, they experience further existence as hopeless and worthless, as if some crucial quality vital to one's continuing survival had been lost or as if some terrible, morbid burden had been acquired which could only be lifted by ending one's existence. Such hopelessness appears related to a precipitating experience of failed expectations in one's self, in others, or in society and may often involve a brief period of rage at self or objects. But the final, common pathway is that of progressively and rapidly failing self-esteem. Thirdly, these patients seem objectively robbed of energy and vigor; even their muscle tone is diminished. Alternatively, a state of random, unfocused agitation may be present.

Following precipitation by disappointment in, or frustration with, one's self or a current object (particularly one that had been sustaining in either self-selfobject or object libidinal terms), a massive regression occurs revealing a flaw in the nuclear self. Instead of a vigorously invested nuclear self, a weakened, poorly idealized structure is bared, one uncertain of its values and insubstantial in its ideals. Above all, such a self structure is characterized by a lack of the firm, vigorous cohesion that is based on a well-structured imbrication of energies, capacities, and guiding values. What is revealed instead is the repressed core of an archaic infantile self: an empty, hopeless, helpless, and insubstantial self that has overwhelmed the adult self and absorbed whatever energies might have remained in the adult self. It is almost as if actual physical survival in the face of a major selfobject loss is simply not possible, so helpless and incomplete is this (abandoned) archaic infantile self. Even if such an impairment does not result in full-scale disaster, the vitality and assertive vigor of an integrated, adult nuclear self are simply no longer present. If no intervention occurs, this emptied-out self, devoid of sustaining energies and ideals, insubstantial and flat, may next proceed to a state of overwhelming (and even suicidal) despair based on the patient's inability to tolerate indefinitely so painful a state.

Alternatively, incomplete or partial fragmentation may lead to the decathexis and exclusion of a part of the body-self, permitting a shallow reintegration of the remaining self. The hopelessness, worthlessness, and degradation become focused, more schizophreniclike, on the part of the "bad" body-self that has been excluded, thereby predisposing one via psychological disavowal to the actual anatomic destruction of the now useless organ.

Superficially, we might note the resemblance of these observations to the classical psychoanalytic theory of depression, especially to the parallel between an apparent rage at a part of the self-selfobject constellation and rage of the introjected, ambivalently loved object of classical theory. On careful analysis, however, several significant differences can be noted: (1) Any expression of primitive self-directed aggression is the resultant end product of a complex process involving breakdown or regression to a more archaic self state and its accompanying functions. Aggression, per se, is not a primary or linear cause motivating depression, which in turn leads to a deterioration in the function of the self. Rather, aggression is a predictable result of the breakdown of self function and its accompanying depressive affects. (2) The role of disappointment in Kohut's explanation is framed in self terms, that is, in terms of structural problems and processes; it is not a result of the vicissitudes of object libido. (3) Inadequate idealization of the self as an integrated, valued, and cohesive structure is seen to be the ultimate predisposition leading to depression. A predisposition to ambivalence or an inability to neutralize "instinctual aggression"

(Hartmann, Kris, & Loewenstein, 1949) is seen as a speculative assumption playing either a secondary role or perhaps no etiological role at all.

Sadomasochistic Behavior in the Broad Sense. Sadomasochistic behavior is seen as arising from the threats to the integrity or power of a nuclear self, especially as experienced in terms of a threat to the ability to regulate tension following disappointment in current self-selfobject transactions. A pathway of response occurs that is somewhat different from that typifying the two previously mentioned pathological entities. With sadomasochistic behavior, only a partial regression occurs, and it is regression via a kind of lateral movement of the psyche, toward the mobilization of certain age- or phase-determined drivelike residues that operate essentially in the service of adaptive/compensatory mechanisms for tension regulation. Sadistic as well as masochistic behavior is thereby considered to be the product of a complex series of efforts of a nuclear self attempting to restore one or another disabled function, but now relying on derivative mechanisms to regulate tension. A combination of self-soothing and self-stimulation is explicitly present in masochistic behavior. Tying one's self with ropes, head banging, and picking away at one's skin, hair, or nails, for example, are all examples of relatively simple masochistic acts. The restoration of a sense of one's wholeness and aliveness or of the continuity of one's own boundaries by the surface stimulation provided through suffering in pain is self-evident. The choice of behavioral acts and the particular drivelike qualities of the acts are all determined by the specific developmental level or phase in which the primary self-selfobject developmental experience failed. Thus, drivelike, physiological-like efforts at tension regulation constitute evidence of the attempts by the distressed child (in the adult) to substitute physical activity under his own control for psychological functions that were never acquired because of the failed parental selfobject function of an earlier time.

Sadistic behavior is less easy to see in its self-restorative functions because of the presence of an apparent object, but unconsciously this object is usually experienced as a selfobject.

Inflicting pain or suffering on another is, however, not merely motivated simply by vengeance for past wrongs as in narcissistic rage. Instead, it may be utilized as confirmation of one's own cleverness, power, and special entitlement, or it may serve to rob the other of his power over one's self or fantasied control over one's behavior. Ultimately, therefore, one substitutes a safer position of apparent grandiosity as a means of assuaging the threatened self. Once again, the underlying affect state of helplessness, inadequacy, unbearable excitement, or bored emptiness is forestalled by the erection of its apparent opposite. Even more than with the first two forms of pathology, however, an understanding of an individual's sadistic or masochistic actions requires considerable empathic work to discern what lies behind and beyond the erotized or aggressivized excitement that is so frequently the common denominator of both of these forms of behavior.

The following example illustrates a complex combination of sadistic and masochistic behavior.

An inhibited and shy young man, suffering from an overall restriction in his capacity for loving and working, had been raised by a rather passive father and a most aggressively bizarre, even grossly sadistic, authoritarian mother. She was a woman who, in many ways, represented an exaggerated caricature of the qualities of her own primitive, European peasant background. When, as a frightened, inadequate, lonely adolescent, he would return home from school, having experienced some academic setback despite his superior I.Q., or having been rebuffed in his awkward efforts at athletic endeavors, he would retreat in anguish and hopelessness by going down to the dark, quiet basement. As is typical with adolescents who have suffered such blows to their self-esteem, he would masturbate regularly at those times. If his parents were out of the house, however, the following additional sequence took place. He would dress himself in his mother's clothes, especially her old undergarments. He would then tie himself to a post in the basement, straining tightly against the ropes, heightening his masturbatory excitement until he would have an orgasm, dirtying her clothes. This would be accompanied by an unclear beating fantasy. Following this, he would untie himself and destroy the garment, again experiencing an outburst of sexual excitement. This sequence of events would eventually lead him to feel more comfortable and calm, and better able to manage his lonely tensions and his vague hypochondriacal-like discomfort.

It is genetically significant that upon beginning school, when he suffered a childhood phobia, his mother, in an effort to shame him, dressed him in an older sister's clothes and whipped him in an effort to "motivate" him to go off to school like a normal six-year-old. Beatings would often by given for very minor infractions of her bizarre rules and expectations and they were endured passively, silently, hopelessly. Following such experiences, the patient would retreat to a lonely, dark, quiet corner of the basement. During late latency, he discovered that his father, too, would retreat on occasion from his mother's unbearably hypomaniclike rages by going down to the basement and quietly drinking. The patient would silently sit in the father's presence, occasionally being permitted to snuggle up to him. Later, in analysis, he was able to reveal his own episodes of severe alcoholism and hypochondriasis, often preceded by unmanageable experiences of tension and helplessness that had been precipitated by unsatisfactory attempts to establish relationships with women. Intermingled with these experiences were occasional periods of depressive helplessness. Paralleling the childhood situation, he would retreat to his darkened apartment for lonely drinking episodes. Initially, he would drink himself into a state of alcoholic agitation and stupor, including elements of cognitive disorganization and hypochondriacal anxiety. On occasion, a gradually clarifying state of integration and calmness would ensue, after which he would be able to go to sleep. In the course of the analysis, when faced with the threat of hypochondriacal regressive reactions and unmanageable tensions, he began to substitute calls to the analyst and the fantasized experience of receiving calls from the analyst. Eventually, the stabilizing transference relationship with the analyst obviated the need for an actual phone call by either party, permitting the patient to calm himself by simply reminding himself that the analyst would "be there" the next day.

Health

The problem of what constitutes "healthy" or "mature" aggression cannot be solved by the simple citation of ex cathedra generalizations. Rather, it can best be explicated by exploring a series of relevant issues, focusing on the origins, circumstances of expression, and structural relationships involved in assertiveness.

1. Assertiveness in the service of one's general self goals is seen as the focused expression of a nonideational, nonaim-equipped, elementary building block, present as an innate, biological predisposition toward activity.

2. Aggressive behavior as a form of assertiveness is an expression of the whole self in action. Its meaning, whether destructive or productive, regressive or progressive, healthy or unhealthy, is a function of the whole self in its nuclear pattern of ambitions, talents, and goals as well as an expression of the current state of the self in the context of self-selfobject transactions.

3. Healthy assertiveness may take the more obvious forms of ambitious performance activity designed to utilize one's talents to fulfill goals, especially in the areas of creativity, the working world, athletics, or the world of scholarship. Sometimes healthy assertiveness of one's own nuclear self may take the form of nothing more than the ability to value (and thereby share in) the worthy achievements or ideals of others. Personal self-fulfillment via distinguished accomplishments that rely on the assertive use of one's talents is hardly open to all on an equal basis. Many people have to content themselves with self-fulfillment through the idealization of, and identification with, other more talented or more fortunate individuals.

4. On occasion, one's own healthy self-assertiveness will inevitably be in competition with, and even opposed to, the healthy self-assertiveness of other healthy selves. As Kohut suggests, "There really is such a thing as healthy paranoia."

5. Health should no longer be defined primarily with a combination of instinctual and psychoeconomic terms that refer to the discharge or reduction of tension occurring under the umbrella of heterosexual genital primacy. Such dimensions may be intrinsic

and necessary as components of a general definition of health, but there are more significant dynamic-ideational components that must be added to any definition. I refer to the capacity for selective assertiveness plus achievement plus toleration of disappointment — all in balanced proportion and in relationship to one's own unique nuclear patterns. Optimally, this should occur in conjunction with the sense of the value, firmness, and reasonable certainty — or tolerable uncertainty — of one's own self.

6. Drive theory is not merely reductionistic as a theory of individual behavior but, as our society grows increasingly complex, it is incomplete as an explanatory system with respect to the problems of mass behavior and mass gratification. In light of the increasing number of people on earth and the decreasing natural resources, gratifications, however selective, must now take into account these changed social circumstances. Thus private gratifications compatible with, or capable of being fulfilled through, satisfactions associated with group identity will become increasingly important in the future.

Some Developmental Aspects of the Self with Emphasis on Aggression[2]

One can think of the id in a number of ways: (1) Classically the id is the source of instinctual drive cathexes of both an aggressive and libidinal nature. (2) The term "id" may represent the nonideational, prepsychological, genetically patterned propensities that man shares with animals. (3) The term "id" may refer to the oldest or innermost area of psychological experience organized by the primary process and the consequent effect that this inner core of experience has on later behavior, especially via transferences.

1. From the standpoint of self psychology, the assertiveness of the self in pursuit of lawful needs is a fundamental, governing principle. But that does not answer the question regarding the

[2]These considerations of development, although generally applicable throughout childhood, primarily emphasize preoedipal experience.

ultimate bedrock situation out of which aggressive behavior and especially destructive behavior flows.

2. If, by "bedrock," we mean that structural level in the understanding of human behavior beyond which attempts to break it down further destroy its fundamentally human, psychological nature, then the bedrock is the cohesive infantile self maintained as part of a self-selfobject configuration with the parenting figures.[3] If a cohesive infantile self is missing, there is no unmistakable human psychology as such, but only restricted, stimulus-response transactions often oriented around tension regulation, involving simpler perceptual modes of organization, and probably genetically prepatterned.[4]

3. Thus, if the bedrock is the achievement and maintenance of a cohesive infantile self, then the threat of destruction of this self, once achieved, even on a temporary and incomplete basis, is the earliest and ultimate danger faced by human beings — more fundamental than castration anxiety, separation anxiety, or guilt. However, destruction of the cohesive infantile self by definition can never be the result of ordinary stress or ordinary dangers or difficulties. Instead, it may well arise from a factor that finds expression in Freud's theories. Overstimulation, either from within or without, if massive enough, or the inability to manage at optimal levels quantities of a specific type of stimulation, may produce a traumatic state of such magnitude that it temporarily destroys the cohesive stability of the earliest self. Consequently, the aggressive quality with which an infant asserts its mounting needs may be a healthy signal to the environment that there has been a destabilization of the infant's fragile (physiological) equilibrium and that an increasingly endangering need state exists. At this level, vigorously aggressive crying or other motor activity is a function and a derivative of the firmness and security with which the infant is capable of asserting that it needs something. However,

---

[3]See P. Tolpin, "The Borderline Personality: Its Makeup and Analyzability" (this volume) for a definition of the cohesive infantile self.

[4]This explanation is clearly open to much question depending on the definitions used and the meaning assigned to the rapidly increasing body of data on early infant observation.

if this aggressive signal is inadequately responded to by the self-object environment, an increasing primitivization of the response follows, and it spreads into a mass affect state absorbing components of the crumbling infantile self. The ensuing rage state, in certain ways resembling later narcissistic rage, represents more than a simple fragmentation phenomenon and suggests that a catastrophic traumatic state is imminent.

4. Implicit in Kohut's developmental concepts are a number of assumptions: (a) The holding environment must be pretuned to respond to asserted needs. (b) If there is a disturbance in equilibrium, not only must the infant be capable of signaling, but the signal must be one that is meaningful to the environment. (c) A state of confidence in that environment is reestablished when the selfobject environment demonstrates that it "knows and understands," first through appropriate affective response and then by taking appropriate action to restore the infant's equilibrium.

5. Kohut suggests that nondestructive aggression has a developmental line of its own from the primitive demanding and potentially desperate or even catastrophic type to the selectively focused and mature assertiveness through which the individual can recognize and utilize the separation of methods from goals.

6. Children below a certain age assertively express any individual needs as if the whole self were involved rather than simply a circumscribed wish. Similarly, the young child interprets the parents' response as a response to his whole self and not just the circumscribed need. Thus, the integrity and value of the whole self appear to ride on the outcome of each particular wish that has prompted an asserted behavioral expression. However, as maturity lessens the totality of the younger child's involvement in each assertion of a need, the child gradually becomes capable of separating and shielding the integrity and value of the nuclear self from the environment's response to each and every need or activity. The significance of this in clinical practice is obvious. It is a fundamental error of understanding to repeat the unempathic or out-of-tune parental response of the past by assuming that the asserted expression by itself, whether it refers to a need or an activity, is the focal issue. Instead, the more appropriate under-

standing of these matters is based on a recognition of the relationship between the asserted psychic element and the total context of the self at the moment: its cohesion, its value, its precise developmental status, its current dynamic relationships.

7. From the point of view of development, an outpouring of destructive forms of aggression in later childhood or adulthood does not necessarily constitute a simple return to an earlier stage in the developmental "taming" of an instinct. Instead, it may originate from a threatened breakdown in the integrity of the mature self, arising from problems in the self-selfobject context. With the failure or frustration of functions involving tension management, gratification, assertive expression, or self-esteem, initially "healthy" aggression may be released as a signal of need. But as the threat increases and the environment fails to respond, the self fragments, and an increasingly primitivized transformation occurs in the expression of the aggression; hence the designation "breakdown" product for the released aggression. Two implications of this development require further elaboration.

(a) *Regression.* With mounting threat of imbalance or fragmentation to the self, the signal function itself regresses. Inevitably, the assertive outpouring undergoes modifications in quality and quantity. As it shifts toward action and away from words (corresponding to the regression from secondary to primary process), the goal of the outpouring becomes aggressive alteration of the environment and its objects—dramatically, unequivocally, even destructively. But, above all, it is regression in the state of the self and its functions that underlies the regression in the quality and quantity of the released aggression.

(b) *Fixation.* The expressed aggression typically bears the stamp of the early developmental level at which the original self-selfobject failure occurred. Instead of internalization of psychological increments of self-selfobject experience (in the form of new psychic structure), the child substitutes desperate reliance upon physiological, drivelike "action" elements to serve as functional substitutes for the missing psychic internalizations. Thus, even though such self functions may remain physiological and drivelike, they come within the grasp of the child's own ego, that is, they are no longer predominantly "outside" of the child's self and lying on the parents' side of the self-selfobject context. The capacity for self management has increased, but at the price of unconscious fixation on primitive mechanisms. Thus, the form of aggression that is released upon a threat to the integrity or functions of the adult self not only suggests the specific developmental stage at which the crucial failure occurred, but also carries with it those intrinsically more primitive, developmentally fixated, and conflict-related formal qualities.

Summary

Kohut has opened a door that extends our capacity for understanding complex human experience from the vantage point of depth psychology. Nowhere is this more true than with respect to aggressive experience. In the earliest phases of psychoanalytic theory, aggression was viewed as the product of an incompletely tamed, primitive, distant-from-consciousness, quasi-biological force. Over the years, the selective contributions of later theorists have both loosened and extended this explanation, thereby preparing the way for acceptance of the total revision of the concept offered by Kohut: aggression is one form or quality of the expression of a universal human propensity toward healthy assertiveness that is intrinsic to, and that accompanies, any activity of a cohesive self.

References

Freud, S. (1896a), Further Remarks on the Neuro-Psychoses of Defence. *Standard Edition,* 3:159–185. London: Hogarth Press, 1962.
_____ (1896b), The Aetiology of Hysteria. *Standard Edition,* 3:189–221. London: Hogarth Press, 1962.
_____ (1900), The Interpretation of Dreams. *Standard Edition,* 4 & 5. London: Hogarth Press, 1961.
_____ (1905), Three Essays on the Theory of Sexuality. *Standard Edition,* 7:125–245. London: Hogarth Press, 1953.
_____ (1915), Instincts and Their Vicissitudes. *Standard Edition,* 14:111–140. London: Hogarth Press, 1957.
_____ (1916–1917), Introductory Lectures on Psycho-Analysis. *Standard*

Edition, 15 & 16. London: Hogarth Press, 1963.

_____ (1920), Beyond the Pleasure Principle. *Standard Edition,* 18:3–64. London: Hogarth Press, 1955.

_____ (1923), The Ego and the Id. *Standard Edition,* 19:3–66. London: Hogarth Press, 1961.

Hartmann, H., Kris, E., & Loewenstein, R. (1949), Notes on the Theory of Aggression. *The Psychoanalytic Study of the Child,* 3/4:9–36. New York: International Universities Press.

Hendrick, I. (1942), Instinct and Ego during Infancy. *Psychoanal. Quart.,* 11:33–58.

Kohut, H. (1971), *The Analysis of the Self.* New York: International Universities Press.

_____ (1972), Thoughts on Narcissism and Narcissistic Rage. In: *The Search for the Self,* vol. 2, ed. P. Ornstein. New York: International Universities Press, pp. 615–658.

_____ (1977), *The Restoration of the Self.* New York: International Universities Press.

Moore, B. & Fine, B., eds. (1967), *A Glossary of Psychoanalytic Terms and Concepts.* New York: American Psychoanalytic Association.

Webster's New International Dictionary, 2nd Edition (1958). Springfield, Mass.: Merriam.

White, R. (1963), *Ego and Reality in Psychoanalytic Theory. Psychol. Issues,* Monogr. 11. New York: International Universities Press.

The Self: Social and Psychological Perspectives

Daniel Offer, Eric Ostrov, and Kenneth I. Howard

During the recent past, the work of Kohut (1971, 1977) has stimulated much interest in the psychoanalytic psychology of the self. Although Kohut's theories stem directly from his clinical work, their applications, like those of Freudian psychology in general, are much broader.

In *The Restoration of the Self* (1977), Kohut stated his intention of leaving it to others to bridge his theory of the psychology of the self with other aspects of the psychology of man. His deepest wish, he added, was that the critical elaboration of his work would further the scientific disciplines of psychology and psychoanalysis. It is in this spirit that the present attempt to bridge two disparate aspects of the self should be understood.

As scientists, the questions about the self that appear most crucial are: "How can we know the self? How can we know the selves of other people or even our own selves?" Before going any further, it may be helpful to try to define the self. In the 17th century, according to the *Oxford English Dictionary,* the self was defined in a philosophical sense as "that which...a person is really and intrinsically...a permanent subject of successive and varying states of consciousness." This definition embodies, but perhaps does not make sufficiently clear, a distinction that recurs in later psychological works — the distinction between the self as observer (a subject of "states of consciousness") and the self as something observed (that which a person is "really and intrinsically"). Along these lines, William James pointed out in 1892, the self can be divided into two parts: (a) the self as knower or the "I" and (b) the self as known, or the "me." This distinction arises because humans can be self-reflective. In observing X, therefore, Y must take into account the fact that X can observe himself at the same time. Thus to Y, X appears, to use James's terminology, to be both an "I" and a "me," whereas X, we can assume, perceives himself at any one moment as just a "me," i.e., the person he thinks and feels himself to be.

This distinction underlines the importance of keeping in mind the particular perspective on the self that is being stressed. To the outsider, X is a total person located in a specific social or historical context and possessing certain attributes. One of X's attributes is the way he seems to think and feel about himself. The way others think and feel about X will almost certainly affect how X thinks and feels about himself, but in the last resort it is X's own cognitions and experience of himself that define what he really *is*. It is true that the two points of view on the self usually seem to overlap and interact. You may think X is a man and he may agree with you; X acts consistently with his beliefs about how a man should act, and you confirm his beliefs and continue to attribute that status to him. But it is conceivable that you and X may disagree about what kind of person he is. For instance, X may objectively be wrong about some aspects of himself — X may think he is smart or skilled, whereas in fact he is not. Or he may want you to believe he is not smart and skilled whereas, objectively, he actually possesses these attributes and has proved it to himself by convincing you otherwise.

What then is the truth about the self? How can we know it? As scientists, we are used to verifying truth by appealing to what people agree on (reliability) or what enables us to predict and control the world more effectively (validity). When it comes to understanding the self, the paradigm may break down unless we keep the two points of view on the self clearly in mind. If everyone agrees that X has a certain attribute that may be because X is successfully fooling everybody—he may be the supreme malingerer, the ultimate confidence man. And if our belief that X is smart, loyal, and compassionate enables us to predict accurately his behavior and depend on him in every crisis, we may still never be in touch with how he really experiences himself. We may never know, for example, that X experiences his real "me" as unintelligent and crass.

Because each of us is an "I," we can probably sympathize with the idea of having feelings and experiences that we do not wish to share with others or actively wish to conceal from others. As scientists, however, we may have difficulty conceptualizing a private reality that in some sense is more "real" than the reality that is open to consensual validation. This dilemma is reminiscent of the ancient free-will controversy in philosophy: simply put, as "I's" we experience ourselves as having a choice, but as scientists we necessarily apply a causal model to ourselves, reducing ourselves to the product of historical and contemporaneous forces, and assigning any "free choice" to the wastebin of error. Perhaps it will be necessary to admit that just as physics has discovered that time and motion are relative to the observer's point of view, so psychological truth is in some respects relative to the observer's point of view.

The important conclusion for psychological science is the need to distinguish carefully between outside and first-person views of the self. It is true that as scientists, as outside observers, we can never know exactly how X thinks and feels about himself. But we presumably can come more or less close to an appreciation of his point of view. Moreover, X may be more or less willing to share his point of view with us. What we can know of and conclude about X, then, may depend on our purpose in knowing X and the nature of our alliance with him.

Let us return to our original distinction. X exists as an "I" and a "me." Y observes X and tries to comprehend him. Though X is conceptually the person being observed, X is presumably as capable of observing Y as Y is of observing him and, in particular, X is capable of observing *how* Y observes him. If X understands the world as well as Y, X can potentially manipulate Y's observations to create a false image of himself or at least to obscure certain information about himself. This possibility would exist, incidentally, even if Y used only accurate physiological measurements. Unless X were helpless mentally and physically (i.e., reduced to a nonperson or functioning at such an extreme emotionally that he could not control himself at all), he could control his thoughts and behavior while under observation to create certain impressions in Y's mind.

Of course, there is always the possibility that the object of study may be naive—one who is unaware that he is being observed. But as social psychologists have learned, the number of naive participants in an experimental procedure tends rapidly to approach zero. Given our present level of technology, moreover, we usually wind up learning about people by simply asking them to report on themselves, a procedure that almost all people understand perfectly well. More generally, the fact that the human object of study is potentially aware of when and how he is being studied always raises the question of the potential distortion such knowledge can create. As a result, scientists studying the self live to some extent in a Goffmanesque world. The self they study is the *presented* self, a situation-dependent, audience-dependent, effect-seeking self. The presented self is appropriate for scientific study because it is avowedly public and therefore can be studied empirically and reliably as both cause and effect. Broadly speaking, we are contending that what people choose to present themselves as *is* what they are for some purposes. X chooses to appear to be a hero; he therefore acts bravely and saves people. He thereby *is* a hero and very possibly will continue to act as one. In his heart he may quaver and feel he is only acting out a role, but perhaps all heroes feel that way, and even if this is the case, what is the difference? He is still a hero. And given his prior actions and what he says about himself, we may be able to predict under what conditions he will continue to act like a hero. As one observer remarked: "If it looks like a duck, acts like a duck, and quacks like a duck, it *is* a duck."

But other observers of the self will not be content with this public point of view. The reason is that such observers observe not for the purpose of predicting and controlling the person studied, but for the purpose of helping this person better understand himself. This notion may seem strange in the context of a discussion of the limitations of knowledge about the self available to outside observers. But the fact is that people may be mistaken or confused about themselves, not only in the sense of objective fact (how popular am I?) but in terms of feelings and motives (just how angry am I? why do I keep doing that?). To the extent X's experience of himself is conceptual, it may represent an inaccurate or inadequate representation of feelings, motives, and ways of coping. In addition, X may be motivated to ignore or discount certain things about himself that nevertheless influence his affective experience and behavior. For Carl Rogers (1951), the basis of emotional disturbance is the self's building up of defenses that serve to deny threatening experiences access to consciousness or to distort the meaning of these experiences. This process renders the self image less congruent with organismic reality, with the result that more defenses are required to maintain the false picture held by the self. Sullivan's (1953) concept of "selective inattention" describes a similar process. For Freud, certain feelings and experiences can be unconscious altogether, that is, totally unexperienced by the choosing, aware self either because they are too threatening to be admitted to consciousness or involve feelings or experiences that were never symbolized. In either case, X comes to the psychotherapist to learn more about himself, not in the Goffmanesque sense of learning how he appears to others or how he can successfully manipulate his appearance, but rather in the sense of learning about his "real self," i.e. what he "really and intrinsically" is from his own point of view.

It is in this context that we can understand empathy, and the Kohutian approach to therapy. As an empathic observer, the therapist participates in an alliance with the "I" of the person observed. Empathy can be understood as depending on verbal and nonverbal cues that the observer can identify or, less cognitively, experience, as corresponding to feeling states that he, the observer, has experienced. By enabling the patient to understand more realistically what he is feeling and why, the therapist imparts to the patient the power to integrate more effectively his ongoing experience of his own self over time and with reality. What makes empathy work is that X, the patient observed, allows the therapist access to his "real self" in order to provide confirmation of the therapist's inferences. Given the nature of the alliance, the therapist can usually trust that the patient is, to some extent, not trying to manipulate the therapist's impressions of him. The patient, on his part, must feel comfortable enough and perhaps needy enough eventually to share his experiences with the therapist or to explain them as truthfully as he can. As a result, as the patient progresses in therapy, the therapist will perceive not only a change in how the patient feels about himself, but a change in the quality of the patient's experiences as an "I" in the direction of a greater sense of integration and mastery.

A useful approach to grasping the distinctions we have been discussing is to look at the self developmentally. For G. H. Mead (Strauss, 1956), humans develop the capacity to represent themselves to themselves by the process of learning a language through which they ultimately learn to regard themselves from the point of view of other people. Language forces the speaker to represent reality in terms which, in order to make communication meaningful, must evoke in others, in an anticipatory way, the same response the communication does in the speaker. In other words, to speak effectively, a person must continuously know that his words will evoke in others the same responses that they do in himself. Reality then becomes very much a social reality, imbued with commonly accepted meanings. One such part of reality is the self, which the person represents to himself linguistically and learns to react to in commonly accepted terms. Thus if X learns he is male and black he will tend to accept those definitions and tend to see himself as possessing the attributes commonly associated with these terms. Moreover, as a corollary, since X is able to anticipate the reactions of others, he can act in ways calculated to maximize the possibility of their reacting to him in certain ways.

From Kohut's point of view, on the other hand, the self is basically an organization of feelings, many based on the prelinguistic experiences of the infant that may not only go unrecognized by the adult, but may never have been symbolized by the adult at all. For Kohut, therefore, the real self largely consists of an organization of feelings about one's person developed since infancy and more or less imperfectly understood by the ego in conceptual or "secondary-process" language. The Meadian self and the Kohutian self can perhaps be assimilated into a framework in which the one is a primarily social self and the other a primarily psychological self.

The Social Self

The social self is how we usually describe ourselves to ourselves and roughly corresponds to how we are described by others. It depends on conscious perceptions that are easily correctable. The corrections take place after the perceptions of others are communicated to the individual. This kind of feedback is essential for enabling people to change their nonconflictual, easily accessible behavior. The social image that emerges is built on an endless transaction between the inner conscious self and the feedback received from others. Much of the behavior of an individual in everyday life is readily predictable when one knows the status and roles of the person. When behavior is not associated with psychological conflict it largely comes under the conscious control of the person. It is also observable, measurable, and codable. The more one knows about another human being, the better one can accurately predict his or her behavior under ordinary circumstances. The schools of thought that deal with this social aspect of the self encompass the work of thinkers like William James, G. H. Mead, Carl Rogers, Erving Goffman, and to a certain extent, Jean Piaget.

The Psychological Self

The psychological self is the nonaccessible, often unconscious part of the self that cannot be directly observed. The psychological self can be studied by an outsider who utilizes inference and has the cooperation of the person observed. If necessary, the outsider can use his own reactions to the person as a guide. The psychoanalytic method seems particularly suitable for arriving at an understanding of the psychological self, for it permits the establishment of a therapeutic alliance that opens the road for the development of a feeling of empathy. The empathic approach makes it possible for one person to gain access to the psychic structure and feelings of another. Empathy describes experiences of each particular person within a framework that permits no predictions concerning the future. The psychological study of the self therefore limits itself to empathic experiential descriptions; it does not concern itself with the understanding of the self as a product of external causal factors. What is common to both views of the self is an implicit "I," the perceiver, the doer, the thinker, that which perceives the social self and experiences self feelings. The "I" is also what is unobservable to X, the person observed, but is part of the person X from the point of view of Y, the outside observer.

To a certain degree, issues concerning the self may be reducible to questions of methodology. As mentioned earlier, we are concerned with how one can know the self. We have postulated that the more social the self, the more directly knowable it is. The heading "social self" contains, most evidently, the "objective social self" that represents what other people think about the person being studied. From this point of view X *is* short or tall, popular or unpopular, likable or unlikable to others. Another perspective concerns how X presents himself in various situations, not how he is "really" feeling, but just the ways in which he presents himself. With this "presented" social self, as with the "objective" social self, our science is comfortable because it can reliably measure these selves and make them the subject of predictive investigations. Another aspect of what we are calling the social self is how X consciously thinks and feels about himself from his own point of view. Since we are still in the realm of what we are calling the social self, what we need for measurement purposes is an alliance with the person studied: we are in essence asking him to share with us his conscious codifications about himself. Presumably, he is able to share these thoughts and feelings about himself with us if he is willing. To the extent that he is unwilling to do so, he will present an image calculated to make a certain impression on us. It is at this point that questions of validity become more intense, for even if X's testimony can be used to predict and control his behavior, we cannot know to what degree it corresponds with his inner reality unless we have the kind of alliance with him that makes the veracity of his testimony plausible. But since, by hypothesis, the self image or conceptions about which we are asking are acceptable or "ego-syntonic" enough to be conscious, the necessary alliance should be achievable even in the framework of the relatively brief encounters of "objective" research.

What about the psychological self? We can hypothesize that just asking X to describe himself will not always suffice. X may not be able to describe certain feelings or may not be in touch with certain feelings; in fact, any broad question that calls for a simple, brief response may necessarily fail to elicit accurate information. For example, the question "Are you sad?" may fail because sadness does not quite describe how X feels, whereas a question such as "Are you usually sad?" that calls for a still greater level of generalization may force X to provide an answer even more remote from his actual experience.

It is at this level that a trusting alliance and the use of empathy prove most effective. Using empathy, the observer, often the therapist, can help X symbolize or cognize himself in new ways that represent more accurately his inner reality and psychological state. This is not to say that the use of empathy is without problems. For one thing, the nonverbal cues used by even an empathic observer may be manipulatable by the observed person, creating one kind of validity question. It is also possible that one person's empathic response may not match that of another—what is sadness to you, may be no more than pouting to me, and so forth. In other words, the reliability of empathic responses is open to question, though to some extent this may be a problem intrinsic to what is being measured. Kohut (1971, 1977), in particular, has elaborated a developmental theory that should be susceptible to scientific investigation so that reliability and validity questions concerning empathy take on special relevance. One tenet that Kohut's theory shares with traditional psychoanalytic theories of development is that experiences in infancy will have appreciable, and even indelible, effects on subsequent feelings in adulthood. Other tenets involve the extremely powerful effect of particular aspects of parental behavior, such as the quality of affective posture, toward the child. However convincing these tenets may be in the framework of case histories, what Kohut has given us, in effect, is the challenge of performing longitudinal and other empirical studies adequate to the task of furthering our scientific understanding of the vicissitudes of the psychological self.

Our own work has been largely concerned with the social self, although we feel we have elicited testimony regarding the self that resonates with our subjects' inner feelings. Our empirical data are based on our work during the past 15 years with the Offer Self-Image Questionnaire (OSIQ) for Adolescents (Offer, Ostrov, & Howard, 1977). This descriptive instrument for self-assessment has been given to over 15,000 adolescents in the United States, Australia, India, Ireland, Israel, Mexico, and Brazil. It has been administered to young and old, male and female, disturbed, delinquent, and normal teenagers from all social classes. In particular, longitudinal data involving eight years of in-depth study of adolescents scoring in the normal range of the test have confirmed the correspondence between testimony offered in the questionnaire and the inner reality of these youths. We should add that adolescence seems a particularly good period for studying various issues that affect self psychology, because it is a transitional stage marked by bodily changes and social changes that must, ipso facto, result in changes in self concept. Overall, our experience with the OSIQ has impressed us with how much can be learned about how a youngster feels about himself in meaningful, first-person terms through a research alliance using a brief, reliable instrument. Based on our work with adolescents, that is, it has been our experience that the psychological sensitivity of the adolescent is sufficiently acute to allow us to utilize his self-description as a reliable and valid measurement of how he broadly feels about himself, at least consciously. We summarize below the major findings from our studies of adolescent self image:

1. Relatively healthy, i.e., nonsymptomatic, adolescents have a better self image than symptomatic adolescents, psychiatrically disturbed adolescents, or delinquent adolescents.

2. Younger adolescents present themselves as having a poorer self image than older adolescents.

3. Adolescents' reported self images correlate significantly and positively with other measures of personality assessment (including clinical interviews).

4. In countries other than the United States (i.e., Australia, India, Israel, and Ireland), adolescent males see themselves as healthier than adolescent females. In the United States, adolescent females describe themselves as having higher moral values than males. On the other hand, adolescent males state that they have better control of their impulses and are happier than their female peers.

5. American teenagers see themselves as considerably happier and better able to cope with their lives than teenagers in other cultures.

All the theories and research methods discussed above are only indicative of the complexities of the study of the self. The strands of knowledge generated by James, Mead, and Goffman have yet to be satisfactorily interwoven with those contributed by Freud and Kohut. Although we have largely confined our discussion to the modern, Western world, discussions of the self should contain historical and cross-cultural perspectives. A discussion of the self in modern America, for example, should not ignore this country's traditional emphasis on individualism rooted in economic developments of the late 18th and 19th centuries. We should also concern ourselves with the experience of self in the People's Republic of China, in traditional Indian tribes, and in preindustrial Europe. By encompassing the experience of self in such varying contexts, our psychology will avoid ethnocentric and ahistorical narrowness.

In addition to these tasks, we need to know more about the development of the self cognitively and affectively, as a function of biological, family, peer, and more idiosyncratic influences. Most of all we should be sensitive to the problems involved in measuring the self. In some sense the self is unknowable: from its own point of view, we can never measure the proactive, choosing, observing self except in terms of what was already chosen. On the other hand, a description of the person can be useful depending on the goal of the observer. Someone "is" a man and the category of manhood is a useful one for certain predictive purposes. What a person claims to think may matter because it can teach us what image that person chooses to project, if only to a certain audience at a certain time. Depending on the alliance, what a person says about himself may also put us in touch with the conscious feelings and self-characterizations that can help us understand him for both scientific and therapeutic purposes. From a psychoanalytic perspective, what a person is motivated *not* to realize about himself is also crucial information about that person, insofar as it leads to behavior that the person cannot explain to himself. Similarly, what a person feels about himself is important whether or not he knows why he feels as he does, or exactly how he feels. Each of these different perspectives on the self implies a different method of finding out about the self as well as different reasons for obtaining knowledge about the self. Generally, the more "psychological" the information sought, the more the investigator must depend on a certain alliance that makes his investigation tolerable. The most intimate knowlege will depend upon a kind of empathic knowing which assimilates data about the actor and his functioning to a framework that is not so alien or threatening to the actor's self concepts that he cannot accept new ways of understanding himself.

All of these ways of characterizing the self raise questions of reliability and stability. The more external criteria are more likely to be reliable and stable. The image a person presents about how he really feels is less easily and reliably measured and less stable, although we have made much progress in obtaining valid, reliable, and stable information by using instruments like the OSIQ. The importance of reliability also pertains to the empathic understanding of what an actor is motivated not to know about himself. For scientific purposes, we must agree on what exactly we are measuring: we cannot compare and generalize if we cannot agree on what is being measured. Insofar as psychoanalytic theory wishes to be scientific, reliable measurement of its concepts is necessary. Stability is an empirical question: Is there stability of self presentation across time and with different audiences? Is there stability of self feeling? These questions, and many others about the self, await further investigation.

In summary, the self, albeit a term in common usage, is difficult to define and forms a complex area of investigation. An investigator must clearly delineate the purpose for which he is studying the self and his particular perspective on the self. From one point of view the actor cannot be objectified, since each actor in some way feels himself to be the viewer, observer, and choosing agent. Another point of view, however, can focus on the actor from an external point of view, including the actor's own point of view "objectively measured." The latter in turn can be differentiated into the actor's view of how others view him and other conceptualizations and conscious feelings about himself. A more empathic perspective allows access not only to conscious feelings, thoughts, and desires, but to aspects of the self which the actor is motivated to exclude from his self conception or which, because of their preverbal origins, he has never symbolized at all. Just as each perspective on the self serves different purposes, each calls for different kinds of assessment techniques. Each perspective, moreover, will generate distinctive measurement problems and research challenges.

References

James, W. (1892), *Psychology*. New York: Holt.

Kohut, H. (1971), *The Analysis of the Self*. New York: International Universities Press.

_____ (1977), *The Restoration of the Self*. New York: International Universities Press.

Offer, D., Ostrov, E., & Howard, K. (1977), *The Offer Self-Image Questionnaire for Adolescents: A Manual* (Revised). Chicago: Michael Reese Hospital and Medical Center.

Rogers, C. R. (1951), *Client-Centered Therapy*. Boston: Houghton Mifflin.

Strauss, A., ed. (1956), *The Social Psychology of George Herbert Mead.* Chicago: University of Chicago Press.
Sullivan, H. S. (1953), *The Interpersonal Theory of Psychiatry.* New York: Norton.

Part III

SELF PSYCHOLOGY
AND ITS
CLINICAL APPLICATIONS

Introduction

PAUL TOLPIN

Psychoanalysis began almost a century ago with a series of case histories. The first of these was the case of Anna O., a day-dreamer: "While everyone thought she was attending, she was living through fairy tales in her imagination...[which] passed over into illness without a break" (Breuer & Freud, 1893–1895, p. 22). Breuer explained that the daydreamer, Anna O., fled from her "puritanical" and "monotonous family" into her "private theater" where she created a more gratifying world for herself. In time, however, "this habit prepared the ground upon which the affect of anxiety and dread was able to establish itself...[and] transformed the patient's habitual day-dreaming into a hallucinatory *absence*" (p. 42). Anna O. developed a grand hysteria and Breuer invented a treatment of attentive listening, which his patient called the "talking cure" or, jokingly, "chimney-sweeping." To this day the case study, the organized and recorded documenting of clinical work with patients, remains a preeminent source of our psychoanalytic knowledge; attentive listening and "chimney-sweeping" continue to be the cornerstone of psychoanalysis as a method of treatment and the source of the empirical data from which psychoanalytic theories of increasing orders of generalization and abstraction ultimately arise.

Continuing this tradition, this clinical section begins with

Evelyne Schwaber's paper, "Self Psychology and the Concept of Psychopathology: A Case Presentation." Dr. Schwaber presents us with a case study, and the self psychological theoretical system which guided her analysis of her patient's pathology. The material serves as a point of departure for several related papers which reexamine the clinical data or expand upon them in new directions, and it also serves as both a link and a contrast with the classical case studies and theories that have informed psychoanalysis from its inception.

Freud's dominant theories of pathology hark back to the description of Anna O.'s personality: "Her states of feeling always tended to a slight exaggeration, alike of cheerfulness and gloom; hence she was sometimes subject to moods. *The element of sexuality was astonishingly undeveloped in her....[She] had never been in love*" (pp. 21–22, my italics). The pathological effects of Anna O.'s inhibited sexual life set a direction for theorizing about the origins of the psychoneuroses that has dominated the understanding of normal and pathological human psychological development for decades and has stimulated a prodigious mass of invaluable conceptualizations about the organization and functioning of the mind. More recently, however, emphasis has shifted from further conceptual refinements of the vicissitudes of the libidinal and aggressive drives and the defenses against them, to different units or aspects of the organization of the mind. Perhaps the origins of this shift can be traced to increasing interest in the preoedipal period, the psychoses, and narcissism; to the Kleinian emphasis on early development; to child analysis and direct child observation; and to the remarkable flowering of understanding about the role of the ego in normal and pathological development. Still, whatever the forerunners, in more recent years a new mirror has been held up to the nature of psychology and the self has been its form.

Defined simply, the self is the essence of one's psychological being, the composite of the interaction of constitutional endowment with what become enduring configurations of developmental experiences with selfobjects and objects that have affective meaning from birth on. The self comprises nuclear ambitions and ideals (the bipolar self) and inherent skills and talents as well as a number of constituents of the mind that have not yet been specifically addressed by self psychology. So far as self psychology is concerned, the formation and transformations of self development play as crucial a role in the understanding of the mind and its functioning as the evolution of the Oedipus complex and the tripartite structure of the mind (id, ego, superego) do in classical psychoanalytic psychology. In self psychology and pathology it is the formation, deformation, and deficiencies of the self that are of central concern, just as the Oedipus complex and its resolution are of central concern in classical analysis. Nevertheless, as with classical psychoanalysis, so with self psychology the source of our primary data remains the patient and what he reveals about himself in his interaction with the analyst.

In her case presentation, Dr. Schwaber describes not a 22-year-old Anna O. and her "private theater," but a 22-year-old Mr. R., a modern young man of the "now" generation who, unlike an Anna O., was not languishing his life away in bed. Instead, he was languishing in his life. His symptoms were those of "'detachment'. . .a feeling of being very far removed from things, [with] dizziness, often accompanied by tremor and headaches." He was apparently not sexually inhibited; he had girlfriends with whom he enjoyed physical intimacy. Yet one could say that he, like Anna O., had never been in love, or, more accurately, that he had never had a strong emotional investment in the young women with whom he was involved. Like the family of Anna O., his family was "monotonous" but, as Dr. Schwaber describes it, the monotony of his family assumed a manifestly different form: his family, particularly his mother, as he experienced her, was emotionally absent in some essential way, and he had fled from the pathogenic effects of that absence, from the empty feeling of his disordered self, into his "private theater." Mr. R.'s theater derived from a modern invention, a modern dream machine—the movies. From boyhood on he attended them with a near-addictive passion because they brought him to life. He said, "As a child, I couldn't wait to be taken to a movie; I approached it with a certain reverence. . .but the intense feeling evoked in movies. . .I don't feel in real life." Mr. R.

had not yet "passed over" into the kind of decompensated illness that Anna O. experienced, but he might well have been on his way toward a latter-day, chronic version of that state when he began his analysis.

It is the investigation of Mr. R.'s inability to relate in a reasonably gratifying way to the real world and the reasons for the consequent collapse into himself that is the central theme of his analysis. In the treatment of Mr. R., however, Dr. Schwaber was guided by principles that differ considerably from those that evolved from the psychoanalysis that had its beginnings in Anna O.'s catharsis treatment. These classical principles formed the basis of a particular form of conflict analysis focusing on the antagonisms between libidinal and aggressive drives and the defenses against them. In contrast to this form of analysis, Mr. R.'s treatment was guided by the findings of Kohut; it used the prism of self psychology to break up the light of the basic data of analysis—the patient's free associations. Mr. R.'s self psychological treatment systematically followed, with a clearer focus and greater intensity, a new model for understanding the patient-analyst experience. This model depends far less on a natural science point of view (the observation of data from the outside) and far more on what Dr. Schwaber calls a "'contextual unit'. . . a construct that recognizes the *immediacy* of the surround as intrinsic to the organization and perception of intrapsychic experience" (my italics). This model makes use of vicarious introspection, of empathy—a confluence of the associative productions of the patient and the analyst experiencing those ideas as if he were the patient—as the critical (though not exclusive) mode of investigation of the patient's associations.

The case study of Dr. Schwaber's work with Mr. R. is presented, then, to illustrate both a method of observation and a theory of personality. The various discussants whose papers follow Dr. Schwaber's presentation were stimulated to examine the clinical and theoretical material from their own particular areas of interest.

Miles Shore uses the paper as a take-off point for the interesting elucidation of an area of applied analysis that concerns "the role of the environment causing mental illness." Using a self psychology framework, he examines the psychopathology of small groups arising in a psychiatric hospital setting, the effect of natural disasters on bereavement, and the effect of extreme isolation on individuals.

Adhering more closely to Dr. Schwaber's clinical material, Sheldon Bach discusses Mr. R. from several points of view not considered by Dr. Schwaber. He elaborates what he perceives as the patient's unconscious fantasy of rebirth as expressed in his fascination with the metaphor of the movie *2001: A Space Odyssey*. It is this fantasy, according to Dr. Bach, that accounts for the massive shift in Mr. R's. self experience and behavior at age 13. He elaborates the theme of rebirth as well as other ideas about perception and the possible role of the Oedipus complex in the patient's pathology.

My own remarks focus on several additional clinical problems: the question of the sufficiency of Mr. R.'s analysis, the role of reactive aggression in the formation of the patient's personality and symptoms, and the technical considerations related to the analyst's empathic misunderstanding of the patient's communications. Dr. Schwaber responds directly to my comments.

Finally, Kenneth Newman uses Dr. Schwaber's case presentation as the referent for a detailed discussion of the status of characterological defenses in self pathology. He draws on several clinical examples of his own to illustrate his ideas.

In addition to Dr. Schwaber's case presentation and the several discussions of it, the clinical section of the book includes original applications of self psychology to the understanding of the borderline personality (Paul Tolpin) and object love (David Terman), along with two papers that deal with the impact of self psychology on the relation between psychoanalysis and psychotherapy (Jacques Palaci and Nathaniel London).

The yield of these clinical contributions, all guided by the findings of self psychology, speaks for the vitality of psychoanalysis today, a psychoanalysis which, invoking a new paradigm, can deal with the Mr. R.s of the world who suffer both from deficit pathology and conflicts deriving not exclusively or essentially from libidinal or aggressive drives, but from the faulty development of the self and the defenses that arise from the need to fill in for or make up for self deficiencies. The rays emitted by the new prism of self psychology are after all not new. They have always been present in the spectrum, but we have not paid enough specific attention to them. Now that we are more aware of their presence and their significance, it behooves us to do what psychoanalysis has done so well in the past: to follow the rays into the particular psychological region that they best illuminate and, just as the authors in this section have done, to examine critically the new objects we find there.

Reference

Breuer, J. & Freud, S. (1893–1895), Studies on Hysteria. *Standard Edition,* 2. London: Hogarth Press, 1955.

Self Psychology and the
Concept of Psychopathology:
A Case Presentation

Evelyne A. Schwaber

We have come increasingly to recognize the extent to which self psychology leads to certain fundamental shifts in conceptualizing pathology as well as adaptation. The concept of the "selfobject" occupies a pivotal position in such a shift, and has significant implications for our mode of ordering clinical data. Bringing together as it does the self and the object, the selfobject concept suggests a system—something I have called a "contextual unit"—between patient and analyst (Schwaber, 1979). It is therefore not to be viewed as a construct pertaining exclusively to failures of differentiation between self and object or to failed recognition of the autonomy of each, but more fundamentally as one which recognizes the immediacy of the surround as intrinsic to the organization and perception of intrapsychic experience.

In this respect, it offers a point of view, the very omission of which in psychological conceptualization has generated some criti-

The author gratefully acknowledges the help of Drs. M. Robert Gardner, Judy Kantrowitz, Samuel Kaplan, and Ana-Maria Rizzuto in formulating the ideas presented here.

cism from theoreticians and researchers. Louis Sander — on whose valuable research data on infancy I draw heavily — has written that heretofore it has been the biological approach that provided the perspective that "the concept of the 'unity of the organism' relates to an organism functioning in its proper environment, i.e., its situation of evolutionary adaptation. A major difficulty in conceptualizing at the psychological level [has arisen] from a tendency to view the organization of behavior as the property of the individual rather than as the property of the more inclusive system of which the individual is a part" (1975, p. 147).[1]

I am suggesting that the selfobject concept offers a way of utilizing such a system relevant to the understanding of *all* transferences, and thereby intrinsic to the psychoanalytic method. It thus offers a deepening dimension to the understanding of empathy and its status as the matrix of the analytic method, a dimension that apprehends the analyst — experiencing from *within* the patient's experience — and the patient, as a system.

Viewed in this broader dimension, the concept of the selfobject offers a way of listening and organizing clinical data in which the analyst's contribution, silent or stated, is seen as meaningfully influencing and ordering the nature of the patient's response — of the transference, of memory, and, essentially, of *ongoing* regulation within a system.

While remaining attentive to this aspect of the patient's response, which emanates from within an interwoven matrix, we must recognize that concomitantly there is a fundamental need on the patient's part to express his own integrity, continuity, and stability. "From the cell upward," Sander notes, "living organisms are actively self-regulating and, at the same time, of necessity exist in a continuous intimate exchange with essential support factors provided by the surround. There is an obvious polarity inherent in this view; attention to either cannot be given at the expense of the other" (1975, pp. 134–135).

This polarity obliges us to seek out in our listening both a "contingency" — how one event, one being, impinges on the other — and a "synchrony" — a stability of self-regulation. The degree of such stability would be a central determinant in the person's ability

[1] Sander's research studies rely on data which recognize the "embeddedness of the human infant in a microscopic and macroscopic interactive regulative system."

to experience a wide range of autonomous choices.[2] Drawing on this framework, we may then consider a concept of pathology which suggests that within a particular locus of concern, the self-regulating processes are not sufficiently stabilized, thereby necessitating heightened attention to the restoration of stability with the surround.

Kohut, in his illuminating notion of the bipolar self, essentially notes that there are two broadly defined developmental phases, two chances for stable self-regulation to ensue—with the responsively mirroring selfobject and with an appropriately idealizable one.

In the following case presentation, I shall discuss a patient for whom there were, sadly, failures in both areas, though he was able, belatedly, to find a way for his father to rally on his behalf. At least by the time of adolescence, that is, the father could offer himself for a somewhat more comfortable idealization, and this provided the child with sufficient sustenance to maintain some stability of his self-regulating matrix.

Mr. R., a student at a local college, working also as a salesman in a camera shop, came to see me when he was 22 years old, shortly before his graduation. He sought psychiatric help at the recommendation of his internist, whom he saw because of abdominal distress, which had begun two years previously when he had left college to work in a more distant city as a photographer for a very well-known magazine. At that time the question of a peptic ulcer was raised, though not confirmed. No particular treatment regimen was prescribed. The psychiatric referral was prompted by very uncomfortable, at times frightening, accompanying symptoms of what the patient called "detachment," that is, a feeling

[2]Sander (1975, p. 131) has stated: "Psychopathology can be viewed as a failure of integrative mechanisms just as easily as it can be viewed as a consequence of conflict." He notes further that Ashby points out "the self-organizing core could gain relative 'disjoin' as a subsystem and thereby possibly a 'temporary and partial independence.' Under these conditions such a subsystem would be capable, within limits, of participating in ensuing perturbations of adaptive encounters with the surround without the perturbations spreading over the whole complement of subsystems that constitute the more basic biological functions of the individual. Ashby's argument thus provides the rationale that a 'self' or a self-organizing subsystem is essential to the regulation of adaptive behavior in a system at the critical level of complexity" (p. 152).

of being very far removed from things, as well as dizziness, often accompanied by tremor and headaches. Mr. R. had not thought of these symptoms in psychological terms, but he came at the suggestion of his physician. Reflecting back, he considered that such symptomatology may indeed have occurred in fleeting moments for years — in fact, as far back as he could remember.

This patient was referred to me by a colleague as an "extraordinarily gifted photographer," though he did not presently feel well enough to pursue that profession.

I saw Mr. R. in a face-to-face setting for several weeks prior to his beginning analysis. He was a pleasant-looking young man, with a golden brown hue to his moderately long hair and full beard, somewhat short of stature, casually and neatly dressed. His manner from the first was informal, with no visible manifestation of anxiety or of any shifting affective response. Thus, though direct, friendly, and thoughtful, he could be described as cool or "detached" — a word used in his own description of his inner experience. He seemed intelligent and articulate, though he had never consciously attempted any introspection.

The patient had thought of remaining in the South, as he enjoyed his job and did not want to return to school, but his symptoms prevented this. He mentioned, only in passing, that he had lived there with one girlfriend and was presently living with another. When I asked about each of them he revealed no depth of feeling. He said that having a girlfriend would not be a factor in his decision about where to go after graduation. He was going to do what he was going to do, and neither his girlfriend nor anyone could keep him from that. When I asked him how he would feel at separating from her, he said he did not anticipate it would be a problem. Otherwise, apart from conveying the importance to him of the "smart doctor" he had seen in that southern community, who seemed to know what he was experiencing (as in guessing about his headaches), he tended to speak only of himself. He did not see his problems as bearing on any relationships.

During the second hour, Mr. R. said that since the last meeting it occurred to him that there had been a shift in his development somewhere around age 13. At that age, he changed from being weak, unathletic, and shy, to becoming newly competent, aided perhaps by a newfound ability in gymnastics. During that same period of time, encouraged by a particular teacher, he had also become interested in film development and in music. Presently, he reflected that these interests were representative of an intense need for something "external to define" him. He conjectured, moreover, that a less confident self, might exist underneath the "externally defined" one, and that he might be afraid to discover this underlying self. When looking at pictures or hearing tapes of himself as a child before the age of 12 or 13, he experienced unbearable dizziness along with the other described symptoms. He could recall no specifically unpleasant childhood memories, beyond a sense that it had always been difficult for him to leave home. Indeed, he then recounted one summer when he had experienced deep humiliation because he had had to leave camp early. In some profound way, he felt no continuity with that part of himself that was a child.

Mr. R., born to an Italian family, was raised in a small midwestern city. His father was a dentist; with his office attached to the home; his mother a schoolteacher. His one sibling, a sister five years older, was a law student at a midwestern university.

Mr. R. spoke spontaneously of his father, indicating his need to feel that his father approved of me as his analyst. Although there had been friction between them in the father's urging him to study more, to "*do* something, *be* somebody," Mr. R. also felt that they were very similar in certain ways. They both pursued numerous hobbies, were very easy-going, and tried to please everyone.

The patient's mother, on the other hand, was never mentioned in these early hours unless I asked about her directly. On these occasions, he described her and his relationship with her with one word: "fine." He added that she was easy to get along with, though tending to side with his father in arguments. He literally had nothing more to say about her, and when I wondered about this, he said he simply felt "that's all there is."

Though the absence of mother from such an early communication may have any number of meanings, there is nonetheless the surface message "that's all there is." This could convey, at least in the present context, an experiential absence of mother, suggesting the possibility of a detachment from her inherent in the organization of the patient's self. We may further recall that his descriptions of his girlfriends similarly lacked spontaneity and were devoid of content.

Mr. R.'s sister, as well, was only described in response to my direct questioning. Frequently unhappy, she had always been in active conflict with her parents and scorned her brother's need to accomplish. Essentially, he never felt particularly close to her.

During these early hours, Mr. R. recalled some further isolated childhood occurrences. On one occasion, he had been left with a babysitter while his parents traveled; he had also been told that in second grade he had been forced to go to school. During a recent recurrence of his symptoms, he said that he had begun to notice their relation to unexpressed emotion and was quite struck by this. He seemed to have a ready psychological gift and interest. He was anxious at the thought of returning to his childhood years, but he also felt some gratification in beginning to reflect about himself in the way we had. It seemed he was readily drawn toward something in the kind of responsiveness he felt he was obtaining from me. Thus, although he had wanted to leave Boston to facilitate his career, he now accepted the idea of analysis and chose to remain. He felt he needed to get on with his life and to pursue his wish to become a filmmaker, so time was of the essence. Thus, his attitude was "if it has to be done, let's get on with it."

Once on the couch, Mr. R. began to recognize that he had many more misgivings about analysis than he had appreciated. During the course of his sessions, these concerns were frequently manifested in gastric hyperacidity or dizziness, or — another striking response — hearing music going through his mind. He spoke of his fear of losing control.

I shall present some fragments of sessions in the course of this overview of Mr. R.'s analysis. In doing so, I will attempt to communicate the central issues that emerged as I was using a listening stance oriented from within *his* perspective, *his* state, i.e., from the empathic mode as we have come to understand it. Thus I listened to determine where he had achieved a self-regulating stability and how he was utilizing me, whether re-creating the past or creating experience anew, in both maintaining that stability (synchrony) as well as in the contingency sense in which what I offered impinged on the flow of his experience.

The early sessions quickly exposed the central issues of concern and organization.

In one hour, he described his groping for something to talk about and considered what this might mean:

Mr. R.:	It is important to me that I talk of something relevant or significant.
Analyst:	As though what would come spontaneously to mind may not be viewed that way.
Mr. R.:	Yes, like talking of my car or my apartment, that I'm thinking of, would be wasting time.
Analyst:	So there is this feeling of wanting what you say to be relevant, significant, and to not waste time — *time* being an important issue.
Mr. R.:	Yes. I'm struck by that! [We see his immediate affective responsiveness to feeling understood, to having his experience articulated.] It's a perfect description of my own life. It must be significant — and I can't waste time. I can see it at work, my desire for significance...the need for people to take notice is very important...the strong need in me for recognition. This all ties in, in a way that's going to be very hard to describe, having to do with my photography and music...the kind of images I'm attracted to, to point my camera at — all share a certain quality, an *epic* quality.
	There is a sense of something dramatic and big going on. With music, too, what I play has a quality which makes people sit up and take notice...I think this is responsible for the

success I've had in both areas. The film *2001,*
I've seen 30 times...it's a tremendous epic
movie.

I tried to help him see the connection between this wish to experience and to be experienced as significant with its manifestations within the analytic sessions.

Mr. R.'s moods vacillated. Sometimes he spoke of "a feeling
that everything is worthless, everything meaningless...this sense
of despair I experienced last night...thinking consciousness is
just an incredible biological phenomenon and so all the people
doing things may be no more significant than other animals." I
replied: "So despair for you is the sense of no unique human
significance." We had yet to understand to what to attribute these
shifts.

During another hour, the following exchange occurred:

Mr. R.: I can remember way back having the experience
of elation. I can remember it being triggered by
how it might look photographically, as in a
beautiful scene or in music. When I see something that looks good, there is a very strong desire to take a picture and kind of freeze it there,
as with a beautiful sunset. It's an experience of
all of a sudden my sensibilities becoming really
heightened, like I'll notice the pores of
someone's skin and it looks great, and I want to
take a picture and catch it...I know a psychiatrist who became interested in photography
and took it up more and more—on his vacations—finally giving up psychiatry.

Analyst: [My own vacation was imminent at this time
and Mr. R. had not referred to it] I wonder if
my vacation may have been stirring such
thoughts, of my waning interest in my profession.

Mr. R.:   I'm not sure how to understand what you mean. I'm thinking of the joke of the two psychiatrists meeting in an elevator. I wonder if you know the joke and if you do, will you answer... [He spoke more slowly.] I think you responded defensively to the idea of a psychiatrist switching to photography... I didn't mean to be critical...

It seemed his train of associations was derailed; somehow we had gotten off the track. This session ended shortly thereafter, and as Mr. R. walked out I noticed he completely avoided looking at me and his body seemed strikingly shrunken in its stance.

One might hypothesize that I had touched on an area of anxiety about separation which was profoundly resisted, leading Mr. R. to respond as he did. But even if this were so, if we listen from the point of view of Mr. R.'s immediate experience, we can "hear" how jarring my comments must have felt. He had been talking of the wonder of photography, a wonder so great that a doctor might even give up his profession for it. By picking up defensive content, I deflated that idea. It was his subsequent slowed-down response, his going "off track," that served as a clue to me that I had disrupted something between us. (In a later hour, when I similarly "failed," he articulated "this sense of fading away, my whole being folding itself up, like literally... my voice softening...")

There was, indeed, almost a kind of startle response to the idea of separation anxiety, an issue about which he had never thought. Often, such lack of awareness or concern with separation is attributed to defensive needs or to shallowness of relationships. For Mr. R., however, I think it was rather that separation experience had not yet reached, developmentally, a level of cognitive awareness. Separation anxiety may then be felt as a disordering of regulatory or integrative mechanisms — which may be manifested symptomatically — as in disorganized behavior or in somatizations.[3] Mr. R. later was to recall being told that he had

[3] Cf. Basch (1977) who notes, quoting Spelke, that "a child's protest to separation is the result of being exposed to a discrepant event that he cannot assimilate or act upon...."

been "traumatized" by a separation of several weeks at about one year of age, when his parents had left on a trip, returning to find that the babysitter had been insensitive. (The parents, however, continued to take such vacation trips.)

I have commented how, when I missed being in "synchrony" with Mr. R., he did not look at me and his body seemed shrunken. I have observed with other patients as well that bodily stance and grace may be important indicators of the sense of aliveness and of tone of the self, and that postures and movements, including eye contact, may shift in accord with the vicissitudes of the experience of the self.

Looking and being looked at were especially charged experiences for Mr. R. He was very attuned to the "look" on my face. In one particular hour, he was troubled by it, describing it as "neutral, indifferent"—reminiscent of his perception of his mother's expression. Indeed, one may conjecture that this very perception of the indifferent neutrality of mother's "look" became the internalized representation of his "detached" state.

The subject of Mr. R.'s mother, as in the initial interviews, was repeatedly and hastily dropped whenever she came to mind at all, with no apparent awareness of distress. Gradually, often by exploring the subtleties of how I may have failed Mr. R., we began to learn about her. Once, he recalled being told by her how he had feigned illness as a child to avoid going to school and what a difficult child he had been. I commented that his mother seemed thereby to be communicating displeasure with him.

> Mr. R.:   I hadn't thought about that...[pause]...that sort of idea fits with the idea I've expressed of life being meaningless and that I've devoted my life to providing the meaning...a hint of that indescribable feeling I get in thinking of my childhood...a kind of sorrow...it's sort of a physical feeling...it's kind of like the bottom falls out of everything...

At this point, Mr. R. felt dizzy and had to pause. When he

spoke again, it was of his father and of work. What seemed to have happened was that the childhood feeling of his mother's displeasure with him, or perhaps my comment about it—that is, a memory of the original failure of the needed selfobject or a repetition triggered by the analyst—evoked a rather fragmenting response, perhaps a kind of "disintegration anxiety." This was relieved when his thoughts turned to father and photography, a shift that paralleled the actual turn in his life that was to sustain him. It was evidence of his own capacity for self-regulation.

As was indicated by his description of mother's "neutral" look —and even earlier, by the absence of her in the history—the painful perception of his mother, increasingly reaching awareness, went far beyond his perception of her as critical; it was a view of her as being indifferent and distant.

> Mr. R.: When I was home recently and mother was very upset about my sister, I was thinking of putting both arms around her...that seemed too much while father was watching...I eventually put one arm on her shoulder, but even that was hard to do. *She seemed so far away*—crying, neither of us moving...she was more separate from us than I would have liked...That statement seems to have frightened me. I can't even remember now what I said, as though I haven't said it... but I can re-create the detachment...

We saw here the poignant link between Mr. R.'s experience of mother as so distant, from which he began to shift away, and his experience of detachment. This description was also interesting from the point of view of its oedipal constellation—the perceptions appearing as defenses, perhaps, against such stirrings. But it was precisely the nature, the quality of the "oedipal" experience that was so indelibly stamped by the more *total* self configuration, as Mr. R. so vividly expressed here. His symptomatology, then, however representative of differing elements or levels of conflict, was still a metaphoric equivalent of the self in trouble.

The pathological interaction with mother had, in addition, a certain subtlety, which, particularly as there had been little overt conflict, might be easily overlooked by the casual observer and perhaps also by the child, as it seemed to have been by Mr. R. in his childhood. In thus not reaching awareness, it became the more insidious, not affording the opportunity for anger or differentiation of his own self experience. Instead, it led to a diffuse kind of helplessness. The following exchange my offer an illustration:

Mr. R.:   [Describing a dream] I was standing on a street corner. . .two kids were threatening me, pulling a gun out. It turned out to be just a toy gun. [In his associations]. . .the kids feel like me, that I feel very threatened by my own childhood. . .my fear of vomiting. . .this brings up a sadness about my life again. . .I remember a time I vomited, then I felt better. I was carried upstairs by mother and I asked, "Am I going to miss Lassie [on TV]?" The sad feeling seems to be from thinking about my saying that—like I need to reject that I said that, almost that I can't accept that I was once a little kid. That question I asked of my mother. . .my sounding so cute. . .

On this occasion I was jarred out of the experience Mr. R. was evoking, and so I interrupted: "Cute? You had conveyed it was sad."

Mr. R.:   Yes, well, the word "cute" seems appropriate. . . sort of like "cute" belongs to what a child feels.
Analyst: Oh, so this is like the weapons that turn out to be toys, a kind of negation of the validity, of the intensity of the feelings a child may have.
Mr. R.:   [Now excitedly interrupting me, which, as we have seen, he does when I have "recognized" the nature of his experience] Exactly! Children's feelings are not taken very seriously. . .I can

easily imagine someone's saying, "Oh, that's cute," and kind of laughing at the child.

It seemed that in this unempathic, asynchronous way, not meant to be malevolent, the child's actual experience had not been "validated."[4] This may have led to the quality of vagueness and of unreality, the lack of differentiation of what was himself, the "slight detachment" he had begun to notice was always with him. We then understood his meaning when he said, "I wouldn't mind a strong physical sensation, like being stung by a bee."[5] I also recognized the search for the grand and the significant as offering a way in which he felt real and perhaps "alive."

As I have implied, this feeling of uncertainty about the centrality of what was his own experience also spoke to his failure to attain a sense of autonomy, a center of his own initiative.[6]

Mr. R.:   I was shy until 13 or so...never said "no"... looking at the picture of me as a child and not being able to make a connection to that child... a feeling of being very controlled. I know I didn't want to do something, and then I'd do it; an image of me being dressed up to go somewhere and not wanting to, but going...If I should happen to see a child, a male child, I think of an open-mouthed "What's going on?" expression—like "Who am I?"...subject to many forces...I saw this four- or five-year-old in Har-

[4]A word used in this context by Sander in a personal communication.

[5]We may wonder if there is a parallel to the deprived baby's head banging, as indicative of an attempt at stimulation.

[6]Sander (1975, p. 138) notes, "The strength of intentionality or goal-directedness in guiding action here first becomes recognizable at times when exploratory aims are blocked. The mother experiences a first active bifurcation in the direction of the child's initiative; toward her, or away from her. (Mahler describes this phase as the 'hatching process.') This early level of active independent organization of his world often meets a very basic ambivalence in the mother. The baby's activity can be interpreted as aggressive, rejecting, or naughty, on the one hand, or precocious, gratifying and stimulating, on the other, with consequent patterns of reinforcement or interference becoming characteristic for the pair."

vard Square who looked like that. He was smaller than the others, pushed around, being led by his mother. It struck me that's the way I might have gone on in much of my life then, moved by the currents. I can't stand to think of myself that way...

This issue became central to Mr. R.'s concern within the analytic situation. He often did not know whether he or I had initiated an idea, and he dreaded feeling pushed by the idea or by me. When I made what seemed to him a "correct" interpretation, as we saw, he often remarked on how "struck" he was by my accurate observation. Thus, though he felt correctly understood at one level, he also at times described the feeling of being taken "off guard." Since what he had been experiencing had not been in his awareness, that is, his newfound insights also felt not quite in his control. This was a phenomenon that occurred particularly in the analysis of his dreams, in which he was often amazed at the "remarkable" discoveries he was making, yet did not feel he was the initiator. (To be sure, it was also crucial for him to feel that if he could not maintain control, at least I could.)

Mr. R. had recurrent airplane dreams which were understood as metaphors for his experience of the analytic process at any given point in time. In one such early dream he reported the following:

Mr. R.:   The feeling of the plane is familiar; it's going over the runway...dangerous high-voltage lines... There was no way we could regain altitude without cracking away from these lines...Some were flying off at tremendous speeds...The pilot was in control, but it was very dangerous nonetheless...We gained altitude very fast and the pilot got up and said it had been dangerous... [In his associations] I had thought years ago that there was something about my life, that it was being directed not by my own choice...the idea of analysis as a risk...not having control... fear of helplessness...

This concern about being taken over reverberated to Mr. R.'s father as well. He was initially experienced as critical and disappointed in his nonathletic and nonacademic little boy. Yet, as we know, he was not felt as unavailable, especially when by adolescence Mr. R. had acquired new abilities and interests:

Mr. R.:   If I want to please my father, I know what to do; but if I feel like even not pleasing my mother — I wouldn't have the slightest idea what to do. With my father, at least there are things I can do to please; like here, if you're quiet and I think I'm not pleasing you, I will talk of something else... but still, this comes back to the old question of how much I do is me and how much is someone else.

Gradually, Mr. R. began to develop a capacity for experiencing the world with a sense of his own ability to initiate and effect, which we understood as a subtle but critical indicator of the analytic progress. We further saw how Mr. R. thereby became more certain of his own feelings, and this in turn permitted him to experience a greater closeness to others, including his father.

Mr. R.:   Yesterday, telling you about the letter from my father, that he cared about me, caused the lump in my throat to grow very great; the sensation itself brought back memories...the whole experience felt great...it brought a smile to my face, even as my eyes choked up. I just felt I loved my father a tremendous amount and that something had changed in the way I thought about him; this feeling is the opposite of detachment...I feel connected...with my father...I didn't want to have much to do with him, for fear of not being able to act on my own; I'm beginning to feel more able to have him come into my life without feeling threatened by his telling me I

should or shouldn't do...it was good to be able
to cry, thinking of him.

To cry or not was an intensely charged question for Mr. R.
Dreams expressed a life-and-death concern about it. Bottled-up
tears and the sensation of a lump in his throat were feelings pervading the entire analysis. There was a sense of something potentially overwhelming.

> Mr. R.: When my parents went away, they said, "Be
> grown-up, don't cry." Crying is weak, childlike.
> Like crying at summer camp. Since I've been in
> analysis I've cried a lot more...I see my emo-
> tions are now closer to the surface. I haven't had
> the detached feeling in some time.

By the end of the first year of analysis, Mr. R. met Jill, who
was to become his new girlfriend. She was in some ways a personification of the analyst, with her psychological mind and her
medical background. Their relationship afforded a yet closer view
of the link, within and outside the transference, between the
response to him and his subsequent experiential state. Sexual
themes emerged more sharply, juxtaposing the little boy who
wanted to cry and who had as a child wet his bed with the sexual
man who must not. Sexuality seemed to offer some of the quality
of the bee sting: it entailed a prerequisite search for sensation to
counteract detachment.

Mr. R. returned to work as a free-lance photographer and acquired a beeper, which gave him a sense of status. He kept the
beeper on during his hours; occasionally a message came through.

The second year of analysis was marked by Mr. R.'s increasing conviction of feeling *real* and of having more control over what
he was experiencing. He began to recognize that his lifelong style
of forgetting and procrastinating was not as passively determined
as it at first seemed to be. Instead, we came to understand it as a
means of opposition to the sense of feeling aimlessly pulled. A sign

of strength thereby reasserted itself as he came to see his motivated negativism within the transference.

Anxiety about separation was not yet affectively felt; it was still inferred from his symptomatology. But he was beginning to perceive the connection between his bodily and his psychic experience. He could almost feel, he once said in a moment of revelation, how "detachment is loneliness made physical."

With this kind of recognition, Mr. R. began to address himself more directly to the question of who I was to him, as he had heretofore been aware of me only when I was out of synchrony, or, to use a communications model, was providing him with negative feedback.[7] The way he referred to "your technique," for example, was a clue to his machinelike view of me which was intensified when I questioned him in ways that made him feel I perceived something being wrong with him. More positive awareness was expressed in his first undisguised dream of me: "I was on this couch and you were leafing back this pad to look something up I'd said a couple of months ago. I found that very nice that you could do that. The overall feeling was that it was comfortable and pleasant. . . the feeling in the dream of great benevolence, from the notebook." Another time, he said, "I think of you not as a doctor nor as a person, but as a personification of a comforting process." These steps in awareness seemed to indicate an increasing ability to view and tolerate me as having a center of volition "outside" him, as he felt a strengthened sense of his self as center of its own initiative—perhaps a step in the development of his own capacity for empathy with another. Concomitantly, he evidenced a deeper experience of and a greater ability to acknowledge feelings about separations.

As sexual themes appeared still more vividly, many with triangular configurations, I began to pursue more actively the seemingly disguised manifestations of an "oedipal transference." Mr. R.'s response to these attempts was telling. For example, he had a dream of me as a barber to whom he had come for a haircut, but

[7]Cf. Basch (1975): "Conscious awareness of self occurs when negative feedback is needed to correct unsuccessful actions."

who proceeded of her own accord to cut off his beard as well. In another dream, he reported himself "in a helicopter with a woman pilot who laughed so much she couldn't handle the controls properly." He associated to: "mother laughing at my 'cuteness'; in all my airplane dreams, there's the question of the competence of the pilot."

As with the earlier example in which Mr. R. was jarred when I questioned whether his thoughts about the psychiatrist-turned-photographer had to do with separation concerns, I saw again how his responses indicated I had stepped outside of his perceptual frame of reference and superimposed my own, that is, my theoretical concerns as to what themes he was defending against. Again, this need not negate the possibility that I was "correct" in my interpretations and that he was indeed defensive. But still, we must heed the nature of the patient's response, which indicated a specific transference revival of the unempathic mother. In fact, it is this idea of the total self experience indelibly coloring whatever oedipal configuration might appear that I want to underscore (in line with Kohut's description of the psychology of the self in the "broad" sense [1977]).

We may also note here that Mr. R.'s response to what he felt as an empathic failure was now no longer so fragmenting and disorienting; it took the form, instead, of a dialogue with me, expressed symbolically in dream imagery, and experienced as more autonomously initiated.

Mr. R. and his girlfriend separated after the second year of analysis. The relationship had become strained, and, perhaps, had also outlived its usefulness in providing an outside embodiment of me. Mainly, Mr. R. could separate because he felt able for the first time to live alone, and he felt good in this newfound capability. The *need* for a girl for sustenance had abated.

During this time the role of photography within the patient's psychic organization, within his self experience, was increasingly elaborated. I shall try to weave together some of these ideas.

Mother's looks, the failed "gleam in her eye,"[8] may be the

---

[8] A phrase used by Kohut (1971).

forerunner of Mr. R.'s camera interest. We can conjecture that the eye was hypercathected as touch was minimized. In his wish to "freeze" a look, to capture a moment's look forever in its slightest nuances, which he felt especially when in a detached state, the camera served in some way to maintain a merger—as a medium for connection. He spoke of the eye as a camera.

But it was his father's very real involvement with photography, "the thing we really came together on," that provided an affirmative aspect for this mode of expression.

The characterological style of Mr. R.'s perceptions and defenses was imbued with the sense of his self as photographer. What he noticed about my office were the pictures; when he described seeing a child on my lawn, he spoke of the "scenes" outside my home. When, late in the analysis, he had fantasies of my family interactions, they were again described as "scenes." When I observed this with him, he agreed that he experienced such scenes as though they were from a movie; he even imagined a mechanical movie viewer, winding and rewinding the film, each time he reviewed such a scene.

Childhood imagery also returned to him as though in a picture, although actual pictures from childhood, as we know, had caused him severe distress. When he thought of himself in his classroom he felt as though he were not on the same plane as the others. Instead, he felt he was higher up, looking down and photographing.

But it was movies, much more than still photography, that held the essence of his exhilaration.

Mr. R.:   As a child, I couldn't wait to be taken to a movie; I approached it with a certain reverence. When I got a look like "are you crazy?" I felt like I would lose something...I've come to see my intense love of films as coming from feeling inconsequential, small...movies have a way of imitating life, or is it life imitating movies?...the distinction seemed blurred; but the intense feelings evoked in movies, as the terror in *Jaws*, I don't feel in real life. So it's like a bee sting...

Mr. R.'s dreams were expressed as movies, creatively drawn and intensely and pleasurably responded to; they lent a major dimension to the analytic work. It seemed that moviemaking held the hope for the future, though he did not yet feel ready to pursue this goal.

> Mr. R.:   It has a tremendous sense of power; one can reach out and grab the audience and do anything one wants with it...[there is] drama, a sense of the grand, like *2001*.

Stanley Kubrick, the director of *2001,* was a major idealized figure for Mr. R., though he only gradually permitted himself to expose Kubrick's importance to him. With much embarrassment, Mr. R. eventually revealed the way he patterned his life after Kubrick's, often asking himself, "What would Kubrick say about this?"

> Mr. R.:   Kubrick embodies the two trends of being very rational, serious, yet his films are full of the imaginative, crazy, fantasy—like taking life on another planet seriously and dealing with it rationally.[9]

As we know, Mr. R. saw *2001* more than 30 times. When, during the course of his analysis, he saw it again, he understood more deeply its hold on him.

> Mr. R.:   The misty, wandering quality so like my child-

[9]I recently came across an old *Newsweek* article on Kubrick (Zimmerman, 1972) which begins in this way: "From the beginning, he has struggled to control both his work and his world, as if the uncertainties of the human condition would rip him to pieces if he relinquished his hold for even so much as a second. But it is precisely this inexhaustible drive to orchestrate even the smallest details of his life and his art that has made Stanley Kubrick the most provocative and brilliant of today's American directors."

> hood dreams...There is a scene in which the astronaut is lying there in the spaceship under a sunlamp, directing the computer as to how to turn him; and his parents call, telling him small talk; he sees and hears them, but they can't see and hear him; his mother, the schoolteacher, tells him the kids think he's famous; they tell him other small talk. He seems impassive. Then they sing "Happy Birthday," and he visibly cringes [as Mr. R. did as a child]. Then they go off into a dot on the screen...He directs the computer to return the sunlamp...

Thus, we saw Mr. R.'s view of the omnipotent grandeur of the astronaut, his concern with physical appearance and the drama of technology; we saw also his view of his parents' isolation from this and his sense of detachment from them.

Mr. R. was told that when he was two years old his grandmother would show him the moon. The moon had always held a special epic, grand fascination for him.

In the last year of his analysis, the patient was feeling rather well, successful in "still" photography work, and making new friends. He was somewhat exhilarated by all this, frequently to such an extent that it seemed hard for him to end the hours. In fact, he had a dream during this time that concerned a "fear of a bomb going off." He said he felt ready to do what he hoped to be able to do in therapy—to move to California. However, because I believed there were some as yet scarcely touched issues, and also because of his exhilarated feeling, I wondered if his wish to leave might represent a desire for premature flight. He did feel, he said, that there was a risk of getting "too comfortable" here, which could keep him from getting on with his life's task. I felt this concern, too, needed further work.

And so for a number of months we were somewhat at odds. I pursued what seemed to me Mr. R.'s defensiveness toward the oedipal issues, the sexual and aggressive themes that seemed to be expressed with increasing sharpness in the transference, and toward any sustained experience of the sense of intimacy. He reminded me directly, or implicitly via retreat, that I was mistaken in my pursuit and that it was precisely because he was capable of richer and more "real" feelings, which so pleased him, that he felt he could go. After a time, he expressed, "I feel like you've been after me lately, since I've been talking of going to California."

Kohut's writings on termination helped me better to understand and trust the patient's feeling about this issue. Kohut has described the appearance in the transference at the time of termination of a "brief oedipal phase," which may be felt "despite its anxieties and conflicts, as a joyfully accepted reality" (1977, p. 229). Whether or not these "oedipal" themes arose *de novo* in the case of Mr. R., what was joyful for him was his newly acquired capacity to experience such themes with rich affective expression, perceived on a psychic rather than somatic level. Kohut has further mentioned his respect for the analysand's "capacity to assess his own psychological state...[and his willingness] to trust a patient's wish to terminate his analysis, especially when...I am able to formulate...the dynamic-structural situation constituting the matrix of the patient's wish" (pp. 19–20).

We saw that Mr. R. was feeling strengthened and freed from the depleting merger with mother, as represented by his feeling of "detachment" that expressed her "indifferent" view of him. This allowed him to reflect more comfortably on other aspects of his mother and to be sympathetic to her as well. He could accept a bond with father which now enabled him to use his childhood idealization to develop his own, now more autonomously experienced, values and ideals. He had achieved a sense of inner continuity through his life span, that is, a stability of self-regulating processes. These changes gave Mr. R. a wider range of choices, including the capacity for deeper affective experience, less dependent on external contingency. He could go on now with the creative pursuit of his deeply rooted life task — to go to California and be a filmmaker.

I am aware that the argument can be made that despite these gains, the analysis was incomplete and that the desire to terminate was a flight from further regression better explored through additional analytic work. For Mr. R., this question could only be hypothetical, as he had made up his mind. What was apparent, however, was that we returned to much deeper, more meaningful analytic work when I resumed the listening mode of trying to "recognize" him[10] rather than trying to teach or "cure" him.

Looking at the issue over which we had struggled then led to further elaboration of the experience of detachment.

> Mr. R.: I see now what detachment is...that with mother and her looks, I felt a stranger...the most essential part of me was not understood! I think of crying...the lump in my throat...I had a dream of going to Spain, a place she'd talked about ecstatically when she went there on a trip; the dream says if I went to Spain and loved it, maybe then she would understand because she felt that way...I cried when she went on the trip ...[there was] a sense a child's tears have no real meaning, are of no import. I was told I cried every night for one and a half years and that I didn't talk until two.
>
> [Another session] a dream of mother laughing while I was telling her something serious; I was getting furious...Like the superficial way my parents treat my plans to move to California...the experience of anger instead of vagueness or detachment is new...A dream of feeling your arms around my neck and you kissed me, and I turned around and kissed you; there was a feeling of less self-consciousness, I didn't need to be so in control...the search for someone who understands.

There followed a dream in which Mr. R. needed to put down

[10]A term used in this context by Kohut.

the thermostat. Thus, he wavered back and forth, increasing the intensity of his sexual and of his angry feelings, while yet recognizing that he must be wary, so as not to risk irreversible loss of control: "I see how these emotions make a major contribution to my creative life, like I have a reservoir which I tap, of a tremendous well of emotions, and I can regulate the flow..."

The frightening airplane dreams, which had been charting the course of the analysis, were now more clearly hopeful.

Mr. R.:   I was in a plane, and there were all kinds of obstructions to our flight. My survival depended on the skill of the pilot. There were many high-power lines...it was really close...the plane had suddenly to reverse directions and stopped just short of the ground. I thought, "What a great pilot!" It was the kind of happiness, that I'd come through all these dangers okay... analysis, with you as the pilot...It is that I feel better and stronger, and so I can go...[Another airplane dream]...a hopeful, good dream; it was a variation on my airplane dream. The theme change started with its being a helicopter and I was in the *same compartment* [i.e., connected, rather than detached] with the pilot. I was always told helicopters are harder to fly than planes; I was being taught to fly this thing and learning; I was doing some...it was scary, also fun; I knew that if I couldn't do it, the pilot would take over. I was learning how to steer it; at one point, the pilot taught me certain kinds of moves to make in particular kinds of situations, like disorienting situations, where it's hard to figure what's up and what's down. I said, "How do you become oriented to what's up and what's down?" and the pilot said, "Simply open the curtain and take a look." It was amazing! There were no tricks. I could just look and see what's up and what's

down. [And then he associated] That's analysis!
Maybe I'm feeling I can fly this thing, that is, my
life...I feel so good this morning.

A termination date was set about four months in advance,
and Mr. R made plans for his move to California.

Mr. R.:   Remembering now that scared, little boy at
               camp, with the lump in his throat, it feels so
               good now to remember without dizziness, feel-
               ing connected. There is a growing sense I am
               really going to miss this...the lump in my throat
               ...an incredible sense of well-being. The differ-
               ence in me is incredible between how I was when
               I first came and now. I see how shallow my re-
               sponses to women had been, and now I am able
               to be concerned with their feelings. Although I
               may speak impersonally about analysis, yet the
               gratitude I feel is not for the process or for
               Freud, but for you. I think of giving you a
               screen credit on a film, thanking you in some
               way...like "Thanks to Dr. Evelyne Schwaber;
               without her help this film would not have been
               made."

During one hour, the beeper went off, and we looked once
again at its meaning. He added another dimension: "The beeper
means that in a certain way analysis must still be in second place,
that I can't turn my life around for analysis."
    I think the beeper means that for Mr. R., his creative life had
to take priority over relationships. Freed to follow this pursuit, he
no longer felt the need for analysis.
    In his final analytic hour, Mr. R. said: "I feel sad; I'm going to
miss it intellectually as well as emotionally. I also feel excited. I
feel grateful that this feels like the right decision; this is great, like
terrific! I have a feeling of breaking out, an *expansiveness* that
feels good. I also feel good that I feel sad; there's a pride I have in

having feelings — like I feel like showing off my new capabilities, that I have feelings...I was looking around a lot, at the waiting room and wall, like taking a last nostalgic look — a combination of sadness and excitement. *It's like taking off a cast* — or how I imagine it to be — concerned about its removal, but also a feeling of freedom, which I sense now, which is nice..."

Perhaps the idea of the cast, a device for healing a broken body part, offered an especially meaningful analogy of the analyst's role in healing Mr. R.'s fragmenting self; perhaps also of mending the first 13 years of his life together with the rest.

I had a letter from him about six months later, in which he wrote that he felt quite pleased with his work. He had already made a film which was well received by the production studio. "I feel so in the right place, doing the right thing," he wrote.

For Mr. R., it is the making of the film which represents a creative translation, the ultimate expression of the sense of "reconnection" of his self on a continuum.

Before I close, I want to attempt once more to relate this clinical material to the view of the infant researcher. I wrote Dr. Sander, asking for his conjectures about what may happen to a baby like Mr. R. in adulthood. I provided him only with the information that Mr. R was from a middle-class professional family, and that his parents told him that he cried for the first year and a half and did not talk until age two. Sander replied:

> Drawing upon the information that this was from a middle-class professional family, I would believe that the basic biological needs of hunger and warmth and so on were not at issue, that the crying would be principally for social interaction, then, not physical care. If we are to speculate what the "archaic" elements of the transference might be, I would say first of all that this infant was exposed to states of overwhelming disruption, unrelieved by any outside input. There would be a basic fear, then, of annihilation, or disruption, or explosion, or fragmentation that would follow from the states of overwhelming physical disorganization that go with such

crying. One might say there would be a fear of being over-whelmed by one's own state, and that there would be a sense of helplessness if such states threatened. There might be a great deal of recourse to self-stimulation — in contrast to the impotence he had experienced in producing contingent effects elsewhere in his world. . . . The necessity to be in control of his life situation himself, lest there be an overwhelming state which might ensue. Thus there would be a great need to control situations potentially triggering his own feelings and his own world. . . . the lack of response of his world to his crying would be connected with a sense that relationships are not to be counted on to come *to* him. That they would be available only if he could elicit them. This would be connected with a certain "distance" that would go with his lack of basic trust in the possibility of anyone "meeting" him from a point outside himself. He would really have had fundamentally to get on by himself, distant from social relationships.

The parallels between what was discovered in the analytic situation and what was predicted by the infant researcher are striking. I believe it is the viewpoint of a depth psychology of the self, with its utilization of the selfobject concept as a mode of listening, which offers opportunity for such concordance of data of these early developmental phenomena.

I will close on a more philosophical note, wondering if Mr. R. represents today's Everyman: man of the computer age, the space age; man using a machine — a camera, a beeper, a mechanized experience of the transference — as a way station to connection, in some way trusting the machine more than the person; man searching beyond himself and other men — for the moon.

References

Basch, M. F. (1975), Toward a Theory That Encompasses Depression: A Revision of Existing Causal Hypotheses in Psychoanalysis. In: *Depression and Human Existence,* ed. E. J. Anthony & T. Benedek. Boston: Little, Brown.
_____ (1977), Developmental Psychology and Explanatory Theory in Psychoanalysis. *The Annual of Psychoanalysis,* 5:229-263. New York: International Universities Press.

Kohut, H. (1971), *The Analysis of the Self.* New York: International Universities Press.

———— (1977), *The Restoration of the Self.* New York: International Universities Press.

Sander, L. (1975), Infant and Caretaking Environment: Investigation and Conceptualization of Adaptive Behavior in a System of Increasing Complexity. In: *Explorations in Child Psychiatry,* ed. E. J. Anthony. New York: Plenum.

Schwaber, E. (1979), On the 'Self' within the Matrix of Analytic Theory—Some Clinical Reflections and Reconsiderations. *Internat. J. Psycho-Anal.,* 60:467–479.

Zimmerman, P. D. (1972), Kubrick's Brilliant Vision. *Newsweek,* Jan. 2.

Discussion of
"Self Psychology and the Concept of Psychopathology: A Case Presentation" by Evelyne A. Schwaber

Self Psychology and Problems of Technique and Termination

PAUL TOLPIN

Dr. Schwaber's stimulating case presentation raises a number of questions for which answers, or at least some further discussion, are in order.

One area of concern, which to some extent has already been dealt with by Dr. Schwaber, is whether, within the framework of the treatment of disorders of the self, this relatively brief, three-year therapeutic effort can be considered a satisfactorily completed analysis; or whether, despite Dr. Schwaber's and the patient's sense that major areas of pathology had been adequately dealt with, and that the patient had developed the ability to move ahead in his chosen vocation, the termination was premature, ending with a flight into health that left significant sectors of pathology insufficiently dealt with. As Dr. Schwaber has pointed out, the issue, practically speaking, is a "hypothetical" one since the patient "was

capable of richer and more 'real' feelings" and was firm in his decision that he had accomplished as much as he needed to; and
because of the valuable help he had already received, he was now
ready to move to California.

Dr. Schwaber indicates that she herself was initially in doubt
about the wisdom of, and reasons for, the patient's decision, and
that she and the patient were "at odds" for a number of months
while she attempted to deal with what she initially saw as resistances to further analytic work. The patient's attitude did not
change, however, and Dr. Schwaber, realizing Mr. R. was giving
her a "message" she had previously been unable to hear, and
reasoning that her patient knew something about himself that she
should heed, accepted his decision to stop treatment. In support of
her position, Dr. Schwaber turned to Heinz Kohut's comments
regarding the analyst's need to respect the patient's "capacity to
assess his own psychological state. . . [and his willingness] to trust a
patient's wish to terminate his analysis, especially when. . . I am
able to formulate. . . the dynamic-structural situation constituting
the matrix of the patient's wish" (Kohut, 1977, pp. 19–20). Dr.
Schwaber does provide such a formulation when she refers to Mr.
R. as "freed from the depleting merger with mother. . . . He could
accept a bond with father. . . ." Dr. Schwaber also notes the her-
alding appearance, corresponding to Kohut's findings for *some*
terminating patients, of a brief oedipal phase that was experienced, "'despite its anxiety and conflicts, as a joyfully accepted
reality'" rather than a source of conflict to be freed from its defensive structures and adequately worked through.

These studies cannot, of course, prove a theoretical position;
they can be used only to illustrate it. They are necessarily tendentious and can be judged, I believe, only on the basis of the clarity
and relevance they impart to the ideas they are meant to support,
and on the strength of their explanatory power. So far as this case
is concerned, it must be accepted as a given that the author's basic
intention was not to argue for or against self psychology or structural (conflict-oedipal) pathology. She was essentially convinced of
the applicability of the former to this patient and was interested in
demonstrating the vicissitudes and the progressive development of

a particular set of idiosyncratic problems within this framework.

On at least two grounds, it is difficult to determine whether, within the framework of self psychology, Dr. Schwaber's case report demonstrates the sufficiency of her patient's analysis. The first consideration is a general and practical one deriving from the limitations of an abbreviated and necessarily elliptical case report. Such reports lead to the omission of the more detailed data that would perhaps have provided a greater sense of process and increased the reader's ability to assess the author's contentions for himself. Little can be said regarding such omissions. The reader must gauge their significance for himself and, as with any case report, make the most of what is available to him.

The second area of consideration arises from the more crucial question: were the patient's core problems optimally analyzed? Several areas of pathology inviting further evaluation come to mind. The first relates to the patient's continuing and increasingly severe and painful detachment from the real world and from involvement with people, and his search for safe affective relationships in the several-times-removed (un-)reality of the movies. This is particularly well demonstrated by his addictionlike involvement with the movie *2001*. In addition to the repeated viewing of it, Mr. R. was particularly fascinated with certain specific features of the movie which resonated with his own deficiencies, defenses, and attempts at revitalization. Consider, for example, the "mind-blowing" grandiloquence (hyperbolized bee stings?) of its music, and its splendidly realized space-age, time-warp visual effects that offer nonspecific, ambiguous intensity as an alternative to somatizations and emptiness or inner "deadness." The music and these visual effects may be used as substitutions for involvements Mr. R. wants but cannot obtain, involvements with real people, such as with the girlfriends he never feels close to. These elements of the film, in brief, substitute a make-believe (sometimes) grandiose, fantasy life for an in-depth experience with others or for a sense of inner fullness and self-stability.

Mr. R. clearly recovered his ability to allow himself to feel meaningfully for another person by way of the transference mobilization of affects in relation to the analyst. The patient's sense of cosmic isolation is exemplified by the self-absorbed, sun-bathing astronaut cut off from his vapid childhood past. The in-difference and emotional distance of his mother, her "absence," is replaced by a gradually increasing ability to experience the world via his experience of the analyst as responsively reliable. The lump in his throat changes to tears and he recognizes that he has not felt "detached...in some time." Later he is able to feel within the transference undefensively close to the analyst and to experience his involvement with her comfortably—he even says, openly, that he loves her. He has found someone (again) who understands him as he at some time (early in life?) presumably had felt understood. His true feelings (not the synthetic, prettified ones he experienced with his mother) and his nuclear self, his ambitions and ideals, have been stimulated and acknowledged.

The dangerous course leading him out of the protective but isolating withdrawal into a private "movie world" can be charted by way of his recurrent airplane dreams. Early in treatment he feared "losing control." I believe that by control he meant control over selfobject wishes that were already beginning to be mobilized. Such mobilization, he felt, endangered a relatively safe, though in-creasingly unsatisfying, defensive position. An early airplane dream illustrates this danger. He fears the dangerous high-voltage lines into which he is about to crash, although he (or the analyst) still retains some control of the vehicle. He thinks about the fear of being taken over and directed by something outside of himself "not by my own choice...fear of helplessness." Like the cosmic, spaceship entry into another world of *2001,* he is overstimulated by his remobilized feelings for the interested analyst. He fears the regression because then he will be endangered not just by the inten-sity of his feeling but by the repeated, traumatically painful exper-iences of loss of the transference-revived, needed selfobject, be it mother or father. Near the end of his treatment his airplane dreams have been decidedly altered. He is able to relate to a depen-dable and idealized pilot with whom he sits "in the same compart-ment." The pilot had taught him how to steer, how to orient him-self, how to take care of himself "without tricks," how to fly his life. Of course one dream implying success in the management of one's self does not make a completed analysis, but the case material is necessarily sketchy and at the very least it points in the direction one might hope the analysis of such a patient would take.

Related to the patient's greater ability to fly his life, to make use of his nuclear ambitions and ideals, is his greater "sublimatory" ability, comprising, among other psychological properties, his innate talents. Luckily, these talents were able to resonate with an area of encouraging relatedness to, and a reinforcing identification with, his father, "the thing we really come together on." It seems clear that this mainly (but not exclusively) idealizing pole of his bipolar self was indeed strengthened or at least became less hampered in the course of his analysis. From his postanalytic message to the analyst we can gather that he was able to begin his (life's?) work with some initial success. It remains an open issue whether he used these father-related skills as a healthy compensation, or whether some hidden defensive avoidance of the resolution of the earlier mother selfobject needs was mixed with these compensatory abilities.

With the available information, I do not believe the issue can be resolved. This issue does seem to be an important one, however, insofar as the patient's future is concerned, and it is contingent upon the relative completeness of his analysis in two critical areas: (1) the thoroughness of the working through and Mr. R.'s ability to deal with, in a healthier fashion, his pathogenic relationship to his mother; and (2) the intensification of his identification with, and the maturation of his mirroring-idealization experiences with, his father as a crucial psychic development not only in its own right, but also as a force available as compensation for certain of the unalterable insufficiencies of the maternal relationship. Again, these questions are unanswerable at present. But to return to the question of the general adequacy of the analysis in these two areas, it does seem clear that the patient was helped considerably by the analytic work and the working through.

Leaving now the larger issues regarding the sufficiency of the analytic effort in this case, there are several more circumscribed technical and conceptual issues that may repay further consideration. I shall limit myself to two such issues. Both arise in relation to one analyst-patient exchange that came up early in the analytic case material. I am referring to Dr. Schwaber's comments about the patient's presumed concern about her upcoming vacation when he was talking about his passion for photography.

The first point has to do with Mr. R.'s felt injury at Dr. Schwaber's response and the vicissitudes of Mr. R.'s anger in terms of his early history and his current reaction to the analyst. As Dr. Schwaber suggests, "the absence of mother in such an early communication [in the analysis] may have any number of meanings," several of which she mentions. However, another possibility might be considered here. The patient's terse "that's all there is" may very well have been an expression not only of an experiential absence of the mother because of her emotional absence from him, but an in-effect absence arising from reactive anger that had become chronic and had changed to cold indifference or even to a repression-effected nonawareness of her. This might have been the pathogenic consequence of "one and a half years of crying" (a hyperbole that nevertheless communicates a severely disturbed and unsatisfying early mother-child relationship) as was reported to the analyst and commented on by Dr. Louis Sander. One could reasonably imagine that the patient's initial rage had been transformed to a rage-form of characterological, cold indifference which then, secondarily, protected him from the revival of early selfobject longings whose revival in the present, he (unconsciously) felt, would only lead to an insupportable increase of the emotional pain he had had to cope with recurrently for many years. So when Mr. R. was confronted with his analyst-mother's misunderstanding (in terms of his immediately relevant affective investment) of the reasons for his talking about photography, he felt terribly injured, and experienced the injury as a loss of contact with a needed selfobject. Because his life had begun so painfully with unremitting tension states (the crying), one would expect that he would be highly vulnerable to the later "insensitivities" perpetrated by his self-centered mother and other "insensitive" caretakers of later periods of his life. Such insensitivity was inadvertently repeated by the temporarily "self-oriented" analyst who spoke about vacations when Mr. R. was expatiating about photography, that is, when he was happily describing a highly meaningful, highly valued aspect of his self. When he attempted to reprimand the analyst with a "who listens" psychiatrist joke, but became anxious that he might have offended her, he backed off with, "I didn't mean to be critical." He did not want to risk further offense, further alienation, and perhaps a more intense recrudescence of his childhood rage. At any rate, neither his specific injury of feeling misunderstood (which was subsequently recognized by the analyst and discussed in her presentation) nor his anger, were addressed at that moment. Regarding the issue of his anger, I would like to underscore how at a particular moment in the analysis (a moment that is paradigmatic of a number of other such moments), the focused joining of the issue of the patient's felt injury and his possible angry reaction to that injury might (then or later) have more fully opened up the analysis in a direction that would have allowed for greater self-understanding and working through.

The second point I would like to discuss has been foreshadowed in the preceding comments about Mr. R.'s anger. It is related to the specific issue of an empathic break and its technical handling, whatever the reactive affects that it gives rise to. To repeat, the patient had felt injured, thrown off course, by the analyst's derailing "separation anxiety" comment. It would have been useful at the time of its occurrence or soon after to explain to the patient how the analyst understood what had happened, specifically, how when the patient spoke with great feeling about one thing the analyst had confused and disappointed him by talking about something else, thereby ignoring his train of thought and his feelings (perhaps adding the genetic reconstructive link, "that seems to be like what your mother did"). It should have been explained how, as a consequence, the patient had felt confused, injured, angry, and had finally collapsed into himself. A clear, factual acknowledgment of the empathic disruption and its adverse effects on the increasing selfobject-transference intimacy would have helped to repair the disruption and facilitated the growing alliance with and trust in the analyst which this patient had been cautiously approaching; it would have encouraged the resumption in the transference of his increasing attachment to the analyst as more "in tune" with him, as the reliable selfobject he had lacked in his development. And it would have encouraged and supported his ability over analytic time to deal with the transformation and management of his anger.

Nonetheless, it is clear from the subsequent development of this case that Dr. Schwaber was in general sufficiently in touch with this patient's most crucial difficulties to enable him to move ahead quite rapidly in his psychological development and to overcome his previous feelings of mounting isolation, self-preoccupation, detachment, and somatization.

This finding leads to the last point I would like to make. Granting the success of the patient's treatment, how does one account for the rapidity with which he improved? Again there can be no sure answer to this question since there were probably a number of factors operating in the patient's favor. The first derives, perhaps, from his youth and the psychological flexibility that youth optimally retains. It is as if Mr. R., despite his age, was still an adolescent, and was still in the process of realigning some of the forces that were the constituents of his personality. Chance may play an important role in the manifest forms and perhaps even the deeper organization of certain areas of the personality. His analysis may have indeed played the role in his mental organization that adventitious, less structured life experiences play in the lives of others. Without analytic help, he had been moving toward an increasingly pathological dead end, a 2001 spaceship filled with technical instruments and processed foods but which provided no opportunities for a viable, sustaining attachment to objects. His nuclear self was hidden behind a repression barrier buttressed by complex defenses. Through the generally correct therapeutic response that acknowledged and thereby helped to mobilize his deepest affects, he was still able to build on, and rebuild from, the best of his childhood experiences. And he was able more accurately to become aware of what had been injuring him, thereby acquiring the ability to distance himself from those injuries and to use his new awareness and the healthier sectors of his personality to carry him toward a new and stronger organization of his functioning self.

Reference

Kohut, H. (1977), *The Restoration of the Self.* New York: International Universities Press.

Discussion

A Reply to Paul Tolpin

EVELYNE A. SCHWABER

Dr. Tolpin's discussion raises a number of critical questions which warrant further reflection. I am grateful for the chance to enter a dialogue, to review and extend my own thinking, and to share some of my ideas with you. Many of my comments, then, are intended to take advantage of the opportunity afforded by Dr. Tolpin's remarks and are not necessarily an index of disagreement with him.

Dr. Tolpin's focus is on the sufficiency of the analytic effort — whether significant defensive mechanisms still remained hidden, and on the technical interventions employed. I shall try to address some of these issues. I would like, however, to underscore what I feel to be the central thesis of my paper. I sought to demonstrate a particular mode of analytic listening — the empathic-introspective mode and its implicit interconnectedness with the self psychological point of view. I further wished to elucidate how the selfobject concept is derivative of this mode. Elsewhere (Schwaber, 1979a), I have defined empathy as "an introspective awareness arising within the context of a selfobject phenomenon." This selfobject concept, originally formulated in the analytic situation with patients suffering from a specific form of psychopathology, has profound implications as a way of perceiving and ordering our clinical data which I feel go far beyond diagnostic considerations.[1]

Thus, in my presentation of the case of Mr. R. I was not focusing specifically on matters of technique or on nosological distinctions. I was not arguing for the selective applicability of the self psychological model to this patient. Rather, I was arguing for its general applicability — the utilization of a particular perceptual stance — the observer within the system, the "contextual unit," the heightened attention to the surround, the sharpened focus on certain immediate experiential phenomena. As I have indicated, it is this mode of observation which defines the psychoanalytic concept of empathy. The analyst, placing him- or herself into the other's intrapsychic reality, views himself as being used and being responded to as part of the context of that reality. I further noted that this point of view dovetails with the "systems" approach to the study of development that considers the infant and caretaker each as part of a unit.

Empathy, then, is implicitly used here as a mode of perception, not as a technique per se. The technical choice then arises secondarily as a translation of understanding based on that perception.[2] It is the enrichment of our observable data through empathic perception which I have chosen to emphasize. Indeed, self psychology as a theoretical system arose as an outgrowth of the systematic use of the empathic-introspective mode as *the* scientific matrix of clinical observation; it is this mode which permitted the discovery and unfolding of a more multidimensional, broad-ranging understanding of transference and opened new vistas of subtle phenomenology for psychoanalytic exploration.

For me, the beauty of this mode of data gathering lies in its creative potential. In sharpening our attentiveness to each person's individuality, to the recognition and articulation of the pa-

[1]It is noteworthy that Kohut (1979) recently suggested that the "self-object" be spelled without a hyphen, in order to "give expression to a significant firming of this concept — that we express more unambiguously the fact that we are dealing not with an ad-hoc construct but with a viable concept which we hope will find an enduring place in analytic thought."

[2]I would like to thank Dr. Robert Michels for helping me arrive at such a distinction.

tient's frame of reference, we minimize the superimposition of inferential leaps based on a theoretical model from without. Often, it has seemed to me, when a patient has felt an empathic failure on my part, it arose from the imposition of *my* view of reality, *my* frame of reference, instead of responding from that within the patient. All of our theoretical models share this risk of superimposition, and many authors have described the erroneous reifications of our theoretical systems and the unfortunate foreclosing of clinical material that can thereby ensue. To reiterate, then, rather than speaking to the applicability of a specific theory for a particular patient, I was addressing myself to the empathic method of clinical observation and the kinds of data that it highlights.

Elsewhere (Schwaber, 1978, 1979b), in an attempt to consider differing modalities by means of which we gather our clinical data, I have spoken of the distinction between the use of empathy and that of "inference." The limits of empathy, if there are not defensive processes mitigating against it, are defined by the experiential similarity between the observer and the observed (about which Kohut had written in 1959). I have noted that listening to the coloquialisms of one whose native language differs from our own, to the descriptions of some of the physiologically based bodily experiences of the opposite sex, or to the plight of survivors of massive trauma are examples of phenomena which move beyond these limits. Inference can be used to fill this gap of dissimilarity.[3] Observations based on such inference may prove correct, but it is nonetheless important to recognize by what means we are making them.

Let me now respond to some of Dr. Tolpin's specific comments. Addressing Mr. R.'s investment in movies, Dr. Tolpin notes its defensive aspect — the retreat from involvement with people to the "several-times-removed (un-)reality of the movies."

---

[3] In a cogent and most illuminating discussion of empathy, P. Ornstein (1979) has recently further considered such a distinction. He notes that the "inferential-extrospective" vantage point, contrasting with that of empathy-introspection, serves as a reasoning process from without, leading to a more "mechanistic-experience-distant" view.

It was precisely my intention, however, to consider the greater complexity of meaning involved in this intense interest, beyond the issue of defense against relationships. For Mr. R., movies represented a deeply rooted locus of experience of the core of himself which he longed to express in an active, not only passive, form. Indeed, it was because of this inhibition of his creative capacity that he was seeking help. Here, again, it is the thrust of the self psychological point of view to have extended these dimensions to our understanding of such phenomena, and to have impressed upon us that such creative pathways, originally linked to early childhood selfobjects, may be seen as developing in their own right. Mr. R. was striving to fulfill and realize his ideals and ambitions as the ultimate expression of his essential self experience; this was the quest that his symptoms impeded.

Commenting on Mr. R.'s fear of losing control of his feelings and of being overwhelmed by them (as Mr. R. later speaks of a need for a "thermostat"), Dr. Tolpin suggests that the fear here may be not only that of overstimulation, but also of loss of the needed selfobject as revived in the transference. This is an important consideration and may be quite correct. Again, however, emphasizing the method of data gathering, this possibility must be recognized as a speculation—perhaps an inference based on the observations of others. More specific data indicating that it was such fear of loss for this patient are lacking.

A word about the locus of the transference: Dr. Tolpin speaks of Mr. R.'s relationship to his father and the analytic work done in that regard, wondering about as yet unresolved difficulties with his mother as selfobject. My own feeling about this (and I believe Kohut has spoken to this idea) is that, in general, the more stable working transference reinstates itself around the healthier parental relationship—in Mr. R.'s case, with the father. Mr. R. spoke, for example, of how with his father, *as* with the analyst but *unlike* his relationship with mother, he knew just what to do to please or displease. When there was a rupture of this transference experience, we were offered a closer look at the nature of the painfully perceived experience with the mother and Mr. R.'s vulnerability to its recreation, perhaps with father as well as with others. We saw more clearly how the patient's "detached" state was interwoven with an inner representation of his "detached," that is, "neutral, indifferent," nonaffirming mother. As he attained a deeper, affectively meaningful understanding of this perception and the circumstances of its re-creation, he developed the capacity for more autonomous experiencing as well as for a more empathic view of his mother. Nonetheless, there is surely more work that could be done regarding his relationship with her, and I think it is an open question as to whether or not he will encounter future difficulty in this area.

Considering Mr. R.'s response to his mother, Dr. Tolpin suggests that he had repressed his chronic "reactive anger...the pathogenic consequence of 'one and a half years of crying'... [which may have] been transformed to a rage-form of characterological, cold indifference." This idea touches on a critical question having to do with the primacy of rage experience, secondarily repressed or transformed, in this patient's psychic life. We may note, in this regard, that Dr. Louis Sander in his letter never spoke of rage, but of "states of overwhelming disruption," fear of fragmentation, or disorganization. The implication is that the quality of the infantile affective experience is of a different order, developmentally more primitive and perhaps more threatening, than one described by a more defined emotion such as anger. Mr. R.'s "detached" feeling had the quality of a sense of spatial isolation, as if he was on a different geometric plane than others, or lost in outer space, disconnected from the capsule. Listening to his description of this state, I do not think it can be equivalently characterized as "cold indifference."

Another patient with a history of parental unresponsiveness in infancy has related to me, "When I feel devastated, finally being able to feel anger becomes a way of coping." Anger, for her, was felt as a more advanced emotion than the diffuse helplessness she otherwise experienced. In this respect, Basch (1976) has written, "It is premature to attribute an emotional life to infants, inasmuch as they have developed neither a symbolic concept of self nor the capacity for symbolic operation, which make reflection possible.... The older child may eventually learn to abstract particular proprioceptive feedbacks associated with attempts to cope with a situation that frustrates his attempts to organize it adaptively, and let the abstraction, labeled 'anger,' symbolize the experience. But this does not mean that babies are subjectively sharing such an emotional experience when they exhibit similar behaviors; we may infer that they are attempting to cope with some disorder, some frustration of their sensorimotor expectations, but not that they are 'angry' in the symbolic sense" (pp. 768–769).

Concomitant with the relinquishment of disrupting states and their somatic expressions, Mr. R. ultimately came to experience anger along with affective awareness of this emotion. This occurrence did not appear to be a matter of lifting repression, but rather a part of a newly achieved maturational step. One may speculate here on the possibility of its relationship to a widening symbolic capacity.

We can see that as we talk of the subtleties of Mr. R.'s experiences, whether the issue has to do with his affect states or his relationships or his fascination with movies, we are responding to them, beyond the search for defensive content, as meaningful in their own right. It was a similar idea that I suggested when I called attention to the patient's "that's all there is" response regarding his mother. Whatever its defensive meaning, this remark may also convey an experiential absence. That is, I was trying to emphasize that Mr. R.'s description, be it in words or through affect, may communicate an important assessment of his experiential state – in any event, his inner subjective reality.

These ideas may be considered further with reference to the session concerning my vacation, when Mr. R. retreated with a statement, "I didn't mean to be critical." This may not necessarily imply that he sought to defend himself against hostile feelings – certainly a possible formulation – but that he perceived something which was meaningful to him in the analyst's response; she appeared to him as though defensive. Thus, it was *his* perceptions, rather than *my* inferences about hidden motives, which led us in the particular direction we then pursued.[4]

---

[4]In attempting to direct attention to this mode of listening, we have seen that

Let me briefly elaborate some additional elements of the hour at issue. When Mr. R. spoke of the joke of the two psychiatrists, I did not ask him which joke he had in mind. I assumed he was thinking of the one about the psychiatrist who, on being told by a colleague, "Good morning," thought, "I wonder what he means by that." The idea is that the first psychiatrist is so caught up in his own work and ideology as to be unable to comprehend the point of view and interest of the person relating to him. This was the essence of Mr. R.'s ubiquitous concern. When I responded from within the issues of my profession and my vacation, I re-created this old injury. His wish was precisely that I invest myself less in my work and more in *his* (or in him).

These ideas touch on some further observations I have made in my own introspection, regarding the occurrences of empathic failure. Often, such failure comes about when I have experienced some violation of my *own* self-integrity and, not immediately cognizant of this inner experience, feel a need to rally to my defense. To paraphrase myself, "What, do you believe I will not think about you while I am away?!" Thus, my response came from something stirred within *me,* something I felt was being challenged. I thereupon introduced *my* perspective rather than deepening my recognition of *his.* I think it crucial that we attempt to heighten our self-awareness regarding such occurrences—whether we feel a violation or flattery to some aspect of our selves.[5] Thus, this point of view,

---

certain data are given sharpened listening focus as, for example, Mr. R.'s change in state, tone, etc. In the subsequent reporting of these data, such aspects as the relation of the patient's response to the analyst's intervention may appear to the reader as self-evident if not simplistic. This "straw man" image, however, is an artifact of the condensation of the observational elements in the reporting. What then appears obvious is only so in *consequence* of a particular attunement.

[5]Sander refers to the developmental concept of the establishment of "regulatory mechanisms." Basch (1975) writes of the infant's need for an "ordering of patterns." We may speculate as to whether such concepts have any bearing on the patient's repetition of a certain pattern or style of behavior, anticipating a particular familiar response. Thus, the analyst, responding as "object" (or "target") acted upon, may experience himself as antagonized, bored, enmeshed in a struggle, feeling pushed to answer a question, etc. —any of which may meet the patient's expectation, although not necessarily his wish that things will be different this time. A response from such a vantage point can serve as a clue that the

in emphasizing the "contextual unit," directs added attention to the analyst's role as intrinsic to the understanding of transference and resistance and as necessitating a sharpened introspective attunement.

The concept of "empathic failure" is intended to convey a *perception* of rupture within the contextual unit. It is not, in itself, synonymous with a "technical error," although that may indeed follow, particularly if the attempt is not made to understand its meaning. But there is no way, even in the ideal, to eliminate failures of empathy, because introspective attunement not-withstanding, one cannot always know ahead of time what will be *felt* by an individual patient as a "failure."[6] Its recognition will, as Dr. Tolpin notes, permit a deepening understanding of the patient's self experience and perception; indeed, it becomes the pathway for delineation of the patient's unique responses.

Thus, I fully agree with Dr. Tolpin regarding the technical handling of an empathic break when he suggests an endeavor to look with the patient at the possible re-creation of a past injury. In the case of Mr. R., however, I did not yet know and chose not to infer that I was felt as repeating an injury the patient's mother had inflicted; I was only just learning to recognize *how* an injury was experienced.

In considering the technical stance, I wish to comment on what may be an ambiguity in Dr. Tolpin's phrasing, "encouraging...increasing attachment to the analyst as *more* [my emphasis] 'in tune' with him, the reliable selfobject he had lacked in his development." The ambiguity lies in the possible implication that the analyst may deliberately and specifically offer herself as someone who corrects for an injurious past. Although I believe Dr. Tolpin would agree that this was not his meaning and

---

analyst has stepped outside the patient's perspective and has thereby lost empathic contact — even though the repetition feels familiar. Responding from within may, in contrast, feel disconnecting at first, until the patient has a chance to integrate the new experience.

[6]The word "felt" is underscored to convey that it is always the intra-psychically perceived reality to which I refer when I speak of the patient's perception.

indeed, that this is not the nature of the analytic task, I feel it is important to underscore this clarification.

Regarding Dr. Tolpin's concluding question about the rapidity of Mr. R.'s improvement, I would agree that his youth—the spontaneous continuity of his own development—may have been a significant factor. We must bear in mind that to some extent Mr. R. had foreshadowed the termination at the outset, when he said he was "going to do what [he] was going to do and no one could stop [him]"; that is, when he had achieved a psychological capacity to seek his self-initiated goal. In addition, we know that a major aspect of his self experience had to do with the need for significance and the mastery of time. Beyond its defensive possibilities, his analytic work expressed this central wish—to have the analysis be meaningful and to not waste time. Finally, Mr. R. was a gifted man, who was perhaps able to use his gift creatively in the introspective process as well.

Again, I would like to thank Dr. Tolpin for his challenging inquiry and the opportunity of a dialogue afforded by his stimulating remarks.

References

Basch, M. F. (1975), Toward a Theory That Encompasses Depression: A Revision of Existing Causal Hypotheses in Psychoanalysis. In: *Depression and Human Existence,* ed. E. J. Anthony & T. Benedek. Boston: Little, Brown.

_____ (1976), The Concept of Affect: A Re-Examination. *J. Amer. Psychoanal. Assn.,* 24:759–777.

Kohut, H. (1959), Introspection, Empathy, and Psychoanalysis: An Examination of the Relationship Between Mode of Observation and Theory. *J. Amer. Psychoanal. Assn.,* 14:243–272.

_____ (1979), Notes for Workshop on Self Psychology. (Unpublished manuscript.)

Ornstein, P. (1979), Remarks on the Central Position of Empathy in Psychoanalysis. *Bull. Assn. Psychoanal. Med.,* 18:95–108.

Schwaber, E. (1978), Reflections on "A Psychoanalytic Overview on Children of Survivors" by J. Kestenberg. Unpublished presentation at the Symposium on *The Holocaust: Psychological Effects on Survivors and Their Children.* Brandeis University, May.

_____ (1979a), On the 'Self' Within the Matrix of Analytic Theory—Some

Clinical Reflections and Reconsiderations. *Internat. J. Psycho-Anal.,* 60:467–479.

———— (1979b), Narcissism, Self Psychology, and the Listening Perspective. Unpublished presentation at Staff Conference, Mt. Auburn Hospital, Cambridge, Mass.

Discussion

Defense Analysis and Self Psychology

KENNETH NEWMAN

Dr. Schwaber's paper points to the present lack of agreement or consensus about the role, and hence the technical management, of defenses in the pathology of the self. In considering her patient's lack of awareness or concern with separations or his feelings of detachment, Dr. Schwaber discusses the possibility of these states being defenses, but ultimately she attributes them to experiential deficiencies and to the internalization of a maternal attitude of detachment. She sees the experiential deficiencies as originating in deficiencies in the self that did not allow her patient to experience the world with a sense of his own ability to initiate and influence it. I am in overall agreement with Dr. Schwaber's understanding, but I feel that it leaves out elements of defensive layering and painful affect states that her patient must have experienced, needed to wall off, and even partly handled by some identification with a detached mother. It is my intent here to discuss various aspects of defenses and their technical handling.

Kohut's investigations have broadened our understanding of the disturbances that result from the thwarting of needs by unempathic, insufficient, or unavailable parents. Patients who present with a variety of symptomatic and chronic character complaints can now be understood to be suffering less from conflicts explained in terms of a drive-defense model than from self pathology—

263

pathology that renders them vulnerable to alterations in self-cohesion and that is catalyzed in particular by empathic failures on the part of needed selfobjects.

It is common for pioneering scientific work to focus on one area, while neglecting other areas for a time. Freud's early investigations dealt with overt clinical behavior and its relation to unconscious content. Similarly, the study of the self has focused on the nature of the patient's core anxiety, the variety of reactions designed to counteract fragmentation and maintain cohesiveness, and the understanding of regressive alterations in the self-selfobject unit consequent to narcissistic injuries.

The motivation for defenses according to the self model differs from the motivation according to the conflict model. In the former case, defenses are not erected specifically to ward off superego anxiety, but to counteract the underlying awareness of painful affect or tension states associated with the reexposure of structural deficits or an enfeebled self. Some of Kohut's most relevant ideas are concerned with the misapplication of the drive-defense model to disorders that reside in the self. Specifically, selfobject transferences early in the treatment often reveal what appears to be a paucity of references to the therapist and are thus quite different from object-libidinal transferences. These narcissistic transferences, however, may indicate not an absence of transference reference but a specific kind of functional relatedness. If considered in terms of the traditional structural model, these initial transference presentations will be seen as defenses rooted in a character pathology which might be categorized, for example, as phallic-narcissistic, and which therefore may be thought of as concealing latent rivalrous and enviously destructive impulses. Similarly, the earliest presentations of idealizing transferences may be viewed, erroneously, as part of a reactive character defense, masking, for example, hostile impulses.

From our understanding of the self and its development we recognize that these tentative idealizing transferences or reactivated needs for mirroring responses should not be viewed as defenses. In fact, Kohut warns against too zealous an adherence to defense and resistance interpretations lest the therapist interfere with the mobilization of these transferences.

Moreover, if the patient's first attempts to utilize the therapist in the service of the self are viewed as defenses—for example, if a merger transference is erroneously interpreted as a defense against the unfolding of a classical transference because of its silent use of the therapist—this may recapitulate earlier traumas or reactivate memories of narcissistic parents who in some way demanded deflection of interest upon themselves.

Another possible danger is that if the patient detects that the therapist considers that his being treated as a selfobject is a resistance, the patient may think he should give up this "defense." The unspoken message may be conveyed that object-libidinal transferences are acceptable, but that narcissistic transferences are regressive or defensive.

A further difficulty in treatment when the drive-defense model is used exclusively with patients suffering from low self-esteem is that, given the initial lack of cohesion and security of the patient's self, the emphasis on defensive posture and character armor may be experienced as criticism. To tell the patient, "You are warding off this..." "You are defending yourself against that..." will reevoke the feeling that he is not doing well enough. The patient feels that he is "bad" and in the presence, once again, of a rejecting parent.

I believe there is now a need for a deeper exploration of the defensive organization of the narcissistic personality disorder. The current relative downplaying of analyzing character defenses is, in part, a reaction to the excessive reliance on resistance analysis that had proved counterproductive to the goals of treatment in patients with narcissistic disorders, insofar as the stress on defenses against impulses proved inimical to an atmosphere facilitating the mobilization of narcissistic transferences. In essence the mistaken reliance on interpretation of resistance has been replaced by a mistaken reluctance to interpret even narcissistic defenses.

Kohut (1971, 1977) stated that the traumatic frustration of the phase-appropriate wish or need for parental acceptance leads to the intensification of this wish or need. This intensified wish, together with the external frustration, creates a severe psychic imbalance which leads to the exclusion of the wish or need from further authentic and consistent participation in the rest of the psychic activities. A wall of defenses is subsequently built up which protects the psyche against the reactivation of the infantile need for acceptance because of the fear of renewed traumatic rejection. Depending on the psychic location of the defenses, the resulting cleavage in the personality may be (1) a "vertical" split, which separates a whole segment of the psyche from the one that carries the central self and is manifested either by states of grandiosity that deny the frustrated need for approval, and/or states of low self-esteem or emptiness; and/or (2) a "horizontal" split, which is the result of repression and is manifested by coldness and remoteness.

The understanding of the vertically split-off segment of the psyche as carrier — albeit in disguised, distorted, and intensified form — of the original narcissistic configurations is of great significance for our therapeutic approach. We must remain aware that, although the split-off surface presentation is related to the thwarted infantile needs, the cruder manifestations should not be mistaken for the more authentic but repressed core.

The personality of Citizen Kane in Orson Welles's classic movie of 1940 affords a beautiful illustration of how the vertically split-off part of the psyche becomes the carrier of the repressed core needs. The overt aspects of his character — his bombast, arrogance, need for control, his addiction to wealth and power — represent the vertically split-off archaic grandiosity which aims both at preserving a precarious sense of self and providing an outlet for aspects of the thwarted needs. These same character traits also serve as a massive protection against the revelation of these underlying yearnings for love and approval. The authentic core of his libidinal wishes for human contact and concern is condensed in the conceit of "Rosebud," evocatively portrayed as a memory trace of a boy with his sled in an icy setting, which poignantly highlights the moment at which young Kane was separated from his mother. This was the crucial trauma that caused him to wall off his genuine needs for responsiveness and left his experiencing self forever frozen and empty.

The technical implication is that it is the "Rosebud" experience that has to be reengaged, and that the surface manifestations of Kane's character must not be confused with the quintessence of the narcissistic experience.

In therapy, it is quite obvious that certain patients need, at least initially, to reenact relationships with narcissistic parents who have been inadequately empathic. Other patients, however, present with extremely subtle forms of this deteriorated, although stable, compromise bond, and in these cases it is extremely important to distinguish between the overt and underlying narcissistic needs. The concept of the patient forming a narcissistic bond with the faultily empathic parent imagoes and then addictively seeking to reinstate this bond in treatment is comparable to Winnicott's (1960) formulation regarding the true and false self. The false self character emerges from the matrix of the patient's faulty infantile experiences with the mother. The false self is a consequence of the child's seduction into a compliant bond with the parent at the expense of nurturing his own spontaneous needs. It promotes a form of relationship which, like that resulting mainly from excessive disappointment in the originally needed selfobjects, provides an illusion of connectedness and self-maintenance, but is never genuinely enlivening or emotionally nurturing because the child's own self and his needs are walled off in a noncommunicating state (Winnicott, 1963). Accordingly, it is essential that the analyst recognize the forms of transference that emanate from the vertically split-off part of the psyche (or false self) because the transferences (really the defense transferences) which are established result in a form of relating that precludes the use of the object (or selfobject) (Winnicott, 1971).

I do not believe these comments effect a complete reconciliation of the work of Winnicott and Kohut, nor am I suggesting here that a one-to-one correlation in fact exists. Nevertheless I do believe that the concepts of the false self and of a vertically split-off part of the psyche can be linked in the context of the early development and adult presentation of certain patients encountered in psychoanalysis.

Although Kohut's work can be compared to, and at times

interdigitates with, the work of other contemporary theoreticians, he has made significant and unique contributions which have caused us to reexamine the nature of a host of clinical phenomena from the model of the theory of the self.

Kohut has reexamined the nature of drive manifestations, and has concluded that often what we are witnessing are not healthfully expressed, psychologically integrated biological (drive) urges but fragmented by-products which are hypercathected (often requiring secondary defenses) to provide relief from narcissistic tensions. Treatment in classical neuroses has stressed the defensive meanings of unneutralized drive demands, particularly when they appear to be regressive forms of drive fixations serving as retreats from later developmental conflicts. With our increased grasp of the central position of the self as the ultimate organizer in drive initiation and integration, we have recognized that common drive manifestations, at times appearing in crude sexual forms, should not be considered the core of the pathology. In many cases where self pathology is pivotal we will see the expression of drives as an attempt to remedy a disordered self, i.e., to counteract the feelings of inner depletion.

To illustrate a characterological attitude which becomes exaggerated and hypertrophied at crucial emotional moments, and which heretofore would have been considered indicative of a compromise between an anal-sadistic drive and defense components, let me cite the case of a patient who often referred to himself as being compulsive and "anal." One of his most painful early memories was of the time when he had had a bowel movement in his pants and his mother had called him a "dirty little piggy." What is of interest is that at times of potential humiliation in relation to his performance and acceptance by others, or following a rejection or lack of response from needed others, this patient became extremely contemptuous, emphasizing the sloth of his rejectors and assuming a more arrogant and hypercritical attitude. He felt himself to be far above a world which was grimy and semiliterate and which could not appreciate his ordered and perfectionistic mind.

In the total context of this young man's personality development and central anxiety — the feeling of being insufficiently valued in his own right and the fear of reexperiencing traumatic rejections in his attempts to gain acceptance and admiration for his own sense of uniqueness and individuality — we can see that the *emergency* shift in attitude has a meaning beyond that of anal-drive-and-defense explanations and includes larger affective reactions. To handle the excruciatingly painful sense of humiliation that accompanies a devalued sense of self, he shifts into a position that represents an admixture of identification with his perfectionistic mother and his self-righteous father. In this stance, he is able, with almost sadistic pleasure, to maintain temporarily his narcissistic balance and to redress present and past humiliations. It is true that the painful memory recalls the anal period, but we can now expand our understanding of character development by recognizing that the mother failed at this period to provide an acceptance for her young son's total body self, instead providing a conditional, selective approval based on more conventional, performance-oriented ideals. The narcissistic injury, as well as the rejection of her son during the crucial anal period, interfered with the development of a secure sense of self-acceptance and self-cohesion. To counteract the hurt, despair, and rage, the patient often turned to self-soothing activities, but he also developed a character style that exaggerated cleanliness and that could be extremely critical of shortcomings in others. This identificatory style was consistently hypercathected during periods of potential or actual narcissistic injury.

Another consideration of the present theory of the self concerns the role of affects and complex affect states, and how they influence final character formation. I shall restate the problem in terms of a dilemma. As mentioned previously, in line with the insights and implications of a separate developmental line of the self, it is considered theoretically and therapeutically unsound to begin analysis by focusing on resistances and interpreting defenses. Many of the patients we see, however, manifest strong but often subtly expressed defenses which, in turn, forestall deeper mobilization of authentic transferences and the intense frightening feeling states associated with the memory of early frustrations. We have, somehow, to reconcile the two horns of this dilemma. To date writings on narcissistic disorders have not sufficiently addressed the problem of conceptualizing techniques that would recognize the defensive structure, especially when it is specific and tenacious, while also acknowledging the fragility of the self, its vulnerability to criticism, its sensitivity to being reengaged with a self-serving parent in the form of the analyst, and its propensity for psychic imbalance.

At this juncture I should point out that one motive for developing a theory and technique of self pathology was to provide alternative explanations for clinical phenomena which, viewed from the structural model, were described as negative therapeutic reactions deriving from repressed conflicts over unconscious guilt and hostility.

To date most of the case illustrations by authors using the self model have described patients who, when provided with the proper atmosphere and acceptance, drop fairly readily their broad resistances and enter into stable narcissistic transferences. It is those patients who do not fall into this category, however, who now require our attention.

Fear of protracted fragmentation experiences and paralyzing apathetic depressions are often the cause of paranoid or schizoid organizations, suggesting that the patient is unanalyzable. Given the fact that, over time in treatment, many patients respond to the therapist's empathic receptiveness and eventually provide evidence of a sufficiently cohesive self and become analyzable, we now should confront the question whether our present theory of the self is sufficiently comprehensive to account for those particular patients who react paradoxically to the analyst's empathy. By confining our interpretations of these negative reactions and defensive postures to the patient's fear of merger to the analyst's empathic failure, do we not overlook a variety of other possible experiences which may require a wider range of explanations?

There are a number of patients who, while revealing the usual general resistances to mobilizing their deeper transference needs and making use of the analytic setting, evidence their greatest difficulty not in spite of the analyst's empathic attitude but, paradoxically, because of it. (I am referring to empathy here not only as a concept signifying the mode or tool by which we collect analytic data through introspection, but also as the attitude of the analyst as he communicates his understanding to the patient.) By analyzing such patients further, I believe we can provide satisfactory answers to critics of self theory who mistakenly assume that the self psychological model of treatment accounts for all unexplained, sudden disruptions in the analysis in terms of the analyst's empathic failures. For the patients I have in mind, the analyst's empathic stance awakens deeper experiences which the patient has longed for, but which have ultimately failed to be reliably satisfying in the past. Their current reaction, then, may be to withdraw, to distort the analyst's intent, or (temporarily) to react negatively, as by demonstrating increased "resistance" to the unfolding or deepening of the transference. Naturally, it requires the continued empathy of the analyst to understand the meaning of the patient's temporary imbalance and the genetic roots of this unexpected resistance. Nevertheless, the major point is that the patient's reaction reveals not just the problem of having been failed by his past infantile objects in his legitimate needs for their appropriate emotional availability, but also a continuing sensitivity to the dangers that an empathic atmosphere can remobilize.

After revealing a particularly shameful aspect of her life, a young woman patient appeared to feel touched by an emotional response I made in attempting to understand her feelings, both then and now. She left with tears in her eyes, but several hours later she called me, incensed at something I had said earlier in the hour. She felt I had related some material to my own experiences, in effect denying the reality of her own. I acknowledged this criticism, but her tone seemed to lack the bitter narcissistic rage and disappointment I had come to know so well in response to my previous empathic failures. I asked her if she had had any reaction to my emotional response at the end of the hour, and, startled, she replied that she could not remember it. After I reminded her of the moment, she said in an entirely altered tone of voice that it was unbelievable to her that she had forgotten it, and added that my understanding had made her very anxious. During the next few sessions she came back to this episode repeatedly, each time adding depth to our understanding. She found the thought that I really cared about her more disturbing than the safe experience of viewing me as detached. She then recovered memories and feelings of such great sadness and such unrequited yearnings for love from her mother that she felt overwhelmed. She learned that the greatest danger was to permit herself to feel cared about, to admit the intensity of this need, and then to recall with fear past occasions on which she had been forgotten and left alone with the intensified feelings of hurt, emptiness, and rage. The event of my previous emotional response helped us gain further insight into why a positive experience so quickly gave way to a negative or "spoiled" reaction. Heretofore we had understood her reaction as due to the feeling that the current positive responses were inadequate to overcome the feelings of underlying emptiness and unlovability. Now we could expand this insight to see that she almost automatically had to shift into a paradoxically negative view of the experience or the object in order to defend herself against more deeply feared affective states. The emphasis here is on the term "affective state," which may include melancholic depression, a sense of utter helplessness and despair, and primitive rage.

Currently at least, the self model seems to have categorized the dangers to which the self is exposed in terms of diffuse tension states and fragmentation threats. Kohut has referred to the masochistic bond as an indication of faulty empathy, a breakdown product consequent to failure in the early self-selfobject dyad. I agree with this view, but I also feel that the overdetermined motives for maintaining or repeating this form of bond have not yet been fully investigated. I see such a bond not only as a needed restitution, but as a defense against a primary depressive experience, one that can be activated not only by the loss of a "bad" object but also by the gratifications of an empathic one. I believe this restitutional relationship is rooted in the early parent-child experience and is addictively sought out — at times in the hope of reversing or mastering the original traumatic experience. Most significantly, these paradoxically negative reactions are frequently encountered and must therefore be understood in their total complexity, and this entails distinguishing them from reactions to empathic breaks. (Note how this differs from Kernberg [1976], who conceptualizes the relevant issues in terms of defenses against envy, greed, and oral sadism.)

Technically, I feel we need to conceptualize how best to intervene with such patients, and how best to preserve the delicate balance between the need to respect the restitutional organization as it protects the self and the eventual need to interpret this organization as a maladaptive defense posing as resistance. The matter of intervention in such cases is complicated, since maintaining the restitutional bond often precludes internal reorganization and, on the other hand, unempathic interpretations can prematurely lead to traumatic overwhelming of the patient's psyche.

Although in its strictest definition an empathic break may be occurring when the patient's equilibrium is disrupted following an intervention, it is not always a failure of an analyst's grasp or understanding that leads to this imbalance. The real test of the analyst's empathy is not his ability to protect his patient from reexperiencing the affect states that underlie the negative reaction, but his ability to understand and to help his patient recognize the intrapsychic source and genetic roots of these reactions. Through the further study of patients who have specific difficulties, at least initially, in making use of the analyst and the analytic setting, we can profitably broaden our discussions to explore both the analyst's as well as the patient's contributions to these negative reactions. Having so recently been released from the sterility of relying on only one major concept to explain unexpected resistances or regressions, we must now guard against an excess in the other direction and beware of assigning all responsibility to the analyst's failures.

Kohut (1977) postulates that, in the treatment of many patients, an understanding phase of therapy may have to precede an explanatory phase. This position challenges traditional theories of technique that favor an early interpretative approach to character resistance. According to Kohut, the patient who has self pathology needs a dependable selfobject to provide sufficient cohesion if he is to feel secure enough to accept interpretations about his character or the nature of his relationships with others. Negative reactions to resistance interpretations, such as lethargy, rage, or withdrawal, have been seen as signs of narcissistic imbalance, activated by the failure of the analyst to grasp the nature of the patient's transference needs. With reference to such reactions, Kohut differs from Hartmann (1950), who argued that the hostile reactions are confirmatory of the positive effect of resistance interpretations in that they signal an increased need for resistance to the acknowledgment of unacceptable drives. Although Kohut's understanding includes the recognition of the patient's needs and the motives for resistances, the emphasis of self psychology seems to be on empathic data gathering and the provision of an accepting atmosphere that allows the transference to unfold, rather than on the complexity of the defensive character organization. As a result of this focus on acceptance and spontaneous development, a misunderstanding may arise which unduly dichotomizes the understanding and explanatory phases. I feel we now have to redress the balance and study the role of the specific complex defensive organizations and the appropriate and tactful manner of interpretative interventions that derives from our understanding of these organizations.

We have yet to detail and spell out how we approach the important early and middle phases of treatment. I do not believe we can completely separate the understanding from the interpretative work. I do not believe it was Kohut's overall intent to maintain this division, but I do not think he has placed enough emphasis on the nature of the two-step process in the analyst's work.

Finally, I would like to comment on the specific affect of rage and its role in self pathology. I believe that positing narcissistic rage as a fragmentary by-product of frustrated but legitimate assertiveness or as an isolated drive experience secondary to the breakup of the self is to limit its role in the psychopathology of symptoms and character. While keeping the selfobject concept in its pivotal position, for example, we could speculate on a sequence of events in which disappointment in selfobjects leads to overwhelming affect states, including frightening rage, and these affect states, in turn, lead to feelings of fragmentation. A further consequence would be that, either as a result of defense or by decathexis, the patient gains an altered view of the object and of himself. This shift in conceptualizing the sequence would make the role of affects a more central one, rather than merely a secondary reaction to the breakup of the self.

A corollary would be that various aspects of character formation could be viewed as admixtures of attempts to maintain self organization and to control narcissistic and melancholic rage. As against the view that the bedrock of self pathology is not rage (i.e., not a constitutionally given, innate aggression) but the early sense of hopelessness and despair in not being responded to, rage may have a larger part to play than has to date been considered in the pathology of the self.

The following case will illustrate to what extent the character of a patient can be overlaid by reactive hostility. My intention is to show that it is not only the repressed needs of the unmirrored core self (horizontal split) that find a distorted outlet in the open grandiosity of the vertical split, but also the damaging effects of unintegrated and walled-off narcissistic rage that find expression in this outlet and can markedly influence the capacity to relate to and be sustained by others.

A male patient sought analytic help for problems which included uncertainty about his own sense of purpose and initiative, but centered around his inability to maintain a positive feeling for any one woman. His pattern was to provide himself with a steady source of admiration by successfully wooing an endless number of girls. His ability to ensure a response was in part based on a formula that had evolved from childhood experiences with his mother. Not being sure that his spontaneous, genuine masculine assertiveness would be accepted by his mother, he had learned most artfully how to create an image harmonious with her conscious and unconscious expectations. This image, reminiscent of Winnicott's (1960) "false self," involved being a sensitive, warm intuiter of the needs of women. He used this part of his personality in an almost addictive fashion to gain the responses needed to counter his gradually revealed feelings of uncertainty, lack of a sense of direction, and intense but mostly buried and denied rage. On receiving the desired responses, he immediately shifted into partially rationalized but nevertheless bewildering feelings of contempt and scorn for the girl, who was then felt to be inadequate to his intellect and sensibilities. His urgency to rid himself of this devalued object was checked only by feelings of duty and guilt. He reported noting that often, as soon as he had succeeded in having intercourse with a girl for the first time, he would be overcome with these sudden, unexplained, rageful feelings toward her. Beyond the explanation that the girl, once conquered, proved disappointing and inadequate to fill his underlying emptiness, we concluded that deep feelings of hurt and rage were always present, and the need for admiring responses from women was an attempt to curb their expression. It was not simply a rage emerging out of the current disappointment, but a chronic, embittered reaction stemming from infantile experiences in which his mirroring needs had been subordinated to the needs of his mother. The women he now seduced into forced mirroring were already transference figures. The sequence of performance and response was an attempt to counter his feelings of injury and rage, but the latter would inevitably leak out in the bewildering aftermath. Following separations (vacations) he complained of my incompetence and ineffectiveness and made plans to leave me. Interpretation of his dreams around these vacations led to an increased understanding of his earlier experiences. It then became clearer that his contempt for me was a manifestation of his reactive hostility and represented a shift into an identification with an aspect of the mother of his childhood. He had felt seduced into a relationship as an extension of her, and then abruptly dropped or unexpectedly criticized.

Here, in the transference, we could see the overdetermined nature of his character development and the multiple factors contributing to his identification as both the narcissistic, performing extension of his mother and then as the ultimate rejector. The attempt to gain gratification for his originally thwarted needs and to curb his chronic injured self found partial outlets in these shifting identifications. In disdaining the women who responded to him in the present, however, he repeatedly rendered them useless as sources of genuine gratification, and he continued to feel isolated and empty. Rage, here, is a major source feeding this complex personality, and to recognize its genetic origin as a reaction to the thwarted needs of the emergent self may be crucial to undoing its distorting effects on the patient's current object relations. This understanding, in turn, may influence treatment in that the reworking of affects and especially the provision of new structures (internalized selfobjects) for managing affective states may be of great significance in a number of patients.

Summary

There are of course many other areas that could be explored but in closing I would like to make the following remark. Although I have critically examined areas of character pathology that I feel have been neglected, I feel in overall harmony with a great deal of Kohut's position. It seems that if our patients are to relive and ultimately rework states of traumatic disappointment and narcissistic injury then their original needs (whether of a dependent, symbiotic, or narcissistic sort) must be mobilized. Only in this context will the reactive feelings of loss, rage, and fragmentation be most compassionately understood. Our ultimate goal is eventually to give meaning to heretofore irrational behavior and thereby to lead to internal changes in microstructures.

The theory of the self has already made significant contributions to psychoanalytic thinking. Its acceptance as an alternative explanation for a variety of clinical phenomena has extensive ramifications for all aspects of current theory and technique. We are now in a position to study in greater detail and in greater depth how the new emphasis provided by the self model affects our established views of all the essential components of the psychoanalytic process. In turn, self psychology has to be extended to encompass the complexities and subtleties that are unique to different patients and their treatment needs. In this paper I have attempted to consider some modifications and amplifications that should be made to extend the present concepts of self psychology to include a wider range of approaches to character and defense analysis.

References

Hartmann, H. (1950), Comments on the Psychoanalytic Theory of the Ego. In: *Essays on Ego Psychology.* New York: International Universities Press, 1964, pp. 113–141.

Kernberg, O. (1976), *Object Relations Theory and Clinical Psychoanalysis.* New York: Aronson.

Kohut, H. (1971), *The Analysis of the Self.* New York: International Universities Press.

—————— (1977), *The Restoration of the Self.* New York: International Universities Press.

Winnicott, D. W. (1960), Ego Distortion in Terms of True and False Self. In: *The Maturational Processes and the Facilitating Environment.* New York: International Universities Press, 1965, pp. 140–152.

—————— (1963), Communicating and Not Communicating Leading to a Study of Certain Opposites. In: *The Maturational Processes and the Facilitating Environment.* New York: International Universities Press, 1965, pp. 179–192.

—————— (1971), The Use of an Object. *Internat. J. Psycho-Anal.,* 50:711–716.

Discussion

Perspectives on Self and Theory

SHELDON BACH

I am impressed with Dr. Schwaber's clinical acumen, sensitivity, and her skillful and empathic handling of the case of Mr. R. She raises certain specific questions about the case which, as we know, have larger implications: Was the analysis prematurely terminated? Was the oedipal transference analyzed or even engaged? Were the anxiety and aggression absorbed in acting out? and so forth. I do not propose to address these issues directly, although I must note my admiration for Dr. Schwaber's awareness of the problems and her candid report, in the best clinical tradition, of her pragmatic and experimental testing of alternative approaches.

But instead of discussing theory, I would prefer to turn to the clinical material itself, in the hope that when examined closely it may suggest a view that can supplement the one Dr. Schwaber proposes.

As I began to look and listen more closely to the data, I became impressed with the fact that Mr. R. was also a looker and listener, a gifted photographer and a musician. The striking shift in competence at age 12 or 13 occurred when he was encouraged by a particular teacher to become interested in photography and music. He reported that when looking at pictures or listening to tapes of himself before the age of 13, he experienced dizziness, detachment, tremor, and headaches. One might say that we are presented here with a discontinuity or gap in development, the first 12 or 13 years being correlated in the patient's fantasy with weakness, incompetence, shyness, and psychosomatic disintegration, that is, with dizziness, tremor, and headaches, and the subsequent 10 years preceding analysis being correlated with a newly found ability in gymnastics, a new feeling of competence, new interests, and the sense of a mission in life, accomplished by means of an audio-visual synthesis and reintegration.

Let me anticipate my point by calling Mr. R.'s new sense of engagement a fantasy of rebirth, and referring to the frightening gap as a fantasy of the death of the self — thus, a fantasy of death and rebirth at a higher level of integration.

This is, of course, the theme of the film *2001,* which is about two rebirths. In the first episode, occurring four million years ago, we see how a group of prehominids achieve a higher level of visual-motor coordination and become men through the intervention of a mysterious slab or teaching machine sent by a higher civilization somewhere in the universe.

The major part of the film, which takes place in the millenium 2000, deals with modern man, who has become the master of technology but remains an animal at heart. On a space trip to the moon, another mysterious slab is found which indicates that man should proceed to Saturn. On this subsequent trip, the computer, symbolizing man's guilty and murderous nature, goes beserk and, in a veritable world-destruction fantasy, kills everyone aboard except young David Bowman, who manages to deactivate it and assume control. Our hero then passes through the Star Gate and is taken in charge by mysterious forces who give him a glimpse of unimaginable vistas of space and time, of the cosmic scale of life. He then experiences a death and rebirth; he regresses, dies, is reborn as a cosmic embryo star-child, and begins his journey back to Earth where he will arrive in the year 2001 as the new Messiah, Nietzsche's Superman, a harbinger of the next transformation and metamorphosis of mankind. All this takes place to the musical accompaniment of Strauss's *Thus Spake Zarathustra.*

The film's creator, Stanley Kubrick, whom the patient so idealized, is also the son of a doctor and was also a magazine photographer before he turned to films at the age of 22, the age at which Mr. R. came for analysis because he did not feel well enough to continue work as a magazine photographer. If, as I have suggested, the age of 12 had witnessed a fantasied first rebirth from prehominid to human, or child to adolescent, then his coming to analysis at 22, just before graduation, a decade or millenium afterwards, was to witness a second rebirth from human to superhuman, or from adolescence to manhood. With the help of Dr. Schwaber, playing the new Eve to his new Adam, he could now go off to create film-babies which would carry both their names, and indeed he reports his first successful production nine months after the termination date had been set.

I will not belabor the obvious implications of this material but shall instead turn to a question that interests us no less than it interested Mr. R. Given the two segments of his life, the prepubertal, in which he experienced himself as weak, uncoordinated, incompetent, and from which he felt cut off, and the rebirn, more highly coordinated and competent postpubertal segment: How is one to get a perspective on or to integrate and synthesize these fantasies or aspects of self? I propose a related question as well. How is one to get a perspective on or to integrate and synthesize the discontinuity between the inner, subjective, or emotional life from which Mr. R. felt cut off, and the outer, objective life of reality in which his task was clear? Yet one final question may also be raised. Given the empathic, selfobject, or "systems" mode of analysis that Dr. Schwaber has so skillfully employed and so beautifully described in her paper, and given the external, objective, systematic knowledge *about* people which we have accumulated in almost a century of psychoanalytic research and which enables us to entertain conclusions about the patient's dynamics simply from hearing the scenario of his favourite film — how are we to gain perspective on or to synthesize and integrate these two modes of observation or knowing? I believe that it was partly in an effort to achieve such a synthesis that the patient first came to analysis, and I would be happy if, in our effort to understand this, we were to achieve even a small part of the satisfaction that the patient so clearly obtained from his treatment.

Let us then return to the patient as photographer, keeping in mind not only the dynamic connection between scoptophilia, exhibitionism, and fantasies of birth, rescue, and primal scene, but also the particular value of photography as a transitional or restitutional phenomenon, a bridge between self and object. For this patient, the distal receptors of sight and sound played a far more prominent role than the proximal receptors of touch, taste, smell, and even proprioception, as we might expect from an infant who apparently lacked close mothering and cried continually for the first year and a half of life. Indeed, the regressive longing and fear that overwhelmed Mr. R. when looking at pictures or hearing tapes of himself as a child before the age of 13 was expressed as a regression from the distal to the proximal senses, with symptoms of dizziness, tremor, and headache; a regression from a more adult to a more childlike mode of being. It was obviously one of the great achievements of the analysis that he could learn to cry again, to feel the lump in his throat, and to dream of being kissed and kissing the analyst in return.

Dr. Schwaber has suggested that for this patient "the eye was hypercathected as touch was minimized," and I would only add that the audio-visual system, the usual distal receptors, were made to function in both a distal and proximal mode, allowing the patient in his particular way to be both near and far and thus to create his own distance and space within the world. Two examples should illustrate what I mean.

Among his symptoms Mr. R. reports "detachment...a feeling of being very far removed from things." Recalling his childhood, "When he thought of himself in his classroom he felt as though he were not on the same plane as the others — [but rather] higher up, looking down and photographing." The perceptual experience being described is that the patient is large in size and observing from a distance an object which is small and far away. In the language of the cinema this is called a "long shot," in the language of clinical psychiatry it is called "micropsia," and in the language of psychoanalysis it is known as "Gulliver" or "Lilliputian" fantasies." In my experience these distortions of size constancy reflect distortions of self constancy. They tend to occur in patients with problems of the self and are often related to the mirroring transferences and states of grandiosity, whether defensive or developmental. The world is, as it were, "all me."

The opposite perceptual experience is one in which the patient is very small in size and observing from nearby an object which is magnified and enormous. In the language of the cinema this is called a "'close-up," in the language of clinical psychiatry "macropsia," and in the language of psychoanalysis "Brobdingnagian fantasies." Here we may recall Gulliver's reaction:

> I must confess no object ever disgusted me so much as the sight of her monstrous breast. . . . It stood prominent six foot, and could not be less than sixteen in circumference. The nipple was about half the bigness of my head, and the hue both of that and the dug so varified with spots, pimples, and freckles, that nothing could appear more nauseous. . . . This made me reflect upon the fair skins of our English ladies, who appear so beautiful to us, only because they are of our own size, and their defects not to be seen but through a magnifying glass, where we find by experiment that the smoothest and whitest skins look rough and coarse, and ill coloured [Swift, 1726, pp. 294–295].

We may contrast this defensive Swiftian disgust reaction with Baudelaire's poem, "La Géante," in which he dreams of curling up like a Lilliputian on the maternal giantess, peaceful and secure in the valley between her mountainous breasts. Here the mood of quiet elation reminds us of Mr. R.'s description of comparable moods: "It's an experience of all of a sudden my sensibilities becoming really heightened, like I'll notice the pores of someone's skin and it looks great, and I want to take a picture and catch it . . ." This mood is most clearly expressed in his relation to the cinema: "As a child, I couldn't wait to be taken to a movie; I approached it with a certain reverence. . . . I've come to see my intense love of films as coming from feeling inconsequential, small . . ."

Here the subjective feeling of smallness, the close-up view of a giantess with enlarged pores, or a silver screen or dream screen

filled with a larger than life image, the mood of reverence or elation, all suggest aspects of the idealizing transference or, as in the
passage from Gulliver just quoted, of defenses against the idealizing transference.

Ferenczi, who in 1926 first remarked on such distortions of
self and object size constancy, noted their relationship to fantasies
of rescue, rebirth, and also of incest: the little man, substituting
his whole body for his phallus, can sleep with impunity on the
body of the giantess and even be reborn in her womb without fear
of castration. Phyllis Greenacre (1955), in a later consideration of
such phenomena, has connected them especially with creative personalities such as our patient, and emphasized the importance of
anal fantasies and above all the family romance, but tempting
though it is to pursue this path, I am afraid it would take me well
beyond the limits of this discussion.

The patient is a photographer, and his developmental history
and possibly genetic endowment obliged him to become his own
self-regulator and to concentrate on mastery and control through
the distal senses. I have tried to describe his two perceptual modes,
the "close-up" and the "long shot," which enabled him respectively
to maintain a connection and to achieve distance, to be one and to
be separate, in the language of rapprochement to "shadow" his object and to "dart away" and, most essentially, to work in the
idealizing transference, where the subject is small or relevant only
as part of the larger object, and to work in the mirroring
transference where the object is small or relevant only as part of
the larger subject. I summarize these modes somewhat crudely,
leaving it to the reader to make the necessary amplifications and
corrections on the basis of his own experience.

What I am arriving at, however, are two modes of perception
or ways of knowing: the first, as if one were part of what is being observed or known, and the second, as if one were separate from what
is being observed or known. The first is the empathic, subjective,
selfobject mode, the "contextual unit" as Dr. Schwaber calls it. The
second is the detached, objective mode which has characterized the
triumph of 20th-century science, but which is beginning to present
difficulties of its own even in the physical sciences.

This problem of multiple ways of knowing has been considered by the great minds of the century and remains, I believe, as yet unresolved. It has been characterized in many ways: as a problem of self-reference, going back to the original statement by Epimenides the Cretan that all Cretans are liars; as a problem of perspective summed up in the statement by Niels Bohr that "we are both actors and spectators in the drama of our existence"; and as a problem of empathy versus causality, or of understanding versus explanation.

Among the psychologists, it was perhaps Piaget who first insisted that the child is confronted with a double or complementary task: of establishing a sense of self as a center for action and thought, and of viewing this self in the context of other selves as a thing among things. What is required is both a subjectification and an objectification, two different perspectives on the "same" self. Further consideration suggests that there may indeed be a multiplicity of such perspectives because, since the self is both subject and object of self-perception, the partition between observer and observed may be drawn at an infinite number of positions and may shift from one moment to the next.

Indeed, I believe that for all of us, the relation between observer and observed is constantly shifting, from moments when we are totally absorbed in something and unaware of ourselves, to moments when we are acutely conscious of ourselves as if we were observing ourself from the outside or through another's eyes.

In all cases of self pathology that I have seen, there seems to be some fundamental disturbance in this mechanism. Either the patient is acutely aware of himself and has lost the ability to become absorbed or concentrate, or he is totally self-absorbed and unable to view himself objectively or, most commonly, there is a disturbance in his ability to use these two modes in a flexible, integrated, and appropriate manner, with particular difficulties at the points of transition.

The case of Mr. R. provides instances of this latter type. For example, the patient at first views his whole childhood from a detached and "objective" perspective. When he remembers vomiting and asking mother: "Am I going to miss Lassie?" he sees this as "cute" and unimportant, that is, he sees himself objectively through the eyes of his fantasied mother rather than experiencing himself subjectively as a child. Conversely, when totally absorbed in the wonders of photography, he mentions a psychiatrist who gave up his profession to become a photographer, he is in a state of subjective awareness and cannot make the transition to the analyst's objective response.

Naturally, in retrospect we can see that what was needed was a mirroring response to validate his self-absorption; the objective response that the doctor is going on vacation, that the patient is just one person among others, and that the analyst has her own needs is *incomprehensible* and, indeed, he does not understand what she means. Although the crucial issue is no doubt separation, the analyst was emphasizing Mr. R.'s fear of her loss of interest, whereas I believe that what Mr. R. was experiencing was the *closeness* which he wanted to freeze, photographically, like a beautiful sunset. Perhaps when his parents went away on vacations they came back with photographs which became transitional or restitutional phenomena. Loving his analyst the way he does, he is incapable of understanding how she could not feel that way too—how she could not love photography as much as he does.

I should make it clear that such misunderstandings are inevitable and serve a useful purpose; Dr. Schwaber has emphasized them precisely in order to provide us with food for thought. My point is that the patient has difficulty in moving from a subjective to an objective view of himself or, conversely, from an objective to a subjective view of himself.

I believe that this can be seen not only as a defense against narcissistic humiliation, rage, and separation anxiety, which it is, but also as a cognitive difficulty, a developmental problem which makes the switch from subjective to objective self-awareness and back again so difficult for these patients and deprives them of the freedom to move flexibly back and forth among multiple perspectives on themselves and their objects.

Those who have been subjected to home movies made by a beginner, so typically filled with out-of-focus close-ups, with heads or arms or other body parts cut off, with abrupt switches to long shots where something is going on but the action is too far away to be comprehensible — those individuals will have some idea of the phenomenal world of these patients and their difficulties in focusing, modulating, and making transitions between subjective and objective self-awareness. With these patients, the camera of the self has not yet achieved a stable homeostasis. It is the analyst, as an empathic and modulating selfobject, who fills the gaps in the continuum that will eventually allow for smooth and reversible transitions between the subjective and objective perspectives, between the inner and the outer, and between self and object.

And it is this function that Dr. Schwaber has so beautifully performed, not by editing the patient's footage, nor yet by directing his shots, but rather by providing the fluid, transitional medium in which he could learn to regulate himself — to join, to separate, and to develop his unique set of multiple perspectives on himself and his object world.

I have tried in this discussion to supplement Dr. Schwaber's paper and to emphasize a complementary approach that will bring together both the old and the new, the subjective and objective perspectives in psychoanalysis, just as the patient was trying to articulate subjective and objective perspectives, to bring together the parts of his life, and to be reborn in some higher synthesis. This issue presents as many problems and as much excitement for psychoanalytic theory as it does for each individual analysis and, like the analyses, it promises to be a fascinating, despairing, joyful, conflictual, and ever unfinished task.

References

Ferenczi, S. (1926), Gulliver Fantasies. In: *Final Contributions to the Problems and Methods of Psycho-Analysis*. London: Hogarth Press, 1955.

Greenacre, P. (1955), *Swift and Carroll: A Psychoanalytic Study of Two Lives*. New York: International Universities Press.

Swift, J. (1726), *Travels into Several Remote Nations of the World by Lemuel Gulliver*. In: *The Portable Swift,* ed. C. Van Doren. New York: Viking, 1948.

Discussion

Self Psychology and Applied Psychoanalysis

MILES F. SHORE

With disarming simplicity, Dr. Schwaber has made a radical assertion with regard to our understanding of psychopathology. At least in the specific area of pathology of the self, she has invited reality into the consulting room. Selfobjects, "those archaic objects cathected with narcissistic libido... which are still in intimate connection with the archaic self" (Kohut, 1971, p. 3) are assigned a role as co-participants with the self in the organization and perception of intrapsychic experience. She also implies that the separation between self psychology and structural-dynamic psychology may be difficult to maintain in practice and that the influence of selfobjects may be manifest in all transferences.

Dr. Schwaber's introductory remarks and illustrative case material are clearly intended to establish two matters. First, she presents the familiar idea that the breakdown of emotionally important relationships constitutes a threat which must be dealt with by the psychological means available to the individual. Second, she offers the novel idea that the capacity to deal with emotional distress is itself interfered with by a breakdown of important relationships. Thus, like the cell whose metabolic activity requires the proper osmotic and electrolyte environment, the self is dependent for effective regulation of experience upon the ambient climate of selfobject relationships. Dr. Schwaber is careful to restrict the

289

compass of her paper to the consulting room and the delicate nuances of the transference contained within it. Emboldened by Kohut's recommendation of playfulness in scientific inquiry (1977, pp. 206–207), I would like to foray outside that hermetic setting to explore the way in which one aspect of reality may be illuminated by the concept Dr. Schwaber has described.

Traditional psychoanalytic theory has been uneasy about reality. The mechanical model of metapsychology implies an impermeable boundary between the mental apparatus and the outside world. Cathexis emanates from the person and attaches itself to outside objects. When those objects fail, the released cathexis and the secondary aggression must be dealt with by the metabolism of grief work so that new objects can be cathected. The slings and arrows of existence are conceived of as outside forces to be dealt with by an apparatus with a structural configuration and functional capacities reflecting innate potential and developmental experience.

In this model, psychopathology results when the adaptive capabilities of the mental apparatus are exceeded by the demands of the external situation. This may be because the reality is more demanding than the expected average as in repeated traumatic losses, or extreme social environments such as concentration camps, combat, and certain forms of higher education. The imbalance between capacity and demand may also result from vulnerabilities in the apparatus. These may reflect a generalized "ego deficiency" disease as in the psychoses and borderline states or more localized areas of vulnerability to the revival of unresolved conflicts as in the neuroses and neurotic character problems. Ego regression may take place in certain situations of extreme imbalance but this, too, is explained as reflecting ego impairment, that is, a basic flaw in the construction of the apparatus.

Thus, the traditional model postulates the existence of an imaginary machine, a psychic apparatus with its individual attributes vis-à-vis a reality conceived as a system with its own forces and dynamics, completely separate from the individual.

This model has come under increasing attack from a number of quarters and for a variety of reasons. Roy Schafer (1976) has taken issue with the mechanistic metaphor which, he contends, has captured psychoanalytic thinking and destructively distorted our perception of psychological events in vivo. Ethicists have long been offended by a schema that seemed to discount free will. During the social revolution of the 1960s, the traditional model drew heavy fire for a melange of social and political reasons. Institutions were being held accountable by young people and by the socially disadvantaged for most human unhappiness. A psychological system that seemed to blame the victim was ripe for challenge. And, of course, the identification of psychoanalysis as a treatment primarily for the well-to-do and educated made it a natural target.

The role of the environment in causing mental illness now, as then, is hotly debated. But the debate is largely political and politicized. Its very vehemence has tended to obscure the fact that there *are* certain psychological phenomena which the traditional model has not accommodated very well. They are phenomena that reflect the surprising responsiveness of behavior and psychological regulatory processes to external forces. Let me give you some examples.

A research project in geriatrics was being organized in a psychoanalytically oriented department of psychiatry in a major teaching hospital. The research group consisted of the chairperson of the department, who was in the final year before retirement, the associate head of the department, the chief psychologist, a consultant in geriatrics, and several ambitious junior staff psychiatrists. It was primarily a clinical department; very little organized research had been done there and the leaders of the team were therefore inexperienced in this sort of activity, even though the chairperson was a distinguished analyst and teacher. All of the members of the team were analysts, or had been analyzed, except for the junior members who were advanced analytic candidates. Meetings of this group were protracted and diffuse. The developing research protocols which were assigned to junior staff members were criticized and revised endlessly, but never completed. The members of the team, particularly the junior ones, became increasingly frustrated and depressed and began to compete with one another for recognition by the seniors. There were feelings that some members of the junior staff were favored over others; friendships of many years were strained and in some cases permanently impaired.

The participants in this project were strongly motivated, talented, and mature people who were sensitive to their own and others' motivations by reason of their basic personalities and extensive training. Yet their self-esteem, their appreciation of each other, and their mood and behavior deteriorated strikingly in this poorly organized group effort.

I submit that the traditional psychoanalytic model has difficulty in dealing with this rather striking reaction. It could be formulated as follows: The chairperson and associate chairperson reacted to the former's imminent retirement by resolving to work on one last joint project. The content of this project was related to the impending retirement, but neither person had the requisite skills to implement it. Their criticisms of the junior members reflected both a displacement of their own limitations in research and their envy of youth and ambition. This situation in turn stirred up oedipal strivings and sibling rivalry among the junior staff, each member of which was scrambling to be the favorite junior person. But what in this traditional formulation accounts for the extent of the depression and the loss of self-esteem? Most significant, how is it that these well-motivated people, whose psychic machinery was not only well constructed but had been so finely tuned, could not accommodate each other more easily and arrive at an understanding of their common external problem?

A second relevant example of the limitations of traditional psychoanalytic explanations emerges from studies of bereavement and natural disasters. In 1970, Bennet reported the results of a controlled study of survivors of the floods in Bristol, England, that had occurred in 1968. He found in 12 months an increase in morbidity and a 50 percent increase in mortality in people whose homes had been flooded as compared with those whose homes were not affected. Even more impressive are studies by Rees and Lutkins (1967) of a small community in Wales. A cohort of 903 close relatives of patients who had recently died were identified as experimental subjects. Eight hundred and seventy-eight subjects from the same community matched for age, sex, and marital status were used as a control group. During the year of bereavement, the death rate in the bereaved subjects was seven times that of the controls. Finally, the well-known recent work of Holmes and Masuda (1974) indicates that the risk of developing physical illness is correlated with the severity of life change. In these studies life changes are rated and a cumulative score developed that could be correlated with risk. Changes include not only obvious loss of important objects such as the death of a spouse. Changes such as a job change, the move from one house to another, and even ordinary traffic violations also are weighted as significant events.

Traditional structural-dynamic theory can account for the loss of a spouse or other strongly and specifically cathected objects. I think it is less capable, however, of explaining convincingly the effect of house flooding, changes of home or job, and many of the other more general life changes which have been shown to affect the individual.

A third set of data which is not well explained by traditional theory derives from the observations of individuals in extreme isolation. In the latter part of the 19th century Captain Joshua Slocum of Fairhaven, Massachusetts, wrote a classic true adventure story entitled "Sailing Alone Around the World" (1905). As promised by the title, it described his solo circumnavigation of the earth in a 40-foot sailing vessel, the Spray. On the evening of July 26, 1895, sailing in high winds to the leeward of the island of Pico in the Azores, he developed abdominal pain after a meal of White Pico cheese and plums. As he put it, "When I came to as I thought from my swoon. . .to my amazement I saw a tall man at the helm. His rigid hand, grasping the spokes of the wheel, held them as in a vise. His rig was that of a foreign sailor, and the large red cap he wore was cockbilled over his left ear, and all was set off with shaggy black whiskers. . . . 'Señor' said he, doffing his cap, "I have come to do you no harm. . . I am one of Columbus's crew.' He continued 'I am the pilot of the Pinta come to aid you. You did wrong, Captain, to mix cheese with plums'" (Slocum, 1905, p. 51). Slocum's was a particularly colorful account of hallucinations in response to fever, fatigue, and social isolation. His observations have been frequently replicated, though less artfully reported, by other solitary voyagers on the sea and in space.

This demonstration of the intimate relationship between intact ego functioning and social input does not fit easily with the traditional model of a psychic apparatus that functions separately from the environment.

Dr. Schwaber's paper presents a different model of psychic functioning and psychopathology. She posits a close *interdependence* between self and objects in a *system,* the selfobject, which is the unit of functioning and the locus of psychopathology.

She has presented us with detailed and empathically derived clinical material that documents the characteristics of the selfobject within the vicissitudes of the psychoanalytic situation. She makes it abundantly clear that the self is exquisitely sensitive to changes in the selfobject climate in the analytic situation, changes that follow the different developmental stages of the self that are recapitulated during therapy. Assuming the hazardous prerogative of a discussant, I would like to pursue this idea a little further without, I hope, doing violence to her fascinating assertion.

It seems to me that the selfobject provides us with a bridge between the individual and reality that can help to conceptualize certain hitherto mysterious connections. Let me return to the examples which I have already presented.

As Levinson (1976, pp. 71–73) has pointed out, the leader must merge his or her own ego ideal with that of the organization in order to set organizational goals. These are cathected by individuals in the organization to bind aggression and to channel self-aggrandizing energy in constructive directions. A complex set of dynamic adjustments takes place which makes the organization extremely important to its members and which adds up to the meaning of work for the individual. In the process, leaders become invested by members of the organization with narcissistic libido and they take on certain of the characteristics of selfobjects. The essential psychological functions of leaders include mirroring, i.e., evaluating the performance of their subordinates in an atmosphere of basic approval and admiration. They also serve as models for idealization by virtue of their embodiment of the goals and their technical skills. This psychological role of leaders is particularly characteristic of organizations of professionals where there is inevitably a much more intense and precarious balance between narcissistic aims and organizational goals.

In my first example, the leaders were intensely invested as selfobjects by the junior staff. The juniors understood the importance of the project to the leaders. They saw it as an unusual opportunity to be close to the leaders, to learn how to do research, to perform well, and to be praised for it. The research was seen as a vehicle for their advancement within the department and the profession. The problem was that the leaders were unable to provide either satisfactory mirroring or an opportunity for idealization. Their lack of adequate research skills coupled with their own depression and sense of impending loss made it impossible for them to provide their young colleagues with the selfobject functions which were essential to maintain relationships in that group in a robust state of health. In that climate of selfobject failure, the junior staff responded with disappointment, diminished self-esteem, depression, and some projection. They lost their sense of where they stood in the department, what their role was, and what their future prospects might be. Their capacity to function in that group was heavily dependent on their relationship with the leaders by virtue of their investment of the leaders with narcissistic libido.

In a similar way, one can understand the devastating psychological effects of natural disasters and life changes. We all live in a rich and nutrient broth of selfobjects. Our edges overlap a great variety of narcissistically invested things and places as well as people. Our favorite chair, a painting with special personal appeal, a faithful car and its hard-won parking spot — all of these help us to orient ourselves and know who we are. They express our aspirations and they gratify us by being available for that purpose. When they are taken away or damaged or fail us in some way, we lose something of ourselves. Hell hath no fury like the person whose office is reduced in size, whose parking spot is given to someone else, or whose Volvo fails to start. And, of course, loss of home, of neighborhood, or of familiar people means a loss of some part of ourselves with clearly discernible consequences on our ability to function.

Finally, the data from sensorially deprived individuals make the point from a slightly different perspective. Slocum was sailing alone in heavy weather. The Spray, his beloved companion, could, with properly set sheets and rudder, sail herself for long periods of time, but not necessarily in a storm. Slocum's life depended on his own capacity to make the necessary adjustments, day or night. The interpenetration of his self with the Spray was so complete that he would awaken in response to shifts in the wind and sea to change the trim of the boat. His greatest enemy was incapacity to respond effectively. No wonder that his illness resulted in a projection of the highly cathected lost part of the functioning self onto the comforting and protective hallucinatory helmsman who would steer the boat while he recovered.

Most innovators in our field suffer more from their admirers than from their critics. Critics, however hostile, sharpen one's thinking and elaborate one's subsequent presentation of ideas in very useful ways. Well-meaning enthusiasts may inflate ideas to the point that they float off into space, freed from their attachment to the solid ground of clinical data.

Self psychology derives from close attention to the nuances of sensitive analytic work with patients. Its originators have been admirably circumspect, as Dr. Schwaber has been, in keeping close to its origins in the microscopic study of the transference. Its units are small and delicate and it would be a disservice to distort them by enlargement, or to transfer them to alien environments where they cannot survive. Nonetheless, concepts whose effectiveness in the analytic situation is explained by a developmental theory must have some form of existence in the world outside the consulting room. If psychoanalysis is to be more than a metaphorical art, we must be able to observe phenomena in ordinary behavior that reflect and verify our theoretical constructs. The fact that the various wavelengths of light can be measured only by special instruments does not make a rainbow either less real or less beautiful. The idea that the self depends in part for its shape and function on the close environment of narcissistically invested objects, though derived from the very special conditions of the analytic situation, may help us to understand significant phenomena in other settings.

Great care will be necessary in translating such an idea from one setting to another in order to avoid the overinflation that has characterized similar attempts in the past. Such care has been admirably demonstrated by Dr. Schwaber's paper. There is much to learn from her approach.

References

Bennet, G. (1970), Bristol Floods 1968: Controlled Survey of Effects on Health of Local Community Disaster. *Brit. Med. J.,* 3:454–458.

Holmes, H. T. & Masuda, M. (1974), Life Change and Illness Susceptibility. In: *Stressful Life Events: Their Nature and Effects,* ed. B. S. Dohrenwend & B. P. Dohrenwend. New York: Wiley.

Kohut, H. (1971), *The Analysis of the Self.* New York: International Universities Press.

_____ (1977), *The Restoration of the Self.* New York: International Universities Press.

Levinson, H. (1976), *Psychological Man.* Cambridge, Mass.: Levinson Institute.

Rees, W. D. & Lutkins, S. A. (1967), Mortality of Bereavement. *Brit. Med. J.,* 4:13–16.

Schafer, R. (1976), *A New Language for Psychoanalysis.* New Haven: Yale University Press.

Slocum, J. (1905), *Sailing Alone Around the World.* Westvaco, 1969.

The Borderline Personality: Its Makeup and Analyzability

PAUL TOLPIN

Brief Review and Overview

Despite the abundance of literature on the subject in recent years, there remains a continuing lack of agreement about the essential nature of the borderline personality. Beginning in 1953, when the designation "borderline" was popularized by Robert Knight, the term has been used to describe a diverse group of patients whose illnesses did not fit the descriptive categories of the neuroses or psychoses, but manifested certain characteristics of both types of disturbance. Over the years the borderline syndrome has increasingly become a catch-all diagnosis comprising a variety of manifestly diverse disturbances ranging from schizophreniclike illnesses, in which gross mental functioning is impaired and a gross break with consensus reality prevails, to more subtle, neuroticlike disturbances in which defensive capabilities conceal a more malignant organization of the personality. In some borderline types the diagnosis is considered dependent on pathognomonic psychological test findings. Furthermore, because the diagnostic category is usually related to social and behavioral manifestations in which the difficulty of clinical management or treatment has figured prominently, there has not been a clear consensus regarding the pathogenesis of the disturbance. In fact this difficulty in reaching a consensus may in part derive from the loose organizational unity of this syndrome.

In 1975, Gunderson and Singer summarized several consensus features "that most... authors believe characterize most borderline persons." These were: (1) the presence of intense affect, usually of a strongly hostile or depressed nature; (2) a history of impulsive behavior ranging from episodic acts of self-mutilation to drug dependency; (3) manifestly good social adaptiveness; (4) brief psychotic experiences, often of paranoid quality; (5) disturbed (bizarre, dereistic, illogical, or premature) responses on unstructured tests (Rorschach) but not on more structured tests (WAIS); (6) vacillating interpersonal relationships ranging from transient and superficial to intense and dependent relationships, the latter marred by devaluation, manipulation, and demandingness. These features can serve as a useful reference point for further investigation of the borderline syndrome.

In this paper I shall use Heinz Kohut's concept of self pathology and his conceptualization of the organization of the borderline personality as a framework for further discussion of borderline disorders. I shall also offer some additional ideas about borderline conditions, and I will touch on the treatment of certain types of borderline conditions in relation to the talents of the therapist.

In addition to Kohut, recent important contributors to the specifically psychoanalytic understanding of borderline disorders include Zetzel (1971), Mahler (1971; Mahler, Pine, & Bergman, 1975), Kernberg (1967), Winnicott (1960), and Modell (1976). As one would expect, some of these authors, in addition to presenting a more analytically informed phenomenology, have attempted to describe more clearly the pathogenesis and dynamics of the disturbance. In general they have located the origins of the disorder in what would classically be defined as the early and middle pregenital period. The specific terminology employed, however, varies according to the particular theoretical approach of the author. Thus Mahler places the pathogenesis of borderline disturbances in the rapprochement stage of separation-individuation, whereas Kernberg finds it in the problems of the oral period, emphasizing the issues of aggression and the defense mechanism of splitting and their effects on internalized self and object representations.

I believe that most authors at least implicitly retain the idea that borderline disturbances straddle the major psychopathological division of neuroses and psychoses and present symptoms characteristic of each group. And, when looked at quite broadly, most of the authors' notions about pathogenesis seem similar; they relate borderline disorders to problems arising from the psychological separation of mother and child. An essential though sometimes unstated or even unrecognized difference between their formulations arises from the question of whether the primary pathology is based on conflict among structural agencies of the mind, whether it is derived from deficits in normal development, or whether it is a combination of these. Except for Kohut, most authors' conceptualizations are governed by a structural conflict model with varying emphases on regressions from the Oedipus complex or arrests at pregenital levels of development. The main thrust of Kohut's formulation, however, is that the borderline disturbance is primarily a deficiency disease arising from inadequate normal development of the structure of the self. This deficiency is subsequently dealt with through a variety of unconscious defensive measures that maintain the integrity of the self through a peculiarly rigid or distorted organization.

Heinz Kohut's Contributions

The contributions of Heinz Kohut to the understanding of the borderline disturbances derive not only from his brief but significant discussions of borderline pathology (Kohut, 1971, 1977; Kohut & Wolf, 1978), but more importantly, from his fundamental and far-reaching contributions regarding the organization and pathology of the self, particularly his conceptualizations of the nuclear self and the cohesive self. In essence his approach is not based on manifest behavior but on the basic organization of the self as determined by transferences (or the defenses against it) that arise in the course of treatment.

For Kohut, as for others, borderline states straddle the neurotic-psychotic boundary, but not necessarily because they manifest gross or even subtle symptoms of both types of pathology. Rather, they are psychoticlike conditions which, because of the availability and the employment of various protective psychological devices, do not collapse into the massive deterioration and the subsequent self and reality distortions that mark a manifest psychosis despite developmental experiences inimical to the formation of a cohesive nuclear self. The complex defensive equilibrium, the balance between self disorganization and surrounding supportive organizing forces, is maintained even though individuals suffering from a borderline disturbance live close to a breakdown of a stable though essentially deficient self.

Kohut defines borderline state as a *permanent or protracted* breakup (fragmentation), enfeeblement, or serious distortion of the self, which is covered over (or developmentally modulated) by more or less effective defensive structures. In addition, he describes, within the larger borderline category, two well-known characterological forms of the borderline states, the schizoid and paranoid personalities. These designations pertain to rigid, defensive organizations that achieve emotional distancing by, respectively, emotional coldness and shallowness or hostility and suspiciousness. Such distancing protects the personality from the danger of breakup, enfeeblement, or serious distortion of the self.

The borderline personality, then, is virtually or potentially psychotic, but defends against an overt psychosis by various techniques that avoid threatening, in-depth attachments to others. Such attachments would tend to lead to overstimulated or chaotic affect states that are not manageable by the brittle personality organization. While Kohut does not specifically spell out other borderline types that are also the outcome of characteristic deficiencies and defenses, it is not unlikely that emotional distancing (if that is required) may be accomplished by effective defensive means that do not lead to manifest schizoid or paranoid attitudes. These other types should also be considered borderline states if the problem of cohesion (protracted fragmentation, distortion, etc.) of the self is the central pathology.

As Kohut sees it, borderline disorders are considered untreatable by psychoanalysis (though, of course, treatable in psychotherapy) because, although such patients are able to establish varying degrees of *rapport* with the analyst, the disordered, core sector of the self of such patients does not enter into the transference amalgamations with the imago of the analyst that are necessary for the conduct of an analysis. In-depth transferences — the experiencing of reactivated, archaic, childhood affect states in relation to early selfobjects — cannot develop because of the borderline patient's unconscious, fearful anticipation of a massive disruption of a previously attained equilibrium which is, with good reason, tenaciously guarded. Without such transference development, however, and without the associated understanding, interpretation, and repeated revival of deeply resonating, core-near affective states — a crucial step in working through — psychoanalytic treatment cannot take place. From the point of view of self psychology I would designate disorders of this type the *true* borderline disturbances.

In contrast to the true borderline disturbances, Kohut defines the psychotically organized personality as one marked by the *permanent or protracted* breakup, enfeeblement, or serious distortion of a self that lacks the organized defensive capabilities of the borderline personality. In such individuals a crucial sector of the personality, whether for constitutional or experiential reasons (or both), has not adequately experienced, has not strongly invested in, or has profoundly withdrawn from (or a mixture of these), primary, affectively sustaining relations with objects (selfobjects). In some psychotic individuals, more or less extensive, cohesively organized sectors of the personality coexist alongside the core psychotic organization and in some instances, e.g., some paranoid types, a "normal" social facade is maintained. In some instances essentially psychotic disturbances, those that preserve a "normal" facade, will be confused with a true borderline personality that is only virtually or potentially psychotic but does not have an active or unmodulated psychotic core.

Ordinarily, the differentiation of psychosis from a borderline state is not difficult in patients with overt psychotic symptoms or a clear-cut history of them. More subtle, covered-over or sectored core psychoses will perhaps be recognized only after more prolonged exposure to the individual patient. These covert psychoses may be more frequent than is usually thought, and their malignant effects on the healthy psychological development of the children of such individuals may be quite severe.

As with borderline disturbances, it is not likely that a workable in-depth transference will develop in therapy in relation to the psychotically organized sector of the psychotic's personality. Nonetheless, a meaningful rapport with the therapist may be fostered in relation to nonpsychotic personality sectors through the use of a variety of ingenious psychotherapeutic strategies, and these efforts will result in consequent strengthening and greater dominance of these nonpsychotic personality sectors.

On the other (healthier) side of the true borderline disturbances lie the narcissistic personality and behavior disorders, the former manifested primarily in autoplastic, the latter primarily in alloplastic symptoms. Kohut defines these narcissistic disturbances (which have more recently been called self disturbances) as characterized by a *temporary* (transient) breakup, enfeeblement, or serious distortion of the self. The narcissistic personality disorders are manifested by, among other symptoms, depression, hypochondria, and sensitivity to slight; the behavior disorders are manifested by, among other symptoms, perversion, delinquency, and addiction. Despite their sometimes quite florid pathology, such individuals are neither intrinsic psychotics nor true borderline personalities. They range from manifestly disturbed, functionally limited people, to socially well-functioning but privately painfully distressed people.

It should be emphasized here that the increasingly frequent use of the term "narcissistic" or "self disorder" as a synonym for severe pathology—as if all narcissistic disorders represented some kind of near-borderline condition—is seriously in error. Disorders of the self may be no more severe than neurotic (oedipally organized) disorders. The severity of disturbance in either case is a function of a number of complexly interacting variables which both shape the specific type of self or structural pathology and effect the pervasiveness of the disturbance.

The personality is not organized as a homogeneous, monolithic structure. The existence of in-depth organizational sectors of the personality, e.g., specific unique endowments or other complexes of self-stabilizing experiences which permit the coexistence of severe pathology alongside stable, "healthy" personality sectors, should therefore be kept in mind. These unique, self-enhancing sectors may effect a gyroscopic action on the total personality functioning which can overcome or at least ameliorate more pathologically organized and pathology-producing sectors. Again, let me emphasize that the functional severity of disorder is a consequence of a complex, interacting set of determinants. These include constitution, early somatic disturbances, early deprivations of expectable care and emotional responsiveness, defensive diatheses (those predominantly constitutional and those predominantly acquired and the variable interaction of such factors), endowments (talents and skills), the propensity for and persistence of rage responses, tendencies to emotional withdrawal and living in fantasy, the tendency to anxiety, particular health-promoting or pathology-promoting identifications, etc. — each of these in dynamic balance with the others. In other words, functional pathology, whether of the narcissistic (self) or oedipal (structural) type, is built up multifactorially and is the consequence of the confluence of innumerable components. It is not usually constructed from a single or even several psychological determinants, nor should it be considered a unitary psychogenetic phenomenon. (This is in line with Kohut's concept of the basic units of personality organization as complex psychological configurations and not, usually, as simple drive units.) The true borderline disturbance is marked by a *protracted* disturbance of the cohesiveness of the self; the narcissistic personality disorder by a *transient* disturbance of the cohesiveness of the self.

At times it is difficult to differentiate certain disorders of the self (narcissistic personality disorders and narcissistic behavior disorders) from true borderline disorders. The difficulty does not usually arise in relation to the transient disturbances of self-cohesion or the pathological intensification of aspects of the nuclear self that leads to the fragmentations, depletions, and distortions of the self that are regularly encountered in the treatment of narcissistic personality disorders. Although at times these disturbances are quite severe, they are usually self-limited or can be resolved (I am oversimplifying here) by an adequate response of the therapist. Outside of a treatment situation they are also resolved or ameliorated by whatever habitual means the individual has at his disposal in his daily life—through his own autoplastic or alloplastic resources. What is of crucial importance in these narcissistic disturbances is that they are in principle treatable by psychoanalysis since they permit the development of the kind of in-depth selfobject transferences that are mobilized by the analytic situation and the methods appropriate to it. However, the immediate intensity and pervasiveness of such self disorders, however transient, may possibly lead to a mistaken assessment of the essential or pathologically dominant personality organization.

Another large group of "borderline" disorders, not specifically explored by Kohut, clearly deserves further examination here. This group consists of a number of manifestly different personality types and symptomatic and behavioral groupings that apparently have little in common except for their inaccessibility to treatment by various methods including psychoanalysis, psychoanalytically oriented psychotherapy, and a variety of eclectic psychotherapies. The consensus borderline features of Gunderson and Singer (1975) noted above are found among the personality traits of such patients, but the makeup of the group is not limited to individuals with such features.

For most clinicians disturbances such as those just mentioned are felt to be the manifestation of some kind of archaic or primitive, vulnerable, unstable, regression-prone personality organization. Without describing the variety of clinical constellations that might be included in this group of patients, let me suggest that their disturbances represent the "border" of the true borderline personality. They have also been called highly vulnerable personality disorders. That is, such patients do not straddle the boundary between the psychoses and the neuroses (though some seem to come close to that) or avoid a manifest psychosis by the rigid use of specific defenses that keep the personality at a safe distance from in-depth affective involvements with others (as in the case of the true borderline). Instead, these individuals have developed a type of cohesive self and a type of nuclear self, but the nuclear self and its cohesiveness are in some way different in content, and less successfully put together, than those typifying the narcissistic personality and behavior disorders. Still, despite the more blatant social maladjustments that may occur, the individual in this group has a self that is better organized than the self of the true borderline patient. (One example of patients in this group are those individuals who develop massive, almost unmanageable merger transferences — sometimes erotized, sometimes recognized only by their oppositional tendencies or the extremeness of their reactive rage — which, because of their intensity and lability, may severely tax the understanding, equanimity, and effectiveness of the therapist.) What I am suggesting here is a spectrum of the quality of the structure of the self, ranging from the healthy (well-adjusted, well-adapted, flexibly balanced) personality to a near-psychotic personality organization on the other hand. The "border" borderline personalities lie at the sicker edge of this spectrum.

Regarding a diagnosis among these different types, what is most important to keep in mind is that the essential differentiation, which cannot necessarily be ascertained from a brief examination, does not *necessarily* lie in manifest behavior or symptoms, *nor in the form of the disease, its manifest content, or even its social severity*. Instead, the differentiation emerges from a knowledge of the basic structural organization, the psychological makeup of the personality. The correct understanding of the latter may require a test of prolonged evaluation or of treatment, that is, sufficient time for the development of adequate transference clues. And even then, within certain limits (and I want to emphasize this most important variable), honesty obliges the therapist to recognize that his own personality and particularly his own empathic limitations may play a significant role in his assessment of the patient's primary, core disturbance. The assessment is at least in part based on the interaction of two participants in an extended diagnostic or treatment process. It is a process that operates within a two-party system and the therapist may be as important a variable as the patient.

Concept of Cohesive Self and Nuclear Self

As stated earlier, the concept of the self—its formation, its cohesiveness, and the contents and quality of the nuclear self—is central to Kohut's formulations regarding borderline conditions. It will be useful, then, to examine briefly some of the basic developmental issues in self psychology that underlie our understanding of normal personality development, the narcissistic personality disorders, and the borderline syndrome. To provide a simple working definition, let us describe the self as the essence of one's psychological being. It is the enduring configuration of endowment and affective memories of developmental experiences with self-objects and objects interacting from birth onward—though later experiences are clearly less crucial to the formation of the most significant aspects of the self than earlier ones. The operational and experiential dimensions of the self can expand or contract from moment to moment or for extended periods of time, depending, among other things, on its locus of attention or involvement and the kind and degree of affect aroused. Once the self has been substantially formed, however, the arrangement of its contents and the forces that hold it together are experienced as a reliable experiential configuration which is the baseline of its functioning. In some essential way one knows one's self. The cohesiveness of the self and its core constituents—the grandiose self, the ideals of the self, inherent endowments of skills and talents—are the centers around which the varieties of psychological health and illness are formed.

The ability to maintain a baseline cohesiveness of the self is crucial for normal development and minimally normal (non-psychotic) psychological functioning. This ability is a developmental achievement that enables the self to remain reliably integrated, without the continuing availability of a selfobject with whom it can unite to effect a cohesiveness otherwise lacking. When such cohesiveness is preserved, disruptions of various kinds, including disorganization, fragmentation, depletion, and/or enfeeblement of the self, will, within wide limits, be transient; once a particular inimical stress has been removed or has been altered by internal emotional shifts, the essential cohesiveness of the self will reliably return to normal. A self-healing action is autonomously possible for the personality.

The understanding of the concept of a cohesive self is closely tied to the concept of the most fundamental psychic structure, the nuclear self. The nuclear self is the genetic core of the experientially and developmentally augmented self. ("Self" is a more general term that includes the nuclear self.) The nuclear self begins potentially with the first mother-child (parent) interactions and continues into early childhood with the father and other selfobjects taking an increasingly important role in effecting its formation and substantiality. It is constituted of the child's endowment in interaction with the earliest mirroring experiences (mergers) and earliest idealization experiences, and it builds on the continuing mirroring and idealizing experiences of early childhood. The term "bipolar self" emphasizes the grandiose and idealizing qualities that make up the nuclear self. The earliest selfobject experiences have no specific psychological content, only a relative sense of tension or lack of tension. Subsequently they become more defined and more complexly formed. The earliest merger experiences, e.g., of the mother responding to the babbling child by smiling and cooing, evolve partially into the (narrowly defined) mirroring experiences in which the selfobject is expected to respond positively to the child's self, listening attentively to what the child says. Comparably, the earlier diffuse idealizing experiences, e.g., of the mother taking the crying child in her arms and soothing him, evolve partially into more complex idealizing states in which the idealized selfobject is expected to respond positively to a self that seeks inclusion in the idealized selfobject's elevated, powerful world — like the admired teacher on the podium who nods to his pupil in the crowded auditorium. In both instances the requisite experience is derived from the "expectable" and necessary affective responsiveness of the selfobject.

The formation of the cohesive self is not separate from the formation of the nuclear self; it is a quality of the nuclear self (E. Wolf, personal communication, 1978), referring to its state of integration, degree of cohesiveness, degree of vitality or strength (in contrast to enfeeblement), and/or the manner in which it has been formed (its lack of distortion as opposed to being "bent," "torn," etc.). One speaks of a cohesive self primarily when the degree of integration, of cohering of the self, is in question. One speaks of the nuclear self when the qualities of the self, i.e., its identifications, its ambitions, and its ideals, are at issue.[1] In normal development a rudimentary nuclear self is generally thought to be forming by the second year of life and to be reasonably well established by the age of five to six. Later accretions are still possible, but they are of less core significance. Thus the idealizations of latency and adolescence, though crucial insofar as the specific contents of the self are concerned, are probably only further shapings of broader, already existing tendencies. A cohesive self is considered fairly well maintained by around age three when the continued presence of the primary selfobjects is no longer necessary to the maintenance of the child's self-integration; that is, the earliest mirroring and idealizing experiences with the selfobjects have more substantially become self, and the binding, forcelike quality of self-cohesion has been initially, reliably established.

In the true borderline disturbance, as Kohut defines it, the cohesiveness of the self is specious. Cohesion is maintained by complex defenses rather than by a healthy, integrating phase-specific formation. In the self disorders (narcissistic personality disorders), by contrast, a cohesive self *has* been established, though transitory states of fragmentation (the term is used generically here; it includes depletion, distortions of the self, etc.) may at least briefly appear massive enough to cause possible confusion regarding the

---

[1]What is asserted here has not been previously formulated in this way. I am emphasizing the interrelatedness of two aspects of the self that have usually been discussed separately as though they were two independent developmental or organizational entities.

basic makeup of the personality. In the border of the (true) borderline disturbances (i.e., the highly vulnerable narcissistic disorders) the nuclear self and its cohesiveness are qualitatively different and less effectively organized than they are in the narcissistic
personality disorders.

I would like to make one last remark regarding the essential
differentiation of what I have termed the "border of the
borderline" conditions. These disturbances objectively are marked
by the social severity of the disturbance (whatever its particular
form), the intensity of felt disturbance of the self, and/or the
unusual degree of inaccessibility of the patient to analytic treatment. The essence of a core psychotic personality organization,
whether defended against (as in the true borderline), or not (as in
the psychoses), lies in the extremely limited viability of positively
toned primary selfobject experiences. The essence of a non-
psychotic personality organization (including the border of the
borderlines), whatever its manifest form of pathology, lies in the
viable, self-nourishing, selfobject experiences of infancy and childhood. These experiences provide the spark of life that, as one patient put it, "waters my brain," and they make past in-depth relations with others, even when largely confined to fantasy or shot
through with massive rage, a necessary and sustaining condition of
life. Most importantly, these experiences afford a toehold for the
therapeutic rehabilitation of these self disorders.

Analyzability

The question of analyzability was touched on earlier when I
spoke of Kohut's definition of the true borderline states and of the
psychoses, both of which are considered untreatable by analysis
because of the inability of the patient to form an in-depth transference to the analyst. Leaving aside the difficult question of
whether a talented and empathic analyst could foster the development of a workable in-depth transference with such patients, the
issue of clinical talent and empathic capability is still a crucial one
in the treatment of highly vulnerable ("border of the borderline")
patients for at least one important reason. The diagnosis of some

very difficult-to-treat patients may not be possible without a trial of therapy of some duration. Whether a workable in-depth transference can develop, whether the childhood disturbance in relation to primary selfobjects can be revived by way of analogously intense adult experiences, may be as much dependent on the analyst's sensitivity to such disturbances, and on his therapeutic skill in helping the patient experience such primary feelings, as on the patient's pathogenic experiences and consequent deformations of personality. In other words, within certain limits the diagnosis and the treatment of the "borderlineness" of patients are not to be judged from the standpoint of an observer outside the field but from the standpoint of the observer participating in a system — the self-selfobject system of the patient and therapist. Rather than being an index of the patient's actual unanalyzability, a highly vulnerable narcissistic personality disorder might be considered (incorrectly) to be a true borderline condition because of the limitations of even a competent analyst's empathic understanding of certain constellations of severe disorders.

In relation to the issue of the therapist's talent, let me briefly consider a particularly useful and sensitive communication by an analyst to his patient. I believe it is an example of an ideally meaningful therapeutic action, one characterized by the union of emotional depth and effective understanding. It is a demonstration of what is meant by the analyst's empathic capability, and how it can affect the treatment of patients, whatever their diagnoses. Of course, such a capability is invaluable in the treatment of such highly guarded, vulnerable, and fragmenting disturbances as the borderline conditions.

The patient, a middle-aged man with chronic, mild depression, feelings of apathy, fatigue, and low self-esteem, began treatment with me after moving from another city where he had been in analysis for several years. After some months he reported what he considered to be a landmark experience he had had with his former analyst. (So far as the point of this vignette is concerned, the context in which this experience was recalled is not important.) After a three-day weekend interruption, he had returned to treatment (with his former analyst) complaining bitterly about his "bitchy"

demanding wife and his selfish, clamoring children; they had finally gotten to him on Sunday, he said, though he had already begun
to feel increasingly depressed, fatigued, and irritable on Saturday.
By early Sunday night he could barely keep his eyes open as he
watched a "stupid T.V. show just to keep occupied." As he was
telling his analyst in a half-irritated, half-tearful tone about how
he had felt and how he did not think he could ever get over this
often repeated, familiar state of mind, he emphasized his remarks
by waving his hand in the air, his index finger extended. The
analyst broke in and said, "You know, I have the feeling that I'd
like to take your finger in my hand and just hold it." A shock of
surprise and a rush of pleasure swept through the patient and his
mood immediately changed. He was washed over by a mixture of
rapidly intensifying emotions dominated by a relief of tension that
was followed by a bittersweet feeling of pleasure and deep sadness.
He began to cry. When he stopped crying, the irritableness and ex-
haustion of the weekend, his recurrent deep pessimism and sense
of gloom were gone, and he felt infused with vitality again.

The analyst and the patient had understood the effectiveness
of the comment as follows: Because of his remark, the deserting,
neglecting analyst (mother-father) had been reexperienced as
though he were (the patient's associations) Michelangelo's God ig-
niting Adam to life through his index finger, or, closer to home, as
though he were a loving parent picking up and comforting a
cranky child. The statement "I have the feeling that I'd like to. . ."
indicated to the patient that the analyst, unlike his emotionally distant parents, was aware of his (the patient's) distressing
hollowness, wanted to help him deal with it, and was conveying his
understanding of its cause and of the patient's need for the responsiveness he had always wanted but never adequately obtained. The
analyst's remark implicitly meant, "I would like to hold you and
soothe you with my voice and my touch because I see how unhappy you are and how unloved you felt then and how unloved
you feel now."[2]

[2]It would be a misreading of the analyst's comment to understand it as a
demonstration of the "transference mutualization" that Arthur Valenstein (1979,
p. 133) warns about. Both the analyst and the patient clearly understood it to be a

By his comment the analyst had succinctly conveyed his empathic understanding of the cause of his patient's pain, and he sensitively cut through his patient's reactive anger at those current transference objects, his family and his analyst, who were depriving him of their affection. He reminded the patient that he, the analyst, was again available, responsive, and understanding of both the past which had damaged him, and the present which, in the form of the analyst's absence over the weekend, had, by way of the transference, reinjured him. And he remedied both with his message of understanding. The patient's rage was defused, and he was reconnected to the analyst. Like Adam, he was brought to life but, in this instance, to a reborn emotional life.

Summary and Conclusions

I have briefly reviewed the concept of the borderline personality. Generally it has been considered to be a psychopathological state with the organization and symptoms of both the psychoses and the neuroses. While various analytic authors have suggested a specific pathogenesis of the disorder, more often than not the diagnosis has been a psychiatric one based on manifest symptom clusters and the degree of difficulty of management and treatment.

Heinz Kohut's concept of the borderline state is based on the model of a core deficiency or distortion in the development of the self. In what I have called the "true" borderline disturbances, Kohut considers the self to be in a state of permanent or protracted breakdown, enfeeblement, or serious distortion, but its in essence psychotic organization is controlled and concealed by a complex set of modulating, defensive structures, the best known of which are the schizoid personality and the paranoid personality. I have

---

metaphorical statement that condensed the analyst's thoughts into a vivid interpretation of both the reasons for the patient's irritable weekend depression and the remedy that he lacked in the past and still sought in the present. It was part and parcel of the analyst's personal style. It in no way implied on the part of the analyst any wish as such for the action described; it implied only a wish to be a helpful physician who could say to his patient: here is where it hurts and this is the reason why.

suggested that in another large category of heterogeneous "border of the borderline" disturbances (also called highly vulnerable, regression-prone personalities) the self, in contrast to the permanently or protractedly fragmented self of the true borderline disturbances, is essentially cohesive, although its contents and its mode of organization are eccentric, more fluid or brittle, and less successfully put together than in the "healthier" narcissistic personality disturbances. However, whatever the pathology of its organization or the difficulties of treatment, patients in this group are not virtual psychotics whose psychotic organization is modulated by complex defensive structures.

In order to clarify Kohut's concepts of the borderline state, his concepts of the cohesive self and the nuclear self are elaborated and the incorrectness of equating narcissistic personality disorders or disorders of the self with severe pathology is pointed out.

The role of the therapist in determining the analyzability of the true and the highly vulnerable narcissistic disorders is discussed; the empathic abilities of the therapist are suggested as a determinant as crucial for diagnosis as for treatment of some of these disturbances. Finally, a brief vignette of a particularly sensitive therapeutic interchange between an analyst and his patient is presented.

References

Gunderson, J. & Singer, M. (1975), Defining Borderline Patients: An Overview. *Amer. J. Psychiat.,* 132:1–10.

Kernberg, O. (1967), Borderline Personality Organization. In: *Borderline Conditions and Pathological Narcissism.* New York: Aronson, 1975.

Knight, R. (1953), Borderline States. *Bull. Menn. Clinic,* 17:1–12.

Kohut, H. (1971), *The Analysis of the Self.* New York: International Universities Press.

———— (1977), *The Restoration of the Self.* New York: International Universities Press.

———— & Wolf, E. (1978), The Disorders of the Self and Their Treatment: An Outline. *Internat. J. Psycho-Anal.,* 59:413–426.

Mahler, M. (1971), The Study of the Separation-Individuation Process and Its Possible Application to Borderline Phenomena in the Psychoanalytic Situation. *The Psychoanalytic Study of the Child,* 26:403–424. New York: Quadrangle.

_____, Pine, F., & Bergman, A. (1975), *The Psychological Birth of the Human Infant*. New York: Basic Books.

Modell, A. (1976), The Holding Environment and the Therapeutic Action of Psychoanalysis. *J. Amer. Psychoanal. Assn.,* 24:285–308.

Valenstein, A. (1979), The Concept of "Classical" Psychoanalysis. *J. Amer. Psychoanal. Assn.,* 27 (Supplement):113–136.

Winnicott, D. W. (1960), Ego Restoration in Terms of True and False Self. In: *The Maturational Processes and the Facilitating Environment*. New York: International Universities Press, 1965, pp. 140–152.

Zetzel, E. (1971), A Developmental Approach to the Borderline Patient. *Amer. J. Psychiat.,* 127:867–871.

Psychoanalysis of the Self
and Psychotherapy

Jacques Palaci

Psychoanalysis as a therapeutic method of treatment has had as its goal the uncovering of unconscious motivation and conflict and has centered around the concepts of transference and defense. Clinical evidence that a certain group of patients could not tolerate this process of uncovering and had difficulty in establishing a classical transference relationship necessitated the introduction of variations in psychoanalytic technique and led progressively to the concept of psychotherapy as a distinct technical approach for this group of patients. This form of psychotherapy — rooted in psychoanalytic theory — is usually referred to as psychoanalytically oriented psychotherapy. The term "psychotherapy" is also used to refer to any type of treatment based on an interpersonal, insight-oriented, talking relationship, for which psychoanalysis is the prototype. Psychotherapy, as a treatment mode specifically recommended for more severe forms of psychopathology, has had no distinct set of unified procedures, no autonomy of its own, and is often mistakenly considered to be a diluted form of psychoanalysis.

Only recently have independent textbooks on psychotherapy begun to appear (e.g., Tarachow, 1963), including one grounded in psychoanalytic ego psychology (Blanck & Blanck, 1974). Earlier attempts deviated from classical theory, basing their therapeutic treatment recommendations on different theoretical premises, such as the so-called neo-cultural school of psychoanalysis (Fromm-Reichmann, 1950).

In this paper we shall consider whether the new theory of the self has changed our view of the relationship of psychoanalysis to psychotherapy, not only from the standpoint of the problem of defining psychoanalysis — its goals and its limits — but as to whether the new theory implies a modified, more encompassing concept of the transference and a new outlook on technique in general. Before doing so, however, we must consider psychoanalysis and psychotherapy beyond their historical, classical meanings, in terms of how they relate to the theoretical formulations of narcissism and transference which are central to the issue.

Most analysts have believed psychoanalysis to be the treatment of choice for the neuroses, but to be inappropriate for the treatment of more severely disturbed patients. In this they follow Freud's (1914) original distinction between "transference neuroses" and "narcissistic neuroses" (what today we call the functional psychoses), opposing object relations to narcissism, and claiming that the latter group of narcissistic patients was incapable of forming a transference relationship. According to Freud, the phase of primary narcissism preceded the phase of object relations[1] and was a primitive state, in which the infant libidinally cathected itself. It refers to an undifferentiated condition, in which there is no separation between the subject and the outside world. Freud differentiated primary narcissism from secondary narcissism, considering the latter a regressive condition in an individual who had achieved the separation of the self and object — the cathexis of the object — but who subsequently decathected the object and withdrew libido onto the ego (self).

The incompatibility of the narcissistic neuroses with psychoanalytic treatment, definitionally opposing object relations to

---

[1]The concept of whether there is a developmental phase without object relations is currently the subject of increasing debate.

narcissism and assuming that psychoanalytic treatment is founded on the object relation — the transference — did not prevent psychoanalysts, already in Freud's time but more especially in recent years, from undertaking the treatment of patients whose principal difficulty was rooted in the narcissistic realm of the personality (Abraham, 1908; Tausk, 1916, 1919; Federn, 1943).

This, then, is the origin of the debate that has raged during the last decades between those psychoanalysts who want to limit psychoanalysis as a form of treatment to the psychoneuroses, and those who want to apply the psychoanalytic method to a variety of more severe mental disturbances. Those opposed to widening the application of psychoanalysis feel that this would detract from its original and most unique contribution — the discovery of the relation between conscious and unconscious motivation, based on the topographic theory — and with a new emphasis on structure formation and preoedipal issues, transform it into a genetic psychology of development.

This controversy is tied with another, more theoretical, older one, that is not usually associated with it. This pertains to the two concepts of personality theory elaborated by Freud: the topographic theory and the structural theory. Here the argument is between those who have claimed that there is little in the topographic model that could not be explained more satisfactorily by the structural theory (Arlow & Brenner, 1964), and those who feel that the topographic theory is indispensable for its clinical applications (Reik, 1936, 1948; Kubie, 1950).[2] Freud himself became dissatisfied with certain aspects of the topographic theory; in order to take into account the unconscious nature of defenses, and the various processes of internalization and identification, he had to complement his first model with his theory of psychic structure. Although he never gave up the idea of integrating the two, he did not succeed in doing so in his lifetime.

It must be remembered that the topographic theory refers to three localities or psychic systems: the unconscious, the preconscious, and the conscious, each having its particular function,

---

[2]The British school of object relations uses a separate theoretical framework.

methods of operation, quality of energy cathexis, and distinguishable by the nature of its representations. Each system, moreover, is related to the dynamic concept of psychoanalysis, which implies that the systems can be in conflict.

The structural theory consists in postulating the progressive structural differentiation of three systems: the id, the ego, and the superego. This differentiation stems from an unconscious matrix, having its origin in the biological. The id is the instinctual pole; the ego is in charge of the interests of the total, narcissistically cathected person, and the mediator between the demands of the id, the superego, and external reality; the superego, through internalization, is the carrier of the parents' exigencies and their prohibitions. The three systems are related to each other and constitute what is called "intersystemic relations." Each system has its substructures, which can be in conflict and which form the basis for what is designated "intrasystemic relations."

The structural theory should no longer be confined to its classical meaning of explaining psychic functioning in terms of a tripartite structure or system (id, ego, superego), but should extend its investigation to the organization, level, and form of specific mental contents. These different aspects of mental contents subsume ideas, perceptions, and memories, as well as more complex arrangements, such as discharges, thresholds, defenses, controls, and identifications. Structural theory should now be concerned with the formation and stability of psychic structure, with processes of internalization, with self and object representations, with the nature of the internalized objects and object relations (whether archaic or of a higher order), with the cohesiveness of the structures, and with the degree of object constancy. It should investigate the circumstances that can lead to the weakening or disintegration (fragmentation) of psychic structures (in other words to their decathexis), and the conditions that permit their restoration. Conceived within this larger and more comprehensive theoretical framework, structural theory lends itself to the clinical and theoretical exploration of a wider variety of emotional and mental disturbances, and provides the basis for the reformulation of certain psychoanalytic concepts.

During the last few years, Heinz Kohut and Otto Kernberg have explored the vast territory situated between the neuroses and the psychoses. Their research has been inspired by and derives in part from an expanded view of the structural theory, as well as from developmental psychoanalysis, with Kernberg drawing particularly on the British school of object relations (Melanie Klein). This has led them to a reexamination of certain fundamental concepts of psychoanalysis. Kohut has made the important clinical observation that regression is often triggered by a narcissistic injury, rather than by a disturbance in object relations. He has pointed out that even in the most severe psychotic disorders, a certain degree of object relatedness is maintained, whereas a serious disturbance of the narcissistic equilibrium is never absent. Based on these clinical findings, Kohut came to the conclusion, contrary to Freud, that narcissistic patients establish object relations of a specific nature, and are capable of a particular kind of transference — the narcissistic transference — and that the vulnerability of the prepsychotic person will have to be investigated not only from the point of view of the precariousness of object relations, but also in regard to the fragility and degree of evolution of the narcissistic structures. Since the prevailing classical definitions and existing clinical theories could not accommodate his empirical observations, Kohut reformulated the concept of narcissism by postulating an independent line of development for the narcissistic structures. His concept of narcissism and narcissistic transference (1966, 1971), elaborated in his recent work into the more general concept of the transference to the selfobject (1977), has made possible the psychoanalytic treatment of a group of narcissistic patients formerly considered unanalyzable. It is thus an important contribution to psychoanalytic theory and practice which, by respecting rigorous psychoanalytic methodology, has disproved the belief that psychoanalysis is limited to the treatment of the psychoneuroses and thereby reopened the question of the limits between the indications for psychoanalysis and for psychotherapy. Kohut's work demonstrates the potentiality of a broadened concept of structural theory in the hands of a creative theoretician and clinician.

But Kohut has gone still further. Having introduced a method for the direct observation of narcissistic pathology via its particular manifestations in the narcissistic transference, and choosing to dispense with extrapolation, he could now explore the origin, organization, function, and vicissitudes of infantile narcissistic structures and their reactivation during psychoanalytic treatment. This led him to the realization of the inadequacy of the topographic and structural drive theory as applied to narcissistic patients, and the fact that these theories also did not do justice to a variety of psychological phenomena outside the clinical situation. The insufficiency of the oedipal, structural, conflict-drive concept has been felt by many analysts who have tried to work with more severely disturbed patients—especially borderline and psychotic patients—but it is among Kohut's achievements that he broke through the limitations of traditional metapsychological conceptualizations. While Freud, on the basis of empirical observations, felt the need to complement the topographic theory with the structural, Kohut recognized the necessity to complement the structural conflict-drive concept of psychoanalysis with the structural defect-restoration concept of self psychology. He was thus able to extend psychoanalysis to encompass clinical observations that cover the spectrum of the most frequently observed psychopathologies today and "to accommodate the multiplicity and diversity of phenomena observed with regard to the self" (Kohut, 1977, p. 15).

The concept of the self arose out of clinical necessity as psychoanalysts attempted to resolve the problems which confronted them in the analytic treatment of narcissistic, borderline, and severely neurotic patients. Theoreticians with orientations as varied as Hartmann (1950), Jacobson (1964), Winnicott (1960), Khan (1975), Guntrip (1968), and many others made use of the concept in their theoretical formulations, yet without the benefit of a precise, agreed-upon definition. The attempts at conceptualization of the self have met with theoretical difficulties and with questionable degrees of success. In order to stay within the framework of classical psychoanalytic theory, Kohut first conceived of the self, not as a constituent of the mental apparatus, but as a cohesive structural organization, with topography and cathexis, similar to the "system ego" but at a lower level of abstraction, closer to experience. Despite its controversial nature, it seems that the concept of the self is indispensable to present-day psychoanalysts and it is rare to find a paper in the recent psychoanalytic literature where the concept of the self is not made use of from one or another of the different theoretical positions. Does this represent a reaction against the mechanistic foundations of Freudian metapsychology (with its origins in a physicalistic psychobiology) that culminated in certain dehumanized aspects of structural ego psychology, or an effort to rid metapsychology of the anthropomorphism that has pervaded it since its beginning? Freud himself felt confined by his natural science model, did not consistently adhere to it, and was in constant danger of anthropomorphizing (Schafer, 1973).

The theoretical discussion of the problem of the self would take us far beyond the scope of this paper. (For theoretical analyses, however, see Levin, 1969; Schafer, 1973; and Panel, 1976.) Let me simply repeat that the concept of the self was derived from empirical data as a clinical matter of necessity; it was not invoked as an abstract scientific concept. Furthermore, the differentiation between self and ego has had far-reaching implications in calling attention to the distortions, limitations, and alterations of the ego. It has led to the exploration of narcissistic pathology and to the more comprehensive theoretical concept of the psychoanalysis of the self.

In his recent work, Kohut perceives the essence and meaning of the self in these terms:

> The self, whether conceived within the framework of the psychology of the self in the narrow sense of the term, as a specific structure in the mental apparatus, or, within the framework of the psychology of the self in the broad sense of the term, as the center of the individual's psychological universe, is, like all reality — physical reality...or psychological reality... — not knowable in essence. We cannot, by introspection and empathy, penetrate to the self per se; only its introspectively or empathically perceived psychological manifestations are open to us [1977, pp. 310–311].

We have observed that the application of psychoanalytic knowledge to more severe forms of pathology is not new. It has been the concern of psychoanalysts and psychiatrists who, since the early days of psychoanalysis, have been dealing with the psychotherapy of borderline and psychotic patients (Federn, 1943; Sullivan, 1931; Fromm-Reichmann, 1950; Searles, 1963). However, since these practitioners believed that the development of a transference neurosis was an essential condition of psychoanalytic treatment—and these patients did not develop such transference neuroses—they usually had recourse (often intuitively) to deviations from the classical model that risked altering psychoanalysis at its foundations, i.e., the concepts of the unconscious and of psychic structure formation.

The opposing viewpoints of those who would apply psychoanalytic treatment to more severely disturbed patients and those who would not stem from two different theoretical models. Those who would not usually link narcissistic pathology with deficiency states (London, 1973), whether or not culminating in psychosis. In the opinion of these authors, the treatment of such deficiency states necessitates the restoration of structures, a process for which they believe psychoanalysis is not indicated and possibly even anti-therapeutic. What is needed is the introduction of "parameters" (Eissler, 1953) for the treatment of less severe cases (those approaching neurosis) and psychoanalytic psychotherapy for the others. The parameter in this context represents a controlled, minimal, technical variation (a deviation from the classical model) suggested and necessitated by the structure of a particular patient's ego. The parameter is employed in treatment which remains classical in all other aspects, i.e., that consists of the search for conflicts related to the cathexis of objects in the context of the transference neurosis of the oedipal-phallic phase. The parameter should lead to its own dissolution before the end of treatment, and its effect on the transference is always to be eliminated by interpretation, by the revelation of the unconscious latent meaning. The idea is that the use of parameters can help these patients to develop the transference neurosis necessary to the treatment.

In opposition to this viewpoint, the group of analysts in favor of extending the range of psychoanalysis believes that the narcissistic disorders and, in extreme cases, the psychoses, are differentiated from the neuroses only by the nature and depth of their conflict, and by the fact that the defenses they elicit are more extreme, rigid, and primitive.

Both groups rely on Freud's theoretical formulations, though they quote different periods of his writings (the group that opposes the extension of psychoanalysis cites the metapsychological papers of 1915; the group endorsing it cites papers of 1894 and 1911). This latter group also departs from Freud's position in claiming that the psychotic does establish a transference relationship, but one that is difficult to recognize and interpret, because as soon as the psychotic gets close to the object he becomes confused and threatened by the loss of his capacity to differentiate self from nonself (Rosenfeld, 1952; Sullivan, 1931; Federn, 1943; Searles, 1963). Psychoanalysts who regard the psychotic disorders as the result of defense mechanisms, though more archaic and primitive, see in psychoanalysis not only the treatment of choice for these patients, but consider the technical recommendations of those seeking to limit the scope of analysis as harmful (Boyer & Giovacchini, 1967; Arlow & Brenner, 1964; also the work of the British object relations school, stemming from Melanie Klein: Rosenfield, 1952; Segal, 1962; Heimann, 1960; and others). Kernberg's (1975, 1976) approach can be situated somewhere between the two opposing positions.

Kohut has dealt with this problem in an unexpected and novel way. His concern since the introduction of the psychoanalysis of the self has not been whether a given technical approach should be classified as psychoanalysis or psychotherapy, or whether or not it is indicated for a particular case. For Kohut, *it is not a matter of accepting or disowning the classical position, but of ascertaining how well certain concepts and existing models of psychoanalysis permit the integration of our expanding clinical observations and experience in a changing world, and whether a reformulation of concepts and a diversification of models would increase our efficiency in dealing with patients and make psychoanalytic technique more suitable for a wider variety of present-day psychological disturbances.*

The traditional recommendation for psychoanalysis as opposed to psychoanalytically oriented psychotherapy has been based essentially on the diagnostic aspects of the case, with psychoanalysis being limited to the psychoneuroses, where a sufficient degree of structuralization has taken place and where the therapist is dealing with a fully developed, well-functioning ego. In such cases, the fundamental psychological difficulty is centered around structural conflicts arising from libidinal and aggressive wishes which a well-defined, cohesive, clearly differentiated self directed toward early childhood objects. Such cases also involve higher-level defense mechanisms, with repression a major defense. In these typical cases, the oedipal-structural-conflict-drive concept has usually proven adequate, though even here the theory of the self has provided a more comprehensive understanding of the neuroses and a more proficient technique. The importance of the role of the Oedipus complex as an organizer of the neurotic, as well as of the psychotic, structure is evident.

In the narcissistic disturbances, on the other hand, the Oedipus complex is no longer the only organizing principle, and it is precisely the ascent of the oedipal phase that is in fact impeded. The main psychological disturbance pertains to the cohesiveness of the self and to narcissistically cathected archaic objects. We are dealing with the threat of temporary fragmentation of the self and of the intrusion of archaic forms of grandiosity and of narcissistically idealized archaic selfobjects. A lack of psychic differentiation between self and object typifies these disturbances. Treatment for such patients with insufficient structure formation (the so-called structural deficit) was until the past 10 years confined to psychotherapy, though this prescription did not entail a clear set of technical procedures. Some vague recommendations were associated with such psychotherapy, such as strengthening the ego, emphasizing reality, reinforcing defenses, and avoiding the uncovering of unconscious material. These recommendations were based on deviations from strictly psychoanalytic procedures, however, and their application was left to the intuitive skill of the experienced therapist. It is only with the contributions of developmental psychoanalysis (Mahler, 1968; Mahler, Pine, & Bergman, 1975; McDevitt & Settlage, 1971;

Spitz, 1953, 1957, 1959, 1965), the progress in the theory of object relations (the British object relations school: M. Klein, 1939, 1952; Fairbairn, 1954; Winnicott, 1954, 1955, 1965; Guntrip, 1961, 1971; Bowlby, 1969, 1973), the progressively broadening structural theory (Hartmann, 1964; Hartmann & Kris, 1945; Rapaport, 1951, 1967; Jacobson, 1964; G. Klein, 1972, 1976), and the exploration and reformulation of fundamental concepts like internalization (Schafer, 1968; Kohut, 1971), narcissism, and the transference (Kernberg, 1975, 1976; Kohut, 1966, 1971, 1977) that the understanding of the process of structure formation has advanced, preparing the ground for widening the scope of psychoanalysis. It is in this area that the psychoanalysis of the self is making its major theoretical and technical contributions. The concepts of selfobject and selfobject relationships, fragmentation of the self, narcissistic transference or, more generally, transference to selfobjects, transmuting internalizations, defensive and compensatory structures, vertical and horizontal splits, the development of the constituents of the nuclear self and the bipolarity of the self; these are among the most important concepts introduced by the psychoanalytic theory of the self. Though these concepts originated from clinical data and observations pertaining to the narcissistic disorders, their applicability is not limited to narcissistic pathology but has far-reaching implications for psychoanalysis and psychotherapy in general.

By complementing traditional metapsychology (with its exclusive focus on structural conflicts), these new concepts have increased the efficacy of psychoanalysis in the treatment of neuroses and extended its therapeutic reach to patients with defective structures who had generally been, until then, relegated to the realm of psychotherapy. In addition, psychoanalysis of the self, thanks to its framework of rigorous psychoanalytic methodology and its range of new conceptualizations, can confront the task of structure building, *if only for a limited group of narcissistic patients.* Central to self psychology is the concept of the transference to selfobjects (the narcissistic transferences) and the understanding of the reestablishment of empathic closeness to responsive selfobjects as fundamental to the restitutive process. This unique and boundary-breaking contribution of the psychoanalysis of the self cannot be overestimated. As the transference is the core of psychoanalytic treatment, any theoretical or clinical innovation must focus on this concept. I can deal here only with some of the theoretical implications of this contribution as they relate to the limits of psychoanalysis and psychotherapy.

The clinical observation of a new kind of transference phenomenon, one that does not fit the existing classical formulations, has enlarged the therapeutic range of psychoanalysis, prompted the exploration of the pathology of the self, and led to the recognition of the theory of the self as supraordinate to the oedipal-structural-conflict-drive model. As a result of these observations, moreover, the question of the definition of psychoanalysis, its range and limits, and its relation to psychotherapy, has been reopened.

Narcissistic transferences stem from primitive forms of the early phases of the development of object relations, and from the vicissitudes of the progressive psychological separation of the child from a state of merger (of biological unity with the mother) to a relatively independent psychological existence. This involves the formation of psychic structure through complex processes of internalization (transmuting internalization), and its disruption through deficient empathic responsiveness. The concept of empathy is central to the theoretical elaboration of the psychoanalysis of the self, and lapses in empathy are considered the cause of temporary or permanent disruptions of the analytic process.

Elsewhere (Palaci, 1975), I pointed out that this clinically based, new conception of transference and countertransference did not fit any of the prevailing definitions of classical transference, and proposed a reconceptualization of the transference that would encompass the narcissistic transferences. As long as psychoanalysis was limited to the treatment of the psychoneuroses, the classical conceptualization of the transference seemed adequate. This conceptualization identified the transference as a one-dimensional, unified phenomenon of varying complexity, based on the content of the unconscious in a repetitive dynamic, and referring fundamentally to advanced phases, to oedipal levels of the development of object relations. It was insufficient, however, for certain patients who, according to the theoretical and technical progress of psychoanalysis, were now believed to be treatable. A concept of transference limited to structural conflcts, i.e., to the "systems" of the psychic apparatus dealing with the sexual and aggressive wishes of the individual, his ideals, and the prohibitions and injunctions governing his life, required relatively advanced, clearly structuralized object relations. It was plainly insufficient for these patients. Preoedipal conflicts, which originate at an earlier developmental period prior to psychic structure formation, necessitated a concept of transference that could take into account the period of structure building, the development of the self and object representations, the phases of internalization of archaic objects and of object relations and functions, and their transformation into psychic regulatory systems. These preoedipal, prestructural conflicts have to do with wishes and primitive narcissistic idealizations, with prohibitions and injunctions which are not experienced as part of the self. They concern archaic representations of part-objects, selfobjects, or primitive object relations.

The broadened concept of transference should include not only the object-instinctual cathexis as displayed in oedipal object relations but the preoedipal aspects of object relations. For both preoedipal and oedipal object relations, it should follow the course of development, assess the degree of structuralization, the separation between self and object, the nature, cohesiveness, and stability of the structural configurations, the type and level of the defense mechanisms employed. The meaning of the transference will not be limited solely to the reactivation and projection of earlier phases of psychosexual development of oedipal object relations, which derive from successful separation of self and object, but will also take into account the tensions resulting from an unsuccessful preoedipal individuation process. This aspect of the transference will deal with the patient's attempt to resume the interrupted developmental process of psychological separation and structuralization in the hope of achieving it in the transference reactivation of the unresolved, preoedipal, narcissistic relationship. This process of structuralization will be aided by a particular aspect of internalization, the so-called transmuting internalizations that bring about an alteration of the projective-introjective interactions and an evolution of the defense mechanisms, which in the narcissistic disturbances remain primitive (splitting, denial, projective idealization, omnipotence, devaluation, etc., as opposed to repression). This attempt, if successful, should lead to the formation, evolution, and stability of the psychic structures, to the establishment of individual boundaries, and to a sense of identity.

Such a comprehensive view of the transference is set forth in the psychoanalysis of the self (see Palaci, 1975). One of Kohut's fundamental clinical contributions is to complement the classical meaning of the transference with the introduction of the concept of the transference to the selfobject. During psychoanalytic treatment, the transference will no longer be taken to refer solely to the revival of the drives and of the oedipal conflicts through the repetition compulsion. In addition, it will be understood to reveal, by the kind of interaction with the psychoanalyst, the level and nature of object relations and the degree of evolution of the narcissistic structures in relation to the drives.

The transference, conceived in this multidimensional form, is adequate both to the therapeutic functions of traditional psychoanalysis, with its emphasis on the resolution of oedipal conflicts and other incestuous and aggressive strivings, and to those of psychoanalytically oriented psychotherapy, which attempts to build structures and restore structural defects. If we consider that psychoanalysis of the self, relying on the "depth-psychological principle of complementarity,"[3] retains both explanatory approaches (Kohut, 1977), and deals with both oedipal and self pathology, we will appreciate the need to rethink the traditional separation between psychoanalysis and psychotherapy.

[3]Bohr's principle of complementarity (or Polanyi's concept of disjunction) is of central importance to psychoanalysis: "The same phenomena can be understood by means of two different mutually exclusive systems of meaning, if we use the epistemological device of complementarity, a device that accepts basic dualities without straining for mutual dissolution or reduction" (Modell, 1978, pp. 656–657).

With the psychoanalysis of the narcissistic personality disorders, the premise underlying the sharp division between psychoanalysis and psychotherapy has been challenged by clinical data. Still theoretical differences between them cannot be denied. If we choose to stay within the boundaries of the classical definition of the transference and define psychoanalysis as a therapy to be used exclusively for neuroses, we will have to question whether the treatment advocated for the narcissistic personality disorders is legitimate psychoanalysis, and whether the narcissistic transferences are valid transferences. If we answer these questions in the negative, we will have to relegate the narcissistic transferences to the secondary position of "transferencelike phenomena." This view is not supported by empirical evidence or by the strict respect for psychoanalytic methodology evidenced by Kohut. It is not simply a matter of terminology or definitions, but of *two quite different alternative formulations of the theory and technique of clinical psychoanalytic work*. Kohut and Kernberg have both chosen to maintain the term "transference" as it applies to narcissistic personality disorders, and have justified this use on the basis of their clinical experience.

It is not my intention to review the various attempts at defining psychoanalysis and psychotherapy, or to explore further the indications for one or the other form of treatment. These questions have been dealt with by many authors and have been the subject of a number of panel discussions (Glover, 1931; Panel, 1953; Bibring, 1954; Rangell, 1954; Fromm-Reichmann, 1950; Blanck & Blanck, 1974). Wallerstein (1969) has succinctly summarized the issues. Freud, despite his clearly defined position of regarding psychoanalysis as the treatment of choice only for the neuroses, nevertheless showed interest in the various directions in which psychoanalysis and psychotherapy could evolve. He stated:

It is very probable, too, that the large-scale application of our therapy will compel us to alloy the pure gold of analysis freely with the copper of direct suggestion; and hypnotic influence, too, might find a place in it again, as it has in the treatment of war neuroses. But, whatever form this psychotherapy for the people may take, whatever the elements out of which it is compounded, its most effective and most important ingredients will assuredly remain those borrowed from strict and untendentious psycho-analysis [Freud, 1919, p. 168].

In a recent contribution, Goldberg (1978) has suggested that the separation of psychoanalysis from psychotherapy lies less in the method than in the goal of treatment: psychotherapy consisting of the repair of the self and psychoanalysis constituting a reorganization of the self. In this connection, it has been pointed out that the demarcation between repair and reorganization cannot always be clearly ascertained, and the setting of goals should be determined by process criteria rather than by an a priori "decision in favor of psychoanalysis or psychotherapy" (London, 1978). I am in full agreement with the latter view and would further question whether, given the theoretical framework of psychoanalysis of the self with its dual-complementary model and its multidimensional concept of the transference, the a priori separation of psychoanalysis and psychotherapy is still a clinical necessity for the broad spectrum of patients who do not fit into the clear-cut categories of the neuroses or the psychoses. Would it not be preferable instead if our method of treatment were guided by the varying emergence of the dominant psychological disturbances in either the object-instinctual or the selfobject transference as the treatment process evolves and the patient's needs unfold?

References

Abraham, K. (1908), The Psychosexual Differences Between Hysteria and Dementia Praecox. In: *Collected Papers,* vol. 1. London: Hogarth Press, 1948, pp. 64–79.

Arlow, J. A. & Brenner, C. (1964), *Psychoanalytic Concepts and the Structural Theory.* New York: International Universities Press.

Bibring, E. (1954), Psychoanalysis and the Dynamic Psychotherapies. *J. Amer. Psychoanal. Assn.,* 2:745–770.

Blanck, G. & Blanck, R. (1974), *Ego Psychology: Theory and Practice.* New York: Columbia University Press.

Bowlby, J. (1969), *Attachment and Loss. Vol. 1: Attachment.* London: Hogarth Press.

_____ (1973), *Attachment and Loss. Vol. 2: Separation.* London: Hogarth Press.

Boyer, L. B. & Giovacchini, P. L. (1967), *Psychoanalytic Treatment of Charac-
terological and Schizophrenic Disorders.* New York: Science House.
Eissler, K. R. (1953), The Effect of the Structure of the Ego on Psychoanalytic
Technique. *J. Amer. Psychoanal. Assn.,* 1:104–143.
Fairbairn, W. R. D. (1954), *An Object-Relations Theory of Personality.* New
York: Basic Books.
Federn, P. (1943), Psychoanalysis of Psychoses. *Psychiat. Quart.,* 17:3–19.
Freud, S. (1894), The Neuro-Psychoses of Defence. *Standard Edition,*
3:45–61. London: Hogarth Press, 1962.
_____ (1911), Psycho-Analytic Notes on an Autobiographical Account of
a Case of Paranoia. *Standard Edition,* 12:9–82. London: Hogarth Press,
1958.
_____ (1914), On Narcissism: An Introduction. *Standard Edition,* 14:73–102.
London: Hogarth Press, 1957.
_____ (1915a), Instincts and Their Vicissitudes. *Standard Edition,* 14:
117–140. London: Hogarth Press, 1957.
_____ (1915b), The Unconscious. *Standard Edition,* 14:166–204. London:
Hogarth Press, 1957.
_____ (1919), Lines of Advance in Psycho-Analytic Therapy. *Standard Edition,* 17:159–168. London: Hogarth Press, 1955.
Fromm-Reichmann, F. (1950), *Principles of Intensive Psychotherapy.* Chicago:
University of Chicago Press.
Glover, E. (1931), The Therapeutic Effect of Inexact Interpretation: A Contri-
bution to Suggestion. In: *The Technique of Psychoanalysis.* London:
Bailliere, Tindall & Cox, 1955, pp. 353–366.
Goldberg, A. (1978), Self Psychology and the Distinctiveness of Psychotherapy.
Internat. J. Psychother. In press.
Guntrip, H. (1961), *Personality Structure and Human Interaction.* New York:
International Universities Press.
_____ (1968), *Schizoid Phenomena, Object Relations and the Self.* London:
Hogarth Press.
_____ (1971), *Psychoanalytic Therapy and the Self.* London: Hogarth Press.
Hartmann, H. (1950), Comments on the Psychoanalytic Theory of the Ego.
The Psychoanalytic Study of the Child, 5:74–96. New York: International
Universities Press.
_____ (1964), *Essays on Ego Psychology.* New York: International Universities
Press.
_____ & Kris, E. (1945), The Genetic Approach in Psychoanalysis. *The Psy-
choanalytic Study of the Child,* 1:11–30. New York: International Univer-
sities Press.
Heimann, P. (1960), Counter-Transference. *Internat. J. Psycho-Anal.,* 31:81–84.
Jacobson, E. (1964), *The Self and the Object World.* New York: International
Universities Press.
Kernberg, O. (1975), *Borderline Conditions and Pathological Narcissism.* New
York: Aronson.
_____ (1976), *Object Relations Theory and Clinical Psychoanalysis.* New York:
Aronson.
Khan, M. M. R. (1975), *Le Soi caché.* Paris: Gallimard.

Klein, G. S. (1972), The Vital Pleasures. In: *Psychoanalysis and Contemporary Science*, vol. 1. New York: Macmillan, pp. 181–255.

_____ (1976), *Psychoanalytic Theory: An Exploration of Essentials*. New York: International Universities Press.

Klein, M. (1939), *Contributions to Psycho-Analysis*. London: Hogarth Press, 1948.

_____ (1952), The Origins of Transference. *Internat. J. Psycho-Anal.*, 33: 433–438.

Kohut, H. (1966), Forms and Transformations of Narcissism. *J. Amer. Psychoanal. Assn.*, 14:243–272.

_____ (1971), *The Analysis of the Self*. New York: International Universities Press.

_____ (1977), *The Restoration of the Self*. New York: International Universities Press.

Kubie, L. S. (1950), *Practical and Theoretical Aspects of Psychoanalysis*. New York: International Universities Press.

Levin, D. C. (1969), The Self: A Contribution to its Place in Theory and Technique. *Internat. J. Psycho-Anal.*, 50:41–51.

London, N. (1973), An Essay on Psycho-Analytic Theory: Two Theories of Schizophrenia. *Internat. J. Psycho-Anal.*, 54:169–193.

_____ (1978), Discussion of Arnold Goldberg's "Self Psychology and the Distinctiveness of Psychotherapy." *Internat. J. Psychother.* In press.

Mahler, M. (1968), *On Human Symbiosis and the Vicissitudes of Individuation*. New York: International Universities Press.

_____, Pine, F., & Bergman, A. (1975), *The Psychological Birth of the Human Infant*. New York: Basic Books.

McDevitt, J. B. & Settlage, C. F., eds. (1971), *Separation-Individuation*. New York: International Universities Press.

Modell, A. (1978), The Nature of Psychoanalytic Knowledge. *J. Amer. Psychoanal. Assn.*, 26:641–658.

Palaci, J. (1975), Transfert et narcissisme. *R. Française Psychanal.*, 42:39–64.

Panel (1953), The Essentials of Psychotherapy as Viewed by the Psychoanalyst, reported by O. S. English. *J. Amer. Psychoanal. Assn.*, 1:550–561.

Panel (1976), New Horizons in Metapsychology, reported by W. W. Meissner. *J. Amer. Psychoanal. Assn.*, 24:161–180.

Rangell, L. (1954), Similarities and Differences Between Psychoanalysis and Dynamic Psychotherapy. *J. Amer. Psychoanal. Assn.*, 2:734–744.

Rapaport, D. (1951), *Organization and Pathology of Thought*. New York: Columbia University Press.

_____ (1967), *Collected Papers*, ed. M. M. Gill. New York: Basic Books.

Reik, T. (1936), *Le Psychologue surpris*. Paris: Denoel, 1976.

_____ (1948), *Listening with the Third Ear*. New York: Farrar, Strauss.

Rosenfeld, H. A. (1952), Transference Phenomena and Transference Analysis in an Acute Catatonic Schizophrenic Patient. In: *Psychotic States: A Psychoanalytical Approach*. New York: International Universities Press, 1965, pp. 104–116.

Schafer, R. (1968), *Aspects of Internalization*. New York: International Universities Press.

_____ (1973), Action—Its Place in Psychoanalytic Interpretation and Theory. *The Annual of Psychoanalysis,* 1:159–196. New York: Quadrangle.

Searles, H. F. (1963), Transference Psychosis in the Psychotherapy of Chronic Schizophrenia. *Internat. J. Psycho-Anal.,* 44:249–281.

Segal, H. (1962), The Curative Factors in Psycho-Analysis. *Internat. J. Psycho-Anal.,* 43:212–217.

Spitz, R. (1953), Aggression in the Establishment of Object Relations. In: *Drives, Affects, Behavior,* vol. 1, ed. R. M. Loewenstein. New York: International Universities Press, pp. 126–138.

_____ (1957), *No and Yes.* New York: International Universities Press.

_____ (1959), *A Genetic Field Theory of Ego Formation: Its Implications for Pathology.* New York: International Universities Press.

_____ (1965), *The First Year of Life.* New York: International Universities Press.

Sullivan, H. S. (1931), The Modified Psychoanalytic Treatment of Schizophrenia. *Amer. J. Psychiat.,* 11:519–540.

Tarachow, S. (1963), *An Introduction to Psychotherapy.* New York: International Universities Press.

Tausk, V. (1916), Diagnostic Considerations Concerning the Symptomatology of the So-Called War Psychoses. *Psychoanal. Quart.,* 38:382–405.

_____ (1919), On the Origin of the "Influencing Machine" in Schizophrenia. *Psychoanal. Quart.,* 2:519–556.

Wallerstein, R. S. (1969), Psycho-Analysis and Psychotherapy. *Internat. J. Psycho-Anal.,* 50:117–126.

Winnicott, D. W. (1954), Metapsychological and Clinical Aspects of Regression within the Psycho-Analytic Set-Up. In: *Collected Papers.* London: Tavistock, 1958, pp. 278–294.

_____ (1955), Clinical Varieties of Transference. In: *Collected Papers.* London: Tavistock, 1958.

_____ (1960), Ego Distortion in Terms of True and False Self. In: *The Maturational Processes and the Facilitating Environment.* New York: International Universities Press, 1965, pp. 140–152.

_____ (1965), *The Maturational Processes and the Facilitating Environment.* New York: International Universities Press.

Discussion of *"Psychoanalysis of the Self and Psychotherapy"* by Jacques Palaci

NATHANIEL J. LONDON

There are two separate dimensions to Dr. Palaci's paper. On one hand, it is a contribution to the metapsychology of self psychology with respect to its relation to psychoanalytic structural theory (ego psychology). At the same time, it is a contribution to the clinical applications of self psychology with respect to the widening scope of psychoanalysis, particularly insofar as it pertains to psychoanalytic psychotherapy. Although these two topics can be related, I shall consider them separately in this discussion.

Structural Theory

Palaci places self psychology squarely in the context of psychoanalytic structural theory. He informs us, in this respect, that he is not referring to Freud's original formulation of the tripartite model of id, ego, and superego. Rather, he deals with the further elaboration of this theory, particularly by Hartmann (1964) and Rapaport (1967), in terms of the study of mental functions and psychic organization. He further asserts that Kohut's (1971) researches were inspired and in part derived from this theory. Yet, Kohut's concept of the self, Palaci reminds us, was derived from

337

empirical data, as a matter of "clinical necessity" and not as a scientific concept. That is to say, Kohut's conclusions with respect to the self arose from the exigencies of the psychoanalytic situation, his organization of these conclusions was strongly influenced by structural theory, but the comprehensive theoretical model of self psychology represents a new formulation. Kohut's theory of the self was conceived originally in structural terms "similar to the 'system ego'...but closer to experience." Thus, Kohut is credited with complementing the "structural conflict-drive concept" of psychoanalysis with the "structural defect-restoration concept" of self theory. The overall sense of Dr. Palaci's argument is that self psychology is not just an extension of structural theory but a distinguishable further development arising from new considerations based on clinical experience. Accordingly, Palaci's subsequent discussion of self psychology is fully integrated with structural theory but focuses on the transference.

In assessing Dr. Palaci's position, one has to decide whether structural theory does indeed provide an essential matrix for the psychology of the self or whether he has emphasized structural theory only in order to preserve the historical continuity of psychoanalytic metapsychology. Schafer (1970) has noted that Hartmann consistently underestimated the degree to which he disagreed with Freud in order to maintain continuity, and Kohut has been viewed as presenting his initial formulations in structural terms for similar reasons. It certainly would be more popular today to conclude that the new paradigm of self psychology should not be encumbered with old theory. Many students tend to view Hartmann's ego psychology as an anachronism; overly abstract, complex, and remote from clinical experience. My view, on the contrary, which follows Schafer's (1970) critical assessment of Hartmann, is that Hartmann succeeded in defining his task from a certain point of view and carried it as far as he could go. That his contributions are complex is not a pejorative reflection on the theory, but a reflection of the complexity of human behavior. It is true that ego psychology became overly abstract, but this problem derives from certain limitations inherent in the theoretical assumptions and points of view. Palaci has convinced me of the correctness of his position; that structural theory is essential to comprehend and apply self psychology. My discussion here is not designed to document this judgment but rather to clarify the relationship between ego psychology and self psychology on the basis of epistemological considerations.

The connecting link between self psychology and ego psychology is the theory of object relations. I have always assumed that self psychology belongs to object relations theory and I have never understood those who feel otherwise. Perhaps the problem is that "object relations" is a loose term. Object relations, in common usage, traditionally has designated the subjective or intrapsychic correlate of social interactions — or of "interpersonal relations," to use the neo-Freudian term. At the same time, a growing body of empirical data pertinent to the subject's experience of self and objects has been organized theoretically. Within the British school of object relations, these data were organized largely from the psychodynamic viewpoint. The observations pertinent to object relations were incorporated into structural theory most notably by Hartmann (1950), Jacobson (1964), and Mahler (1968). In this context, Hartmann introduced the concept of self representation as a metapsychological correlate of object representation. Object relations theory, being limited to a specific category of psychoanalytic observations, is, like the theory of the defenses, on a different level from the broader scope of structural theory. Within structural theory, the vicissitudes of object relations can be considered in the context of defenses, cognitive schemata, etc.

Schafer (1968), in reviewing the empirical referents for the concepts of self and object, asserted that there was as yet no metapsychological base for these concepts and that they should be considered experiential terms. In fact, he took Kohut to task for defining the self simultaneously in metapsychological and experiential terms. Kohut (1977), however, has persisted in this position, justifying the manifest incongruity on the basis of the need for flexibility and theoretical open-mindedness. The self, in Kohut's narrow definition of the term, refers to a specific structure in the mental apparatus. In his broad sense of the term, however, the self is an experiential concept, the center of the individual's psychological

universe and an independent center of initiative. This juxtaposition of structural theory with an experiential concept provides a
clue to understanding the epistemological status of the contributions of self psychology.

Self psychology has been formulated first and foremost from
the clinical vantage point of the psychoanalytic transference. The
selfobject formulated in such a context involves the same mixture
of metapsychological and experiential ingredients as the concept
of the self. The self to which the selfobject relates is conceived in
one sense in structural terms. However, the selfobject is embodied
in the actual presence of the analyst as experienced by the analysand in manifold ways that help to sustain and consolidate his self.
Potentially, these experiences with the analyst, through transmuting internalizations, may become the basis for new structure
formation. The experiential "self" of the analysand, then, is first of
all, *in the mind of the analyst.* Through empathic as well as objective modes, the analyst organizes his experiences with the analysand into such a conception of self. Such an organization provides
the means to establish contact and to track the analysand through
the analytic process. Of course, this "self" is also in the mind of the
analysand, particularly as he becomes increasingly a co-therapist
in the treatment. Ultimately, the sum of the experiences in the
interaction between analyst and analysand provides the data base
for defining the analysand's "self."

The point is that self psychology does represent a new paradigm in psychoanalysis. It is not that self psychology is closer to
clinical experience than ego psychology (sound structural theory is
not remote from observation), but rather that it approaches the
clinical data from a different epistemological vantage point. Structural theory is oriented to subjective experience with respect to
adaptation to an objective environment. That is why the subject's
organization of reality is emphasized in structural theory. Self psychology is, in addition, oriented to the clinical interaction and to
its developmental antecedents. That is why empathic experience
receives a new emphasis. Such a different viewpoint leads to a
different view of subjective experience (or the intrapsychic focus)
and a different view of the role of the environment (as in the conse-

quences of empathic failures), not to mention redefinitions of transference and countertransference. The juxtaposition of structural concepts and experiential concepts in self psychology does present theoretical and semantic problems. Perhaps the classical metapsychological points of view, which organize the subject's psychic activity from objective viewpoints in the Cartesian sense, should be supplemented by an experiential-interactional point of view. In any case, structural theory remains integrated with self psychology. Self psychology has neither redefined nor discarded ego psychology. Rather, it has advanced psychoanalytic structural theory with new data derived from an experiential-interactional viewpoint.

Psychotherapy

In his presentation, Dr. Palaci is concerned with what has been called "long-term psychoanalytic psychotherapy" as an alternative to psychoanalytic treatment. He has not discussed a range of goal-limited psychotherapies, particularly those well defined in psychiatric academic settings. In this discussion, I too will only consider long-term intensive psychotherapy.

Dr. Palaci focuses on only one aspect of the distinction between psychotherapy and psychoanalytic treatment. His concern is with those patients who may fall within the widening scope of psychoanalysis. These are patients who, because of the extent of their psychopathology, have in the past been considered unsuitable subjects for psychoanalysis but suitable for psychoanalytic psychotherapy. Dr. Palaci refers to the broad spectrum of patients who cannot be classified at the extreme poles of the typical neuroses or the psychoses. He asks if, from the theoretical framework of the analysis of the self, the a priori separation of psychoanalysis and psychotherapy is still a clinical necessity. It is implicit in his view that there are indications and contraindications for initiating and continuing psychoanalytic treatment. However, he holds that the emergence in the treatment process of the predominant psychological disturbance, be it oedipal pathology or pathology of the self as reflected in an object-instinctual or a selfobject transference, should not determine whether the treatment is *called* psycho-analysis or psychotherapy. Rather, these developments should provide guides to the optimal psychoanalytic technique for that particular patient.

Dr. Palaci's argument is familiar and convincing. Self psychology has indeed contributed to the widening scope of psycho-analysis. Patients who would previously have been considered in-appropriate for psychoanalytic treatment are now regularly treated with success. The treatment of such patients, while benefiting from advances in technique, is in full accord with the essentials of psy-choanalytic technique. In fact, self psychology allows a more ac-curate assessment and response to the psychoanalytic process, par-ticularly with regard to the vicissitudes of transference and resistance. Dr. Palaci has fully reviewed the theoretical advances of self psychology, particularly with respect to transference and structural deficits, which have allowed this widened scope. Being in full accord with his position, I will only add a few words of cau-tion. The advances in technique of self psychology have not yet stood the full test of time. In addition, the technology for treat-ment evaluation continues to lag far behind the technology for treatment. Accordingly, the effectiveness of psychoanalytic treat-ment for these new patient populations is as difficult to establish as it continues to be for patients with classical neuroses. In addition, research in goal-limited psychotherapy, using the concepts of self psychology, has not progressed to the point where it can establish the degree to which the advances of self psychology may be used optimally with psychotherapeutic strategies that are more modest and less costly than psychoanalysis. Beyond these cautionary con-cerns, my further comments are directed to issues in the distinction between psychoanalysis and psychotherapy which include but ulti-mately transcend self psychology.

The argument that opposes Dr. Palaci's position should be mentioned, if only to be challenged. It maintains that the differ-ential indications for psychoanalysis and psychotherapy have wor-thy origins that remain valid today. According to this argument, patients unsuitable for psychoanalytic treatment should not be selected for such treatment, because to do otherwise would be a a disservice to the patient and a discredit to psychoanalysis (Freud, 1913). This position further holds that the definitions of psychoanalysis and psychotherapy as different treatment modalities remain valid. Psychoanalysis is the most comprehensive treatment available for the structured neuroses: specifically for developmental arrests related to insufficient resolution of oedipal conflicts. There are other ways to help people, however, and there are other populations in need of help — we recognize the value of treatment modalities other than psychoanalysis. But to introduce a new modality and call it psychoanalysis can only serve to confuse and dilute the very definition of psychoanalysis.

The perception of such a threat to the very core of psychoanalysis has been at the heart of every rejection of so-called "dissident schools." It is not the *valuable* contributions of a dissident school that threaten psychoanalysis. The threat is when a dissident school, as an organized professional movement, attempts to redefine psychoanalysis into a new modality. It is as important to recognize the danger of such a threat as it is to recognize that overzealous efforts to resist such "threats" can lead to dogmatism and stifle the advances of new paradigms — to threaten progress in psychoanalysis. There is little doubt that self psychology, like any new paradigm that can be conceptually separated on some terms from standard psychoanalysis, could become the focus of a dissident school, whether we like it or not. It could be misused to scotomatize the significance of oedipal conflicts, regardless of whether such conflicts emerge in a particular psychoanalytic investigation as independent, dependent, or intervening variables. Self psychology in itself, however, need not meet the definition of a dissident school because it does not redefine psychoanalysis. Rather, applications of its contributions are fully consistent with the technical and process criteria of psychoanalytic treatment. Its applications contribute not only to the widening scope of psychoanalysis but to significant refinements in technique with respect to the structured neuroses. In other words, whether self psychology is used in a dissident school or as a new paradigm for psychoanalysis is a subject for the sociology of professional organizations rather than a problem for psychoanalytic theory. Having concluded that self psychology belongs in the mainstream of psychoanalytic investigation, it is now appropriate to turn from the definition of psychoanalysis to problems regarding the definition of psychotherapy.

What does it mean when a patient is considered unsuitable for psychoanalysis but is referred for what is termed long-term intensive psychoanalytic psychotherapy? The recommendation for treatment is shifted from a very well-defined modality — psychoanalysis — to one that has remained vague with respect to technique, process, and goals, as well as subject to considerable idiosyncratic variation from one clinician to another. Patients considered unsuitable for psychoanalysis because of the extent of their psychopathology are often referred for intensive psychotherapy with the implicit assumption that the goals of an analysis can somehow be reached. It is not infrequent that such psychotherapies become interminable or have inconclusive or poor results. Such unsuccessful psychotherapies, generally understood by the general public to be psychoanalytic treatment, have been harmful to the reputation of psychoanalysis. These psychotherapies are all too frequently merely supportive or relationship therapies. What is disturbing is that such supportive treatment — an adequate holding environment — can be provided by means much less costly than continuing psychotherapy of three or four times a week.

The problem of intensive psychotherapy is also complicated by the fact that it is not unusual that such treatments prove highly successful. The therapist may be an analyst or a nonanalyst, and it is possible that the goals of an analysis may have been reached. In such cases, it is possible that an analysis has been conducted and only designated psychotherapy. In some cases, the patient may have been misdiagnosed initially but nevertheless improved with psychotherapy. In other cases, the patient would no doubt have fared poorly in an analysis strictly oriented toward a structured neurosis, and the success of treatment can be explained in terms of self psychology or perhaps some other theory.

I am prepared to acknowledge, if only to register my dissent, the argument that the advances of self psychology constitute a

welcome contribution to intensive psychotherapy, but that psychoanalytic treatment should be preserved as a modality reserved for
the structured neuroses. Foremost among the reasons for my disagreement with such a position is my conviction that psychoanalysis as a treatment modality should be defined by the activity
of the analyst, by formal features of technique, and by process
criteria rather than by diagnostic considerations. Consider a sur-
geon who performs a laparotomy, fails to find the diseased appendix he anticipated, but corrects another condition responsible for
his patient's distress. He has not performed an appendectomy but
he has performed an effective and successful surgical procedure.
Similarly, a psychoanalyst who establishes a psychoanalytic situation has conducted an analysis, whether the central pathology
proved to be oedipal conflicts or disturbances in the bipolar self.
While the importance of accurate diagnosis cannot be overestimated, the indications for analytic treatment transcend diagnostic assessment of the central pathology. Neither pathology of
the self nor oedipal conflicts are in themselves sufficient to decide
to undertake an analysis. The justification for an analysis ultimately rests in a conclusion that the central pathology, whatever it
might be, can be significantly and decisively resolved, within a
framework of limited goals, to a degree that cannot be accomplished by any other less ambitious or less costly modality.

A treatment conducted by a psychoanalyst in which full use is
made of his psychoanalytic knowledge and the process criteria of
an analysis are met should be designated psychoanalytic. The inclusion of free association among these criteria may merit separate
discussion, but the mobilization and resolution of a therapeutic
regression, a regressive transference, and a transference neurosis
are generally included. Transference neurosis, in this sense, is by
no means defined only as the repetition of oedipal conflicts. Certainly, the reactivation and repetition of past pathological experiential patterns in the transference is one of the defining characteristics of a transference neurosis — whether the transferences are
oedipal or archaic. Yet, I would emphasize equally the process criteria for defining a transference neurosis: the development of the
therapeutic split, the analyst and the analysis becoming central in

the analysand's life, symptomatic improvement outside the analysis, and the coalescence and intensification of significant themes in the impetus of the ongoing process. These are all significant features that transcend diagnostic considerations and specific ideational content.

What if these defining criteria for an analysis are not met? The situation can only result in an unsuccessful or a partly unsuccessful analysis. For example, a transference neurosis may not develop and the analysis may still prove highly effective. To conclude, as is often the case, that the treatment is "only psychotherapy" confuses the issues. It makes no practical difference whether the treatment is called psychoanalysis or psychotherapy. Consider a situation where the patient is obviously progressing, yet where an analytic situation has not developed. There is no utility in noting that the treatment is "only psychotherapy." The practical question is whether the patient's progress could be equally well advanced in a less costly manner — say, once- or twice-weekly psychotherapy. This is a difficult question but an important one. Perhaps advances in peer review procedures will provide new data, new concepts, and new organizational structures for answering such questions. That vague modality designated long-term intensive psychoanalytic psychotherapy has only served to obscure matters — and this was the case long before the advent of self psychology. It is worth noting that an analysis conducted or attempted by a nonanalyst is commonly labeled in this way. In such cases, training criteria rather than intrinsic criteria serve to define the modality. Such issues should be clarified. To my view, the definition of "long-term psychoanalytic psychotherapy" should be drastically restricted or perhaps even eliminated. If preserved, it should designate a valid modality clearly differentiated from psychoanalysis. Of course, this suggestion is provocative and requires further exploration and discussion. It is based on an expectation that effective peer review criteria can be developed for a range of psychoanalytic psychotherapies as well as for psychoanalysis and that these modalities can be differentiated by process considerations.

Self psychology, as Dr. Palaci has explained, has decisively widened the scope of psychoanalysis. Hitherto unanalyzable patients are now analyzable. This fact does reduce the area for intensive psychotherapy, insofar as that vague modality formerly provided an umbrella for helping patients with pathology of the self. Self psychology along with all aspects of psychoanalysis contributes both to the psychoanalytic situation and to a range of modalities designated psychoanalytic psychotherapy.

References

Freud, S. (1913), On Beginning the Treatment. *Standard Edition,* 12:123–144. London: Hogarth Press, 1958.

Hartmann, H. (1950), Comments on the Psychoanalytic Theory of the Ego. In: *Essays on Ego Psychology.* New York: International Universities Press, 1964, pp. 113–141.

_____ (1964), *Essays on Ego Psychology.* New York: International Universities Press.

Jacobson, E. (1964), *The Self and the Object World.* New York: International Universities Press.

Kohut, H. (1971), *The Analysis of the Self.* New York: International Universities Press.

_____ (1977), *The Restoration of the Self.* New York: International Universities Press.

Mahler, M. (1968), *On Human Symbiosis and the Vicissitudes of Individuation.* New York: International Universities Press.

Rapaport, D. (1967), *Collected Papers,* ed. M. M. Gill. New York: Basic Books.

Schafer, R. (1968), *Aspects of Internalization.* New York: International Universities Press.

_____ (1970), An Overview of Heinz Hartmann's Contributions to Psycho-analysis. *Internat. J. Psycho-Anal.,* 51:425–446.

Object Love and the
Psychology of the Self

David M. Terman

Psychoanalysts have long been concerned with the nature and vicissitudes of "object love," but less explicitly with "love" per se. Leon Altman (1977) recently noted that the subject of love as such has been neglected by analysts. He pointed to the fact that "love" is not listed in the American Psychoanalytic Association's *Glossary of Psychoanalytic Terms,* and voiced his dissatisfaction with the equation of love with libido. "If love is libido," Altman observed, "then love is a well-concealed maneuver of the sexual instinct to find expression. And surely love is more than that" (p. 38).

The *Glossary* does have an entry for "object love," which it defines as "The type of love relationship with another person which occurs when that individual is cathected (invested) with *libido"* (Moore & Fine, 1967, p. 58). In addition to Altman's objection that love is more than libido, one would have to raise the additional objection that the model employed is incorrectly extended. The concept of object love does not describe a "relationship" at all. It describes an inner psychological state. The state presumably has some correlation with the interpersonal *relationship,* but the two are *not* the same. Libido is an intrapsychic process that can never be interpersonal.

349

This confusion between the intrapsychic and the interpersonal has persistently troubled analytic investigators, despite periodic reminders of conceptual confusion and exhortations for theoretical clarity. This would suggest that our topographic and structural models may not be adequate to conceptualizing properly either the source or the development of this important interpersonal process that we call love or object love.

What is object love? At times Freud used the term to denote the outcome of sexual development. He noted, however, that its origins and composition were not strictly sensual. In 1912, Freud described two "currents" to account for its genesis: the "affectionate" current and the "sensual" current. He wrote that the affectionate current "springs from the earliest years of childhood [and] is formed on the basis of the interests of the self-preservative instinct and is directed to the members of the family and those who look after the child" (p. 180). In *An Outline of Psycho-Analysis* (1940, p. 188) he reiterated that "love has its origins in attachment to the satisfied needs for nourishment." The affectionate current was, in 1912, responsible for the high valuation of the love object.

In "On Narcissism: An Introduction" (1914), Freud seemed to incorporate this affectionate current into the concept of narcissistic libido; it was narcissistic libido that gave value to the love objects, not object libido. But, again, in 1921, he reiterated his position of 1912, noting, "The depth to which anyone is in love, as contrasted with his purely sensual desire, may be measured by the size of the share taken by the aim-inhibited instincts of affection" (1921, p. 112). Here, it seems, Freud was again deriving the affectionate current from aim-inhibited object libido.

The origin of the affectionate current within the libido theory is almost wholly dependent on inner energies. If it is conceptualized in terms of aim-inhibited object libido, its origins conform to the drive discharge model, with the tensions in question being the pregenital sexual instincts. If it is understood as a product of narcissistic libido, its origins are both autochthonous (the cathexis of the ego) and related to the early satisfaction of basic biological needs.

These equivocating conceptualizations lead to an important

confusion noted by Saul in 1950 in his discussion of the origin and experience of object love: that between "loving" and "being loved." Saul understood the importance of being loved, noting that "to be loved is the basic need of childhood."

Curiously—yet understandably—the experience of being loved is hardly considered in the theory of either the dynamics or genesis of object love. The concept of an affectionate current does not adequately conceptualize the process of being loved, for it does not include the qualitative nature of the experience or the experience of helplessness or dependence that ensues when one cannot provide an experience of an essential affect state which must emanate from *another* person.

There is another important limitation of the libidinal perspective for understanding the state of being loved: the relative neglect of the effect of the response of the love object. The object, in a drive discharge model, is important only as it delays or facilitates discharge. The object of infantile drives must always be frustrating, for frustration and failure are intrinsic to the infantile situation, both as a result of the immaturity of the infant's physical equipment and the conflicts with the nurturant objects that such drive discharge would bring.

Such a conception leaves little room for the experience of gratification and its role, if any, in the evolution of object love. Outside of the satisfaction of basic biological needs, the parental response, in theory, has little significance. Freud's attitude toward parental love was, at best, barely tolerant. There is a somewhat pejorative ring to his description of it, for he seemed to regard it with some skepticism. He saw it both as erotic ("The 'affection' shown by the child's parents and those who look after him, [which] seldom fails to betray its erotic character" [1912, p. 181]) and narcissistic ("Parental love which is so moving and at bottom, so childish, is nothing but the parents' narcissism born again" [1914, p. 91]). Freud did not explore it further.

Ferenczi was more interested in the developmental importance of parental love in "Confusion of Tongues Between Adult and Child" (1933). He described a stage of "passive object love" or of tenderness in which the child "plays" at taking the place of the parent of the same sex in order to be married to the other. He emphasized, however, that "this was merely fantasy. In reality the children would not want to, in fact they cannot, do without tenderness, especially that which comes from the mother. If more love, or love of a different kind from that which they need, is forced upon the children in the stages of tenderness, it may lead to pathological consequences" (pp. 163–164).

Here Ferenczi explicitly called our attention to children's need for certain kinds of parental responses. He connected the need for such responses with the development of object love, but he did not attempt to pursue the metapsychological implications of the need. He was content with the incisive clinical observation that "passionate" reactions of adults—either of love or anger—are traumatic and lead to "splits in the personality."

M. Balint, following Ferenczi, emphasized and developed the importance of what he called "passive object love"—i.e., the wish to be loved. He postulated that this passive form of love was the source of "active object love." In "The Final Goal of Psychoanalytic Treatment" (1936), he noted that "One should never forget that the beginnings of object libido pursue passive aims and can only be brought to development through tactful, and in the literal sense of the word, 'lovable' behavior of the object. And even later one must treat these newly begun relations indulgently, so that they may find their way to reality and active love" (p. 188). The active role of the parental response in the development of object love can hardly be more clearly emphasized.

The Balints described the nature of this passive love—which M. Balint later termed "primary love"—as a "naive egoism" (A. Balint, 1939, p. 95), in which the needs of the object were not considered or perceived and in which one's own needs and wishes were automatically met. The gratification of the need led to quiet contentment, whereas nongratification led to "passionate" reactions— i.e., rage and protest (M. Balint, 1933, p. 48).

The Balints claim the active object love develops out of this passive or primary matrix by virtue of both gratification of the primary needs and an increasing "reality sense" that gradually educates the child about the "other's" needs. For A. Balint (1939), the reality sense developed by virtue of a kind of maternal rejection of the child's "naive egoism":

> The child who has outgrown his infancy is no longer so agreeable to the mother....nevertheless he clings to her and does not know any other form of love but that of his naive egoism. This naive egoism, however, becomes unbearable, because now there is no mutuality, which was its basis. Thus the child is faced with the task of adapting himself to the wishes of those whose love he needs. It is at this point that the role of reality starts in the emotional life of man [p. 103].

The Balints emphatically detach this development from the vicissitudes of genitality:

> Tact, insight, consideration, sympathy, gratitude, tenderness...are the signs and consequences of the extending strength of reality sense in the sphere of emotions. The real capacity for loving in the social sense is a secondary formation created by an external disturbance (i.e., the maternal withdrawal from the primary egoism). It has nothing to do with genitality [A. Balint, 1939, p. 102].

M. Balint tried to place these phenomena into the metapsychology of libido theory. He asserted that these early wishes "to be loved" are libidinous but not "sensual"; they are tender wishes, and they can be gratified. However, as I have noted, Freud's concept of object libido cannot accommodate such phenomena with consistency. To agree with Balint that "I shall be loved always" is the final aim of all erotic striving, is to change totally Freud's concept of the source and nature of erotism.

Might one subsume Balint's phenomena under the category of narcissistic libido? Balint explicitly chose not to do this for one important reason: passive love in essence relates to *objects*—the experience of another's affects—namely, the experience of another's love. The object relatedness of the experience, the sense that another human being had to be part of the experience, apparently precluded a consideration of it as a narcissistic phenomenon.

In summary, the Balints' hypothesis is the following: "Active love," or loving, develops from "passive love" or "primary love." Primary love is egocentric, takes the satisfaction of its needs "for granted," and when gratified, leads to feelings of contentment. Though primary love is termed "libidinal," its aims are passive and it is *not* essentially erotic or self-preservative. It is concerned with "being loved." Finally, this "primary love" becomes "active" love by means of a series of rejections.

Self psychology may help clarify the nature of the phenomena to which the Balints drew our attention in 1936. There is a great similarity between the experiences which they describe as primary love and Kohut's description of a selfobject relationship. One of the hallmarks of the selfobject relationship is the certain availability and use of its "object": the object is taken for granted because it functions as part of the self. Further, some of the functions of the selfobject correspond very closely to the elements of "primary love." The parent's approval, pleasure in the child, availability to ease his or her tensions, and concern, for example, are experienced as mirroring selfobject functions. Inasmuch as they are truly taken for granted by the child, they can fairly be included as aspects of "primary love." Kohut has, of course, elucidated their role in self development.

Kohut has, however, insisted on separating the lines of development of self and object love. He has, rightly, I think, insisted that self development follows a course of its own and that the goal and pinnacle of self development should not be a state of object love. In discarding Freud's "U Tube" analogy of the relationship between narcissistic and object libido (Freud, 1914, p. 76), Kohut has explored and described the rich series of transformations and formations of narcissism that are not only complex and varied in their own right, but result in the most valued aspects of maturity. The consolidation of the poles of the self—of its ambitions and ideals—is an important developmental task, one that surely should not be abandoned for the sake of object love.

Kohut has continued to explore the establishment and vicissitudes of the self, and, in *The Restoration of the Self* (1977), has continued to separate these self phenomena from object love. He has elaborated the differences and labeled the two resulting frameworks as applying, respectively, to "Guilty Man" and "Tragic Man." Guilty Man is described as living within the pleasure principle, attempting to satisfy pleasure-seeking drives and to discharge the tensions that arise in his erogenous zones. Kohut declares the structural model sufficient and appropriate to explain pleasure-related aims and conflicts (1977, p. 132).

Yet Kohut subsequently wavers a little in the contention that such pleasure conflicts can all be understood in the structural framework when he raises the question in his discussion of the Oedipus complex: "Could it not be that we have considered the dramatic desires and anxieties of the oedipal child as normal events when, in fact, they are the child's reactions to empathy failures from the side of the self-object environment of the oedipal phase?" (1977, p. 247). Here, Kohut echoes his earlier assumption that the "infantile sexual drive in isolation is not the primary psychological configuration...[but that] the primary psychological configuration (of which the drive is only a constituent) is the experience of the relation between the self and the empathic self-object" (p. 122). In questioning whether all such oedipal conflicts are really pleasure-derived, Kohut is questioning whether conflict over pleasure may be a sign or symptom of a deeper or broader issue pertaining, even in the case of the Oedipus complex, to self construction and the requisite selfobject participation. Elsewhere (1975) I have described the Oedipus complex as a phase of self construction in which the relevant issue is not the relative fragmentation or cohesion of a whole, nuclear self, but the differentiation of important gender-related goals and ambitions. According to this thesis, the experience of pleasure at this time is in the service of phase-appropriate self expansion, while excessive conflict over pleasure or the failure to transform archaic, infantile, oedipal goals is symptomatic of selfobject failure. To simplify my argument, identification, with the requisite, appropriate parental response, is the motivation for, rather than the resolution of, the oedipal anxieties.

If object love were solely or mainly pleasure-derived, then we could segregate it from self development. We could, in that case, simply classify the Balints' phenomena as another description of selfobject relationships to be separated from the development of object love. The metapsychology of pleasure-derived love, however, repeatedly leads to theoretical confusion between the intrapsychic and the interpersonal, and does not adequately account for the experience of being loved. The Balints contend that being loved is somehow related to love, and there is a striking similarity, indeed, an identity, between the *qualities* of the selfobject and essential components of the inner attitudes and behaviors of "loving."

One link between them might be formulated in the following way: the processes and experiences that foster self development also comprise the foundation and sources of object love. It is this inner experience of love, this selfobject function—i.e., parental attitudes of care, concern, pleasure in the child, availability, and empathy—which partially corresponds to Ferenczi's "passive love" and Balint's "primary love." These formulations represent primary emotional gestalts essential both in the construction of the self and in the development of object love. These processes, elaborated by self psychology, give us a way to conceptualize the development of object love without an energy psychology and without reducing this development to purely somatic sources. It is a way, moreover, that can systematically encompass the experience of being loved.

Both self and love arise from the self-selfobject matrix. Self—which includes ambitions and ultimately values—arises out of the matrix as the overriding, guiding inner structure. Love is the need to replicate actively and/or reexperience the originally fused and then gradually differentiating self-selfobject state. The need to replicate the experience—i.e., through active loving—would have to be organized through the still more nuclear patterns of ambitions and ideals—i.e., the self—and would have to become one of the goals and needs of the self. Its position in the hierarchy of goals and values of the self would and could vary. Some individuals would have highly elaborated aspects of self and goals which did not prominently include the need to be an active replicator of self with another person. The place of both loving and being loved in the self equilibrium of most people, however, should not be underestimated. The mutual exchange of self-sustenance fostering is the goal of most intimate relationships, and the satisfaction when such a balance is achieved is very great indeed. For though it is subsidiary to overall goals, loving bears a special proximity to the conditions of our psychological birth.

Hence the lines of self development and object love appear to be intimately related, the latter being an aspect of, or derivative from, the matrix of self formation. Object love is a way to reproduce and reexperience that matrix in action once separation and differentiation have been achieved.

If object love arises out of the conditions of self formation, what is its relationship to pleasure and erotism? G. Klein's (1976) proposal to separate the phenomena of sensuality and pleasure from the drive discharge theory may point to the direction in which the answer lies. Klein reaffirms the value of understanding the intensity of adult sensual pleasure with earlier childhood sensual experience as Freud outlined in the *Three Essays on the Theory of Sexuality* (1905). For Klein, however, the elaboration of those sensual phenomena into a drive discharge theory detracts from the understanding of the evolution and place of sensual experience. Similarly, the derivation of object love from this theory has minimized the understanding of nonsensual but extremely essential experiences in the genesis and structure of object love, and has linked it too rigidly with erotism. Divorcing both the epigenesis of sensuality and the evolution of the valuing, caring aspects of object love from the drive discharge theory may permit a clearer account of each phenomenon.

In this framework of self formation, we can account for the source of love, its development, and the later vicissitudes of its communication and transaction. In this light, the source—being loved—is the performance of selfobject functions by another that foster, protect, enhance the self, especially in its mirroring functions. Appreciation, approval, pleasure, the willingness to merge and feel one with, empathy, and care—these are all examples of such functions. The parental capacity to perform these functions in their subtle, specific, and constantly changing course permits the child's construction of his self, and is the basis for the need to experience derivatives of the self-constructive process both passively and actively in later life.

The development of love must depend on sufficient self-selfobject separation to recognize the former selfobject as an independent center of initiative. I would question whether this gradual separation and wish to turn passive into active is only or chiefly a function of "maternal rejection." Surely, as noted by many authors — Lichtenstein, Mahler, and Kohut among them — increasing selectivity of parental response helps the child mold his own experience of himself and his needs, but an important ingredient of separation is the simple accretion of function as it has been properly and repeatedly executed within the selfobject matrix. There is, I believe, a spontaneous growth of patterning that is crystallized out of the matrix and that *necessitates* independent and separate function. Hence, there is a compelling, natural growth of separation that follows the increasingly complex inner patterning that precipitates out of the matrix.

The relationship with the newly experienced independent object is not only concerned with pleasure. A new awareness of negotiation between independent entities is certainly important. The awareness of the voluntary nature of what had formerly been experienced as a matter of course may contribute to the idealization of the parent and lead to a new sense of vulnerability and the consequent need to "court" the parent. Any "gratitude" that may emerge at this or a later period is related less to an overcoming of envy than to the simple awareness — very laboriously acquired — of the essential and voluntary nature of functions previously experienced as automatic.

Once partial separation and awareness have occurred, the necessity for continuing response and dialogue has not ceased. Indeed, a special quality of the inner experience of both separateness and fusion may occur simultaneously — something like the musical experience of a fugue — which gives the development of love a special property and intensity. Kernberg (1977) has noted the importance of the contradiction of both overcoming and heightening awareness of self boundaries, especially in sexual passion. Like so many other realms of development, self formation is not absolute and total. All through childhood the process of self delineation and growth continues, along with the consequent necessity to experience some aspects of others—especially parents—as functions and hence as selfobjects.

The main thrust of any active loving wish in childhood still serves self construction. The positive oedipal desires, for example, are less for the sake of the mother (i.e., they embody less the true capacity to hold oneself in abeyance for the sake of another) than for the sake of experiencing oneself as "lover." That is, the oedipal wish is less for the sake of love than for enlarging self experience.

In this connection, the response of the parent to the early expression of love is an important component in its further development. Either indifference or overexcitement is likely to cause difficulties in the formation of loving relationships later in life. One male patient had great difficulty maintaining a consistent attitude toward the many women with whom he became involved. As he became increasingly involved with a woman, he would suddenly and unaccountably become very critical of her appearance or habits. After some time, genetic reconstruction indicated that his mother had been preoccupied with compulsive, cleaning details and had responded to his childhood expressions of affection with coolness, criticism of his failure to live up to her standards of neatness and decorum, and isolated preoccupation with certain of his physical attributes. It was even longer before he could bear to experience such tender wishes and shy affection in the transference.

The reconstruction in the analysis of another patient—a married woman—indicated, on the contrary, that her mother had responded to her with overexcitement and enthusiasm at the least expression of childhood warmth or talent. The mother did not cling to her child, but excitedly approved of the appropriate developmental steps. As a young lady, therefore, the patient was a person of warmth, charm, and enthusiasm herself. However, she would easily become overstimulated, anxious, and phobic when deeply experiencing warm feelings for her husband, and at such times she became almost comically critical and overanxious with him.

In both these instances the parental response became part of the later expression of the loving function and its malfunction. For both patients, the earliest nucleus of self and the impulse to re-create the conditions associated with this state were present. Later development was thereby rendered problematic.

For most, gratitude and explicit awareness of the role of another's functions in the birth of self are not conscious and cannot be formulated in specific ideational terms. Perhaps this is because the earliest matrix is experienced in sensorimotor terms. Nonetheless, it is both the awareness of "otherness" and the sense of the essential role of the "other" in the core of one's existence that prompt reciprocal feelings of caring for and valuing another.

The full development of the capacity to care for and value another can only occur after most of the work of self construction has passed and at a time when obligatory selfobject function is no longer unilaterally required. The capacity for mutuality is a late acquisition, and the road from the early awareness to the mature capacity is long.

Summary

I have suggested that object love in the sense of the active, reliable, meaningful caring for and valuing of another is neither derivative of any somatic tension (pregenital or genital), nor an outgrowth of the satisfaction of biological needs. Rather, the source of such a development lies in the inner experience of being psychologically cared for. That experience coincides with the selfobject matrix out of which the self is formed. Hence, the source of object love is self genesis. Selfobject functions, when they are actively reproduced, are expressions of love. After self development has proceeded sufficiently, the motivation to reproduce selfobject functions actively arises out of the passive experience of love that one can conceptualize as discrete only retrospectively. It arises, that is, from the experience of adequate and appropriate selfobject response.

The development and vicissitudes of loving can be best understood as an outcome of the continuing interplay of selfobject functions. The special intensity of love arises partly from its reproduction of the early essential fusion and from the later tension between facilitative, nonobligatory fusions, and greater differentiation.

What are the advantages of such a conceptualization? (1) It frees us from an energy theory that is increasingly called into question by modern analytic theorists. (2) It allows us to think beyond the somatic processes and helps refocus attention on the interactional affective processes, whether experienced in terms of self or as independent entities. (3) It can theoretically account for later loving interactions in a more parsimonious and less confusing way. As such, this conceptualization may provide a theoretical framework that better describes the importance and nature of the inner, intrapsychic experience of interpersonal interaction both in development and in maturity.

References

Altman, L. (1977), Some Vicissitudes of Love. *J. Amer. Psychoanal. Assn.,* 25:35–52.

Balint, A. (1939), Love for the Mother and Mother-Love. In: *Primary Love and Psychoanalytic Technique,* by M. Balint. New York: Liveright, 1965, pp. 91–108.

Balint, M. (1933), Critical Notes on the Theory of the Pre-Genital Organization of the Libido. In: *Primary Love and Psychoanalytic Technique.* New York: Liveright, 1965, pp. 37–58.

_____ (1936), The Final Goal of Psychoanalytic Treatment. In: *Primary Love and Psychoanalytic Technique.* New York: Liveright, 1965, pp. 178–188.

_____ (1948), On Genital Love. In: *Primary Love and Psychoanalytic Technique.* New York: Liveright, 1965, pp. 109–120.

Ferenczi, S. (1933), Confusion of Tongues Between the Adult and the Child (The Language of Tenderness and of Passion). In: *Final Contributions to the Problems and Methods of Psychoanalysis.* New York: Basic Books, 1955, pp. 156–167.

Freud, S. (1905), Three Essays on the Theory of Sexuality. *Standard Edition,* 7:123–245. London: Hogarth Press, 1953.

_____ (1912), On the Universal Tendency to Debasement in the Sphere of Love. *Standard Edition,* 11:179–190. London: Hogarth Press, 1957.

_____ (1914), On Narcissism: An Introduction. *Standard Edition,* 14:73–102. London: Hogarth Press, 1957.

_____ (1921), Group Psychology and the Analysis of the Ego. *Standard Edition,* 18:67–143. London: Hogarth Press, 1955.

———— (1931), Female Sexuality. *Standard Edition,* 21:221–246. London: Hogarth Press, 1961.

———— (1940), An Outline of Psycho-Analysis. *Standard Edition,* 23:144–207. London: Hogarth Press, 1964.

Kernberg, O. (1977), Boundaries and Structure in Love Relations. *J. Amer. Psychoanal. Assn.,* 25:81–114.

Klein, G. S. (1976), The Vital Pleasures. In: *Psychoanalytic Theory: An Exploration of Essentials.* New York: International Universities Press, pp. 210–238.

———— (1976), Freud's Two Theories of Sexuality. In: *Psychoanalytic Theory: An Exploration of Essentials.* New York: International Universities Press, pp. 72–120.

Kohut, H. (1971), *The Analysis of the Self.* New York: International Universities Press.

———— (1977), *The Restoration of the Self.* New York: International Universities Press.

Moore, B. & Fine, B. (1967), *A Glossary of Psychoanalytic Terms and Concepts.* New York: American Psychoanalytic Association.

Saul, L. (1950), The Distinction Between Loving and Being Loved. *Psychoanal. Quart.,* 19:412–413.

Terman, D. (1975), The Self and the Oedipus Complex. Unpublished paper delivered to Chicago Psychoanalytic Society, May.

Part IV

SELF PSYCHOLOGY
AND THE SCIENCES OF MAN

Introduction

MARK J. GEHRIE

This section of the book reflects our conviction that in order to grow and flourish psychoanalysis must be actively pursued as a theory and a method relevant beyond clinical applications. Although this is not a new proposition (as illustrated amply by a considerable number of Freud's own major works), it is one that has been diminished and left fallow for want of a *modus operandi*. As suggested by a number of the contributions in this section, the psychology of the self may not solve all the problems of applied psychoanalysis, but it does offer a new perspective or framework from which some of these problems may be approached.

In large part, the contributions of the psychology of the self to applied analysis may be seen as interpretive: the cultural and historical data with which the world presents us may now be assessed and appreciated in a new way. The vision of man as primarily motivated by a need for a sense of completeness and wholeness of the self, rather than by (conflicting) drive aims, lends a new dimension to the understanding of these data. To date the methodological problems of applied analysis all relate to the failure to clarify fully how best to apply psychoanalytic theory to nonclinical data. A major advance which the psychology of the self provides, however, is based on a contribution it has made to clinical psychoanalysis as well: its emphasis on the centrality of the empathic-introspective stance in data collection and evaluation. The anthropologist or historian who approaches his material empathically will experience it on a fundamentally different plane than the anthropologist or historian who objectifies it. The work of Collingwood (1956) in history, and Malinowski (1967) and Devereux (1967) in anthropology, are particularly fine statements of the value and impact of the empathic perspective. The willingness and ability of the scientist in any given field to allow himself to become involved with the materials under scrutiny, rather than purposefully distancing himself from them, will be critical for the development of that field. Especially in the case of psychoanalytic theory and applied analysis, the empathic method presents a paradigm that underlies the positive accomplishments of these fields. Without it, we are relegated to cognitive inventions that do justice neither to psychoanalysis nor to the other sciences of man. The contributions presented in this section represent but a small sample of the range of interpretive strategies of applied self psychology.

References

Collingwood, R. G. (1956), *The Idea of History*. New York: Oxford University Press.
Devereux, G. (1967), *From Anxiety to Method in the Behavioral Sciences*. The Hague: Mouton.
Malinowski, B. (1967), *A Diary in the Strict Sense of the Term*. New York: Harcourt Brace.

The Self and the Group: A Tentative Exploration in Applied Self Psychology

MARK J. GEHRIE

Since the time of Freud's provocative ventures into speculative anthropology, there have been many efforts to tie psychoanalytic theory to explanations of cultural materials. Investigators
from many disciplines have frequently felt little constraint in
treating historical events, cultural myths and symbols, and group
behavior of many types — to say nothing of the works of artists and
biographers — as if they were the productions of a patient free-as-
sociating on the couch. As a result, efforts in "applied psychoanalysis" often brought cries of "reductionism" from audiences
unwilling to accept the primacy of the Oedipus complex in such
collective, cultural matters. Many also found it difficult to accept
the implication that all human interaction as well as artistic,
creative, and scientific productions could be "explained" by reference to the instinctual drives and their vicissitudes.

Psychoanalysts themselves often share the disquieting feeling
that many of these appied efforts do justice neither to the cultural
materials in question nor to the theory that is being used to explain
them. I have long felt that such efforts are doomed from the start
unless a reliable method, appropriate to both the data and the
theory, is available to practitioners of applied psychoanalysis. If

we are to go "beyond the basic rule," then we must do so with a conviction that our results will have a validity that approaches the validity of our clinical findings. It is with an eye to arriving at such a method that I offer some tentative comments on a new approach to group psychology. In this area, I feel that the psychology of the self may offer an approach that builds on Freud's (1921) basic ideas, while increasing the explanatory power of Freud's theory and bringing psychoanalysis closer to the social sciences.

In *Group Psychology and the Analysis of the Ego* (1921), Freud described the organization of groups on the basis of libidinal relations between objects, highlighting the regression from object choice to identification. Relying heavily on the influence of a loved leader in accounting for group cohesion, Freud noted that individuals take this leader in place of their ego ideal, and in so doing identify with other group members. This mass identification permitted regression in the group, and it helped Freud explain the observable features of much group behavior.

In his effort to relate the psychology of primordial groups to the psychology of early man, Freud highlighted the defensive role of group membership in the face of separation anxiety, as well as against envy and jealousy. He explained group spirit as a derivation of mutual envy, and stressed that the demand for equality between group members "stems from the original wish to be ruled by one person: the leader" (1921, p. 121). Hence, the explanation of group identification as the basis for mutuality in groups depends — in Freud's central thesis — on the singular importance of the leader.

We are still faced, however, with the problem of explaining group cohesion in instances where membership is not primarily based on the tie to the leader. Unless we are to consider the structure of social groups as invariably reflecting in a larger sense the original organization of the family — an assumption on which Freud based his hypothesis — then a further explanation of cultural group dynamics is required. The need for such an additional explanation is further highlighted by the increasing evidence from many sources that the significance of familial interaction in the life of the individual is decreasing, and that the role of the family in contemporary Western social life may itself be on the decline.

This does not in itself disprove the validity of Freud's explanation of group psychology, but it does underscore the need for a supplementary explanatory model that can account for both the sense of belonging in leaderless (cultural) groups, and the nature of increasingly significant group ties outside of the family.

It is not true, of course, that cultural groups lack leaders or institutional hierarchies to which a leadership role might be assigned. The question, therefore, is not whether Freud's way of thinking is at all applicable, but rather if it is as applicable to communities that bind themselves together irrespective of the influence of the leader (and whose individuals remain fundamentally tied to each other even during chaotic leaderless periods) as to the kind of leader-oriented communities Freud originally had in mind.

According to Freud's hypothesis, the loss of the leader-father led to the "totemic community of brothers" (1921, p. 135), and forced an identification between the brothers in the service of mutual self-preservation. The authority of the new fathers of each family became limited by the rights of the other fathers. Although contemporary social struggles are often viewed as the renewed competition between these brother-fathers for the position of primacy, the fact remains that access to influence and power seems to be increasingly sought through membership in what appear to be nonfamilial groups. There also appears to be a corresponding decline of the relevance of the family in an increasingly broad range of political, economic, religious, and social activities. Certainly a degree of individual independence now exists that was unknown in primitive societies and social organizations and atypical even in 19th-century Western civilization. Consider, for example, such recent social phenomena as the student movement, the women's movement, and numerous "ethnic pride" movements. All these movements are experienced by their memberships as expressive of internally known "truths," and they correspondingly place minimal emphasis on conspicuous leaders for the maintenance of group cohesion. On the contrary, it is the "belonging" itself which is celebrated, and which creates a sense of power for both the individual and the group. Perhaps Freud would have seen these phenomena as evidence of the "psychological poverty" of

American culture, where identifications between group members exist without a significant leader (1930, pp. 115–116).

To what, then, may the "sense of belonging" between members of a cultural group be attributed in cases where leaders play an insignificant role in the emotional life of the individual? In Japan, for example, although figurehead leaders of formerly great paternalistic power and influence remain—such as the Emperor who retains considerable charismatic appeal for many Japanese—a shift has occurred since World War II toward a kind of group consciousness that is founded on a sense of belonging that is very different from traditional Japanese familial social organization. These new economic, political, and religious organizations are characterized by the fact that their strength lies in their numbers, their unity of action, and their sense of community, rather than in their devotion to a leader or a cause. If a leader does emerge, his power stems from the sanction of the community, rather than the other way around. In Europe and the United States, comparably, the growth of nonfamilial institutional power appears to be gradually replacing the tie to the charismatic and paternal leaders, whose power to effect meaningful changes is perceived as limited.

It may be that the increasing ways of effecting separation from the family without concomitant loss of access to means of power have promoted the development of extrafamilial group membership. From the point of view of cultural history, it has always been the family that has stood at the foundation of a firm social organization. Therefore we are in a period where change is not only taking place at a different rate, but also in what seems to be a different direction. The child of this new generation, disappointed with his father's limited capacity to be a powerful effector of change, and faced with a multitude of alternatives, may seek what seems to him to be less vulnerable means of maintaining his own grandiosity. Unlike the individual whose grandiosity must eventually be tamed if he is to remain within the family, a nonfamilial group makes no such demands; the individual's untamed grandiosity may gain expression in the form of the group's limitless claims to religious, social, political, or psychological power. In this sense, the leaderless group allows the individual a narcissistic freedom or motivation that is less available within the strict confines of a rigidly organized, stratified, and idealized tie to a single leader. A celebration of the self may be achieved through this kind of group belonging, unhampered by the kinds of restrictions that characterize the more traditional family relation. The opportunity to idealize the group, and at the same time to achieve a sense of personal power or perfection through belonging, may provide a haven for a self that is otherwise unable to tolerate the loss of archaic narcissistic supplies. This kind of "belonging" may also provide access to a pool of selfobjects that can be used in the service of tension regulation, and thereby make certain types of regression an acceptable and even irreplaceable feature of group membership. A man's creative and emotional involvement with his own cultural (or group) ideology may, in this sense, express a fundamental motive to restore or maintain a sense of self-cohesion. Kohut (1978), for example, notes in his correspondence with Erich Heller:

> The myth-formations and communal experiences of man's religions, the meaningful beauty of the integrated symbols of his self in his works of art, the formulations of his various scientific world views, the definitions of the meaning of experience and existence contained in his systems of philosophy, they are all, in the last analysis, motivated by man's "fall from grace," are all, to state the issue again in the language of modern depth psychology, motivated by the loss of the secure cohesion, continuity and harmony of his self [p. 449].

In this sense, the way a person structures his relationship to his own cultural group may be understood as a reflection of the state of his own self.

But what are the implications of this insight for research? If we accept the idea that the maintenance of self-cohesion may be a central dynamic in leaderless group membership, then the use of a culturally informed, empathic-introspective approach allows us access to the group psychology of the individual, that is, the place of the group in the mind of the group member and the relation of group belonging to the cohesion of the self. The empathic-introspective approach would thereby permit us to explore this sense of belonging not only from Freud's perspective of shared identifications, but from the perspective of the role of the cultural or group imago as one feature of the development of a cohesive self. Although the study of groups from an analytic perspective necessarily suffers from the impossibility of free association — "the central instrument for the investigation of the unconscious" (Kohut, 1960, p. 280) — the exploration of the internal role of group belonging is still possible. What is required is a twofold awareness on the part of the analyst: an understanding that cultural or group imagoes may have a role in the celebration of the self that is part of group belonging, and that this experience may function for the individual as a developmental step toward the formation of a self-regulated and harmonious sense of cohesion.

From this perspective, "group psychology" becomes an extension of the psychology of the self. It permits access to certain kinds of group dynamics from an empathic-introspective stance within the realm of the unfolding selfobject transference, group dynamics that might eventually lead to an understanding of that critical "glue" that gives many groups their essential qualities.

Clinical Example

A clinical example will demonstrate how the psychology of the self permits the study of the group psychology of the individual. This example derives from research in the area of long-term psychoanalytic follow-up, and it consists of a few excerpts from the case of a second-generation Japanese-American, or *nisei,* who was analyzed in the period around 1950. Twenty-five years after his termination, a series of six follow-up interviews with the ex-analysand was conducted, in an effort to reconstruct the "fate" of the analytic product. The original analyst collaborated in this research, and after receiving permission from the patient, supplied some information regarding the original treatment.

At the time this research was conducted, one major focus of

the research (beyond the issue of assessment of psychoanalytic change over the long term) was the exploration of the role of cultural dynamics in the patient's personality. We hypothesized that because of the cultural trauma of the relocation of Japanese-Americans during World War II, and the subsequent difficulties in readaptation, the issue of cultural group membership would be prominent in the associations of all our Japanese-American follow-up subjects. We found this to be true, although in an unexpected way. Briefly, in all of the follow-up cases in our small sample, the issue of cultural group membership and a "sense of belonging" was prominent in a negative sense. Japanese descent, that is, was experienced by these individuals as something to be deemphasized. In every case, efforts to "assimilate" and to feel a part of the larger white-middle-class society were freely acknowledged, and references to the World War II relocation were made with a manifest sense of shame. Without going into the details of each case, it is safe to say that many *nisei* suffered a traumatic depreciation of their cultural background from long before World War II until well after it. This depreciaton, combined with the limited acculturation of many of their parents, the *issei,* often resulted in a noticeable decathexis of the Japanese element in their lives. (It is noteworthy, for example, that out of a population of 20–25,000 Japanese-Americans in Chicago in the early 1970s, only about 1,000 belonged to the Japanese-American Citizen's League, a politically active citizen's group.) Since most *nisei* were already teenagers or young adults at the time of the relocation, however, it seems reasonable to suggest that in some cases the experience of that cultural trauma reverberated with much earlier experiences that had already left them particularly vulnerable.

Most of the research on the subject of the Japanese-American readaptation after World War II stresses the immediate aftermath of the relocation experience, and the unusual capacity shown by many *nisei* to respond actively to, and identify with, the values of the American middle class (Babcock, 1962; Caudill & DeVos, 1956). And, indeed, in most instances, the quality of the reaction of the *nisei* to the wartime relocation seemed entirely appropriate both to the outrageous circumstances of their uprooting, and to the values of the Japanese culture which influenced them as children: anger and shame were teamed with a conviction that unceasing efforts to be "good Americans" would finally vindicate them in the eyes of their countrymen. Witness, for example, the highly decorated, entirely Japanese-American 442nd Regimental Combat Team in Europe, who fought for the same country that had denied them their most basic constitutional rights. For other Japanese-Americans, however, the trauma of the relocation seemed to mirror a more fundamental sense of outrage, and to magnify an already anguished sense of vulnerability. It was as if they did not perceive the issue of the relocation as an affront to a previously well-established set of cultural identifications, but as a trauma to a precariously established sense of self that had never optimally internalized the parental tension-regulating functions, and never completely developed the corresponding psychological structure.

Looking back over the cases selected for follow-up, we might say that there was a "lack of opportunity" in these latter instances for the child or adolescent to idealize and hence comfortably identify with either the culture carriers (the parents), or the culture itself. Alternatively, becoming part of the assimilated mass of the larger "American culture" was not an option, due to the racial tensions of the times. Thus, many in this second generation may have carried with them into the war years a preexisting vulnerability. As a result, the development of the self, based on phase-appropriate attachments to the powerful selfobjects (the grandiose self and the idealized parental imago), may have been interfered with by the traumatic cultural experiences of the parents.

The follow-up case that most clearly illustrates this condition is that of a *nisei* analysand who originally sought analysis at the age of 29 in the year 1950.

The patient was a 29-year-old married male of Japanese ancestry (*nisei*). He was born in America and was a self-referral through the Japanese-American Research Project in Chicago. The original analyst wrote then that the patient's presenting complaints were referable to problems of "character structure." She noted the patient's constant feeling of being constricted, inhibitions, passivity, inability to express himself in verbal and motor areas, inability to express the warmth that he thought he felt, and fear that he would not be able to control the angry feelings he sometimes experienced. He was more critical, withdrawn, and withholding from his wife than he wanted to be, and his warmest and freest contacts were with his two-year-old child.

The patient's father was not the first-born son, which in traditional Japanese life greatly reduced his significance in the family. He emigrated to this country and was here for several years prior to his marriage to the patient's mother. The father, who suffered from a moderately severe asthma, was a weak and somewhat dissolute character in the eyes of the patient; the patient felt his father was unable to cope with this country (he was employed irregularly) and was not as ambitious as most Japanese. The father had gone through bankruptcy when the patient was 17, an event of great shame for the children. The patient regarded him as "a great disappointment." Nevertheless the patient was afraid of his father and had obeyed him implicitly in his early childhood.

The patient's mother died when he was nine. The patient remembered her as hard-working but not in very close contact with the children. His memories of her were considerably blurred.

The patient was the fourth of six siblings; he was not close to any of them although he was active as a child with his two younger brothers. The family was widely scattered at the time. The oldest sibling was a brother, six years the patient's senior; then came sisters four and three years older than the patient, and brothers five and seven years younger. After the mother's death, the children were kept by the father but cared for by neighbors in an irregular fashion until the father married a (Japanese) woman of ill repute, for whom the patient had great feelings of disgust and humiliation. Following the father's remarriage, the family moved to Idaho (as did many Japanese) to avoid the internment camps established during World War II. The father did badly following the move, and although the children were cared for, the situation was unpleasant. The patient's stepmother died of Bright's disease when the patient was fourteen.

The patient was always an able student but was very shy and reserved in his peer relationships. When he finished high school, he worked for a short period and tried to make arrangements to study for a college degree. In 1944, at age 21, he enlisted in the armed forces and was in the army of occupation in Europe for two years. Following his return he entered university, where he hoped to obtain a Master's degree. At the time he began analysis, the patient had been married for three and a half years to a nurse who was a very competent person but also very inhibited. His wife and he were somewhat aware of their isolation from each other, but were unable to remedy the situation. Their child, Mary, was two at the time.

At the onset of the analysis, the analyst recorded the observation that the patient was "a very intelligent and potentially able young man, who presents a very typical picture of the passive, inhibited, male second-generation Japanese. His problem is further complicated by his isolation from women, undoubtedly intensified by the death of both his mother and the stepmother. He presents a more severely traumatic picture by virtue of the father's failure than do most Japanese and his capacity to experience or act upon aggressive or hostile impulses is practically absent."

During the analysis, the analyst noted certain outstanding themes, especially the patient's acutely experienced sense of inadequacy and failure and his sense of isolation from his mother even before her death. The analyst characterized the patient's early history as "very traumatic" and referred to the patient's use of passive defenses against outbursts of rage. The trauma of the loss of the mother was reexperienced in the transference as the patient's defensive struggle against his own intense wish to reestablish a preoedipal, dependent tie with the analyst. It is unclear exactly to what extent his feelings of loss were worked through, since the analyst at 325 hours noted that "he has been able to drop some of his facade...(and) his dependency needs are sharper and...better known to him." At the conclusion of the three-year analysis, the analyst recorded that "he has come to grips with some of his immature dependent reactions...," noting that the patient was still troubled by a negative mother transference to his daughter, seeing her as his "bad self."

At the time of the follow-up, the patient was 53 years old.

Among his first associations was one relating to the quality of the analytic atmosphere as he recalled it. This association brought him to tears:

> I guess another thing that comes to my mind now is [long pause and tears] funny reaction [pause]; I feel quite moved and I'm not sure why. What I was thinking of was I guess the most significant aspect of the therapy as I see it; [it] was my analyst's genuineness and humanity. I hadn't anticipated that kind of reaction [long pause]. I've often thought through the years that probably the personality, the person that my analyst is, the kind of person that she was, was one of the major factors in the whole process. Although I was keenly aware of her techniques because I was a student and really learning and paying attention. I was thinking on the way over that I wasn't very keenly aware of how she, or what I thought, she was doing, was controlling the level of the transference. She never really let it get into some really sticky territory, which I knew it could develop into, and I had the very definite impression that she kept it from going into that kind of level.

It is clear that one of the most profound aspects of his experience of psychoanalysis was the freedom that he experienced from his own rage due to the empathy and responsiveness of his analyst. With her, the "paralyzing anxiety" associated with his own nearly uncontrollable rage was ameliorated. Clearly, what he valued most was what he thought of as her "control," a control that prevented the analysis from getting into what he called "sticky territory."

Clearly, the patient had experienced something with his analyst that had been new to him, and which made an impression that still affected him after 25 years. He said, "I think I was looking for a mother, and I found my analyst." The empathic responsiveness of the analyst had preserved him from an experience which, in his earlier relationships, had caused him to react with his "uncontrollable rage." From the record of the analysis, we already know that this rage was so overpowering that he was frightened about its consequences. He recalls one instance as an illustration:

"I guess I had a couple of striking emotional experiences, one was kind of a mixture of panic and guilt and shame and about realizing my own destructiveness toward my little daughter. I picked her up and I was tossing her in the air and I dropped her on the sidewalk."

Although the analysis had concluded with the therapist's sense that the patient's dependent needs were "more known to him," there is evidence from events in his life that a particular vulnerability persisted after the termination. After years of a rocky marriage, he divorced his first wife and married someone with whom he had experienced a satisfying sense that "it would be the fulfillment of all my desires." Now, two years after his second marriage, he reports:

> When we're together too much we begin losing sight of who's who, and [then] fighting is a way to redefine the boundaries and separate us. And so we've taken to trying to separate from each other very deliberately and consciously, which has helped a bit. But it's almost a continuous task to keep clarifying those kinds of things and for me to remind myself that that's mine to run and not her's.... I look on it as like two drops of mercury—that can only have a relationship if they have separateness. And if they get too close the surface tension breaks. They merge into one, which is what most people do, and destroy both in the process. And then it takes violence to break them apart.

For this patient, the closeness that he experienced with his second wife became terrifying. Although these data are fragmentary, there is evidence, including material from the follow-up process itself, suggesting that the patient sought to establish a merger transference with his second wife and that the merger then became overstimulating for him and threatened to fragment his fragile self. His rage and violent need to "break apart" the merger functioned restitutively on behalf of his endangered self.

It is from the perspective of the patient's anxiety related to his narcissistic vulnerability (fragmentation anxiety) that the issue of his cultural group membership reemerged. It was not until the fifth follow-up interview (out of six) that he made any reference to his ethnic background. He was commenting on his interest in cooking and in preparing Japanese food, at which point the follow-up analyst commented that he had said very little up to that point about his Japanese ancestry. The patient replied:

Yeah, actually I don't know very much about it. I guess that's all something that I've learned only later. My father spoke English very well. And was a good cook. I learned from him. And...I guess I only learned about any kind of impact of the Japanese culture incidentally. My uncle worked with my father and spoke Japanese. My father spoke English quite well and my mother spoke English so that we never learned very much about it even though I went to Japanese school for about a year once. And I must have been about six or seven [pause] but in my later life I've become interested in some things—some of their art. I don't care for a lot of the cultural things. I don't care for the people. I've come to see that Japanese women are...have been slaves for centuries and as such are bitterly resentful and sometimes sadistic in their interpersonal relationships. My stepmother was an exceedingly sadistic woman. And I've seen about two Japanese women from Japan who married GIs here. They are tremendously sadistic people. I've been a little shocked at the destructiveness of these people. And I believe it's characteristic of the culture. There's enough familiarity in what they present with what I've seen in other Japanese women that makes me feel that that is a very prominent part of the culture. I think people who are subjugated like that can't help but be savagely hostile in their own ways. And then I think of nice people which I've come to be very suspicious of...so I don't like a lot of the Japanese culture. It's I guess like all ancient cultures, they build up so many traditions about managing aggression that it's a little difficult to see what they're about. Things that seem so nice really conceal a lot of destructive things. I see the Japanese being interested in flowers and peace and lovely gardens and yet they're the same people who will have been so

brutally sadistic during the war. So they're hiding something
when they're so nice. And I'm very suspicious of niceness. I
would rather someone be much more direct and aggressive.
At least I know what I'm dealing with. I think it's more
honest.

It seems safe to suggest that the patient's rage at his mother was
displaced and projected onto Japanese culture in general and
Japanese women in particular. The intensity and violence of his
association are reminiscent of his depiction of the "violence" necessary to break apart the two drops of mercury that had merged into
one. The reference to the experience of parent loss here in terms of
selfobject dynamics is unmistakable. There is also the reference to
the father speaking in English and being a good cook, and to the fact
that the patient only learned about Japanese culture "incidentally."
But if it was "only incidental," why the merging of his intense rage at
the maternal imago with his attitude toward Japanese culture? It
may have been that the traumatic understimulation suffered by this
man at the hands of his remote and distant mother forced him to
turn toward his father, with whom he was able to form an ambivalent selfobject tie. He felt disliked and depreciated by the father,
however, who, as the patient recalled, tried to use him as "kitchen
help" in the restaurant. His ultimate disappointment with his father
left the patient in a repetitive cycle of over- and understimulation
that was mediated by periodic rageful outbursts or passive resistance
to doing anything.

While the analysis had succeeded in dealing with the portion of
his ego that was tied to the shaky identification with his father, and
to some degree ameliorated his inhibitions, it was not successful in
helping the patient to internalize missing psychic structure, the
absence of which perpetuated his need to seek a selfobject with
which to establish (and anxiously break apart) a merger. His needs
for mirroring forced him to continue to seek selfobjects to reduce
the tension of his chronically understimulated state. His rage at
things Japanese may, in part, be explained by the unavailability of
Japanese culture as a significant source of self-esteem regulation at
the very time that his developing self was traumatically frustrated

by the unavailability of his parents. It may have been that being Japanese-American at that point in history, combined with his family's flight from its cultural ties, was experienced by the child as yet a further "turning away" — like his parents, he may never have felt "a part of" his own Japanese heritage. The unidealizability of "Japaneseness" at that historical moment, combined with the lack of parental mirroring, may have combined to engender the universal sense of unresponsiveness that the patient reacted to with desperate, rageful attempts at restitution. This restitutive device has remained embedded in his personality, to be utilized when self-object failures in the present threaten his self-cohesion.

From the point of view of the group psychology of the individual, this case example supports the hypothesis that without the opportunity to receive phase-appropriate mirroring from, or to establish an idealized attachment to, a culturally cohesive ideology — either via the parents or another institutional vehicle — the child's cultural group membership, like attachment to the parents, may not be permanently integrated into the psyche, and will be experienced with a concomitant sense of foreignness and rejection. The rage of this patient may be but one of many modes of attempting to soothe a persistent vulnerability in the self system that is experienced whenever the issue of group membership is in conscious or unconscious focus. Developmentally speaking, such patients never form true identifications, and their participation in culturally constituted groups never reaches the level described by Freud in *Group Psychology*. A second hypothesis could at this point be developed around the issue of the nature of group ties that such individuals are able to form, and the narcissistic needs that these ties meet at the level of mirroring needs and opportunities for idealization. With the hypothesis that selfobject ties form an ongoing element in the life of the individual, it can be argued that the experience of cultural group membership, and its accompanying "sense of belonging," is an expression of a selfobject tie that is at the foundation of the psychology of leaderless groups.

References

Babcock, C. G. (1962), Reflections on Dependency Phenomena as Seen in Nisei in the United States. In: *Japanese Culture,* ed. R. Smith & R. Beardsley. Chicago: Aldine, pp. 172–185.

Caudill, W. & DeVos, G. (1956), Achievement, Culture and Personality: The Case of the Japanese-Americans. *Amer. Anthropol.,* 56:1102.

Freud, S. (1921), Group Psychology and the Analysis of the Ego. *Standard Edition,* 18:69–143. London: Hogarth Press, 1955.

_____ (1930) Civilization and Its Discontents. *Standard Edition,* 21:64–145. London: Hogarth Press, 1961.

Kohut, H. (1960), Beyond the Bounds of the Basic Rule. In: *The Search for the Self,* vol. 1, ed. P. Ornstein. New York: International Universities Press, 1978, pp. 275–303.

_____ (1978), Psychoanalysis and the Interpretation of Literature: A Correspondence with Erich Heller. *Critical Inquiry,* 4:433–450.

Art and the
Self of the Artist

CHARLES KLIGERMAN

Our topic, art and the self of the artist, is confronted at the outset with the global dimensions and complexity of our subject. In order to reduce our burden to some degree, I am assuming that we all share more or less similar views about what is art, and can therefore dispense with definitional problems in aesthetics and confine ourselves to the self of the artist and its role in the creative process.

An observation that should be made at the outset is that the title of this paper is itself somewhat misleading: *the* self of *the* artist. There is no such unitary formula (although practically every previous symposium and most publications seem to make such an assumption). This point was sharply emphasized at the 1971 International Psycho-Analytical Congress Panel on Creativity (see Panel, 1972). It would seem highly unlikely, to say the least, that one could see much similarity of creative self between Johann Sebastian Bach and Toulouse-Lautrec. Obviously there are many different kinds of artists with differing self structures and differing modes of creative activity. Nevertheless, we still recognize a certain common specialness in artists, a particular drive, dedication, and need to create that sets them apart from the ordinary creativity that is found in

383

many people and, indeed, may be inherent in the entire human race. Is this difference only quantitative? I am reminded of a Viennese sculpture teacher who told his students: "What is the difference between you and Michelangelo? There is no difference; he was just a thousand times better than you." However, I believe there are decisive qualitative differences too, and these differences shade into the entire problem of differentiating talent from genius. We are accustomed to think that genius is born, but is it not more likely that talents are born, whereas the genius-self develops through the vicissitudes of life? Hence, the conventional wisdom that the genius has to suffer in order to become great.

On the other hand, when it is a question of talent of such magnitude that it seems to approach consummate perfection, common usage tends to equate this with genius as well. But the talent alone is not enough. Not many would regard Andrea del Sarto as a genius, but regarding Mozart there is no question. It would be difficult to say much about the incredible musicality of Mozart without claiming that he was born with a divine gift. True, his earliest objects were musicians of high order, and he was encouraged and taught by the greatest musical minds of his day, but few would doubt the primacy of his innate talent. Yet, Mozart's greatness rests equally on the subtle psychological understanding and the profound sense of tragedy that characterized his work more and more in his mature years.

Greenacre (1957) and others have made important studies of the early factors in the lives of creative people that foster particular sensitivities and dispositions to certain creative modalities. Although such studies suggest that talent can be acquired, it is generally agreed that the constitutional factor remains a sine qua non.

At any rate, the subject of talent, perceptual sensitivity, and the facility of certain functions seems to be a problem in ego psychology, whereas genius, or at least the higher forms of artistic creativity, falls mainly into the realm of self psychology. It is an area at once more holistic, complex, and integrative than one encounters in the study of specific ego functions or the resolution of structural conflict. Parenthetically, Freud's famous observation that "Before the problem of the creative artist analysis must, alas, lay down its arms" (1928, p. 177) refers, I believe, to the "talent" part of the artist — the inexplicable divine gift. Actually Freud himself did not lay down his arms and did not shrink from studying the inner depths of creative personalities.

The 1971 Panel on Creativity was notable for the fact that all the participants, although representing very different theoretical orientations, laid very heavy emphasis on object relations in the structure and operation of creative personalities. Some, especially Richard Sterba, came extremely close to the perspective of Kohut's psychology of the self, but stopped short of the key concept of the selfobject. This emphasis on object relations represented a distinct shift away from earlier formulations stressing instinctual conflict and its resolution through sublimation. (Although we should remember that Freud very early linked sublimation with identification.) This is not to suggest that these earlier formulations are irrelevant or invalidated: they have given us much valuable insight in the past, and in the hands of distinguished contributors like Ernst Kris (1952) have been subtle, illuminating, and certainly undeserving of the hackneyed epithet "reductionism" so often imputed to this approach.

But the view of creativity as a vicissitude of narcissism rather than a sublimation of unacceptable pregenital drives comes much closer to our experience of the artist, and especially to his experience of himself.

At this point, I would like to propose a fictional profile of the early development of one kind of great artist. I offer it as a heuristically useful model.

The great artist (and they have mostly been males; Virginia Woolf in her moving essay "A Room of One's Own" gives compelling reasons why the female artists have languished) is the first-born child in a family where the father and perhaps other relatives have already attained some distinction in the field of art. He is doted upon by a very loving, empathic mother who sees him as the most wonderful, beautiful child in the world. (A variation is the narcissistic mother who sees him as an extension of her beautiful self and the future fulfillment of all her exhibitionistic claims.) He early displays the family gift, a development that is eagerly anticipated and encouraged by both parents.

The early disappointments of the great artist are not too catastrophically traumatic, usually involving some physical separation or an emotional estrangement due to empathic failures. The ensuing loneliness leads to the rich development of fantasy as a mode of consolation and self-soothing—perhaps a form of play related to the later artistic activity. On the other hand, the child may attempt to recover his self-esteem and original sense of perfection by reconciliation and merger with the idealized selfobjects.

Often the decisive disappointments occur with the birth of new siblings, when the doting mother is no longer available with her enormously stimulating input. At this point the child often turns more to the father for empathic mirroring and especially as a figure for idealization. I wish to stress for a moment the importance of the physical self in this development. I believe that in many artists there is an unusually strong emphasis on the sheer physical beauty of the child which gives a particular cast to his fantasies of omnipotence and grandiosity. This emphasis probably plays a greater role in the childhood of artists than in other creative workers such as scientists. Almost by definition, the artist idealizes beauty, the scientist truth. Obviously there are admixtures—many artists strive to express fundamental truths in life, and many scientists are intrigued by a certain abstract beauty and aesthetic elegance of scientific solution, but by and large the artist is concerned with exhibiting a beauty that was originally his own (or that of the idealized maternal selfobject). The ubiquitous madonna and child portraits of the Renaissance are perhaps the quintessential representation of such embodiments of the bipolar idealized self. I will take this up later, but in the meantime, here is an anecdote of Goethe's mother:

> Wolfgang was not fond of playing with little children unless they were beautiful. Once at a party he suddenly began to cry and exclaimed: 'Away with that ugly child; I can't bear it!' He did not cease crying until he got home where his mother questioned him about his misbehavior. He could not

get over that child's homeliness. At that time he was three [quoted in Lewissohn, 1949, p. 5].

Thus the future artist was enormously valued in early childhood, first as a beautiful, wonderful, special child. (This is every child's heritage, but the artist's to an exceptional degree.) Later he learns to intrigue his parents with his cleverness or a special talent, often either inherited or the result of an early identification. Goethe learned to tell stories from his mother. Picasso was the son of an art teacher. The child Dickens was called on to sing, dance, and recite to entertain his father's friends.

Such demands result in an enormous overstimulation of the future artist's exhibitionism and grandiosity. This, in turn, necessarily makes him vulnerable to the inevitable experiences of disappointment, lack of empathic mirroring, perhaps even to rebuke or ridicule leading to painful feelings of shame and humiliation. A familiar example of such rebuke is the situation in which a child has amused or tickled his elders with a cute saying or trick. Intoxicated with exhibitionistic delight, the child will insatiably attempt to repeat his triumph again and again, until the bored parents who evoked this overstimulated state unempathically turn against him with harsh admonitions about "showing off." Clinical experience is only too replete with examples of episodes like this that are painfully remembered for life. The ensuing fall from grace is followed by a passionate need to recover the original beauty and perfection, and later on to present the world with a work of beauty (really the artist himself) that will evoke universal awe and admiration. There are thus at least three main currents in the creative drive:

1. An innate intrinsic joy in creating, related to what has been termed "functional" pleasure. This is perhaps the most important factor, but the one we know least about.

2. The exhibitionistic grandiose ecstasy of being regarded as the acme of beauty and perfection, and the nearly insatiable need to repeat and confirm this feeling.

3. The need to regain a lost paradise — the original bliss of perfection — to overcome the empty feeling of self-depletion and to recover self-esteem. In the metapsychology of the self this would

amount to healing the threatened fragmentation and restoring firm self-cohesion through a merger with the selfobject—the work of art—and a bid for mirroring approval by the world.

But we have dealt so far with only one aspect of the bipolar self. The other pole, which concerns the idealized selfobject, plays a crucial role from early development. Kohut has explained in great detail the early oscillation between the grandiose self and idealized object—how when inadequate or unempathic mirroring leads to traumatic loss of self-esteem the child regains his cohesion by merging with the admired idealized selfobject. Then, following optimal disillusionment through transmuting internalization, the values, standards, and ideals of the object become part of the ideal system of the self. This form of identification becomes indispensable for the high standards, need for authenticity, taste, and aesthetic rigor of any first-rate artist. And so we can add a fourth current to the creative drive—the need to regain perfection by merging with the ideals of the powerful selfobjects, first the parents, then later revered models who represent the highest standards of some great artistic tradition.

The optimal development and transformation of archaic narcissism into psychic structures play a crucial role, of course, in the development of a firm cohesive self in any person. The ordinary "normal" person is able to transform his grandiosity into realistic ambitions commensurate with his capacities, and his internalized ideals into reasonable moral and ethical values, subject to the usual human frailties. He defends himself against regression to archaic forms of grandiosity because of the shame tensions involved, and he has more or less come to terms with any illusions of his perfection. With most artists it is quite otherwise. Few approach the fictional ideal I outlined, and many, if not most, have suffered severe strains, perhaps actual structural deficits in their sense of self. In many this is related to the hectic patterns of enormous overstimulation and traumatic disappointment at the hands of unempathic, narcissistic, often inconsistent, parents; in others, an astonishingly sizeable group, there has been an important actual loss of selfobject in childhood. In these artists there is an overwhelming need to feel whole again by reconstructing the ideal self or selfobject as a concrete work of art. This often amounts to a passionate, almost addictive need to create, and in fact nonartists with this kind of structure frequently do become addicts or engage in perverse activities — proclivities to which the artist is certainly not immune.

Thus whenever this type of artist is threatened by a loss of self, be it a structural deficit or a temporary functional enfeeblement, he attempts to feel whole again by offering his product as a perfect self to be confirmed by an admiring world. Of course the ultimate narcissistic blow is death, the negation of one's very existence, and Bernard Meyer (in Panel, 1972, p. 21) tells a touching story of a dying old man who for the first time in his life tried painting, and turned out to have first-rate talent — like Grandma Moses. He lived out his days in a blissful state of creativity. Otto Rank (1932) long ago distinguished between the creative and neurotic parts of the self on the basis of the respective fears of death and of life. This very important aspect of creativity can be considered a restitutive or restorative one, whereas the other currents almost have the zestful quality of instinctual drive gratification.

But even artists who have not experienced such deficits in development are probably never far from the demands of their infantile grandiosity and they too fiercely assert their claim for corroboration by the world. When the demands of infantile grandiosity combine with a passionate and uncompromising devotion to the highest ideals of the art, there arises during the creative process a great deal of lability of self-cohesion, and a strong tendency to regress to archaic states. This tendency brings with it the danger of severe narcissistic tension and at times threatening fragmentation. When out of this turbulent, somewhat chaotic state, the work reaches some level of recognizable articulation, the orderly work ego, guided by the ideals and critical standards of art, takes over to shape and elaborate the project. What is here outlined, you will recognize, is Kris's (1952) familiar formulation of the inspiratory and elaboratory phases of creativity. Artists have greater access to the unconscious, are able to use the intensely mobile cathexes of the primary process, and are able to transform primitive fantasies into a viable work by a regression in the service of the ego followed by a return to the higher critical faculties of the secondary process. These metapsychological formulations are as valid today as when they were first elaborated. Their translation into the framework of self psychology, however, gives a more empathic sense of the actual experience of the artist, permits the possibility of a more accurate genetic reconstruction, and opens the way to a more effective therapeutic orientation to the emotional hazards that threaten the artist.

In 1976, Kohut proposed a three-phase cycle for the activity of certain creative people: (1) a phase of frantic creativity and original thought; (2) a phase of quiet work, of elaboration, in which there is a good equilibrium between the psychic systems and a stable feeling of self-esteem, and (3) a postcreative fallow phase, often characterized by restlessness, emptiness, and increasing precreative tension.

Clearly these formulations are paradigmatic, but there are all manner of variations, combinations, and complicating factors. For example, a few moments of reflection brings to mind a number of artists who fit this pattern admirably along with others who instead seem to work from day to day with no great variation. In the latter case, we are witnessing either a different mode of creativity altogether, or some variation of Kohut's formula. I suspect the latter is most often the case. The artist of this type that comes immediately to mind, the so-called "normal" genius, seems to be Johann Sebastian Bach—solid German paterfamilias, incomparable musician. Bach was an industrious, decent, responsible husband and father, and a reliable worker. In addition to his regular duties as organist and Kapellmeister, he composed an average of 20 pages of score for every day of his life—mostly at an incredibly high level of his art.

With Bach, it would seem that all of the phases outlined above are combined and condensed into a smooth-running, reliable process analogous to an autonomous ego function: if you will, he operates like an expert craftsman who has perfected his skill and employs it every day, without undue creative turmoil. In other words, he works all the time in the mode of the elaboratory phase or in Kohut's second phase of quiet work. Yet it does not take many bars of Bach's great music (like the B-Minor Mass) to convince the listener of the passionate wellspring constantly flowing underneath the music.

Now Bach was not a revolutionary. He absorbed a great musical tradition and carried it to its highest culmination before it was supplanted by a whole new style and direction in the history of music that he actually encouraged in his sons. His creative self was strengthened by his staunch allegiance to an established pattern of artistic ideals, not to mention his devotion to his God, the most idealized selfobject of all. We are accustomed to think of great artists as powerful, original minds who break with tradition and forge new pathways. But some of the most sublime artists remained within an inherited tradition and were not revolutionary.

Few artists have the monumental creative stability of a Bach, and most, whether or not revolutionary, have a more labile self structure and tend to experience degrees of creative turmoil ranging from the mild to the quite severe and often incapacitating. I believe there are two main issues involved here: one involving aggression and dynamic conflict, the other involving an economic issue along the lines proposed by Kohut. In regard to the former, one must note, especially in highly revolutionary artists, a break with past tradition, with established norms and standards that represent a part of both the previous self of the artist and his internalized idealized selfobjects. This leads to a mourning process that is often a major part of the creative turmoil. Also, if there is a strong, defiant, destructive feeling toward the old forms, there can be a deep sense of guilt ranging all the way from primitive archaic "oral" guilt to guilt of more postoedipal varieties. Many writers, such as Melville, speak of a feeling of having done something wicked or evil in writing their books. The role of primitive aggression in creativity is not well understood, and although much of this aggression can perhaps be explained via the dynamics of narcissistic rage, I do not believe this explanation is complete. It is with reference to this dimension of creativity that the Kleinians and other British thinkers postulate the importance of the ubiquitous paranoid and depressive anxieties, and stress the importance of psychotic-type mechanisms like splitting and projective identification. These formulations can be useful in the study of psychotic artists, but they are far less convincing in contemplating healthier types.

The self psychology approach with its essentially economic point of view lends clarity to the whole continuum of artistic types. This approach lays great stress on the early stage of the creative act in which so much energy is absorbed in the creative work that the rest of the self is enfeebled, anxious, hypochondriacal, prone to hypomanic overstimulation, or subject to desperate feelings of loneliness and isolation. (This is theoretically similar to the idea that so much of the superego energy of the artist is devoted to the artistic ideal standards that the other aspects of his superego are weak, and he acts like a delinquent.) At this stage of their creative work, many artists resort to all types of stratagems to stabilize their shaky, enfeebled selves. The forms these stratagems may assume are legion. Some writers employ standardized magical rituals at the beginning of their work. They wear a certain jacket, arrange their pencils in a certain order, and so on. All these external arrangements provide a kind of magical structure, supportive of the self. Others employ an idealized fantasy figure — a muse — to whom they attribute both inspirational ideas and a kind of comforting, spiritual guidance.

There is a beautiful description of this kind of muse in the essay that Pirandello wrote as an appendix to his *Six Characters in Search of an Author*. This lonely, desperate feeling is a result of the artist's discovery within himself of new, uncharted ideas that are so novel that they do not yet seem a part of himself. Kohut compares this feeling to that of a small child in the dark who is alone and frightened. One might even term it a form of stranger anxiety. At this point many such artists turn to another person who functions like an omnipotent selfobject — a person who is soothing, reassuring, and allows a merger that strengthens the enfeebled self while the creative work goes on. Kohut (1976) described this "transference of creativity" in great detail in the case of Freud and Fliess, showing how once Freud had articulated his ideas and reached the stage of quiet elaborative work, he no longer needed Fliess in this selfobject role, and indeed regarded him as a hindrance in his scientific revision.

Now there are myriad variations of this basic principle. In the case of many artists, the relationship may be of much greater duration than that of Freud and Fliess, and it may span the creation of many works. Bernard Meyer (Panel, 1972) has studied several cases of the kind of relation which he terms the "secret-sharer." A notable example is that of Joseph Conrad and Ford Maddox Ford (Hueffer). After his estrangement from Ford, Conrad suffered a severe deterioration both psychologically and in the quality of his artistic work, and he never recovered. Some years ago I theorized that a similar factor was involved in the deterioration of Melville after he wrote *Moby Dick*. He had developed a similar transference relationship to Hawthorne, and his adulatory letters seem to demonstrate that Melville had actually "fused their egos" (Kligerman, 1953) or, in current terminology, had merged with the idealized selfobject. It was my belief that this merger became too disturbing to Hawthorne, who extricated himself by taking a consular post in England, leaving Melville feeling betrayed and devastated.

It is not easy for the other person to play this selfobject role with the artist. If he feels secure in his own omnipotence, as Kohut describes Fliess (but even Fliess moved to a distant city), he may be able to withstand this kind of merger without becoming too concerned about the loss of his own self boundaries. But many have to withdraw to perserve their own intactness. A particularly interesting situation presents itself when both parties to such a merger relationship are artists, and each plays this selfobject role with the other. The result can be a symbiotic relation of extraordinary fruitfulness. But difficulties often arise, especially when one artist is much more famous and successful than the other. Some writers tend to use the other as a sounding board for their own ideas to such an extent that the other feels drained and lacks energy for his own creative work. Such mergers among creative thinkers often lead to ugly situations in which neither artist is sure where an idea originated, or, conversely, each artist is only too sure. But frequently the borrowing is openly and joyfully acknowledged, as when the artist pays homage to a colleague by imitating his style.

Such borrowing can also be used to master loss—when Matisse died, Picasso painted like Matisse for a time.

A special form of selfobject relation for writers involves the translator, literally an alter ego or extended self of the writer in another language. There is an interesting and rather sad account of the relation between writer and translator given by John Nathan, who translated for the great Japanese novelist Yukio Mishima. Mishima, whose youthful works had swept Japan in an unprecedented way, had been faced with declining popularity in his late 30s. His novel *The Sailor Who Fell from Grace with the Sea* was received indifferently in Japan, and when Mishima learned that Nathan had done an outstanding English translation, he was elated. Mishima had a burning ambition to win the Nobel prize, for which he seemed in line, although he had been passed over several times. Naturally an English translator would be crucial to his prospects, as most critics did not read Japanese. Nathan (1974) relates: Mishima "then told me he considered us 'an unbeatable team' and asked me for a promise not only to translate his next novel but to become his official translator and help him win the Nobel prize. I agreed deliriously and we shook hands."

As events transpired, Nathan did not like Mishima's new book and proceeded to sign a contract to translate a novel by a rising young Japanese writer whom Mishima considered his only real rival on the scene. Moreover, Nathan did not tell Mishima of his plans for eight months. When Mishima was finally informed, Nathan states that he "decided to have nothing further to do with me. I left Japan in April 1966, and...wrote a bitter article for 'Life' in which I likened the experience of reading a Mishima novel to 'attending an exhibition of the world's most ornate picture frames.' I never saw or heard from him again, but I did learn from mutual friends that he was gravely offended" (Nathan, 1974, pp. 203–209).

At the time of the publication of his biography of Mishima in 1974, Nathan still seemed bitter and somewhat puzzled by Mishima's reaction, a notable example of what we might call an empathic failure. But there were undoubtedly other issues involved about which we can only speculate. One plausible guess is that faced with an overwhelming personality like Mishima, Nathan felt himself caught up in the web of a powerful narcissistic system and experienced a compelling need to extricate himself.

The subject of Yukio Mishima is a good place at which to return to the theme mentioned earlier as constituting an important aspect in the self structure of many artists: the grandiose exhibitionistic claims of the body-self in terms of personal beauty. One might think that this aspect of my formulation would more accurately apply to actors and performing artists, and indeed there is often a psychological spectrum between creative and performing artists. But aside from the fact that there are special psychological characteristics of performers that cannot be discussed here, many creative artists do often function as performing artists, for the performing arts supply the direct, immediate gratification often lacking in painful creative work. This is most readily seen in composers who also conduct or concertize, but also in writers who at times act in plays or give public readings or lectures.

This need to perform sometimes occurs when the writer feels particularly depressed or isolated and craves a more direct kind of loving mirroring than the prospect of acclaim from an unseen audience. When Dickens was struggling with depression in his final years, he pursued a strenuous series of public readings in a near-demonic fashion, even though he was ill and did so against his doctor's advice.

The need for beauty of body-self and for direct admiration from others was particularly strong in Yukio Mishima. Soon after birth he was virtually kidnapped by his severely pathological grandmother, who kept this prized child for years almost as a prisoner in her bedroom, allowing his parents the most minimal access to him. This unhygienic regime, while fostering his grandiosity as the center of the old lady's universe, also led to the development of a weak, spindly frame that proved to be a source of extremely painful humiliation. At school he idealized and envied the beautiful bodies of some of his athletic comrades, one of the determinants of his early homosexual development. In adulthood he became an ardent physical culturist spending hours developing his body, not unlike a certain type of homosexual who is always working out in the gym in order to attain physical perfection. He developed an impressive physique (although his legs always remained rather spindly). Mishima's obsession with physical perfection was in irreconcilable conflict with his fetishistic attitude toward words. He ultimately decided that one can only feel alive and attain the perfection of beauty by dying gloriously, and he acted out this belief in spectacular fashion in a wild episode culminating in his committing *seppuku (hara-kiri)*. The study of Mishima's life and works constitutes a veritable textbook of self pathology.

In this essay, I have covered a very broad range of artistic types as well as many of the vicissitudes of their development and creative expression. Despite the necessarily cursory treatment of these themes, I feel the examples successfully demonstrate how the self psychological frame of reference can illuminate some of the most meaningful issues in the artistic personality in a holistic and yet thoroughly depth-psychological way. The further application of the empathic-introspective approach to biographical method, and especially to the psychoanalysis of artist patients, promises to enrich greatly our understanding of an area that has always been precious to civilized man.

References

Freud, S. (1928), Dostoevsky and Parricide. *Standard Edition,* 21:177-194. London: Hogarth Press, 1961.

Greenacre, P. (1957), The Childhood of the Artist. *The Psychoanalytic Study of the Child,* 12:47-72. New York: International Universities Press.

Kligerman, C. (1953), The Psychology of Herman Melville. *Psychoanal. Rev.,* 40:125-143.

Kohut, H. (1976), Creativeness, Charisma, Group Psychology. In: *The Search for the Self,* vol. 2, ed. P. Ornstein. New York: International Universities Press, 1978, pp. 793-843.

Kris, E. (1952), *Psychoanalytic Explorations in Art.* New York: International Universities Press.

Lewissohn, L. (1949), *Goethe—The Story of a Man,* vol. 1. New York: Farrar, Straus.

Nathan, J. (1974), *Mishima.* Boston: Little, Brown.

Panel (1972), Creativity, reported by C. Kligerman. *Internat. J. Psycho-Anal.,* 53:21.

Rank, O. (1932), *Art and Artist.* New York: Tudor.

Heinz Kohut and the
Historical Imagination

Charles B. Strozier

Heinz Kohut is the most original and provocative thinker currently active in psychoanalysis. His two books and numerous articles have essentially opened up a new depth-psychological approach, the psychology of the self, that builds creatively on Freud and the work of ego psychologists of the past generation. Kohut's work defines a new metapsychological approach to the clinical data of observation, clarifies the empathic stance of psychoanalytic investigation, and outlines the therapeutic procedures that appear to modify classical technique. He is also a major thinker in the second half of the 20th century who, like Freud, has grappled with fundamental issues beyond the clinical setting. The diversity of papers in this volume suggests the range of Kohut's existing and potential influence on history, political science, anthropology, and literature. When scolded recently by Erich Heller, the distinguished literary critic, for venturing into the treacherous area of psycholiterature, Kohut (1978) responded: "My immediate response is simple. The inquiring human mind, I say, will not be stifled by prohibitions. . . . We don't know what will ultimately come of it, but we do it anyway. This is what man has done since his mind first began to be active. There is a relationship between the child's playfulness and scientific inquiry that no parental disapproval— and that includes your sermon to the analyst-child— will stop."

In this spirit of playful adventure I would like to examine critically the specific ways in which Kohut himself has interpreted historical phenomena. The extent of Kohut's work in history, although not systematically presented, is noteworthy. He has commented insightfully on problems of method and the meaning of evidence; he has provided thumbnail psychobiographical sketches of a number of historical figures; and he has outlined what I think is the most interesting psychology of group behavior since Freud's (1921) pioneering work in this area. Kohut (1978) is forthright in believing his psychology of the self opens new avenues for understanding history and culture generally. But he has also gone beyond mere assertion and dealt with the entire gamut of issues currently facing psychohistory.

Throughout his writings Kohut has occasionally found it useful to provide brief sketches of historical figures to illustrate a theoretical point. One such example is his use of Churchill to illustrate the interplay between the grandiose self, the ego, and the superego in determining personality (Kohut, 1966). Churchill, as a child, attempted to jump across a ravine to escape pursuing playmates. It was days before he regained consciousness and months before he began walking again. Nor was this episode an isolated event in Churchill's life. He seemed to possess an uncanny ability to extricate himself from apparently hopeless situations. Kohut hypothesizes that Churchill's grandiosity was not adequately guided or controlled by his ego ideal, though, "Luckily, for him and for the forces of civilization, when he reached the peak of his responsibilities the inner balance had shifted" (1966, p. 257). As a child, however, Churchill almost died at the hands of his impulsive grandiosity. He jumped the ravine, according to Kohut, because, deep down, he thought he could fly.[1]

At several points Kohut has also joined the chorus of analysts

[1]Kohut returned to Churchill in "Creativeness, Charisma, Group Psychology: Reflections on the Self-Analysis of Freud" (1976, p. 411).

and psychohistorians who have commented on Hitler.[2] Scattered throughout his writings is the kernel of a genuinely original view of this demonic and thoroughly perplexing figure. Toward the end of his first book, *The Analysis of the Self* (1971), and then in a later essay (1976), Kohut develops the idea that Hitler, like Schreber's father, had a kind of "healed-over psychosis." Hitler seemed able to retain his ability to test reality, but his reasoning capacity entirely served his rigid, narcissistic personality structure. Kohut sees Hitler's period of lonely self-absorption in Vienna from 1907 to 1913 as a hypochondriacal phase from which he emerged with the fixed idea that Jews had invaded the body of Germany and had to be eradicated (1971, pp. 150, 256). Of greater interest, however, is Kohut's analysis of the impact of a severely disturbed narcissistic figure like Hitler on his immediate followers and, by extension, on Germans in general. For example, Kohut is struck by the absolute self-confidence of Hitler and his peculiar ability to subordinate the class of rational technicians to his grandiose fantasies of magical-sadistic control over the whole world (1972, p. 382; 1971, p. 150). Thus Hitler served Speer's needs just as Wilhelm Fliess, in another context, filled a psychological vacuum in Freud's period of heightened creative tension (1972, p. 382).

   In such psychobiographical vignettes Kohut has clearly not attempted to provide an in-depth analysis of the figure in question or to write what Erikson has labeled a "life history." The evidence from the biographies of Churchill or Hitler is used selectively and for illustrative rather than analytical purposes. In the process, Kohut suggests new lines of psychobiographical investigation, although at first glance his primary interest appears to be the rather limited one of simply enriching his observational field in much the same way as Freud drew creatively on literary, historical, anthropological, and political examples to enliven his discussion of theoretical issues. Kohut recognizes the limits of such uses of data from history or any allied discipline; they make the allied discipline the handmaiden of psychoanalysis. But as Carl Schorske (1974) and many others have pointed out, psychohistory in the end is just

[2]For the best introduction to this literature, see Loewenberg (1975).

history, though it is hoped a more psychologically informed, sensitive history. If psychoanalysis — of the self or otherwise — helps us frame a historical question, it is still the relentless search for validation in the historical evidence itself that turns a whimsical insight into meaningful history.

But perhaps there is more methodological meat to Kohut's psychobiographical vignettes than is immediately apparent. For one thing, Kohut's careful attention to narcissistic issues opens up categories of evidence from a much later period in a figure's life than we are accustomed to handling in psychohistory. Much as any serious writer strains against the regressive pulls into his figure's childhood (because in the end there simply is no evidence from a dead person's infancy), a theoretical emphasis on drives and object relations far too often forces the psychohistorian into facile reconstruction of developmental issues. Kohut avoids this tendency. Thus his charming analysis of Churchill's grandiosity is firmly based on the leader's own concrete autobiographical report. Furthermore, Freudian drive theory leads the unwary biographer into the very private and largely inaccessible realm of a significant figure's loves and hates, unconscious fantasies, and symbolic interactions with his or her contemporaries. Kohut's approach, indeed his whole psychology of the self, on the other hand, permits the observer to interpret what we actually see: a figure's goals and ambitions, his ideals, and all the complex interactions characterizing his work life, whether they concern Schweitzer in the bush (Kohut, 1960, p. 576) or Hitler defrauding a generation of Germans. Most importantly, however, this presentistic focus on the observable remains a depth-psychological focus that incorporates the most useful elements of the psychoanalytic tradition.[3]

Turning to a somewhat different issue, it is noteworthy that the empathic stance of the observer to his data is at the center of Kohut's psychology of the self (Kohut, 1959; 1977, p. 302). In the area where delicately constructed bridges span psychoanalysis and history, such an empathic stance can of course result in sentimental

---

[3]For an extremely helpful discussion of these methodological issues, see the comments of John Demos in Strozier (1975).

obfuscation (Kohut, 1977, pp. 304–305) or a cover for an identification with one's subject (Kohut, 1976, pp. 382–383). Nonetheless, Kohut asserts that empathy defines our very field of observation; to avoid its disciplined use is to compromise the essence of our endeavors. The key here is Kohut's insistence that the use of empathy be "disciplined."[4] For the researcher, this means at a minimum undergoing a personal analysis (Kohut, 1960, p. 569).[5] For the historian, however, it also requires a knowledge of the sources and an ability to handle historical methodology. As Kohut recently noted: "The valid self-analysis of the psychoanalytic group — or of any group — must rest not only on the clear, nonregressive perception of archaic psychological experiences which arise within the group; it also requires the intellectual and emotional mastery of the material" (1976, pp. 420–422).

And so, with this quote, we come to group behavior, the area of Kohut's most creative contributions to the study of the past. No single issue is of greater concern to psychohistorians generally than how to go beyond a focus on individual biography (see Weinstein and Platt, 1975). Kohut wholeheartedly affirms the necessity of understanding collective behavior if psychohistory is to avoid the curse of triviality (1976, pp. 420–421). In the area of group behavior, Kohut, it seems to me, outlines two different, if clearly interrelated, approaches. The first applies his ideas on the self-object to a reevaluation of the relationship between the charismatic leader and his followers. The second approach develops his ideas on the group self and its formation, cohesion, and fragmentation. I will consider first the question of leadership and followership.

The central theme of his 1976 essay on "Creativeness, Charisma, and Group Psychology" is the examination of Freud's psychological state during his self-analysis in the 1890s. Kohut notes the extraordinary feat Freud performed, but also the strains it imposed on his narcissistic balance. For during such periods of

[4]Erikson also has dealt extensively with this issue in psychohistory. See Strozier (1976) for an examination of Erikson's "disciplined subjectivity."

[5]For a completely different point of view, see Weinstein and Platt (1973, p. 1n).

self is at the mercy of powerful forces which it can-
and its sense of enfeeblement is increased because it
helplessly exposed to extreme mood swings which range
ere precreative depression to dangerous hypomanic over-
ation, the latter occurring at the moment when the creative
stands at the threshold of creative activity" (Kohut, 1976, p.
3). Kohut argues that it is characteristic of creative individuals to
have fluid narcissistic cathexes, that is, to be able to move flexibly
between the poles of merger with a mirroring selfobject and an
omnipotent, idealizing selfobject. However, it is the idealizing
cathexes or the need for merger with an omnipotent, idealized
other that Kohut finds most striking and relevant for the understanding of creativity.

At this point Kohut asks a deceptively simple question that
has far-reaching implications: What kind of person serves as an
idealized selfobject for the creative person? The beauty of the
question is that it makes available for dynamic study the whole cultural and political environment surrounding the individual creative
figure, thereby providing the basis for a broadened psychosocial
understanding of the leader and his followers. In other words, the
question opens up the study of groups in history. Furthermore, as
part of the methodological context for asking this question, Kohut
distinguishes between the endopsychic factors that create the
transference situation in analysis and the situation of the creative
person in which the self is enfeebled and drained of its cohesion-
maintaining cathexes (1976, p. 407). These demands on the creative figure weaken his self-cohesion and make him dangerously
vulnerable to specific idealizing selfobject needs. In clinical psychoanalysis, on the other hand, it is the therapeutic setting that
activates developmentally ancient, endopsychic transference
needs. For the historian, Kohut's approach to Freud is infinitely
more palatable than the classical transference model, because it
focuses attention on the observable present while simultaneously
retaining a depth-psychological approach.

Kohut's answer to his simple question leads him to Wilhelm
Fliess and to some interesting generalizations about the Fliesses of
the world, "who are specifically suitable to be the objects of the

idealizing needs of the creative person's temporarily enfeebled self during a creative spell" (1976, p. 409). Kohut sees these Fliesses as narcissistically fixated persons, bordering on the paranoid. They possess an unshakable self-confidence with enormous, if brittle, self-esteem. Lacking any self-doubts, such figures set themselves up as leaders. Their absolute certainty risks total failure but also makes possible confident leadership. They possess an all-or-nothing character (1976, pp. 409–410). Along with Fliess, one could think of any number of leaders who fit nicely into this narcissistic framework. Kohut mentions Hitler and Schreber's father; I might add Napoleon, Stalin, and Mao.

The point, however, is not to generate a new typology for classifying leaders but to understand the essential psychological bases of the leader and the follower in history. The historical analogue of Freud's depleted narcissistic state during his self-analysis would be familiar situations of social, political, and economic dislocation created by wars and revolutions; demographic disasters such as the effects of the plague in the 14th century; and sudden shifts in social life, such as the impact of industrialization and urbanization in early 19th-century Europe. During these periods of collective narcissistic enfeeblement and tension, a desperate group need for merger with an idealized selfobject creates the political base from which the support of strong, charismatic, narcissistic leaders issues. These leaders then enhance and confirm the enfeebled group self in the same way an idealizing transference situation during clinical psychoanalysis motivates the analysand to seek merger with the idealized selfobject-analyst. Such historical periods of narcissistic tension—"crises" is the term generally employed by historians—and the special leaders who emerge to direct events during such times, alternate with longer, calmer, more stable periods of growth and consolidation At such times another kind of leader meets the psychological needs of the group self. Thus the practical and eminently political Nehru followed Gandhi; the master *apparatchiki* Krushchev and Brezhnev followed Stalin; a shrewd technocrat like Hua takes over after Mao; and Carter may stand in approximately the same relation to Nixon.

The concept of a group self occupies a central position in Kohut's recent thought. As he has recently stated, "Group processes are largely activated by narcissistic motives" (1976, p. 422). Kohut means this as broadly as it sounds. On the one hand, members of a group form and remain together in part because they share an ego ideal (as Freud noted in his work on group psychology [1921]), but more importantly because they share a "subject-bound grandiosity" or a grandiose self. Thus shared ambitions, more than ideals, provide the cohesive glue for the group self (1972, pp. 397–398). At least this was the way Kohut saw it eight years ago. More recently, he appears to have placed greater emphasis on shared ideals—the religious, cultural, political threads woven into the fabric of our heritage—as the basis for cohesion of the group self. Kohut's recent discussion of the psychoanalytic group self, for example, places a great deal of emphasis on the idealized imago of Freud. Such a shared ideal provides a solid safeguard against narcissistic tensions (such as shame) and protects against narcissistic disequilibria (such as envy, jealousy, rage) (1976, p. 389). It seems valid to infer from Kohut's most recent book that he now sees the relationship between the group self's shared idealized imago and its grandiose self not as an either/or choice but in terms of the "tension gradient" between the various constituents of the group self (1977, Chapter 4).

This conceptualization of group behavior provides a range of insights into some very old issues. For example, the idealized group imago of late-19th-century Germany centered around all-powerful, authoritarian, politically and militarily omnipotent images that fused patriarchal family patterns and antidemocratic political traditions. Such idealization spawned political passivity and was in turn fed by rapid military victories, the growth of an empire, and economic dynamism. The other constituents of Germany's group self centered on grandiose notions of world domination and cultural preeminence. The humiliating loss in the war then created extreme, rageful responses because the whole basis of the German group self's cohesion was threatened. Fragmentation, which historically expresses itself as political, social, and economic chaos, resulted. In time, a strutting little corporal provided brittle, but desperately sought, narcissistic nourishment for Germany's bruised self. What followed was a frantic search for revenge that has its analogue in Kleist's story of Michael Kohlhass (Kohut, 1972, p. 362), as "Hitler exploited the readiness of a civilized nation to shed the thin layer of its uncomfortably carried restraints" (1972, p. 377).

This suggestive example provides an appropriate point at which to conclude. For the work of Kohut to be fully appreciated, we need many more.[6] The challenge to historians to learn and to use Kohut's psychology of the self is readily apparent. For some it will not be easy. It has taken historians half a century to start reading Freud, and then it was largely under Erikson's prodding. Now historians need a whole new shelf of books in their studies. But unless I am sorely mistaken, without that shelf our libraries will soon be obsolete.

References

Freud, S. (1921), Group Psychology and the Analysis of the Ego. *Standard Edition,* 18:65–143. London: Hogarth Press, 1955.

Kohut, H. (1959), Introspection, Empathy, and Psychoanalysis. *J. Amer. Psychoanal. Assn.,* 7:459–483.

_____ (1960), Beyond the Bounds of the Basic Rule. *J. Amer. Psychoanal. Assn.,* 8:567–586.

_____ (1966), Forms and Transformations of Narcissism. *J. Amer. Psychoanal. Assn.,* 14:243–272.

_____ (1971), *The Analysis of the Self.* New York: International Universities Press.

_____ (1972), Thoughts on Narcissism and Narcissistic Rage. *The Psychoanalytic Study of the Child,* 27:360–400. New York: Quadrangle.

_____ (1976), Creativeness, Charisma, Group Psychology: Reflections on the Self-Analysis of Freud. In: *Freud: The Fusion of Science and Humanism,* ed. J. E. Gedo & G. H. Pollock. *Psychol. Issues,* Monogr. 34/35. New York: International Universities Press, pp. 379–425.

_____ (1977), *The Restoration of the Self.* New York: International Universities Press.

_____ (1978), Psychoanalysis and the Interpretation of Literature: A Correspondence with Erich Heller. *Critical Inquiry,* 4:433–450.

Loewenberg, P. (1975), Psychohistorical Perspectives on Modern German History. *J. Mod. Hist.,* 47:229–279.

Minnich, N. H. & Meissner, W. W. (1978), The Character of Erasmus. *Amer.*

[6]See, in this connection, Minnich and Meissner (1978).

Hist. Rev., 83:598–624.

Schorske, C. (1974), Unpublished paper delivered at the Conference on the Self in History, Chicago.

Strozier, C. B., ed. (1975), The Self in History. *Newsletter of the Group for the Use of Psychology in History,* 3:3–10.

_____ (1976), Disciplined Subjectivity and the Psychohistorian: A Critical Look at the Work of Erik H. Erikson. *Psychohist. Rev.,* 5:28–31.

Weinstein, F. & Platt, G. (1973), *Psychoanalytic Sociology: An Essay on the Interpretation of Historical Data and the Phenomena of Collective Behavior.* Baltimore: Johns Hopkins University Press.

_____ _____ (1975), The Coming Crisis in Psychohistory. *J. Mod. Hist.,* 47:202–228.

The Psychology of the Self:
Religion and Psychotherapy

RANDALL C. MASON

The staff therapists of the Center for Religion and Psycho-therapy of Chicago have been clearly and definitively influenced by the work of Heinz Kohut.[1] The psychology of the self has helped clarify data previously observed but unexplainable, and called to attention other data previously overlooked. While there is awe-some power in the broad theoretical sweep of the psychology of the self, it is the clinical aspects of Kohut's theories that have pro-ven the most powerful, convincing, and exciting in our work. We have repeatedly seen psychotherapeutic hypotheses translate into clinically observed changes in clients.

This presentation focuses on the influence of the psychology of the self on work at the Center for Religion and Psychotherapy. I will not consider changes in our therapeutic work that might be common to psychotherapy in general, however, but will limit the discussion to three areas relevant to religion. The first concerns our work as pastoral psychotherapists with persons seeking our

[1]We at the Center are most grateful to Dr. Harry Trosman, Professor of Psychiatry at the University of Chicago, Training Analyst at the Institute for Psychoanalysis of Chicago, and a Consultant for the past 10 years at the Center for Religion and Psychotherapy, for introducing us to the psychology of the self and for his continued contributions to our thinking in this area.

407

help. The second concerns our thinking about the training we provide parish pastors in the context of the ways in which the psychology of the self could influence the teaching and ritual practices
of institutional religion. The third concerns the way in which the
psychology of the self has illuminated traditional religious symbolism. In all three areas, the psychology of the self has increased
our understanding of the meaning and influence of religion itself.

Prior to moving to these three areas, attention must be given
to a methodological problem in the discussion of religion. The
definition of religion in an operational way that makes it accessible
to observation and study within a psychotherapy context or from
an intrapsychic perspective is elusive. The difficulty is not as apparent in other disciplines in that the indices of an operational definition are more easily defined and observed. Thus, Max Weber
could label entire countries Roman Catholic or Protestant and
study the rise of capitalism as a function of the Protestant ethic.
Allport, with his focus on conscious attitudes, can determine the
religiousness of a person by asking whether that person believes in
God. The sociologists focusing on the group as a unit can determine religion by recording membership in religious organizations.
The task of the theologians, however, is to describe what religion
ought to be rather than observing what is practiced.

Observers of the intrapsychic cannot accept the operational
definitions and indices of other disciplines, for religion defined in
such operational terms is bound to have quite different intrapsychic meanings for different individuals. Group affiliation, like
church membership, will not mean the same thing psychologically
for those so affiliated. In a therapy session, if a person engages in
God-talk, does one conclude that the person is talking about his
religion, engaged in some form of resistance, neither, or both? If a
person does not talk about religion, do we conclude that he is not
religious, or do we suspect that the religious aspects of his personality are seeking expression in secular equivalents to traditional
religions such as Americanism, capitalism, scientism, communism,
and other modern equivalents that have the power to elicit awe,
hope, and discipline in a way of life?

Such operational definitions are further complicated by

religion's own identity struggles. Let me use an analogy that is intended to be purely illustrative and not explanatory. Religion is like a mother merged with children who have left her. In the early centuries of Christian tradition, as with primitive religions, religion included her children — politics, law, medicine, science, philosophy, the arts, and others — as subheadings within herself. One by one these children, often experiencing great pain, persecution, and the outpouring of rage, moved to establish an autonomous identity governed by their own standards and laws. In the past 50 years theological apologetics have critiqued the assumptions of these disciplines, an action that, while often appropriate, gives the impression of the mother who says, "Look, you still need me." Meanwhile, the children have often made mother epiphenomenal, and even described her as an "opiate of the people" or a "collective neurosis." In the face of all this, you may not be surprised that mother is undergoing a crisis of self identification. Even though she remains powerful and influential, she wonders wherein her autonomy lies, and whether it might be true that she is simply an easily discarded reflection of her children.

It was this situation that Dietrich Bonhoeffer described while in a concentration camp in the book *Letters and Papers from Prison* (1972). His word "God" is best understood as religion:

> The movement that began about the thirteenth century... toward the autonomy of man (in which I should include the discovery of the laws by which the world lives and deals with itself in science, social and political matters, art, ethics and religion) has, in our time reached an undoubted completion. Man has learned to deal with himself in all questions of importance without recourse to the 'working' hypothesis called 'God.' [And elsewhere in the book:] It has again brought home to me how wrong it is to use God as a stop-gap for the incompleteness of our knowledge [pp. 325, 311].

What Bonhoeffer[2] and others within the intellectual religious

[2]Such thoughts led him to reject concern for religion in an assertion of what he was to call a nonreligious assertion of Christian faith. It would be wrong,

community have noted, most of practicing religion has ignored.[3] It has especially ignored (or considered relevant only to the severely emotionally disabled) the implications of the psychotherapeutic. You may understand this when you realize that the world of psychotherapy has claimed autonomy for a child most precious and integral to the mother herself: the care and nurture of persons.

Thus, there is no easy operational definition to inform our discussion, or to answer the question of how religion is related to psychotherapy or the intrapsychic. Within this context, however, let me suggest an operational definition of religion for our discussion: religion has to do with a valuing affirmation of a basic transcending reality that has the power to define the Good Life, expresses itself in ritual and celebration, and results in norms for achieving the Good Life. Such a definition is more useful in the area of psychotherapy than defining religion as belief in God, or by reference to the traditional major religions, or by borrowing definitions from other disciplines. It permits inclusion of the secular religions and may even include the individual system of the paranoid schizophrenic.

Despite outward content differences, such diverse religions appear to serve as psychic equivalents, and their inclusion in one definition begins to clarify a category of psychic phenomena for observation and study, of which traditional religion is but one variant.[4] These religions, despite outward variations, deal in similar fashion with basic psychological issues such as cohesiveness and fragmentation. At their best, such religions may enhance the individual's sense of order and meaning in the universe, and lend

---

however, to interpret his call for a religionless Christianity as a reflection of the concern for definition raised here.

[3]This critique would not apply to those in the pastoral psychotherapy movement or those in the intellectual religious community who are in universities and seminaries. The dialogue between religion and psychotherapy has been quite stimulating, even shaping the work of theology itself, and resulting in numerous publications. However, such persons represent a very small segment of practicing institutional religion.

[4]I believe that religion so defined is adopted through the processes of normal psychological development, and that the autonomous power of such a religion, as distinct from considering it merely epiphenomenal, may be understood from an adaptational perspective.

support to his ideals and ambitions. At first glance, at least, many of the secular equivalents appear to have served this function more successfully than many expressions of traditional religion.

The definition given above is close to that of Browning, who, dealing with similar methodological issues, defined religion in an early manuscript of the book *Moral Context of Pastoral Care* (1976) as "any system of symbols which gives a person 'a general framework or orientation to live' and 'object(s) of devotion.'" Both definitions incorporate Jerome Frank's reference in *Persuasion and Healing* (1973) to systems that define the healer, the causes of illness, and the steps necessary for healing. At this point religion does become relevant to the practice of psychotherapy, as any psychotherapist would discover who sought to compete with a witch doctor in a primitive society or sought to exercise his tools of healing within many parts of the contemporary religious community.

The Psychology of the Self: Pastoral Psychotherapy

The psychotherapeutically relevant definition of religion is basic to an understanding of the way in which the psychology of the self has influenced the first area of our work at the Center for Religion and Psychotherapy—the practice of pastoral psychotherapy. It is also basic to understanding one way in which religion is a part of the Center. We spend about 1000 hours a month seeing clients, generally on a once or twice a week basis. The predominant presenting problems relate to marital and family issues and vocational concerns though many clients come with a vague sense of uneasiness and personal discomfort as well. For the most part, clients fall within some mythical normal range of emotional stability, and are functioning well in most aspects of their lives.

A large percentage of our clients would perceive themselves as the "good people" of the world, involved in helping and taking care of others. Their goodness might even include a horrified concern over the neediness of others or some weakness in their own lives. Many might best be described as presenting a reaction

formation to narcissism. They seek out pastors for help, most likely through some kind of superego identification, or because going
to other mental health workers often connotes some form of illness that they do not want to admit, e.g., "We have problems in
our marriage, but we are not sick."

Our knowledge of the psychology of the self led us to listen to
certain statements that we had previously ignored. One formerly
overlooked term was "selfishness," which clients described with a
punitive attitude when they perceived it as present in themselves or
others. Another term with special meaning was "responsibility."
The sense in which clients used this term can be caught by substituting "responsibility" for "control" in a sentence of Kohut's on
the relation of the grandiose self to selfobjects: "The expected [re-
sponsibility] over such (self-object) others is then closer to the concept of [responsibility] which a grownup expects to have over his
own body and mind than to the concept of [responsibility] which
he expects to have over others" (1971, pp. 26–27).

For clients, concern with being responsible is often accompanied by a genuine horror at the idea of controlling anyone. Their
feeling of responsibility results in a sense of moral failure and guilt
over having inadequately taken care of those around them.
Weakness, vulnerability, neediness, or limits are pejorative terms
when used in relation to the self, even though they understand and
even appreciate such qualities in others. All of these clients are involved in some kind of commitment to be caring "superhumans."
In these marriages I have come to think in terms of "plantation
systems" in which each partner is involved not in meeting his or her
own needs, but in taking care of the spouse, simultaneously feeling
wearied, overwhelmed, and pressured by what can be referred to
as "the white man's burden." What these attitudes add up to is a
moral and intellectual commitment to "hiding the self." What is
awesome is how pervasive, deep, and ingrained these themes are,
and how many of our clients perceive such commitment in terms
of a moral framework.

The commitment to "hiding the self" represents an ethical
norm determining what it means to be fully human and successful
at living. It posits that the assertion of the self and clear delineation

of the boundaries of the self are sinful. Some of our clients would rather steal or indulge in a sexual perversion than assert their selves.

Our experience of the various expressions of the commitment to "hiding the self" indicates that they are undergirded by an unquestioning conviction that adherence to this norm is the way to be good and to achieve the Good Life. To support such convictions clients appeal to one or a combination of four religions that sanction the "hiding of the self": Christian folk religion, Americanism, self-discovery, and liberationism.[5] In various ways these religions call for the caring of others more than the self, unlimited responsibility toward others, the overcoming of vulnerability

[5]The Christian folk religion is what is popularly believed by many Christians, even though the theological community might disagree with its designation as Christian. The theme of self-sacrifice is very strong in this religion and is often understood as self-abasement. Interpretations of the Biblical injunction to love thy neighbor as oneself have more often than not given primary emphasis to the loving of others.

The religion of Americanism often permits self-assertion but denies vulnerability in the business world and denies self-assertion in close personal relations. Stalwartly seeking to be good disciples of the American dream, adherents experience "getting in touch" with their own needs as a selfish thing to do. They come to psychotherapy very often to help out other family members who lack their strengths. They receive moral support from some secular prophets, the newspaper columnists, who now and then give a moral spanking to the trend of self-assertion.

Adherents of the religion of self-discovery are engaged in learning new artistic skills, going into psychotherapy, or perhaps learning yoga. While self-discoverers might appear to be in favor of discovery of the self, they often seek to use psychotherapy as a way of suppressing the self. One observer referred to a cultlike group of the "society of the friends of psychotherapy," whose mission is to direct each other to the right psychotherapist, the opportunity for mission being provided by the endless self-discussions in which the disciples of this religion engage.

Religious liberationists live in the dream of a changed society and often merge with their ideological commitments. They condemn the preoccupation with self of those engaged in psychotherapy as draining from the dream as well as being selfish. They come into psychotherapy only when no other alternatives are available, and do so with shame. For such persons our connections to the civil rights movement have legitimized us as healers, and we see a fair number of them. The physical pain experienced by liberationists during the Democratic Convention of 1968 cannot rival the pain in shame and loss of self that these people associated with the perceived defeat of their cause during that convention.

and weakness, the rejection of self needs (especially in the family setting) and other variants of these themes. Many of these clients remember the common Christian folk teaching to which they were exposed in their youth: "God first, others second, and me third."

Before considering our responses to these religions and their moral teachings, let me stress that I am not raising questions about mature forms of caring or a sense of responsibility in which boundaries are clear and the self is not hidden. Rather, I am pointing to various expressions of the "hiding of self," to grandiosity that has not been adequately modulated to permit the difficult but more mature forms of object attachments, and to merger tendencies that interfere with the development and assertion of the self. Although these tendencies are rooted in child development, their continuation into adulthood is sanctioned by the religions noted above. These sanctions mean that many adherents will not even seek our help, or be able to make full use of our advice if they do reach us. Let me also be clear that, by use of the term "self-assertion," I am not supporting some of the therapeutic evangelists who utilize some theories in order to supplant unlimited caring with unlimited grandiose self-assertion, thereby giving sanction to the more primitive forms of narcissism. The love of neighbor as self implies a balanced empathic awareness of one's own needs and the needs of others, plus the recognition that the self and neighbor are different. I understand this to be one quality of mature object relationships. The psychology of the self has helped us understand what adherence to that norm can mean, and alerted us to the fact that it means neither a "hiding of the self" nor unlimited self-assertion.

Prior to the psychology of the self, we had paid little attention to these ethical concerns or religious systems of our clients. In conflict-structural psychology there were ethical issues surrounding hostility and sexuality, but they rarely emerged as clearly as issues of the self. Awareness of these issues gradually led us to assume a teaching role in our counseling, whereas earlier we were almost phobically committed to a nonteaching stance. Teaching has evoked two very negative images for us as clergy, images associated with being "educative" and "proselytizing." By educative, as applied to therapy, I refer to a moralistic-inspirational exhortation which can occur in muted fashion out of a simple lack of respect for and understanding of the therapeutic process.[6] On the basis of recent clinical experience, I would no longer use the term "educative" as a basis for ruling out all teaching. I suspect that teaching interventions, like therapeutic interpretations, are educative in the pejorative sense and useless when made without empathic understanding of the client, but constructive when informed by empathic understanding. Out of respect for the individual, we are opposed to proselytizing, and whatever teaching is done in relation to ethics seeks to develop and expand the religion of the client rather than that of the therapist.

Let me now give some clinical examples that fall on a continuum. At one end of the continuum are cases where teaching is primary and therapeutic goals minimal. This approach typifies the kind of help given a client who comes for a single consultation. At the other end are cases where therapy is primary and teaching minimal.

Starting with the consultative end of the continuum, the first example illustrates the setting of limits on grandiose responsibility, the second the balancing of self development with merger tendencies, and the third the issue of limits:

1. A couple, ready to move to their retirement home in a southwestern state, came because they did not feel they could move until their daughter received help. Their religion was a combination of Christian folk religion and Americanism in which one worked hard and did one's duties and then retired. The completion of duties was frustrated, however, by a 28-year-old daughter "wandering the streets." Psychologically, the boundaries between parents and daughter were not clear and they could not rest, seeing their daughter's behavior as if part of their own persons were out of control. Intervention focused on how much they had already given, suggested that further attempts would probably be counterproductive, and indicated that the daughter now had to be placed

---

[6]The issue of education may be an especially sensitive one to pastors since that enthusiastic and optimistic pioneer of psychoanalysis, the Swiss pastor Oscar Pfister, was considered by some to have been "educative" in his practice of psychoanalysis in Zurich.

in God's care if she were to be helped. While conveying our understanding and appreciation of their concern, we counseled that the
continuation *of that concern* in a way that truncated their lives
would be taking over God's responsibilities. They were seen for
three sessions after which they were able to resume their retirement
plans. The sessions included some mourning for the separation
from the daughter.

2. A woman in her twenties came to a pastor to talk over a
recommendation by her physician that she enter psychotherapy
because of physical and personal problems. Although she felt that
doing so might be a good idea, financially it entailed postponement
of her plans to enter graduate school to prepare for a Christian
vocation. Furthermore, "If I have truly given myself to Christ's
service, how can I spend all that time worrying about myself and
my problems instead of giving to others?" Her thinking was consistent with a form of Christian folk religion in which the ethic is to
give oneself up in trust to God and His service, while assuming that
all personal needs and problems will be taken care of. Discussion
focused on the meaning of Christian discipleship and vocation,
and how that might include a responsible development of the self.
She came to see her entrance into psychotherapy as a way of
preparing for Christian service rather than an indication of a lack
of faith. With some relief, she was able to become more realistic in
her planning.

3. A young couple came for counseling after a year of marriage. The wife, married to a highly intellectual, isolated male, felt
a sense of urgency to achieve more unity and closeness in the marriage. Psychologically her selection of such a mate had been
appropriate, for she was highly sensitive to perceived insults and
slights, became overly entangled in close relationships, and had
some dim awareness of her need to protect herself from intense relationships. Overwhelming the need for self-protection, however,
was the push toward merger and the need to make over her husband so that he would be more sensitive and tender like her. Supporting the nonprotective side of herself were the ethical norms in-
forming her behavior: these norms derived from the marriage
ceremony suggestion that "the two shall become as one," and the

need to make over her husband rooted in the liberationist religion. The sessions focused on increasing each spouse's awareness of and respect for the vulnerability of his or her partner (which does fit with a feminist liberation religion); and noting that the statement in the marriage ceremony that "the two shall become as one" did not imply giving up independent, autonomous selves. They became convinced that it was permissible not to relate so intensely. They remained in joint marital therapy for three months, terminating after their home life became more relaxed and less pressured.

Moving along the continuum we encounter work with clients in which the model used is more akin to supervision than to traditional therapy, supervision in the sense that the supervisor may be a model and the supervisee is expected to be able to employ new approaches to others growing out of the supervision. If the supervisee is unable to do so, he or she may need to enter therapy. A similar process occurs with clients who gain a vision of new ways of being and have the ego capacities to implement that vision. The changed vision leads to changed behaviors that are self-validating and continuing. If such clients are committed to caring for others, they find their new attention to self an aid to caring and view their former behaviors as destructive.

4. A banking executive came because he felt his marriage was breaking up because of his wife's continual rage. His commitment to care for her plus his understanding of the women's liberation perspective left him feeling helpless and with no right to make any demands on his spouse. Discussion focused on liberation as a process pertaining both to men and women. It was suggested that his suppression of his needs was a subtle form of paternalistic put-down since his wife was so aware of her own needs — thus her rage. He learned how to express his needs in ways his wife could hear, and he was amazed at her positive response.

5. A couple came for marital help with the husband complaining that his wife was too dependent. In paternalistic fashion, he was taking care of her by getting her into therapy. Although both entered individual therapy, he quit after several sesssions. He had become involved with another woman, and was usually unsuccessful in lying about it to his wife. The knowledge of this other

relationship panicked her and she responded by trying to become a better person so that she could better understand and please him. This resolve was often broken through by narcissistic rage at the insult of his involvement with another woman. The resolve was fostered and sanctioned by a Christian folk religion which prescribed caring behavior and disregard for the self. Whenever she expressed her rage her husband was quick to remind her of proper behavior and she would feel guilty for being so selfish and for hurting his "self development." She could not accept the advice of suburban friends to get "rid of him." Early interventions focused on the Christian responsibility to one's own self, and stressed that her efforts to be selfless were destructive both to herself and her husband. She began to acquaint him with the notion that she could handle anything he did. She was finally able to tell him that he indeed had a right to his self development, but that she could not live with him in the process (the continually stimulated rage was highly unsettling and interfered with her everyday functioning). She was firm in demanding that he leave the home until he could be fully present in the home. He left in a state of shock, indicating that he could not believe that she could be so selfish. She subsequently began to calm down.

The shock of his wife actually making him leave home brought the husband back into therapy. The shock was accompanied by separation pain over the loss of a selfobject whom he assumed he controlled. When his therapist suggested that he communicate his vulnerability and confusion rather than lying, he did so with good results, in that his wife, while not satisfied, felt less insulted and less enraged than when he tried to lie. His religion was more an Americanism-capitalism combination. While he blamed his difficulty in communicating his vulnerability to his wife on the business world where vulnerability is concealed or one "will never make it," in fact, this was his own personal religion and ethic. He indicated that his boss had informed him that he did not care which woman he wound up with, but advised him to make his decision quickly and settle down or lose an upcoming promotion. Although this was his boss's statement, it also reflected his own feeling about the way he ought to be able to manage things. Thus, his omnipotence, supported by his business ethic, meant that he could not persist in relating in a new way to his wife. The supervision model did not work. The precipitant for his involvement with another woman appeared to be the overstimulation resulting from several rapid promotions, but he was never able to bring this aspect of his life into therapy, insisting that everything was going well. Actually, he experienced the very fact of being in therapy as an overwhelming insult and he eventually terminated.

Moving further along the continuum, we encounter work with clients in which teaching is present in the earlier stages of therapy but less so in the later stages. The client may in later stages express anguish over selfishness, but it is clear that the problem is the anguish rather than selfhood.

6. A depressed and worried but highly intelligent and well-educated woman in her thirties started therapy both fearing that I would be punitive and judgmental, and doubting my credibility when I was not. In the absence of such judgments, she perceived me as one of the advocates of "anything goes." She had a psychologically sadomasochistic relationship with her husband in which she confessed her misdoings and he provided consistent condemnation — misdoings that were most often a breakthrough and assertion of the legitimate needs of the self. The marital relationship was a recapitulation of an earlier relationship with her dominant and intrusive mother. After some months in therapy the outlines of a vertical split emerged. On the one side, there were the fantasies of the ideal woman she would like to become, along with the energies associated with those fantasies. On the other side, there was a weary woman feeling condemned, constantly under pressure, and unable to meet the demands of others. Her understanding of the Christian religion supported the "reality" life, and her *condemnation* of the "anything goes" morality supported the vertical barrier against the feared chaos and fragmentation of the grandiose sphere. Early discussion focused on supporting her weak (but nevertheless present) moral sense, and advising her that the development of the self was legitimate and did not lead to a philosophy of "anything goes." Subsequently, the vertical split was revealed along with the emergence of the grandiose fantasies, and

the process of integration began. With the development of a mirror transference, she utilized the therapy for calming herself in relation to the overstimulation of the emerging self, and to express appreciation rather than condemnation of the exhibitionism and concomitant reality achievements in her life.

7. An older married male professor felt overwhelmed in his home. For the same reasons as the banking executive discussed above, he was unable to make demands on his working spouse. His manner of caring for the children was influenced by the moral relativism of a cultural pluralism (meaning that all the other kids were doing it) and made it difficult to say "no" to his children and to achieve any order in his home.[7] He lived by responding to the demands of others, and when this orientation was challenged, he strongly protested his desire to be a caring person. His move from simple expressions of helplessness to an exploration of his mergers came as he saw that his method of caring was training his family to be irresponsible, and realized that his caring had to be balanced by attention to the needs of the self.

These brief clinical illustrations depict but a few of the many persons for whom the self psychological perspective proved relevant. We have been amazed at how many clients were struggling with such issues once we had a perspective that permitted us to hear what they were saying. The usefulness of teaching interventions in the moral realm was not something which we had jointly planned beforehand, but more a discovery made individually by each staff member that eventually led to a dialogue of shared experiences. In ending this section, it should be noted that certain clients do come for therapy for whom such teaching is irrelevant or unnecessary.

The Psychology of the Self: Institutional Religion

The second area to be explored concerns the potential influence of the psychology of the self on institutional religion.

[7]This difficulty with the "no" is relevant to Kohut's discussion of the contemporary development of the narcissistic personality in his Epilogue to *The Restoration of the Self* (1977).

Many would maintain that the major impact of Freud lies not in the number of patients for whom he and subsequent analysts provided help, but rather in his development of the analytic method and the cultural impact of his findings. In the past, we at the Center, along with other mental health workers, have worked with parish clergy in the hope of improving their counseling skills. I now think such efforts were misguided because they left a more important task undone: the translation of psychological knowledge into the life of the religious community.

One area where such translation can occur concerns the teaching and preaching of doctrines and ethical guidelines. These guidelines could be expounded, for example, in a way supportive of the development of the self rather than promoting self-denial. The problem with much doctrinal exposition and ethical teaching lies not in its theological or religious roots, but rather in its psychological base in 19th-century rational and voluntaristic psychologies. To change this method, students at the Center are writing papers which develop ethical guidelines using both theology and the psychology of the self as the psychological base. Truby (1978), for example, used Bonhoeffer as theologian and Kohut as psychologist to clarify the ethical issues of male dependency (the macho imperative). Such work leads to a change in the content of preaching and in religious education. Many parish clergy would be open to the influence of the psychology of the self in their preaching and teaching if they could engage in a dialogue with persons who could help them relate the psychology of the self to doctrine and ethics (issues of individual life style) — a more significant way for the mental health community to relate to the clergy than through the teaching of counseling skills.[8]

Such a dialogue would focus in part on rituals, such as the funeral, bearing in mind the special significance of grief reactions for personal dysfunctioning. The content and procedures of the ritual are in many traditions not considered sacred and could be modified in ways that would facilitate the resolution of the loss

---

[8]One, of course, need not agree with the doctrine to discuss its application in a way most helpful to persons.

of selfobjects.

In the area of aftercare, pastors lack a systematic, psychologically informed method for care of the bereaved, despite a tradition that suggests the need for regular visitation and the kind of support that any well-intentioned, intelligent person could provide. Many pastors, of course, overwhelmed by their own feelings of helplessness (which are accentuated by a lack of a clear understanding of what they could do), simply avoid the bereaved. Others make sympathy or "exhortation-to-faith" calls, become frustrated when people do not improve quickly, and then may stop calling altogether. The influence of Carl Rogers has helped some to listen in an emotionally supportive way. They do their best with the available psychological knowledge.

It is unnecessary to dwell at length on the value of a systematic method of caring for the bereaved that has the psychology of the self at its core. Let me just mention among the concepts of self psychology relevant to such a method the regressive effects of mirroring or idealizing selfobject losses, shame and humiliation, transmuting internalizations, empathic understanding, narcissistic rage, and the significance of time itself. Merely to know that what they are experiencing is within the realm of human experience is of major benefit to the bereaved. The visits of pastors are especially welcomed during these times, and they have the right of initiatory access. But how often should they visit, what should they observe, and what interventions should they undertake to promote the resolution of grief?

Let me underscore the significance of psychoanalysis and the psychology of the self in this area by noting that psychoanalysis, through its method, in a relatively unprecedented way in comparison with other psychological theories, has emphasized the central significance of relationships and of continuity and stability in relationships. This begins with the assumption that for some forms of personal growth to occur, treatment four times a week for some years is necessary. This emphasis on relationships continues in the clarification of the significance of empathic breaks that occur within the analysis itself. As Freud noted: "At this point [the point at which resistance blocks therapeutic progress] what turns the scale in [the patient's] struggle is not his intellectual insight — which is neither strong enough nor free enough for such an achievement, but simply and solely his relation to the doctor" (1916–1917, p. 445).

The Psychology of the Self:
Intrapsychic Understanding of Religion

Moving now to the intrapsychic understanding of religion, the psychology of the self enriches the symbolic content of religious themes. Of the numerous examples, only a few will be given here. Conflict-structural psychology does not illuminate like the psychology of the self the centrality of mirroring in the traditional benediction:

> The lord bless you and keep you.
> The lord *make His face to shine upon you* and be gracious unto you.
> The Lord *lift up the light of His countenance upon you* and give you peace.
>
> Amen.

Likewise, note the idealizing issues as well as the feudal imagery in the popular Reformation hymn:

> A mighty fortress is our God, a bulwark never failing,
> Our helper He amidst the floods of mortal ills prevailing.
> For still our ancient foe does seek to work us woe.
> His craft and power are great, and armed with cruel hate,
> On earth is not His equal.
>
> Did we in our own strength confide, our striving would be losing,
> Were not the right man on our side, the man of God's own choosing.

Hymns, scriptures, and liturgy have traditionally begun with the affirmation of the omnipotence, perfection, and holiness of the God figure. A client who is no longer sure he believes in God will still pray three times a day to gain that power and support.

Without seeking to undercut the philosophical issues involved, one might wonder about the possible role of "transmuting internalizations" in the increased popularity of process theology. One aspect of process theology is the idea of a limited God who, as limited, enters into a partnership with man in a mortal struggle whose outcome is unknown. In traditional theology God was omnipotent, omniscient, and the outcome of the struggle was never in doubt. Neo-orthodox theology in both Europe and America recaptured the wholly otherness of God in order to rescue God from becoming a self-extension — as He would be if seen as being on both sides of the struggle during World War II. The emphasis on the otherness of God continued to the point that in the fifties Paul Tillich spoke in symbolic language about "God hiding His face from this generation."[9] Then in the sixties the "death of God" theologians emerged, to be followed in the seventies by theologians increasingly interested in process theology with a limited God. The possible "transmuting internalization" suggested here is not widespread in the religious community but would pertain primarily to some of those within the intellectual religious community who have both experienced God as a selfobject and have been sensitive to the modulating influence of world events.

This presentation has sought to convey the way the psychology of the self has influenced our thinking and work at the Center for Religion and Psychotherapy in the areas of pastoral psychotherapy, teaching, the role of ritual in institutional religion, and finally, in the understanding of religious symbols.

In concluding, let me return to my earlier discussion of the definition of religion. The definition I proposed, while more useful than many, still points beyond itself to the need for a definition that includes a better understanding of the intrapsychic components involved in religiosity. What intrapsychic components make phenomena religious rather than nonreligious? How are we to

[9]Tillich made this comment in a discussion with Rollo May and students at Union Theological Seminary around 1961. The focus of the discussion was the loss of power and meaning of traditional religious symbols in the present age.

understand that people involve themselves in making transcendent assumptions or religious assertions? What is the intrapsychic understanding of the feelings of awe and dread in response to what is perceived as the sacred? (See Otto, 1958, pp. 12–24.)

I think the psychology of the self is especially pertinent to this task in its discussion of idealization and the modulation of idealization in the capacity to value, and in its discussion of grandiosity and the modulation of grandiosity into the prerequisite structures and the instinctual fuel for life tasks. Life tasks, including the crisis of the death of oneself and others, are among the traditional concerns of religion that can be better understood by incorporating these new psychoanalytic concepts.

References

Bonhoeffer, D. (1972), *Letters and Papers from Prison.* New York: Macmillan.
Browning, D. (1976), *The Moral Context of Pastoral Care.* Philadelphia: Westminster.
Frank, J. (1973), *Persuasion and Healing,* rev. ed. Baltimore: Johns Hopkins University Press.
Freud, S. (1916–1917), Introductory Lectures on Psycho-Analysis. *Standard Edition,* 15 & 16. London: Hogarth Press, 1963.
Kohut, H. (1971), *The Analysis of the Self.* New York: International Universities Press.
———— (1977), *The Restoration of the Self.* New York: International Universities Press.
Otto, R. (1958), *The Idea of the Holy.* New York: Oxford University Press.
Truby, T. (1978), An Exploration of the Relationship of Dependency to an Appropriate Image of Manhood. Unpublished certificate prospect paper, Center for Religion and Psychotherapy, Chicago.

The Psychology of the Self and Religion

JOACHIM SCHARFENBERG

As a young theologian I found that most models of pastoral care taught in European universities did not have a sound clinical base. Consequently, my postgraduate work included many courses in psychology. I discovered, however, that most theories of psychology taught in Germany after World War II lacked depth. I subsequently undertook formal psychoanalytic training and discovered what has turned out to be a vital mode of ministry.

Thus, in the course of my training I added to my identity of pastor and theologian that of psychoanalyst. I also attempted to apply the experiences of psychoanalytic psychotherapy to that powerful cultural force called "religious tradition." Religious tradition, in a strong sense, became my "patient." And, in my attempts to understand this patient, I found in Heinz Kohut's psychology of the self an important new tool. As a result of these interests, I am at present a psychoanalyst with an active clinical practice, as well as a theologian involved in research on the psychology of religion at the University of Kiel. It is from these dual

I am deeply grateful to Dr. David M. Moss, III, of the Center for Religion and Psychotherapy of Chicago for his editorial assistance.

427

commitments that my presentation should be understood.

I

It seems to me that the literature dealing with the development of self psychology calls for the use of religious language to communicate certain elementary insights about human nature. The omission of religious language did not characterize the early years of psychoanalysis, but rarely during the last two decades has religious language been explicitly used in the psychoanalytic literature. I think this is a development related to the "aging" of psychoanalysis, but it is also a problem that goes back to Freud's own skeptical view of religion. For instance, his sarcastic remarks that human beings of "old age" tend to be "feeble-minded, pious and credulous" clearly reflects a deep-seated negative attitude (Freud, 1933, p. 54). This type of attitude spawned opinions that eventually separated religion and psychology—a separation that I believe to be unfortunate and ill advised.

It is always important to remember that Freud made several serious attempts to understand the phenomenon of religion in terms of a comprehensive concept of human history. He did this within the context of an intellectual presupposition of his time: the presumed correlation between ontogenesis and phylogenesis. His most elaborate attempt to articulate this correlation is probably *Totem and Taboo* (1913). In that work he stated:

> The animistic phase would correspond to narcissism both chronologically and in its content; the religious phase would correspond to the stage of object-choice of which the characteristic is a child's attachment to his parents; while the scientific phase would have an exact counterpart in the stage at which an individual has reached maturity, has renounced the pleasure principle, adjusted himself to reality and turned to the external world for the object of his desires [p. 90].

Freud linked narcissism with the animistic stage of development, and without exception, placed religion within the framework of the second stage, associated with a regressive revival of infantile parental images centered around the oedipal conflict. However, I think there is an even stronger affinity between the theory of narcissism and religion. In what follows, I shall investigate some of the reasons for this affinity.

Freud articulated his contribution to the psychoanalytic psychology of religion in the context of a three-part critique of religion. The first aspect of his critique is directed against a superego religion that tends to view the violation of religious morals as taboo. For Freud the superego is "the representative... of every moral restriction, the advocate of a striving towards perfection — it is, in short, as much as we have been able to grasp psychologically of what is described as the higher side of human life" (1933, p. 67). Interpreting this form of moral masochism in terms of a revival of the Oedipus complex and, therefore, as a "sexualization" of morals, Freud fought against the taboo nature of religious morals and argued, instead, that ethical decisions should be based on rational insights.

Freud's second criticism is directed against religion as "delusion." The average "customer of religion," he submits, has lost the ability to discriminate between the "notion of words" (*Wortvorstellung*) and the "notion of things" (*Sachvorstellung*). Rather than treating religious symbols as poetic expressions of truth, this customer equates such symbols with reality. This fallacious equation leads Freud to characterize religion as delusional. At the same time, he concedes that religious imaginations do contain a "nucleus of truth" since they symbolize the return of the suppressed oedipal drama as it is manifested in the *Urhorde* or primal constellation of ideas, and with concomitant working through.

Freud's third criticism is directed against religion's attempt to master reality by means of the infantile world of wishes. He sees in religious imagination only seductive temptations of the pleasure principle, stimuli that deal with reality by means of an infantile wish world. In opposition to this, he postulates his program of "training for *reality*." It is from the standpoint of this concept of reality that I would like to begin my critique.

Freud set forth a so-called scientific *Weltanschauung,* according to which a person has "renounced the pleasure principle, adjusted himself to reality and turned to the external world for the object of his desires" (1913, p. 90). This thesis calls for further comment. Since Freud made this statement, the world has changed because the concept of reality has changed. At present, the world is understood primarily in its socioeconomic aspects. Many people in their fantasies and aspirations are now looking for creative alternatives to a deeply unsatisfying and destructive reality. This is particularly true of our younger generation.

All attempts to deal with the presently unsatisfying reality by means of regression to the pleasure principle — as for example, Marcuse proposed in 1955 — have proved to be counterproductive. Yet the weakest point in Freud's negative assessment of religion remains his concept of reality. Religion inherently attempts to transcend reality not only by way of return to the "pleasure principle," but also legitimately by way of the "security principle" of transformed narcissism. In my judgment, the "security principle" of transformed narcissism could be the key to a new way of looking at reality.

A metapsychological concept of the psychology of the self offers a methodological approach to the psychology of religion. That methodological approach permits not only the "understanding" (*Verstehen*) but also the "explaining" (*Erklären*) of religious phenomena since it puts empathy on a solid scientific basis.

Freud's attempt to reduce the phenomena of narcissism to animism seems questionable and, at the very least, in need of more extensive investigation. His critique of religion can be countered with the argument that it does not grasp certain phenomena that lie between animism and patriarchal forms of religion. One can see such intermediate phenomena in various forms of mysticism, in the Far Eastern religions, and in reports on "miracles" where a man has overcome the forces of nature. Such mastery of nature is represented, for example, in Jesus' ascension to heaven and his reported ability to walk on water, in the grandiose fantasies of an artist like Hieronymus Bosch, in certain apocalyptic ideas, and in the so-called "negative theology" of the Medievals. In my opinion, the newer theories about the development of the self and narcissism provide a quite different and very valuable instrument for dealing with these phenomena.

Freud strongly opposed religious ideation and urged that it be given up as an inauthentic source of security. He rigidly believed that mystical and miraculous phenomena (like those listed above) were best understood as animistic fantasies confined to configurations occurring within a narcissistic realm. I contend that this perspective blurs the boundaries between subject and object to which modern science directs our thinking and our feeling. The psychology of the self, on the other hand, offers a framework for understanding religion as the relevant mode for the expression of real empathy. Religion, that is, presents the possibility of envisioning the "archaic self" and the idealized "selfobject" on a grandiose stage of self representation, a place where man is thought of as grandiose.

In this religious sphere, there is not simply a quick discharge of highly tensed, pent-up needs. To the contrary, there is a feeling of security and comfort. The great need for this release and security is cultivated only in very few places. In this context let me quote a statement made by Freud that may be one of his most "religious" comments and which seems consistent with the testimony of many religious mystics: "Turn your eyes inward, look into your own depths, learn first to know yourself! Then you will understand why you were bound to fall ill; and perhaps, you will avoid falling ill in [the] future" (1917, p. 143).

I think that in the future it will be possible to work with material from the history of religion and divide it in a more satisfactory manner than Freud did. For instance, it might be divided into three aspects. First of all, religion can be seen as an expression of a "cosmic narcissism" that belongs in the area of the pre-ego, what Bion called the "0" (1970, p. 26). Secondly, it can be viewed as the differentiation between subject and object symbolized in the great dualistic systems of world interpretation, like the cosmic struggles between gods and demons. And finally, religious phenomena can be interpreted as symbols of the impressive scene of the "three-person relationship" that dominates the pattern of patriarchal religions.

Here we might raise a basic question: In light of these new insights is religion still to be understood as a regression? I have no
doubt that it is. Indeed, one of the functions of a psychoanalytically oriented psychology of religion might be to look for
boundaries and control mechanisms for religious regression
analogous to those characteristic of the psychoanalytic setting
where regression is initiated in the service of the ego. And what
would such a psychoanalytic situation be without empathy? Is it
not a common task — for the analyst and others — to deal with the
narcissistic roots of our own identity, using the great traditions of
humanity to shape successfully our future by working through our
own past?

II

In the remaining portion of this paper I would like to
stimulate discussion of the interrelationships between religion and
the psychology of the self by (1) exploring what I appreciate most
in the psychology of the self, and what I find helpful in understanding religious phenomena; (2) providing some clinical material
that demonstrates how religion and the psychology of the self can
fruitfully ally without losing their separate identities; and (3) commenting briefly on the task of a pastoral psychologist in theory and
in practice.

What I appreciate most deeply in the psychology of the self is
the anthropology that underlies the metapsychology of the self.
This anthropological perspective understands the self not so much
as a content of a mental apparatus but rather as a center of the
psychological universe. With this assumption, one is able to see
new dimensions of humanity. One sees, for instance, that "joy is
more than sublimated pleasure" and that "man does not live by
bread alone," i.e., that "the child needs empathically modulated
food giving and not just food" (Kohut, 1977, pp. 15, 45, 81).

Furthermore, I admire the psychology of the self as a new type
of science that is guided by attempts to use empathy as a reliable tool
of empirical research. If one concedes that insight is more attainable
by empathy than by the nonempathic registration of empirical

data, one understands at once why the psychology of the self has such potential for those concerned with religion: the relevance of self psychology applies to all students of religious phenomena, whether or not they want to discard religion, to understand religion, to cleanse and cure religion from malignant regression, or to acknowledge religion's indispensable value for shaping the future of the history of society. Through the psychology of the self, some kind of objectivity could be introduced to the science of religion that will include "introspective-empathic observation and some theoretical conceptualization of the participating self" (Kohut, 1977, p. 68).

I also welcome the broadening of horizons by which religion is not only explained through the conflict-psychology appropriate for "Guilty Man," but, at the same time, is explained as the creative expression of "Tragic Man," who has to master life despite death and meaningless emptiness. As a result of this approach, the idea that life is meaningful despite failure and death becomes a legitimate target of scientific investigation. From this point of view, it becomes possible to find more meaning in symbols — such as the symbol of the cross or crucifixion — than was possible when religion was reduced to the model of a son rebelling against the father.

There is a playfulness in theory making, as I sense it, partly determined by the fact that one can never get at the truth itself (Kohut, 1977, p. 207). I understand that theology has the same structure because its object is not "given" or "at hand," but represents a task to be undertaken. In a similar way the ego is not given, but needs to be acquired according to Freud's dictum: "Where id was, there ego shall be."

It is interesting to take into account the changing historical situation of man. Psychoanalysis *never* will be an ontology dogmatized into timeless statements about humanity. It only can be the historical response to a historical challenge. The historical challenge for mankind at the turn of the century may well have been the problem of suppressed sexuality or, as expressed by Kohut, the problem of "overstimulation in early childhood." Yet at present, anxieties are certainly more relevant to a fragmentation of the self. The words of Eugene O'Neill, often quoted by Kohut, can also be quoted here: "Man is born broken. He lives his life by mending. The grace of God is glue" (see Moss, 1976).

At this point I would like to present some clinical and religious material through which it can be demonstrated that the difference between neurosis and narcissistic behavior disorders can be shown by the use of symbols in behavior, dreams, and transference. My point is that people suffering from narcissistic disorders require a more highly symbolic way of communicating in order to express themselves properly. Higher symbolization means that the limitations imposed by reality are abandoned and that the appropriate language can only be found in the world of religion or in further states of regression into the world of fairy tales and fabulous beings.

A patient suffering from an obsessive-compulsive neurosis developed a very strange symptom. Every night in bed he felt forced to perform several somersaults forward and backwards and to sing a verse of a spiritual hymn. He could fall asleep only after he performed these strange exercises which, to his mind, had some kind of religious connotation. This symptom can be designated a "symbol" through which the patient prevents a certain unconscious notion behind the symbol from entering consciousness. If we ask how this unconscious idea could become a conscious one, we have to consider the transference. In the transference, we would expect, all the psychic energies that fuel the patient's symptom will be collected as in the focus of a looking glass. The symptom and also the transference are created by the patient to express one thing in terms of something else. In the present case, the patient revealed the transference situation through his manifest behavior. From the first analytic hour, his behavior was extremely unusual in that he displayed many passive-submissive gestures. He was extremely punctual and very exact in respect to the appointments and never dared to express any kind of expectations regarding therapy. He pedantically tried to comply with the basic rule of psychoanalysis to express whatever came to his mind. He always lay down on the couch like a ramrod and never moved a single muscle. In short, his behavior in front of the analyst was *as if* he expected something very painful. As therapy progressed, his excessively cautious behavior took over part of the functions that the symptom had performed for him previously. His compulsiveness diminished somewhat, and on the days of his analytic hour, he could sleep at night without performing his ritual. It is a basic principle of the transference that there is nothing new in the content of the transference. Thus, the reviving of an actual memory will in time replace the symbolic representation.

During the analysis, this patient recalled a certain event that happened on a certain day in a certain place: when he was about five years old he loved to roam around in the house and garden. This, however, was forbidden because his father was ill and had to be protected against noise and excitement. One day he ran around in the garden, slipped, fell down (a kind of somersault), and hit his head against a mailbox. With a heavily bleeding wound on his head he had to be carried into the house. A few days later his father was dead and his mother told him: "If you had behaved well, as you ought to, your Daddy would still be alive."

Here we have an analogy between the symptom and the form of his transference. This transference was analogous to the act of failure in the past as well as to the manifest behavior displayed in his symptom. It is the typical conflict of "Guilty Man," who has failed to master the oedipal drama.

Another patient, a girl with anorexia nervosa, maintained her weight at the beginning of analysis by eating great quantities of food and then inducing vomiting afterwards. This behavior might also be some kind of symbol of remembrance. But this patient did not give any clues that could clarify the transference situation, since her behavior was utterly unobtrusive. I was provided with my first insights into the transference situation by way of a dream: " I meet you at the beach. You say: 'I hate my parents.' I say: 'I can understand this very well because I hate my parents myself.' You say: 'But I have killed them with a walking stick.' I say: 'I wish I had done this too.' I look at you and you are a dragon with several heads and I am a snake. I say: 'You did not kill your parents, but you just cut off two of your own heads. We are all idiots if we only cut off our own heads instead of killing our parents.'"

The transference in this case is much more complicated than

in the previous one. The merger of the personalities of the patient
and therapist is evident but remote from reality. The patient is not
yet able to relate to the analyst "as if" he were one of the important
figures of her past. She needs a symbol that is limited to the early
states of childhood (since mankind seems to have decided not to
believe in fabulous beings like dragons and snakes with some kind
of human personalities). You may not be surprised to learn that in
this case the crucial problem was not a certain incident of
misbehavior on the patient's part but powerful infantile fantasies
about parents who had no empathy for her and did not permit her
to idealize them. In this case reality could not be cathected, but
only the symbols as a "mental representation of drive," or of the
selfobject. In my opinion, one might be able to determine a person's level of consciousness and/or unconsciousness by assessing
his or her ability to approximate symbols to reality. As long as the
mental representations are unconscious (as most of the problems
of narcissistically disturbed persons are) the patient utilizes the
symbols of fairy tales, myths, and religious traditions for exter-
nalization: those symbols that were originally created for the very
purpose of communicating the conflict of "Tragic Man."

Briefly put, the kind of religious material that can be used for
and by modern man to externalize the deepest layer of anxiety is a
symbolism that extends *beyond* the guilt principle. For example,
all fantasies centering around the idea of a paradise lost indicate
not so much the loss of an object, but the fear of falling out of the
symbolic unity with God (e.g., mother). An example of a most
moving religious symbol is contained in a story about a counselee
of Rabbi Chanoch of Alexandria. Every night this man registered
and counted all his belongings, including every piece of clothing he
owned. When he had recorded his possessions he then wrote down
where they were placed. At one point, however, he suddenly realized he could not avoid the question "Where am I?" He could not
find himself, which, in his case, referred to the disintegrating parts
of a self that had never been mirrored to him in the gleam of the
eyes of an empathic mother. Again the words of O'Neill apply: the
man truly felt that he had been "born broken."

What then is the job of a pastoral psychologist? The answer is embedded in a tripartite cluster of functions. The first function is to develop an "empirical theology" that explains what initially has been understood. The second function is to establish a theory of symbols in which the interrelationships between psychological and religious symbols are not only demonstrated but understood and explained. This function also involves working on the development of criteria for a critique of religious symbols. Finally, the third function of such a pastor is to work with people, drawing on the conflict-solving potentialities of religious symbols. This function is especially important in the present, when the symbols of mass media seem to play a dominating role in social strife and social control.

Reflecting on my remarks, the famous words of Goethe provide an apt conclusion: "Those who have science and art also have religion. Those who do not have science and art should have religion" (*Wer Kunst und Wissenschaft besitzt, der hat auch Religion. Wer Wissenschaft und Kunst nicht hat, der habe Religion*).

References

Bion, W. R. (1970), *Attention and Reality*. London: Tavistock.

Freud, S. (1913), Totem and Taboo. *Standard Edition,* 13:1–161. London: Hogarth Press, 1953.

_____ (1917), A Difficulty in the Path of Psycho-Analysis. *Standard Edition,* 17:135–144. Hogarth Press, 1955.

_____ (1933), New Introductory Lectures on Psycho-Analysis. *Standard Edition,* 22:5–182. London: Hogarth Press, 1964.

Kohut, H. (1977), *The Restoration of the Self*. New York: International Universities Press.

Marcuse, H. (1955), *Eros and Civilization: A Philosophical Inquiry into Freud.* Boston: Beacon, 1974.

Moss, D. M. (1976), Narcissism, Empathy and the Fragmentation of Self: An Interview with Heinz Kohut. *Pilgrimage,* 4(1).

Some Possible Contributions of the Psychology of the Self to the Study of the Arab Middle East

MARVIN ZONIS

The writings of Heinz Kohut may serve to narrow the gap between psychoanalysis and the social sciences in a variety of ways. His conceptual, theoretical, and methodological contributions provide stimulating and provocative challenges to social scientists to resume the formerly vital tradition of attempting to integrate psychoanalytic approaches to the study of man.

His work on the development of the self and the narcissistic products of developmental arrests can help us understand a variety of social and political phenomena which have been observed for decades by social scientists. All too often, however, social scientists have been uninterested, or more to the point, incapable, of explaining their observations with the concepts and theories heretofore available to them.

To illustrate this point and thereby to demonstrate the powerful contribution that Kohut's work represents for the social sciences, this paper will focus on the Arab Middle East.

Many of the characteristics that Kohut attributes to patients with narcissistic personality disorders have been used unwittingly by students of the Middle East to characterize their Arab subjects, especially Arab males. Granted that these accounts, written both by Europeans and indigenous social scientists, cover a wide spectrum of modes of investigation, from 19th-century travel literature to the most scientifically inspired contemporary studies. Granted further that the subjects of such studies cover an equally broad social spectrum, from illiterate villagers or peasants to highly educated urban dwellers, as well as a geographical range extending from Morocco to Iraq. This diversity of approaches notwithstanding, what is most noteworthy about these various studies of different peoples in different settings at different times is the startling amount of agreement in their characterizations of Arab males. A common set of qualities shine through the diversity.[1]

One possible explanation, of course, is that all these authors have been bewitched by very powerful stereotypes about Arabs. And certainly such stereotypes do exist and are widely shared by Arabs as well as non-Arabs. But more likely, I think the common characteristics and the stereotypes found in the literature reflect not so much the mental imaginings of the observers, as the fact that something about the psychic configuration of the subjects is indeed being captured.

Before dealing with these psychic configurations it is essential to note two points. First, the language of much of this paper and, of course, of the writings of Kohut himself, is the language of psychopathology. But the use of such language here, and the theo-

---

[1]There are essentially five genres of literature relevant to this paper: (1) ethnographies of the Arab Middle East written primarily by Western travelers and more recently by Western anthropologists; (2) novels, plays, poetry, and an occasional autobiography—works by Arab authors; (3) psychological studies, many of which entail the administration of testing instruments to Arab subjects; (4) psychiatric studies and surveys of villagers, patients in mental institutions, or clinics; and (5) accounts of so-called "national character" or "basic personality." As with any comparable body of literature on cross-cultural psychology, these works vary immensely in quality. There are special reasons, however, to question the literature on the Middle East. Much of it grows out of the "missionary-civilizing" roots of Western scholarship on the Arab world. (For a recent critique along these lines, see Said [1978]). Problems of scholarship are exacerbated by the pall over research on Arabs cast by the Arab-Israeli conflicts and the special position of Americans, in particular, vis-à-vis those conflicts.

retical propositions that underlie such language, is not meant to suggest the presence of pathology among Arabs and Arab males. In the long tradition of psychoanalytic investigations, this paper is predicated on the assumption that the insights gained from the study of a patient population can be useful in understanding psychic processes among nonpatients. Despite the fact that the vocabulary used originates from the efforts of analysts to "treat" their patients, the following comments are intended as a social-scientific attempt to understand Arab subjects.

Second, the characteristics which have been singled out below are, indeed, normative behavior for the Arab male, that is, they may reflect phenotypes rather than genotypes.[2] What must be significant for the analysis of such behavior — whether for psychoanalytic or social-scientific analysis — is the meaning of the behavior. These behaviors, in other words, take on significance to the extent that they relate to or are part of the underlying psychic structure or "personality" of the subject. A second major assumption of this paper, then, is that such a relation obtains here; that these particular behavioral phenotypes would not persist unless they were consonant with and expressive of "deep structure" among Arab males.[3]

The list of characteristics which thoughtful observers have attributed to Arab males is, as with generalizations made of other peoples, virtually endless. I would like to select here six characteristics that have been noted especially often.[4] They are:

1. A pervasive search for heroes and a propensity for attaching themselves to or following political strong men, village chiefs, tribal sheikhs, urban political bosses, as well as national and pan-Arab figures.

[2]For a clear statement of the phenotype/genotype distinction, see LeVine (1973, esp. pp. 115–124).

[3]The validity of this second assumption is, of course, predicated on the idea that common "phenotypes" are widespread in the Arab world. It is worth reiterating that the immense diversity of the Arab world — religious, ethnic, linguistic, economic, and cultural — necessitates a systematic effort to determine the prevalence and distribution not only of these phenotypes but of any generalities applied to that highly differentiated collection of persons grouped under the rubric "Arab."

[4]These characteristics are mentioned so frequently in the literature on Arab males that I have not attempted to cite references for each item.

2. An intense vulnerability to slights, whether behavioral or solely verbal. Perhaps in response to their propensity for feeling slighted an encompassing system of etiquette exists which dictates correct interpersonal interactions as well as proper linguistic codes to be followed on virtually all occasions.

3. Arab men have often been noted for their propensity toward what has been labeled variously as vanity, display, or even exhibitionism, as well as toward dramatic outbursts of emotion that the Western press chronicles from time to time when they take the form of political riots or demonstrations.

4. Arab males have been described as maintaining an intense lifelong relationship with their mothers. A Tunisian sociologist has suggested that the relationship is so intense that the Arab male spends his life longing for a return to the "world of mothers... buried in the depths of an idealized past, and enveloped in fantasies." This longing, he further suggests, is so powerful that the Arab woman has become the "Queen of the unconscious" (Bouhdiba, 1977, p. 113).

5. An intense sexualization of interpersonal relations has also been frequently observed, both among men and between men and women. Arab men have been especially noted for their "Don Juanism."[5]

6. The final characteristic that I would include here is the extent to which observers of the Arab world have unanimously asserted that Arab social relations are governed by the operations of shame rather than guilt. Guilt, such a powerful source of personal control as well as social control in the West, seems relatively absent in the Middle East, whereas shame and the act of shaming seem to be the far more prevalent mechanism. The imbalance between these mechanisms of control is so great that Arab culture has been noted as an archetypal example of a "shame culture" and the Arab man has been referred to as "an Oedipus shorn of guilt."[6]

[5]Peter Dodd (1973) offers an important refinement of the notion of "Don Juanism" as it operates in the Arab world.

[6]See Bouhdiba (1977, p. 136). Bouhdiba is only the most recent of many authors who have alluded to the prominent role of shame as a mechanism of control. See also Ammar, Bazzoui and Issa, Peristiany, etc.

The link between these characteristics and the theoretical and conceptual transformations of narcissism that have been developed by Kohut is so clear that it requires no further elucidation here. What is also fascinating is the widespread reports of certain patterns of childrearing in the Arab world that might be expected to result in an array of narcissistic imbalances among Arab males. Such imbalances would serve as the psychological underpinning of these behavioral and emotional characteristics.

Kohut himself has cautioned us about the lesser utility of etiological investigations in comparison with the genetic approach within the theoretical domain of psychoanalysis (1971, esp. pp. 254n–255n). Nonetheless, in the absence of psychoanalytic data pertaining to the Middle East derived through the genetic approach, I will refer to "those objectively ascertainable factors which, in interaction with the child's psyche as it is constituted at a given moment, may — or may not — elicit the genetically decisive experience" in the hope that, in this case at least, such data will be at least suggestive if far from conclusive.

Perhaps the single most comprehensive monograph on the childhood experiences of Arab males is Ammar's *Growing Up in an Egyptian Village — Silwa: Province of Aswan* (1954). Ammar, who grew up in the village of Silwa, received his higher education in England and returned to the village in order to do research for his Ph.D. dissertation at London University.[7]

In his study, Ammar demonstrates that the goal of childrearing in Silwa (and by something of a gross extension, I would argue, in much of the Arab world) is not to produce a child with a cohesive self that can be "an independent center of initiative." Quite to the contrary, it is to produce a child who can be called, in Arabic, *"muaddab,"* literally, one who is literate. In this context, literacy is not equated with the written word. Instead, it refers

[7]As is the case of the validity of the "characteristics" or "phenotypes" listed above, one must also question the generalizability of Ammar's study for the remainder of the very diverse Arab world. For the purposes of this paper, I believe that Ammar captures at least ideal typical modes of childrearing in the Arab Middle East. In a recent unpublished paper, Leonard Binder details the similarities in childrearing practices described by Ammar with accounts from the autobiography of Taha Hussein and the novels of Naqib Mahfouz.

to the experience of having mastered and succumbed to the dominant cultural definitions of what constitutes appropriate behavior under any given circumstances.

The essential way of producing a culturally literate child is the conscious effort made by the parents to reduce the male child's sense of self-esteem, lest he become too independent. A variety of very specific mechanisms is employed to this end. Each child in a family, for example, is provided with a derogatory nickname by which he is addressed by all his siblings as well as by his parents. Siblings are encouraged to act aggressively toward one other, not merely verbally, but physically as well. Parents are expected to beat their children to maintain discipline, and children are expected and even challenged to violate parental rules with punishment reserved not for those who violate rules per se, but for those who do so ineptly enough to be caught. Children are constantly warned about dangerous supernatural powers, the evil eye, and a special class of mythical ghouls who specifically attack children.

For the first two or three years of life, the child is close, physically and emotionally, to his mother. He receives nearly all her attention and her mothering during this time. With the birth of the next child, however, he is abruptly turned over to the "care" of his older siblings—the quality of which is clearly implied in Ammar's account of the extent to which children are encouraged to aggress against siblings.

The father pursues a different course during this early child-rearing. The principal value for the adult male is leisure, which is time spent in the company of other adult males. The father is expected to be home only to eat and to go to bed. His relation to his children seems limited to administering punishment and teaching his male sons when they reach the age of 10 or so to take over farming duties as a way of increasing his leisure time.

Ammar elaborates this pattern of childrearing at considerably greater length. In the present context it suffices to say that his account of Egyptian village practice seems accurate. Moreover, many elements of his account appear in other reports of urban childrearing practices in the Arab world (Hussein, 1932; Mahfouz, 1966). None of these studies, taken either individually or collectively, provide evidence that directly supports the argument being made here. But they do suggest that if etiological factors generate the genetically decisive experiences among young Arab males, the results would be various insufficiencies in the cohesiveness of the self. The characteristics of Arab males identified by so many observers would be entirely consonant with this interpretation of the childhood experiences that Arab males are likely to have undergone.

The literature on which this case has been made is glaringly thin. It is drawn from a variety of intellectual traditions, rests on questionable data, and manifests diverse biases. Nonetheless, the different contributions are ultimately coherent and complementary. In light of the nature of the literature, then, the case being made here cannot provide conclusive generalizations about Arab males, but it does point to the useful research possibilities that result from "taking Kohut to the field." The tantalizing possibility thus exists that a scientific, genetically oriented study of adult Arab males would confirm these etiologically based hypotheses centering on narcissistic imbalances.

In addition, other exciting research possibilities are suggested. The role that thwarted narcissism plays in sustaining the conflict between the Arabs and the Israelis, for example, seems a natural subject of inquiry. (Attention would need to be focused, of course, not only on the Arab states and the Palestinians but on complementary processes that operate among Israeli Jews as well.) Other possible subjects for investigation in the narcissistic domain would be leader-follower relations and problems in the institutionalization of political development; Arab problems in developing a work ethic as a sustaining input to economic development; and, perhaps, the uses of Islam as target for idealization. Obviously, many more topics present themselves for investigation within the realm of the psychology of the self.

One final observation is in order. Kohut suggests that the psychological problems now being experienced in the West which emanate from the loosening of family bonds will come to be felt in the underdeveloped areas of the world (1977, pp. 276ff). I would suggest that the contemporary alteration of family patterns in the

West does not constitute a stage in the evolutionary development of family relations through which other peoples in non-Western cultures will also pass in the future. Rather, it is a pattern which already characterizes many non-Western peoples, along with the concomitant psychological manifestations that Kohut's contributions have done so much to elucidate.

References

Ammar, H. (1954), *Growing Up in an Egyptian Village—Silwa: Province of Aswan.* London: Routledge & Kegan Paul.

Bouhdiba, A. (1977), The Child and the Mother in Arab-Muslim Society. In: *Psychological Dimensions of Near Eastern Studies,* ed. L. C. Brown & N. Itzkowitz. Princeton: Darwin.

Dodd, P. C. (1973), Family Honor and the Forces of Change in Arab Society. *Internat. J. Mid. East. Stud.,* 4(1).

Hussein, T. (1932), *An Egyptian Childhood.* London: Routledge & Sons.

Kohut, H. (1971), *The Analysis of the Self.* New York: International Universities Press.

―――― (1977), *The Restoration of the Self.* New York: International Universities Press.

LeVine, R. A. (1973), *Culture, Behavior, and Personality.* Chicago: Aldine.

Mahfouz, N. (1966), *Midaq Alley,* trans. T. LeGassick. Beirut: Khayats.

Said, E. (1978), *Orientalism.* New York: Pantheon.

Part V

TWO LETTERS

Two Letters

Heinz Kohut

From a letter to one of the participants at the
Chicago Conference on the Psychology of the Self

September, 1978

Your scientific aside gives me the chance to clarify certain ideas that are important for the understanding of my outlook and I will now respond to it. With reference to a passage in my report on the two analyses of Mr. Z. in which I interpreted his lonely, depressed masturbation as *not* being "the vigorous action of the pleasure-seeking firm self of a healthy child," you suggest that the masturbation could also be seen in accordance with Spitz's theories as "an attempt to separate...as growth-promoting, in the service of separation." And you also say that it could be understood in accordance with the conceptions of Mahler who says that the "empathic mother is attuned to the child's attempts at separation... and can tolerate the necessary accompanying aggression" and that the child of such an empathic mother can therefore neutralize [the aggression] and use [it] for self-gratification." "The child of such an empathic mother is then able to turn to himself, in furtherance of his separation, after which he enters the phallic phase with the capacity to enjoy his newly won ability to gratify himself independently." And you summarize by stating that—apparently

449

as prototypical for healthy development — a sequence of "the separation of self and object leading to drive cathexis" can be observed. All in all, you seem to conclude that Mr. Z.'s childhood
masturbation should be considered as belonging to a "subphase in
the separation-individuation process," thus implying clearly that it
should be considered essentially as a healthy, forward-looking
move, a step in maturation.

I wish I could agree with these propositions. I would even
wish I could at least disagree with them. I can do neither because,
not lying squarely within the realm of that aspect of reality that is
accessible via introspection and empathy — not clearly placed, in
other words, within the conceptual framework by which in my
view depth psychology is defined — I cannot get a firm grasp of
their psychological meaning.

I will underline the importance that the preceding statement
has for me by saying that understanding it means understanding
the essence of my outlook. Lacking this understanding, one can
neither agree nor disagree with my theories. Nor could I engage in
a meaningful argument with someone who does not understand
it — it's the old story of the tiger and the polar bear: they live too
far apart to do battle.

Let me get into *medias res*. The framework within which
Spitz's and Mahler's theories belong and within which their statements find their meaning is the framework of sociology. In other
words, however psychologically insightful and sophisticated these
great contributors are, they deal in essence with social relationships and they must, therefore, formulate their findings in sociological — interactional, transactional — terms. Mahler's term "symbiosis" is fully appropriate within this frame of reference: it means
that two biological units are viable only if they live together ("sym"
means "together"; "biosis" refers to their "life"). The specific emphasis lies, of course, on the survival ability of only one of the two
(the child), but that does not alter the essence of the assertion that
is implied by the use of the term. While the meaning of the term
"symbiosis," because it is placed clearly within an interactional
framework, is unambiguous, that of "individuation" is not. On the
one hand, as a move away from symbiosis, it contains the assertion

that now the living together is not necessary anymore for survival, that separateness has been achieved (by both, especially by the formerly dependent one). On the other hand, however, the term "separateness" does not predominantly carry a biological meaning but a psychological one: the formerly dependent unit is not claimed to have now become independent in the sense of its separate biological or social survival, the independence to which the term refers is one of an inner feeling state — a significant inconsistency has crept in. I believe that the puzzle resolves itself when we realize that the observers who formulate these statements are not only influenced by conflicting commitments to biology and psychology but that they are also implicitly subscribing to a set of values. In a spectrum of values that extends from clinging dependency ("bad" in the value scale of human society, especially Western society) to uncomplaining self-sufficiency ("good" in the value scale of human society, especially Western society) the term "individuation" implies that the weaker member of the formerly symbiotic twosome has made a decisive move from a ("bad") attitude of fearful clinging to a ("good") atittude of fearless self-sufficiency.

Please do not dismiss my arguments as fussy or pedantic. In themselves the inconsistencies of the sociopsychological framework of the external observer of childhood behavior who is also a sophisticated psychologist, e.g., of the stature of Spitz and Mahler, would not bother me. Most important theories in science outside of mathematics show some internal inconsistencies. But I am not complaining about formal imperfection — what is at stake here, as demonstrated by a comparison of the results obtained when the same data are seen from one point of view or from the other, is a decisive difference between the outlook of the child observer and the outlook of the introspective-empathic psychologist, which is mine.

Let us first compare the concepts of "independence" and "individuation" — à la Spitz and Mahler — with the concepts of a "nuclear self" and of the "establishment and firming of the nuclear self" à la the psychoanalytic psychology of the self. You will see immediately that the two pairs of concepts belong to two different world views with two different sets of values. I can perhaps point up the difference of outlook most sharply by stating that from the point of view of the psychoanalytic psychology of the self a value-laden demand for psychological independence is nonsense — almost as nonsensical as would be a demand that the human body should be able to get along without oxygen. At this point one would need to write a book to begin to do justice to the variety of self-selfobject relationships and self-object relationships, both real and fantasied, that characterize a full and successful human life; and I will not attempt to indicate with the aid of examples how this dimension of a good life should be elaborated in the course of childhood and adolescence in order to lead to a fruitful maturity. I will restrict myself to reminding you that the courage which is required for some of the greatest human achievements, the products of those rare moments in the history of humanity to which Stefan Zweig referred as *Sternstunden der Menschheit* (stellar hours of mankind), in art, science, and political action, rests on the relationship — I spoke once of transferences of creativity in a related context — to fantasied selfobjects with godlike power and perfection.

Have I begun to make it clear to you why I find Spitz's and Mahler's formulations unsatisfactory? They are not wrong. But even though derived from the careful empirical observation of the behavior of children, they strike me, from the standpoint of the depth psychologist, as "experience-distant" because they are not derived from the prolonged empathic immersion into the inner life of the observed but from the scrutiny of behavior that is evaluated in accordance with the traditional value judgments of Western man.

If we now, however, equipped with the insights of the psychoanalytic psychology of the self, turn to the childhood of Mr. Z., in particular to his lonely masturbation, which you interpreted in harmony with Spitz and Mahler as being in the service of maturation, you will recognize, I hope, that self psychology allows us to see decisive differences in experience where the observer of childhood behavior sees the same phenomena, and you will understand why I am forced to disagree with your suggestions.

Mr. Z.'s masturbation was not the essentially joyous activity of a strong and cohesive self that can allow itself the experience of intense zonal pleasure without incurring the danger of fragmentation due to the concentration of feelings upon a single body part and of being destroyed by the ecstatic excitement. His masturbatory activities were accompanied — as were Mr. W.'s fantasied excursions across his body — by a melancholy mood, even by a sense of depression. True, they were attempts to provide pleasure for himself. But while there was pleasure, there was no joy since, as the accompanying fantasies testify, even while experiencing bodily pleasure, his body was not his own: it was bought and sold in accordance with the selfobject's whims.

As seen by the psychoanalytic self psychologist, normal development — the varieties of normal development, one should say — does not rest on a "separation of self and object." Apart from brief episodes of self-selfobject confusion when, during the working through of a selfobject transference the analysand responds to an empathy failure of the analyst by substituting an archaic merger for empathic resonance, the *cognitive* separation of self and object is fully achieved by almost all of even the most severely disturbed selves that I have been in therapeutic contact with. And the essential therapeutic task — a conviction that is increasingly establishing itself in me as I am adding year after year of experience of analyzing patients with self pathology — is not the achievement of the separation of the self from its selfobjects but, on the contrary, the reentering into the course of the line of development of self-selfobject relationships at the point where it had been traumatically interrupted in early life. As I crudely outlined already long ago (1966), narcissism is not, as Freud had taught, a precursor of object love, to be relinquished and to be supplanted by the latter — it has its own line of development. Even some of the most individuated of individuals, men and women who are able to express the pattern of their selves most unambiguously in creative word and deed, may persistently search for the selfobject environment that is in harmonious contact with them until, often after prolonged periods of loneliness and a, to outward appearances, bizarrely uncompromising persistence, they ultimately obtain what they need. But when they have securely inserted themselves into the empathic matrix that they require, they are then not only able to receive freely but also to give of themselves in abundance.

An example from literature: Eugene O'Neill's propensity toward alcoholism and shiftlessness diminished decisively and his creative productive life began in earnest after he had experienced several months of empathic care in a tuberculosis sanitarium. And he created his greatest, most deeply moving works — *Mourning Becomes Electra; The Ice Man Cometh; Long Day's Journey into Night* — after he found Carlotta, his third wife, who for many years completely fulfilled his needs for an empathic selfobject. She protected him against traumatizing disturbances and gave him the mirroring responses he required, with a single-minded devotion that must have been the outgrowth of intense, almost perfectly attuned needs of her own nuclear self. O'Neill intuitively recognized the incredible fit almost at their first encounter and pursued her without regard to the suffering he inflicted on his family and to the social disapproval to which he exposed himself. (In contrast to most of the students of O'Neill's life, I would not regard his actions as being "selfish" in the derogatory sense in which this word is customarily employed but rather as being undertaken in the service of his creativity, i.e., as enabling him to reach conditions in which he could simultaneously live out the pattern of his self most fully *and* give to others the best he had to give. At any rate, similar to the pattern of the life of other great men — cf., for example, the self-selfobject unit that Proust established with his servant Celeste — he ultimately found a psychological milieu that became the matrix in which, despite social isolation, conflicts and physical illness [i.e., "beyond the pleasure principle" as I defined the term in *The Restoration of the Self* (1977)], his self could fulfill its destiny.)

The maxim that the self requires a milieu of empathically responding selfobjects in order to function, indeed in order to survive, applies not only in the instances of selves who because of unusual talents and skills are able to express their pattern in a form that has broad social consequences (such as in the cases of O'Neill and Proust), it is even more valid in the case of anonymous Everyman. However insignificant from the point of view of society the inner program of ambitions and goals that forms a person's nuclear self might be, however unimpressive to others the pattern of thought and action that emanates from it, if, surrounded by a nourishing selfobject milieu, that self has developed around a firm core and is able to realize its nuclear aims, it will feel fulfilled, i.e., in tune with the unrolling of its destiny, and ultimately at peace with its inevitable decline — a decline that is then not experienced as leading to meaningless destruction but as ushering in the completion of a meaningful course. And others, too, if they are able to perceive human wholeness and to recognize the unrolling of a cohesive life, will respect the person who has achieved such integrity in the structure of his personality and of the history of his life — however small as measured by objective societal standards the person's stature may be and however narrow the scope of the reverberations of his existence.

As you can see again, I have remained unreformed: despite the criticism to which my work on the psychology of the self has been exposed, I continue to maintain that the sequence of maturing and changing empathic merger relationships between the self and its selfobjects can be fruitfully examined by the depth psychologist, from its archaic inception, via the creative-productive period of the self, to its ultimate wisdom as the world of objects begins to recede, i.e., I continue to maintain that narcissism has its own line of development. Independence from selfobjects, a break with the selfobject world, I might add, is indicative of serious psychopathology — it occurs not only in the clinically ill paranoiac but also in certain character types whose pseudoproductivity is, unfortunately, capable of bringing about destructive consequences, e.g., in the arena of history. The pathological forms of expression of the needs of the self, on the other hand, that we often encounter in our patients with narcissistic disturbances — their enraged demandingness, their arrogance — is no more than a cover, barring access to the legitimate demands for the empathic selfobject environment of which they were deprived as children. It is the very helplessness and despair of those who have almost given up all hope of getting the response they need for their psychological survival that lead to the asocial attitudes that are then, in turn, rejected coldly, angrily, patronizingly, or contemptuously by those who cannot discern the rightful demands that have gone into hiding.

So much for today. I consider this letter not only as a personal response to you but also as a trial run—I very much hope that our Chicago conference will be filled with similar interchanges, enabling us all to see many of the issues and problems of self psychology with increasing clarity.

From a letter to a colleague

September, 1978

I was surprised by one statement in your recent letter concerning the correspondence between Erich Heller and me, a statement on which, since, as you said, you have promised yourself only to applaud but not to enter the field, you did not expand. "As to the historical givens of some of your work, Heinz," you wrote, "it seems to me that empathy can only become a tool of inquiry, once it has ceased to be an immanent part of human discourse and existence."

I pondered your statement which questions the basic position from which I have pursued my work since I first presented my thoughts on empathy more than 20 years ago (Kohut, 1959). And I asked myself what you meant when you used the phrase "the historical givens of some of your work" (*all* of your work, you could have said) and, in particular, when you said that "empathy can only become a tool of inquiry, once it has ceased to be an immanent part of human discourse and existence." Concerning the latter I concluded that, since you obviously imply that empathy still *is* "an immanent part of human discourse and existence," you must feel that it cannot yet serve us as such a "tool."

You may be acquainted with some of my views on empathy; I hope, however, that you will not take it amiss when I now encourage you to (re)read the most important passages in my writings that deal with this topic in order to refresh your memory. There is first of all the aforementioned paper of 1959; then there are the pages devoted to empathy in "Forms and Transformations of Narcissism" (1966, pp. 450-453); then there is the subchapter on empathy in *The Analysis of the Self* (1971, pp. 300–307); and there is, above all, the seventh chapter of *The Restoration of the Self* (1977), especially the subchapter called "What Is the Essence of Psychoanalysis?" (pp. 298–312). These are the most important references. But you might also like to look at the remarks about introspection and empathy in "Psychoanalysis in a Troubled World" (1973a) and at the essay "The Psychoanalyst in the Community of Scholars" (1973b).

As you see I have given a good deal of thought to the role and position of empathy in our field — indeed I consider my views here to constitute the basis for the whole of my work, a conclusion that is not idiosyncratic but was also reached by others who studied and evaluated my contributions to depth psychology. John Gedo and Arnold Goldberg, for example (1973, p. 315), claimed that my views on empathy occupied a pivotal position in the framework of my thoughts, and Paul Ornstein, the editor of my selected writings (the collection bears the title *The Search for the Self* [1978]; originally however it had been my intention to call it *Scientific Empathy and Empathic Science,* a choice which again tells you how crucial I consider my position on empathy to be), assigned the same central role to my views on empathy in his thoughtful introductory essay.

For me — as was true for Freud (1933a, p. 179), who, however, did not follow through consistently in his theorizing here — all empirical sciences belong to one of two categories: there are, on the one hand, the sciences that base themselves on extrospection and vicarious extrospection, and there are, on the other hand, the sciences that are based on introspection and vicarious introspection (empathy). To the first category belong the physical and biological sciences, to the second the psychological sciences, par excellence psychoanalysis, the science of complex mental states. If the orientation about the external world provided to science by our sensory equipment were invalid because the use of our sensory equipment had not yet "ceased to be an immanent part of human discourse and existence," then the nonpsychological sciences would have no observational basis to stand on. And if we were forced for the same reason to consider as invalid the orientation provided to science by introspection and empathy, then psychology would be deprived of its observational foundation.

If various explorers of a country to which we, ourselves, will never be able to go (e.g., because these explorers lived before our time and the area they explored is now obliterated) describe this country to us in the terms of the storehouse of the images and memories that we have acquired through our lifelong previous acquaintance with the external world via the use of our senses (plus, of course, all the relevant experience-distant theories that belong to this dimension of our outlook on the world), then we are in principle able to learn from them, *via vicarious extrospection,* what the country which their reports describe was like. Had we not seen, touched, heard, and smelled the world before we studied their reports, we would not be able to grasp the information they transmit. And the same holds true with regard to psychoanalysis, the psychology of complex mental states, the psychology of inner experience. When our analysands tell us about their inner life, they describe to us a country to which we have never been, a country to which we can never gain direct access. Still, we are, in principle, able to understand their reports *via vicarious introspection (empathy)* because they are given to us in the terms of the storehouse of the images and memories that we have acquired through our lifelong previous acquaintance with the inner world of man through our own introspection (plus, of course, all the relevant experience-distant theories that belong to *this* dimension of our outlook on the world).

As you can see, my conviction concerning the irreplaceability of empathy has remained unshaken. And I will defend it against the view that it cannot yet serve as a tool of scientific inquiry because it is still an immanent part of human discourse and existence, just as I have in the past defended it against the skepticism of those who confuse it with compassion (see 1977, pp. 304–305) and against the skepticism of those who confuse it with intuition (see 1971, pp. 302–303), two aspects of psychic life which are in essence unrelated to empathy.

The confusion with compassion is easily dealt with — it rests on the erroneous assumption that because empathy is a prerequisite for compassion, the obverse must also be true. Empathy is, however, not only employed for friendly and constructive purposes but also for hostile or destructive ones. When the Nazis attached howling sirens to their dive-bombers and were thus able to create disintegrating panic in those they were about to attack, they used empathy for a hostile purpose. It was empathy (vicarious introspection) that allowed them to predict how those exposed to the mysterious noise from the skies would react. If a salesman uses in quick succession both a firmly commanding and a softly cajoling approach, his empathy is not in the service of compassion—it is meant to overcome the sales resistance of the customer. In other words, he—or the supervisor who instructed and trained him, or the industrial psychologist who devised the method—is in empathic contact with the child in the customer who was once made to obey by similar means, i.e., through near-simultaneous command and seduction.

I now turn to the failure to differentiate between empathy and intuition which is as erroneous as the failure to differentiate between empathy and compassion discussed in the preceding. The correct perception of psychological data through empathy proceeds neither more nor less frequently in an intuitive manner than the correct perception of nonpsychological data through vicarious *extro*spection. A person whose use of empathy has become highly trained by decades of familiarity with certain psychological areas may at times grasp some detail concerning the inner life of another person with great speed and apparently without the necessity to gather any evidence. It has happened to me many times, for example—and I am certain that every experienced analyst will corroborate the fact that he, too, is familiar with such events—that in the course of seemingly innocuous ruminations from the side of the analysand I will suddenly remember an incident from the patient's childhood which the patient may have mentioned only once before, perhaps years ago, and that then, five or ten minutes later during the session, the patient will again talk about this very incident. I used to wonder on such occasions whether I had not fallen prey to a retrospective falsification here, whether an unresolved remnant of an infantile wish for clairvoyance or omniscience might not have persuaded me that I had anticipated the analysand's association when in fact I had not. In order to ascertain the correctness of my observation I disciplined myself to commit to paper any suddenly recalled information about a patient — e.g., information concerning a childhood event about which the patient may have spoken only once, years ago. The result was that in not infrequent instances I could indeed confirm the fact that my own associations had been ahead of those of my patient. Should one ascribe such occurrences during analytic work to some unusual and mysterious gifts that analysts supposedly possess and say that they are based on intuition?

The answer to this question is "no." Even though a scientist trained in the use of empathy may himself be unable to spell out the individual data on the basis of which he identified a complex psychological configuration, the process by which he arrived at his perception is, in principle at least, open to rational investigation. We have simply witnessed the performance of a mind that has learned to pick up numerous data preconsciously and at great speed and, like a well-programmed computer, either first to combine the information concerning details and then to arrive at a correct and accurate result or to identify a complex but familiar configuration all at once. But speedy and seemingly direct perceptions are also available to a gifted and/or trained observer of the nonpsychological realm who investigates the nonpsychological dimensions of our surroundings through *extro*spection. If we get a glimpse of a face that we know well, we will recognize it on the basis of the instantaneous perception of a great number of individual details which form a complex but familiar configuration and we are in general not able to spell out the individual data that have enabled us to perform this act. No one, of course, will speak of intuition with regard to our ability to recognize the face of a friend. But how about the single-glance diagnosis of some illness by a seasoned clinician; the seemingly unreasoned choice of an, to others, unpromising direction of scientific investigations that ultimately lead to a great discovery by a gifted researcher; and, yes, even the decisive moves of certain great chess players, military strategists, politicians, and diplomats? In all these instances talent and experience combine to allow either the rapid and preconscious gathering of a great number of data and the ability to recognize that they form a meaningful configuration or the one-step recognition of a complex configuration that had been preconsciously assembled, perhaps in years of silently proceeding work.

Some scientists who are committed to the traditional methodology applicable in certain phases of the physical sciences would say now that these speedy processes will at times also lead to erroneous results. They do, of course. All human achievement is imperfect. And they would probably say, furthermore, that in science we need not only speedy perception but also an accurate and detailed accounting of the methods by which we arrived at our results. And, again, I would agree. Where I do not agree, however, is the implication that such a detailed account is, in principle, possible with regard to the extrospected universe but not with regard to the introspected or vicariously introspected universe of the inner life of man. To my mind there are in this regard no differences, in principle, between the extrospective, nonempathic and the introspective, empathic observational methods that belong to these two realms.

But now I must try to convince you that, despite the fact that it is still an immanent part of human discourse and existence, empathy can be employed by scientific depth psychology—which as you know, means to me, that I want to convince you that a scientific psychology of complex mental states, the only psychology that I consider worth pursuing, is possible at all. Let me first say that I do not deny that there are specific difficulties that stand in the way of man's use of empathy for the exploration and control of the world within us—just as there are specific difficulties that stand in the way of man's use of his extrospective orientation for the exploration and control of the world outside. But admitting the existence of these difficulties does not make me a pessimist with regard to empathy. On the contrary, the mere fact that despite man's ingenuity in the use of physical, psychological, and cognitive tools, there is nothing else at his disposal, that he has no alternative if he wants now through depth psychology to investigate and ultimately control the inner world, as he has attempted to do with the external world via the physical sciences, makes me on the whole rather optimistic. Since we are talking about a process of maturation, development, and growth, the fact that our survival depends on our ability to achieve this maturation, development, and growth increases to my mind the chances that these changes will in fact occur. But what opposes the scientific employment of the introspective-empathic stance? Put in a nutshell: there is nothing wrong with it per se—no more wrong with it, in principle at any rate, than with the use of our senses in extrospection; it is our shortcomings in using it which are the problem.

I don't know whether you are familiar with Hanns Sachs's essay "The Delay of the Machine Age" (1933). His thesis was that, at the time that preceded the end of their political and military supremacy, i.e., at the time that preceded the breakup of their far-flung empire, the Romans had at their disposal the means that could have saved them—if only they had been able to use these means. Yes, they had machines, and they used them—but only for frivolous, peripheral activities: for children's toys, and for their games and theaters. They did not use them to build roads and bridges, they did not use them to transport their legions, they did not use them for the serious business of war. Here they stuck to their marching feet, to their legs and arms with which they controlled their horses, thrust their swords, and held their shields. The reason for their failure to harness the power of machines in the service of the state, a move that might have prevented their downfall, was, according to Sachs, that they prized their own bodies too much and could therefore not give over the performance of the functions of their beloved arms and legs to inanimate machines—at least where life in all its seriousness was involved. To paraphrase the crucial statement of your letter: they could not freely transmute the power of their bodies into the power of machines as proxy for or replica of the body because their bodies were still an immanent part of their existence—or, as I would say, because their self in this sector was still an archaic body-self. (Compare these reflections with the related thoughts I presented concerning the move from eating with one's hands to eating with eating utensils [1977, pp. 111–112].)

But we must return to the main subject matter of this letter and ask whether and, if so, to what extent Sachs's thesis applies also to our use of introspection and empathy, specifically to the use of introspection and empathy with regard to the serious business of life, i.e., above all, to the scientific use of introspection and empathy employed in the service of the attempt to control our destructiveness and thus to ensure our survival. Are we, in other words, whose survival is threatened by our inability to control our narcissistic vulnerability, in particular our inability to curb the narcissistic rage that supervenes when our self is hurt, unable to use a potentially effective tool, indeed a tool that might save us? The tool, of course — I know I am repeating myself, but the matter bears repetition — is the scientific investigation of our inner life in order to understand and control it and thus, perhaps, to prevent the end of civilization via an atomic holocaust triggered, in the last analysis, by an uncontrolled outburst of narcissistic rage in the arena of history.

But now you might say that I have contradicted myself. First, you might say, I point to the Romans who were not able to harness their knowledge about machines to actions that would have allowed them to stem the tide of the barbarians at their far-flung borders, but then, you will add, I express the view that we, in our era, would not be falling prey to the analogous failure concerning the use of introspection and empathy.

There are certainly similarities between the time preceding the fall of the Roman empire to which Sachs referred and the juncture at which Western civilization finds itself at the present time — and, as you know, these similarities have led some thoughtful observers (e.g., Eissler, 1965, pp. 225-228), in harmony with the principles and conclusions of Oswald Spengler (1918-1922) and of Freud (1930, 1933b), to be deeply pessimistic about the survival chances of man. Strange as it may seem on first sight, there is something uplifting about prophesies of unavoidable doom, while a balanced approach that recognizes the extent of the danger but can also consider man's potential ability to deal with it tends not to evoke enthusiasm and gratitude but rather the superior smile of contempt. There is grandeur about the suprahuman position of a seemingly objective, detached pessimism, while the need to recognize the necessity for hard work, and the possibility of failure even then — the price that cautious optimism exacts — is human, all too human. Still, if I were pressed to be more specific about my assessment of the survival chances of Western man I would say that I am neither a pessimist on the basis of a Spenglerian historical or Freudian biological argument nor an optimist on the basis of an unshaken faith in man's rationality and the inevitable victory of civilization. In support of a pessimistic outlook one can say indeed that there are many similarities between the symptoms that are generally manifested by dying cultures and those discernible in our society. And one must also admit that there are similarities between, on the one hand, the inability of the Romans to use the tool — the power of the machine — that might have been able to deal with the external foes who ultimately destroyed their empire and culture and, on the other hand, our inability to use the tool — the power of the insights achieved via scientific introspection and empathy — that might be able to deal with the internal foe, man's unconquered propensity to engage in wars, his propensity, when in the throes of narcissistic rage, to disregard even the danger of total destruction.

There are still further similarities, in particular a crucial one which is, I believe, related to the point that you raised in your letter. Even under the pressure of an adaptational emergency of utmost urgency, the Romans were unable to make a comparatively simple maturational step concerning an aspect of the body-self — a step they needed to make in order to become capable of employing machines in the service of their survival. The inability of the Romans to make this step in adaptation is indeed comparable to our inability to make the analogous maturational step concerning an aspect of our mind-self — a step we need to make in order to become capable of employing the insights of introspective-empathic science in the service of our survival. Or — adopting for the sake of the present considerations the frame of reference within which you arrived at your judgment that empathy is not, or not yet, available for scientific use — we might say that the Romans' inability to give up their archaic body-fixation is similar to our inability to dislodge empathy and introspection from its position as "an immanent part of human discourse and existence," thus preventing us from using it as an autonomous "tool of inquiry."

It is my claim, however—and now I am arguing on the side of a cautious optimism—that the similarity between our difficulties in using introspection and empathy and the failure of the Romans to use machines, or, in other words, that the similarity between the delay of the machine age and the delay of the age of an effectively applied depth psychology, is essentially only a partial one.

First I will mention—admittedly a weak argument—that the danger faced by modern man is greater than the danger faced by the Romans. The Romans were threatened by the loss of their world domination while we, since the introduction of atomic weapons of destruction, are threatened by the possibility of the total extinction not only of one people or one culture but of all of human life on earth. Does the broadening of the danger allow us to assume that man will try harder to institute countermeasures, that, to be specific, he will even bow to the necessity of having to investigate his inner life in order to control his propensity toward destructiveness that might be his total undoing? I do not know the answer to this question, but I assume that the greatness of the peril should be considered as a factor, however small in itself, that might increase man's readiness to take steps to subdue the enemy within himself.

There is, however, another fact to consider, a fact that I would evaluate as more potently on the side of the cautious optimism concerning man's future that I believe to be the realistic assessment of his capacity for survival than his recognition of the enormity of the danger to which he is exposed. Strange as it might seem on first sight, I believe that the very existence of scientific depth psychology—a new phenomenon in the history of science, in human history—is itself a fact that supports the hope that mankind will respond to the threat to its survival by the great adaptational step that is required. True enough, the insights of depth psychology are not yet being employed in the arena of history—at least not on a scale that could be considered as even minimally effective. They are so far employed only—seen in historical perspective one might say they are employed playfully; perhaps in analogy to the Romans' use of machines in the theater and as children's toys—in individual therapy. No doubt, depth psychology is also being used in the investigation of human activities outside of individual therapy. But here, in contrast to individual therapy, there is not yet any serious attempt at translating insight into effective change, analogous to the way by which we proceed in psychotherapy.

In addition to all these acknowledged similarities, however, there is this significant difference. It concerns the attitude of those who hold the key to the storehouse of the new knowledge toward their respective fields of activity: the attitude of the Roman artisans—slaves, I would assume, not free citizens—who designed and built machines toward the field of knowledge about machines, on the one hand, and, on the other hand; the attitude of the depth psychologists of our era toward depth-psychological knowledge. While the psychoanalytic insights concerning man, like the knowledge about machines of the Romans, do not—with minor exceptions, e.g., perhaps in the fields of education, business administration, and jurisprudence—yet make significant contributions to the conduct of public life, psychoanalysts, at least a group among them, unlike the task-oriented slave-technicians in Rome, are workers in a forward-moving, yet broadly based and theory-supported science who, despite the many internal and external obstacles that stand in their way, continue to pursue their research and to expand the scope of depth-psychological knowledge and of its potential application. Indeed I believe that, however hard it may be to dislodge the use of introspection and empathy from its archaic commitments as "an immanent part of human discourse and existence," this great and indispensable tool of our science is already beginning—especially since the advent of the psychoanalytic psychology of the self—to provide us with insights about man's inner life that have a chance of giving him increased control over his actions, in particular over his destructive actions.

You know—to express myself more specifically now—that I do not believe that man is to any pragmatically significant extent motivated by an unconquerable death instinct; that I believe instead that he has been the victim of his still unconquered tendency to react to injuries to his self with often boundless narcissistic rage. But while, as I said, this tendency has not been mastered, I cannot see why our increased scientific knowledge—obtained with the aid of the increasingly disciplined employment of introspection and empathy as tools of observation—should not ultimately lead us to further progress that will allow us to obtain effective control over human aggressivity.

Whether we will or will not be successful in this endeavor may indeed depend ultimately on our ability to increase the scope and depth of our scientific empathy. Will scientific depth psychology in general, will the new psychoanalytic psychology of the self, in particular, be able to attain its goals? I do not claim the ability to predict the future. All I wanted to say is that a favorable outcome of man's attempt to deal with his destructiveness is in principle not impossible. And I derive from this conclusion the injunction that the depth psychologist must not retreat to a position to sterile pessimistic superiority but that he must continue to strive to penetrate into man's inner life and to illuminate it as broadly and deeply as possible and, furthermore, that he must fight courageously for the effective integration of his insights into the broader awareness of society—despite the opposition, in particular despite the painful ridicule, which his attempts will elicit and, last but not least, despite his own tendency to remain fixated on that developmental level in which the scientific use of introspection and empathy and the results that are obtained via their use are shunned as a threat to man's wholeness instead of being welcomed as a chance to buttress his disintegrating self. It is this last-named uneasiness, I suspect, that prompts even such well-meaning people as you to take sides with Professor Heller against the psychoanalyst's attempt to use his empathy for the scientific scrutiny of man's self and of the products of its creative activities. But this use of empathy will neither weaken man's self nor destroy the beauty and significance of the creations that emanate from it; nor will empathy lose its position as an immanent part of human discourse and existence by becoming a sharply focused tool of disciplined scientific inquiry. Most, if not all, great achievements of man—not only in art and in the world of action but also in science—certainly the very greatest of them, are brought about by psychological functions in which a total sector of the psyche participates. They are not produced by isolated surface activities of the mind but through the unified cooperation of all psychic layers, including the deep and archaic ones. And these conditions, I know, prevail also with regard to scientific empathy as employed by the depth psychologist. It engages, on the one hand, simultaneously and/or in rapid alternation, empathic responses that go back to an earliest nonverbal communion between a rudimentary self and its selfobject which has as its goal the nurture of psychological well-being and the furtherance of development and, on the other hand, highly disciplined, sharply demarcated empathic responses that satisfy the standards of scientific objectivity. Psychoanalysis explains what it has first understood, I said some years ago. Restated in the terms of the framework that your remark provided for me: psychoanalytic empathy can be a tool of scientific inquiry while yet remaining an immanent part of human discourse and existence.

I will close by telling you that I am grateful to you for having expressed your doubts about my position in such a friendly and tactful, yet open, way. I hope that my response clarified my views on empathy, this crucially important tool that is potentially available to man in his quest for knowledge, mastery, and, it is hoped, survival.

References

Eissler, K. R. (1965), *Medical Orthodoxy and the Future of Psychoanalysis.* New York: International Universities Press.

Freud, S. (1930), Civilization and Its Discontents. *Standard Edition,* 21: 64–145. London: Hogarth Press, 1961.

_____ (1933a), New Introductory Lectures on Psycho-Analysis. *Standard Edition,* 22:5–182. London: Hogarth Press, 1964.

_____ (1933b), Why War? *Standard Edition,* 22:199–215. London: Hogarth Press, 1964.

Gedo, J. & Goldberg, A. (1973), *Models of the Mind.* Chicago: University of Chicago Press.

Kohut, H. (1959), Introspection, Empathy, and Psychoanalysis: An Examination of the Relation Between Mode of Observation and Theory. In: *The Search for the Self,* vol. 1, ed. P. Ornstein. New York: International Universities Press, 1978, pp. 205–232.

_____ (1966), Forms and Transformations of Narcissism. In: *The Search for the Self,* vol. 1, ed. P. Ornstein. New York: International Universities Press, 1978, pp. 427–460.

_____ (1971), *The Analysis of the Self.* New York: International Universities Press.

_____ (1973a), Psychoanalysis in a Troubled World. In: *The Search for the Self,* vol. 2, ed. P. Ornstein. New York: International Universities Press, 1978, pp. 511–546.

_____ (1973b), The Psychoanalyst in the Community of Scholars. In: *The Search for the Self,* vol. 2, ed. P. Ornstein. New York: International Universities Press, 1978, pp. 685–724.

_____ (1977), *The Restoration of the Self.* New York: International Universities Press.

_____ (1978), *The Search for the Self,* 2 vols., ed. P. Ornstein. New York: International Universities Press.

Sachs, H. (1933), The Delay of the Machine Age. *Psychoanal. Quart.,* 2:404–424.

Spengler, O. (1918–1922), *The Decline of the West,* 2 vols. New York: Knopf, 1945.

Part VI

REFLECTIONS ON
ADVANCES IN SELF
PSYCHOLOGY

Reflections on
Advances in Self Psychology

Heinz Kohut

In discussing some of the contributions to this volume, I will not attempt to summarize all the material that was presented. I could neither do justice to such a job nor do I really think that I would perform a useful service in undertaking it. I will instead share with the reader my personal responses to some of the papers, focusing sometimes on this or that detail of an individual contribution, sometimes on those aspects of a topic under scrutiny that, in my opinion, were either neglected or insufficiently emphasized or that I consider of such importance as to require additional emphasis. I hope that these personal reactions will, by demarcating certain recurrent clusters of uncertainties and questions that emerged in presentations and debates, make a contribution to our future investigations by identifying the various directions in which the future development of psychoanalytic self psychology might proceed.

The first section of the book, "Self Psychology and Development," is of great importance because it addresses some of the crucial issues that self psychology is currently raising. These issues do not concern the clinical application of self psychology but rather topics of more general significance. The first question, raised by the Shanes, and later incisively discussed by Marian Tolpin, is whether the time has come for self psychology to give up its isolation and to acknowledge that it is not the only modern school of psychology that attempts to explore certain areas that have been insufficiently explored by classical analysis. In acknowledging this fact, these contributors consider whether we should now select the best portions of these various contributions and amalgamate them with one another, undoubtedly with the silently made assumption, or at least with the hope, that this effort would result in a new whole greater than the parts contributed by any one individual school. The second issue concerns our theory, in particular the question whether it has been proper for us to assign the central position in our theory to the self rather than, as had been true for classical analysis, to the drives and, par excellence, whether the stress that self psychology lays on the empathic mode of observation and its influence on theory is not a regression from rigorous, scientific objectivity to sentimental, nonscientific subjectivism.

I will first give you my thoughts about the question of whether self psychology should or should not attempt to integrate its findings, concepts, and theories with those of other modern schools, especially with the findings, concepts, and theories of those analysts who exerted their major impact on our field via their contributions to child analysis and child observation, in particular with those of Mahler and Winnicott. Before attempting to address myself to the essential obstacle that, as I see it, stands in the way of the integration advocated by the Shanes, I will briefly focus on a point which, although not by itself conclusive in settling the issue at hand, deserves mention.

It is my impression, specifically with regard to Mahler and Winnicott (whose contributions the Shanes particularly commend for integration with self psychology), that however valid and important their findings and insights, they focus on circumscribed periods of individual development and, with the exception of certain applications in pathography (see, for example, Lynch, 1979) their work does not furnish us, as does classical analysis and self psychology, with a broad concept of man that would illuminate human pursuits and human fate "beyond the bounds of the basic rule."

I believe that this is a significant point which deserves further thought. But I will admit that, while it might weaken the Shanes' position if it were raised as an argument against their advocacy of integration, it would not fully invalidate it—it would simply restrict an attempt at integration or synthesis to the circumscribed areas of child development which Mahler and Winnicott have illuminated through their work. In its essence, if I understand it correctly, the Shanes' argument is based on the opinion—with which I fully agree—that the genetic data obtained by reconstructions from the analyses of adults and the findings obtained by psychoanalytically sophisticated child observers and child analysts should be allowed to cross-fertilize each other. Let me stress again that I not only consider this point of view legitimate, but that I also hope that the task it advocates will soon be undertaken. (I should like to mention here that Sander's work in particular [e.g., 1975] promises to enrich self psychology and, in turn, to be enriched by it.) It is, however, my view—and this is the major point of my argument against the position taken by the Shanes—that, in order for this task to be carried out successfully, i.e., in order that it eventuate in significant results, the basic stance of the child observer and those who reconstruct childhood experience via the analysis of transferences must be compatible.

But before I elaborate the decisive reason why the integration of the work of Mahler and Winnicott and psychoanalytic self psychology cannot lead to fruitful results at this time, I would first like to look briefly at two other reasons why self psychology has, to date, generally proceeded on a relatively independent course— independent, that is, except insofar as self psychology (a) seeks to remain firmly based on the methods of traditional psychoanalysis and its modes of thinking, and (b) strives to preserve the sense of an unbroken continuity in the development of psychoanalysis, one characterized by slow advances, step by step, in response to new discoveries and the need for theoretical concepts engendered by them. The two explanations I have in mind may, in fact, be considered two sides of the same coin. They communicate the same meaning, but do so in an inimical-accusatory tone in one instance, and in a friendly and vindicatory tone in the other. Is it not simply conceit on our part, some might ask, that we are going it alone, that we think we cannot learn from others, and that we do not make the attempt to integrate our findings with theirs? Or, expressed in terms meant to justify our lack of responsiveness to the work of other modern investigators, could we not argue that it is necessary for us to go it alone for a while in order not to interfere with the momentum of our own discoveries by withdrawing our energies prematurely from our primary research commitment, and channeling them to the important but secondary obligations of scholarship, including the attempt to correlate our findings with those of others?

Concerning the possibility that vanity is the culprit, I can only testify to my awareness of the motivating potential of this flaw, and my belief that I have done everything in my power to avoid succumbing to the petty desire to have the stage to myself. It may come as no surprise to you when I now tell you that I believe that the second explanation—I have referred to it as a friendly and vindicatory one—has much to recommend itself. As a matter of fact, I have advanced it in the past when, with regard to my own work (cf. 1977a, pp. xix–xxi), I tried to explain why I could not, with the limited powers at my disposal, be both a devoted investigator who scans the psychological field with a new instrument of observation *and* a detached, conscientious scholar who compares, objectively evaluates, and ultimately integrates his discoveries with those of many others who work with different observational and conceptual tools. I concluded that this was work that should be done, but that it should be undertaken by others and should await a later, more consolidated stage in the development of psychoanalytic self psychology.

But now I will leave these issues behind me. I have dealt with them sketchily, but they deal at most with secondary impediments to the integrative task that we are asked to do and not with the primary, overriding obstacle that, even if undue pride and the need for elbowroom are discounted, would still block our way. What is the real obstacle that precludes our participation in a move toward the integration of our findings with those obtained by other methods, the move that was so competently and persuasively recommended by the Shanes and which, on the face of it, seems so desirable?

Many years ago, perhaps in the late '60s, Otto Kernberg asked me during a friendly chat what I thought was the difference between his work and mine, and it was not long after that occasion that Margaret Mahler touched on the same issue in a letter. I still remember clearly my replies. To Dr. Kernberg I said that he looked on narcissism as in essence pathological, while I looked on it as in essence healthy; to Dr. Mahler I wrote that we were digging tunnels from different directions into the same area of the mountain.

I could still endorse these old statements of mine, though it may not be readily apparent why I would not offer them at present in response to questions of this type. In fact, such questions, in their disarmingly simple form, and inviting as they do concise replies, would today cause me some embarrassment. The differences between self psychology and the schools of thought represented by the two aforementioned investigators now appear to me to be much more basic than they did a decade ago; there is too much that would need to be said to permit the kind of brief reply that I felt able to give 10 or 12 years ago.

Returning to the issue that we are discussing at present, I can say that I do not consider the differences that I mentioned in my responses to Dr. Kernberg and Dr. Mahler 10 years ago as unbridgeable obstacles blocking the integration recommended by the Shanes. Whatever my shortcomings, I am not a pedant. If anything, I tend toward a looseness of formulation that makes for a relativistic stance. Why not emphasize the pathological aspects of narcissism? And why could this traditional attitude not now be integrated with an approach that stresses, in addition, the role that narcissism plays in mental health? The latter approach had, after all, already been discussed by Federn, though, unfortunately, in an idiosyncratic way which diminished the usefulness of his valuable contributions. And why — a point that is of specific relevance in the present context — should the approach of the child observer and that of the adult reconstructor of childhood not lead to results that can be integrated? Yes, there are conceptual difficulties to be overcome. But I have no doubt that if we are not overly puristic here, accommodations can be made and inconsistencies disregarded, to the mutual benefit of those who investigate the child's behavior in depth and those who gain access to the depths of the child's psyche via the memories of their adult patients.

What then *is* the unbridgeable obstacle? It is the basically different outlook regarding the scientific evaluation of the nature of man and the significance of his unrolling life.

In view of the fact that the basic discrepancies between the conceptions of the self psychologist and the conceptions of those who emphasize the primacy of hostility and destructiveness in human nature and, consequently, man's propensity to be beset by conflict, guilt, and guilt-depression, are not relevant to the presentations in this volume, I will not discuss the question of whether this approach (of which Kernberg's work represents a specific and influential variety) can be integrated with that of self psychology. Some of my later remarks concerning drive psychology and the complementarity between the psychology of Guilty Man and Tragic Man, although dealing only tangentially with the self psychological outlook on aggression, will I hope, be relevant to this issue. What I must directly focus on, however, is the question with which the Shanes confront us. Why not build a bridge between the findings of psychoanalytic self psychology and those of the psychoanalytic child observers, in particular with those of Mahler and Winnicott and Spitz? Rather than attempting to spell out the views on man in general and on the child and his move toward adulthood in particular, which are held by Mahler, Winnicott, and Spitz, I will summarize the self psychological outlook with regard to certain basic aspects of the human condition and trust that this will allow the reader to draw his own conclusions concerning the question of whether it is possible to build a bridge between self psychology and the findings of these child observers.

In the view of self psychology, man lives in a matrix of selfobjects from birth to death. He needs selfobjects for his psychological survival, just as he needs oxygen in his environment throughout his life for physiological survival. Certainly, the individual is exposed to the anxiety and guilt of unsolvable conflict and to the miseries of lowered self-esteem following the realization that he has failed to reach his aims or live up to his ideals. But so long as he feels that he is surrounded by selfobjects and feels reassured by their presence — either by their direct responses to him or, on the basis of past experiences, via his confidence in their lasting concern — even conflict, failure, and defeat will not destroy his self, however great his suffering may be. Self psychology does not see the essence of man's development as a move from dependence to independence, from merger to autonomy, or even as a move from no-self to self. We do not disregard man's anxieties and depressions, in infancy, in adulthood, and when face to face with death. And while we certainly do not ignore man's greed and lust or his destructive rage, we see them not as primary givens but as secondary phenomena due to disturbances in the self-selfobject unit. Accordingly, we do not focus our attention on the baby's anxiety vis-à-vis strangers (Spitz), his clutching of substitutes for the unresponsive or unavailable mother (Winnicott), or the affective and ideational swings that accompany his reluctant move from symbiotic existence to individuality (Mahler) as if these phenomena represent primary and circumscribed psychological configurations. From the vantage point of self psychology, these phenomena are secondary, their meaning and significance becoming understandable only when seen from the point of view of man's abiding need for selfobjects throughout the whole span of his life. What we have begun to study, therefore, and what we hope, in the future, to investigate in fruitful cooperation with others, is the sequence of self-selfobject relationships that occur throughout life. As part of this undertaking, we will ask how in tune with the small baby's specific needs the responses of the selfobject were at the beginning of extrauterine life. We will determine whether the selfobject responded with proud mirroring to the infant's first strivings toward physical separateness. (It should be noted that while we speak now of greater physical distance from the selfobject, we do not speak of a lessening of the empathic bond.) How, we will further ask, does the selfobject milieu respond to a person in the subsequent stations in his life, in adolescence, for example, or in middle age? And, finally, how does the selfobject milieu respond to a person's dying? Does it respond with pride in him for being an example of courage in pain and decline, or by withdrawing its mirroring from him at this ultimate point in the curve of life? You will have noticed that I have referred only to the selfobject's mirroring functions in sketching out our research task. In view of the fact that responses of alter-ego selfobjects and of idealizable selfobjects may be present side by side with those of mirroring ones, and that twinship support and the devotion to ideals often supply the major sustenance that is obtained from the selfobjects, it is clear that the roles of alter-ego and idealized selfobjects during the various phases of life deserve as much attention as the role of the mirroring ones.

In contrast to the self psychological position that I have outlined, a position which not only influences our therapeutic strategy but also determines our investigative aims, it is the unquestioned — and even unmentioned because it is taken for granted — assumption of all the schools of child observation that are not guided by the self psychological point of view that man's life from childhood to adulthood is a move forward from a position of helplessness, dependence, and shameful clinging to a position of power, independence, and proud autonomy. And, furthermore, in complete harmony with the preceding outlook, this assumption takes for granted that the undesirable features of adulthood, the flaws in the adult's psychic organization, must be conceptualized as manifestations of a psychological infantilism, i.e., as manifestations of psychic immaturity due to the failure to move forward in development or due to a person's frightened return to the weakness, dependence, and clinging attitudes of the child.

There is a value system hidden here (paraphrasing Hartmann, one might refer to it as a "maturation morality" or as a "developmental morality") that is quite in accordance with the prevailing value system of Western civilization. I will add that I believe it achieved its dominant position in depth psychology via the teachings of Freud, who placed knowledge values (the ability to see inner and outer reality clearly despite unpleasure, the acceptance of the scientific world view as the ultimate step from the pleasure principle to the reality principle) at the top of his hierarchy of values and saw man, both in his individual development and in history (cf. *Civilization and Its Discontents* [1930]), as submitting only reluctantly to the domesticating influences of civilization and as falling woefully short of the moral-developmental ideal which demands that he tame his drives and assert his intelligence.

I do not intend to argue the superiority—i.e., the greater relevance with regard to man's actual problems—of the self psychological outlook on man and on his life over the views about man and his life held silently and matter-of-factly by those whose findings we should integrate with ours. While I believe that our viewpoint indeed has much to recommend itself and is in fact more relevant with regard to man's fate in our time and in the foreseeable future, our present focus is not on the comparative value of these two positions. In the context of the Shanes' recommendation, however, this *is* the appropriate place for pointing out that the differences between these two outlooks are basic and that they are of such magnitude that we would have to demand from either the other schools of thought or from self psychology the relinquishment of the central value system that determines the content of scientific observation and the significance assigned to the data. "Kohut's baby," as Marian Tolpin put it humorously in her discussion, is not dependent, clinging, or weak, but independent, assertive, strong—it is psychologically complete so long as it breathes the psychological oxygen provided by contact with empathically responsive selfobjects and, in this respect, it is no different from the adult who is complete, independent, and strong only as long as he feels responded to.

If we accept the presence of a milieu of responsive selfobjects as a necessary precondition of psychological life, if, moreover, we acknowledge the fact that the healthy, normal human being is psychologically constituted in such a way that he survives only in such a milieu and is equipped with the ability to search for and find such a milieu, then our outlook on man—on his psychopathology and on his behavior in the social and historical arena—will be determined by this basic assumption. It is quite in harmony with this assumption that we have come to the conclusion that some of the greatest achievements of adult life become possible only if childhood functions have remained accessible, or have become accessible again, perhaps due to the renewed availability of whole-some selfobject responses. Some and perhaps all creative achieve-ment, for example, rests broadly on the functional patterns that are the essence of happy playfulness in childhood. If, however, the requisite selfobject matrix is absent later in life, whether in adoles-cence, adulthood, late middle-life, or in old age, then the self will be endangered, may lose its cohesion, and, as pride and assertive-ness are gone, creative-productive activities will cease.

We now shift from the issue of integration of our findings and theories, as advocated by the Shanes, to consider certain forceful criticisms that others have directed at self psychology. By our tendency of assigning too significant a role to empathy, it is said, we are endangering the scientific status of psychoanalysis and are jeopardizing the gains that psychoanalysis has made dur-ing many decades of hard work and rigorous devotion to objec-tivity. This argument proceeds to dissociate our clinical contri-butions from our theories, praising the former as progressive, while condemning the latter, in particular the theories elaborated in *The Restoration of the Self* (1977a), as retrogressive. I believe that proponents of this position misunderstand one aspect of our theoretical stance completely, however conscientiously they may have studied our work. As I have argued elsewhere (see my sec-ond "letter to a colleague" in this volume), I do not believe that assigning a central role to empathy (defined by us as "vicarious introspection") as the requisite observational tool of psy-choanalysis can endanger the scientific status of psychoanalysis. The question is not whether empathy should or should not be employed or whether we should consider empathy as the basic observational tool of analysis. Since a psychology of complex mental states is unthinkable without empathy, the only question one can legitimately ask is whether a psychology of complex mental states can ever be scientific. If we express our conviction that it can, we have in the same breath acknowledged our acceptance of empathy — an operation which is indeed not just a valuable tool of the psychology of complex mental states, but defines its essence and determines the content of its field. We must, therefore, not attempt to disavow empathy but must examine it and study its applications with the ultimate aim of cleansing it of any impurities that would disqualify the discipline that employs it as a basic operation from counting itself among the sciences.

I will repeat now the three points I made in my "letter to a colleague" because I am convinced that, once understood, they will protect us against the fear that the use of empathy is, ipso facto, irreconcilable with the outlook of science:

1. Empathy (vicarious introspection) is in essence neutral and objective, it is not in its essence subjective. Its analogy in the physical sciences is vicarious extrospection, i.e., a process by which data extrospectively obtained by others and reported to us are integrated into the context of the organized system of the data that we already possess. Empathy must, therefore, not be confused with either sympathy or compassion. Empathy is surely a necessary precondition for our ability to experience compassion; and compassionate acts, in order to be effective, must be guided by the accurate empathic assessment of the recipient's needs. But the same can also be said with regard to many of our hostile-destructive feelings; in order to be effective, certain destructive actions—those that aim at inflicting psychological wounds—must be guided by the accurate empathic assessment of the victim's sensitivities.

2. Empathy is not intuition and must not be confused with it. It is occasionally employed in an intuitive fashion (e.g., by an experienced psychoanalytic clinician), that is, with great speed and without the awareness of intermediate steps, just as extrospection may be employed intuitively (e.g., by an experienced medical diagnostician). In its scientific application, however, intuition cannot be allowed to stand by itself. The intermediate steps that lead to a conclusion in a science that relies on empathy and introspection (psychoanalysis) have to be brought into awareness and spelled out for our scrutiny, as is the case in the sciences that must rely on extrospection and vicarious extrospection (biology, physics, etc.).

3. Empathy is employed only for data gathering; there is no way in which it could serve us in our theory building. In the clinical situation the analyst employs empathy to collect information about specific current events in the patient's inner life. After

he has collected these data with the aid of empathy, he orders them and gives the patient a dynamic or genetic interpretation. In arriving at his formulations he does not employ empathy, indeed he could not possibly employ it, even though he continues to deal with that aspect of reality that is accessible only via introspection and empathy. I might add, however, for the sake of completeness, that the analyst may use empathic testing maneuvers (thought experiments) after he has tentatively formulated his dynamic and, especially, his genetic interpretations, before he decides to communicate them to the analysand.

My argument, up to this point, seems to me to be beyond controversy. If it is open to any reproach, it could only be, I believe, that it is unnecessary even to advance it, i.e., that the claim it supports is obviously correct and that my defense was unnecessary. How is it possible for perceptive colleagues to criticize self psychology for its emphasis on empathy? And how can it be explained that on two occasions I myself have referred to empathy, beyond its scientific use as a value-neutral tool of depth-psychological observation, as an ingredient of certain broad human attitudes to which I personally happen to subscribe?

I could dismiss my own seeming inconsistencies by pointing out that these loosely framed remarks on empathy were made on two festive occasions when I addressed nonprofessional audiences (Kohut, 1973a, 1973b). But while it would thus be easy enough for me to dismiss these two references as nonscientific *obiter dicta* and point to the many statements in my work in which I make my scientific position on empathy clear beyond the shadow of a doubt, I believe that, perhaps as so often happens in science, these misunderstandings and inconsistencies point to a yet unfinished task.

The task, as I see it, is not to abandon the strict scientific position concerning empathy that we have espoused, but to investigate the relationship between this scientific empathy, on the one hand, and the cluster of ill-defined meanings, calling forth associations of friendliness and emotional warmth, that the term "empathy" tends to evoke. Here lies indeed a task for the future, challenging self-psychologically informed theoreticians and clinicians to move us toward a deeper understanding of these relationships.

At this point, I can do little more than repeat with greater clarity and preciseness what I may have insufficiently elaborated in the past. First, I will once more underline that when we speak of scientific empathy as a mode of observation and as the definer of a specific field of scientific investigation, we are pointing to a value-neutral *process* (Warren Bennis was, I believe, the first to suggest that we introduce this terminological refinement) or, as I prefer to say, to an *operation*. In other words, whatever term we choose, we must clearly distinguish empathy from the result to which the empathic operation leads. Thus, empathy, as process or operation, can lead us to either correct or incorrect, accurate or inaccurate results — a spectrum of possibilities that is also found in the realm of vicarious extrospection, the analogous operation occasionally used by the nonpsychological sciences.

But how then is this definition of empathy in science related to the popular meaning of the words "empathy" and "empathic"? In popular usage, e.g., in such phrases as "he or she is empathic," it seems to be taken for granted that the operation used by the person in question either led or is leading to correct results or, to say the least, is usually leading to correct results. Experience-distant logic tells us that we should disregard the popular use of the term and, by repeated emphasis, insist that our definition be accepted, at least as far as scientific depth psychology is concerned. And indeed this is what we have been doing and must continue to do. But experience-near reflection bids us not to dismiss these popular statements and biases out of hand, especially when even the scientific mind is easily confused by them. Is there perhaps some psychological truth hidden in the popular usage of this term?

I believe there is. The confusion between the strictly defined meaning that the term "empathy" has for the depth psychologist — that it is an instrument for the acquisition of objective knowledge about the inner life of another person — and the hazy popular meaning of the term evoked by the expression that someone "is an understanding or empathic person," is, I believe, accounted for by the genetic fact that already at the very beginning of our existence we survived and thrived only because a matrix of empathy was immediately established between us and the adult who took care of us. The term "empathy" tends, therefore, to evoke preconscious associations concerning the early relationship between mother and child. For most people this relationship is an exalted one; we need only think of the glorification of the relationship between Mary and baby Jesus, and of its celebration in innumerable works of art in Western culture, to convince ourselves of the truth of this assertion. But why, we must ask ourselves, do we, Freud included, tend to cling to this glorified picture in the face of our knowledge that these early relationships are by no means flawless, that, indeed, many babies are severely traumatized by defective parental empathy and by parental hostility toward them? This is a psychological question that needs to be carefully explored. There is, of course, some truth to the ubiquitous notion — most babies after all do survive. But I think that there is also a large defensive element in the romanticized image; witness the fact that it is often overly sweet and cloying, betraying our unconscious recognition that we must counteract some doubts. It may well be that these doubts pertain to our deepest and most intense fears — fears of not surviving because our basic environment is not in tune with us — and that we try to evade them via the mechanism of denial, buttressed by the defensive emphasis of the positive aspects of the relationship between mother and child. It is in consequence of these maneuvers that we, secondarily, tend to equate empathy in general (which can be correct or incorrect, accurate or inaccurate, present or absent) with perfect empathy (always correct, always accurate, always present).

There is still another point to be made in defense, or at least in explanation, of our tendency to obfuscate the difference between empathy (a value-neutral process that may serve either friendly or destructive aims) and compassionate understanding (a process that prompts us to console a sufferer). I believe that there is, in addition to the genetic connection of which I have spoken, a particle of truth contained in this otherwise basic error. It is indeed psychologically correct to say that under certain circumstances exposure to an enemy whose hostility is fed by selected empathic perceptions is better than exposure to an enemy who destroys without any empathy. The deepest horror man can experience is that of feeling that he is exposed to circumstances in which he is no longer regarded as human by others, i.e., in a milieu that does not even respond with faulty or distorted empathy to his presence. The deepest horror evoked by Nazi destructiveness—the death of anonymous millions in gas chambers—is contained in the concept of "extermination," i.e., of the victim's facing a machinelike destruction, of feeling himself wiped out as if he were a lower animal or a noxious inorganic substance.

Thus, the claim that empathy, even if it is flawed and distorted, has a wholesome effect, that it is, in a broad sense of the word, therapeutic, can by no means be dismissed. For some people, perhaps up to a point for most, the mere exposure to a situation, such as that provided by most forms of psychotherapy, in which one person has committed himself for prolonged periods to extend his "empathic intention" toward another (cf. Kohut, 1959), will have a beneficial effect. And I will only emphasize once more that the nonspecific benefits that accrue from feeling oneself within an empathic human environment apply even in situations in which the empathy that is extended to us is used for inimical purposes—there *are* some chronic fault-finders among psychotherapists—or in which it leads to inaccurate results and faulty responses—e.g., when certain theoretical misconceptions distort our image of a patient.

To summarize the preceding reflections, I need say only that the role of empathy in psychoanalysis is twofold—nonspecific and specific. Its *nonspecific* beneficial effects form a part of the ambience of the psychoanalytic treatment as, indeed, they do in almost all forms of psychotherapy, with the possible exception of those approaches (behavior modification) which try to hold understanding to a minimum and deal with the patient's problems via the manipulation of reflexes. In its *specific* employment in analysis, empathy, purified of any admixture of compassion (consoling) or hostility (fault-finding), is in the service of the analyst's cognition. It is a data-gathering operation, the skillful use of which can, via instruction and experience, be gradually improved, thus allowing the analyst to make increasingly correct, accurate, and relevant observations about the inner life of his analysands. These observations provide the psychoanalytic researcher with the data for the formulation of experience-distant theories which he communicates to his professional colleagues and the psychoanalytic clinician with the data for the dynamic interpretations and genetic reconstructions which he communicates to his patients. I will end my reflections about the use of empathy in analysis by stating once more that they appear to me to be beyond controversy — that if they are open to any reproach, it could only be that they are obvious and trite.

I feel the same way about the claim that the domain of the psychology of complex mental states — by which I refer to psychoanalysis without excluding, sight unseen, other scientific approaches to the same field that may yet arise — is in essence defined when we say that it is that aspect of reality that is accessible via introspection and empathy. Again, this statement seems to me to be beyond controversy and, if anything, all too obvious. It simply asserts that the science of complex mental states, as the science that investigates the inner life of man, is psychology and not chemistry or physics or biology.

Why then the controversy? I do not believe that it is explained by any real ambiguity in our approach to the field — we *are* psychologists. But, although Freud, too, adopted consistently a psychological approach in the explorations he pursued after he had turned from neurophysiology and neurology to the investigation of the field that had been opened by Breuer's and Anna O.'s discovery, he was not always consistent in his statements. While on many occasions he spoke directly and unambiguously of psychoanalysis as psychology, he was never able to give up completely the thought habits of his first professional commitments, and, as a result, he elaborated some of his theories within a syncretistic framework — put less kindly, we might also speak of a mésalliance — that has come to be known as psychobiology.

In the web of tenets and theories called metapsychology, the crucial issue in this context is the concept of the drive, a concept which, if understood biologically, introduces all kinds of confusion and ambiguity. Still, we have all learned to live with these inconsistencies and are able to close our eyes to them. And, although such seemingly unobjectionable statements as "the mind (or the psychic apparatus) processes (or tames or sublimates) the drives" should disconcert us since in the middle of the sentence we are suddenly pitchforked from one level of discourse to another, we take them calmly because we know approximately what message they attempt to convey; we do not fuss about the fact that, so long as we consider the drives as part of our biological equipment, the controlling mechanisms of these drives could only be provided by our brain and its functions but not by our mind. While I believe that there is a way out of this dilemma, namely, to derive the drive concept from the experience of drivenness and thus provide it with a purely psychological meaning (Kohut, 1959), I have hardly ever felt the need to exert myself on behalf of absolute consistency in this respect. Correspondingly, my emphasis on the basic position of empathy did not interfere, for 20 years after I had pointed out the theory-defining role of this operation, with my acceptance of the central position of the drives and of their primacy in theory. That I ultimately (1977a) began to see drive manifestations as secondary is, therefore, unrelated to my conviction that introspection and empathy are our basic tools of observation or that analysis is defined by the fact that it deals with the data that are accessible to observation only through introspection and empathy. The reasons for my assertion that drives, psychologically conceived, occur secondary to the break-up of the self are empirical. I advanced this theory not to serve as a further step away from the inconsistencies of psychobiology, but because I believe that it fits the data of observation while the theory of drive primacy does not.

Speaking in more general terms, I believe, in retrospect, that there are two seemingly contradictory reasons that accounted for my increasing dissatisfaction with classical metapsychology and the ego psychological extension of the tripartite model.

The first reason was that there seemed to be little connection between, on the one hand, the theories which for more than 15 years I taught to my students at the Institute in a two-year course on metapsychology and, on the other hand, the clinical experiences they encountered. I did what many of my colleagues did and undoubtedly still do: I revised the classical theories here and there and twisted their meaning to give them relevance to clinical work. But I know that, as the years went by, I became increasingly uncomfortable about my equivocations, without yet having the courage to speak openly to others about my problems or even to tell myself that something was wrong. It would be a challenging and fascinating task to investigate the nature of the gap that separates classical theory and our day-to-day experiences in the clinical situation. But I will not try to address this topic here, not only because I believe that the preceding remarks have already struck a familiar chord in many of my colleagues but also because their further elaboration would not be directly related to a critique of the theories of self psychology. The other discomfort that I felt increasingly about the body of classical theory was that, by illuminating starkly one aspect of man while paying scant heed to another, it distorted the analyst's perception, both as a clinician and as an investigator. In the first role it distorted his perception of his patients and in the second his perception of the personalities that he scrutinized outside the clinical setting and of the events, e.g., in history, that he sought to explain. Psychoanalytic theory, as I saw it, was not adequate to deal with some of the most important dimensions of the human condition.

As I mentioned earlier, certain critics of self psychology applaud our clinical work but reject our theories. To them, I would reply that theory and clinical work are too interwoven to allow for such a separation, and that the theoretical system which the analyst espouses affects the mode in which he conducts his analytic work — par excellence the concept of mental health which, by shaping the goals that he thinks his patient can reach, influences his assessment of the progress that his analysands are making and the point at which he can consider them ready for termination.

It will not be surprising to hear that I associate such theoretical issues with a value system that is contained in the seemingly objective statements of classical psychoanalytic theory. The principal tenets of classical analysis which are the carriers of these values and which, subtly but effectively, lead the analyst toward a specific value-laden stance vis-à-vis his patient are: (1) the theory of the primacy of the drive and the theory of drive taming that is correlated to it; and (2) the theory that there is a single line of development which leads from narcissism to object love.

If we consider the drives—primitive (pregenital) sensuality and primitive destructiveness; man's untamed, uncivilized animal nature—as basic, then we will consider drive taming—the gradual domestication of the animal in us—to be our task. It is the task of the individual in psychotherapy, reluctantly undertaken but eventuating in partial success with the aid of the analyst who makes conscious via defense interpretations the patient's rejected animal part. It is also the task of society, reluctantly undertaken (cf. Freud, 1930), and, again, as with individual psychotherapy, leading to only a partial success (cf. Freud, 1933). Must it not be expected that this conception of man will determine the climate that prevails in therapy? It does, and, however mitigated by the humane forbearance of most analysts, it is impressed upon the patient and determines the goals that the patient, guiltily, strives to reach.

And the theory that there is a single line of development leading from narcissism to object love? How, again, can it help but color the outlook of the analyst who has made it his own? And, furthermore, how can it help but determine the formulation of the therapeutic aim? Let me at this point take up briefly a rejoinder—I would expect analogous objections to my remarks regarding the theory of drive primacy—that I now expect to hear from some of my colleagues. Most analysts, I will be told, will behave toward their patients as if these theories did not exist. And it will be said, with specific reference to the theory of the single-line development from narcissism to object love, that all analysts will act in accordance with their conviction that healthy forms of heightened self-esteem are welcome and are not to be considered as fixations on the infantile and immature. I would reply that if our observations demonstrate to us that there is a line of development from immature to mature narcissism, then our theoretical formulations should reflect this fact, i.e., we should openly and unambiguously discard the theory of a single line of development and drop the morality-soaked claim that normal development is characterized by the transformation of narcissism (with a pejorative connotation) into object love (considered as a praiseworthy developmental achievement).

I do not oppose these theories—the theory of drive primacy and drive taming and the theory of a single line of development—on theoretical grounds. They are not only internally consistent but also in harmony with the traditional Judeo-Christian value system of the Western World. But they do not fit the data about human life that we in fact obtain—at least not all of them, especially insofar as they concern that aspect of man we refer to as Tragic Man.

Theory cannot be judged by internal criteria alone. Although, undoubtedly, the beauty and inner consistency of a theory are not only aesthetically pleasing but suggestive of validity, the decisive questions—whether there is correspondence between the theory and the events in nature it claims to reflect; whether our mastery over the events in nature which it purports to explain is increased by its use—have to be answered through observation. It is one thing, however, for a scientist to affirm abstractly that he will always assign the role of ultimate arbiter to observation; it is quite another thing, at least under certain circumstances, for him actually to utilize observation in this way. Once theories have been with us for a long time, for example, and we have adjusted to living with them, we are prone to close our eyes not only to internal inconsistencies but also, and especially, to lack of correspondence with the data we gather. Theoretical systems tend to become rigid, take on the quality of dogma, become imbued with moral qualities, and, instead of being the helpmates of the observer, stand more and more in his way, interfering with his ability to perceive formerly unrecognized configurations in the aspect of the world under investigation, or to alter his understanding of configurations that were formerly misunderstood. As you can see, I am stressing a certain point, namely, that in certain phases of scientific progress, specifically when a new viewpoint allows us to see new aspects of the field that we investigate, theories become secondary and fluid: they are devised ad hoc and are open to change—the accumulation of new data and the drafting of experience-near formulations that delineate their interconnection take precedence.

This is the stage self psychology is at now and the stage, we hope, it will remain at for some time to come. It is not theory that will, for example, tell us who is healthy or cured—it is health and cure, however naively perceived at first, that we try to explain in the experience-distant, carefully considered terms for which we usually reserve the name "theory." If we see that great works are created, great thoughts thought, and great deeds done, under conditions that our established theory considers unhealthy, then we should question the theory, try to understand whether it indeed fits the facts, and, if not, reshape it to accommodate better the data. If, to continue with our example, we recognize—as we do—that some of the greatest achievements of man occur in settings in which the gigantic achiever, during one of those "stellar hours of mankind," to quote Stefan Zweig, is intensely involved with a self-object, often perceived in archaic distortion, with whom he has merged, then we should question the encompassing validity of the theory that gives scientific respectability to the, in essence, moral tenet that the move from dependence to independence, from narcissism to object love, is *the* move toward health and maturity. And once we begin to take a more relativistic attitude toward the aforementioned moral-theoretical tenet, we necessarily begin to introduce a deeply significant shift in our attitude in the clinical setting and in the way we approach the investigative field outside our office.

Freud's relationship to Fliess—his overestimation of Fliess during the years when he made his most daring steps forward into new territory; and his realistic reassessment and subsequent dropping of Fliess after he had made his decisive discoveries—may serve as an example of what I have in mind. But it is not only Freud; there are innumerable others in whom we can observe this phenomenon we characterize as a "transference of creativity." There is Nietzsche's attachment to the idealized Wagner during the time when he prepared himself for the great outpouring of his most original works. And there is O'Neill's lifelong, desperate search for the selfobject that would satisfy his need for perfect "mirroring," for that "gleam in the mother's eye" which his drug-addicted mother had not provided for him. When he finally found it in his third wife, he was able to create his best works: not only *Mourning Becomes Electra,* which brought him the most notable public recognition of his life, but also, and especially, the two deeply stirring plays in which, by drawing on his own experiences, he depicted the central existential problem of modern man. I am referring to *The Iceman Cometh* and *Long Day's Journey into Night,* to my mind the greatest dramas of our age. And let me add to these examples of scientific and artistic creativeness the heroes of another sphere: those survivors of the concentration camps who did not lose their humanness during their dehumanizing ordeal because they felt themselves connected with personified political or religious idealized figures (cf. Matussek, 1971). During the years in the camps they remained human beings—sharing their rations, for example—and when they eventually returned to freedom they were relatively free of the permanent psychological damage sustained by almost all other survivors. And then there were those touching isolated resisters to Nazi tyranny, standing up alone or in small groups (such as Jaegerstetter in Austria and the Scholls in Munich), who, again, were supported by a feeling of merger with personified ideals. They gave over their total selves to these ideals during the time when they performed some of the most awe-inspiring acts of courage of our age. They had prophetic dreams in which God spoke to them—they were undoubtedly not "realistic," "mature," or "independent" in the conventional sense of those terms—and the support that sustained them came not from loving "objects" but from their deep involvement in the narcissistic dynamics of self-selfobject relationships.

Mind you, I am not advocating that the theoretical structure of depth psychology should be changed in order to be in harmony with the experiences of only the very greatest of men. But these great ones furnish us with clues that aid our observation of ordinary people. Once we begin to shed the old bias, we can see in everyday life, among average human beings, the same sequence of phenomena—a search for selfobject support and improvement of functioning if it is found—that we observe in the life of some very exceptional individuals. The ordinary person too, must have sustaining selfobjects in order to be active and productive. We need mirroring acceptance, the merger with ideals, the sustaining presence of others like us, throughout our lives.

And what is the conclusion that is to be drawn from these experience-near insights, if indeed it still needs to be spelled out? It is that we must have the courage to alter some of the experience-distant theories that we have inherited so that they fit the facts that we observe and the experience-near meaning that we derive from them. And if, to close the circle, we apply our revised theories to the clinical situation, we can say, *in nuce,* that we have come to see that our patients must not be educated to dispense with selfobjects but be allowed to learn the lesson that their specific pathological childhood had prevented them from learning: that one can never be completely autonomous and independent, that the self can live only in a matrix of selfobjects, and that it is not immature and contemptible to search for them and to elicit their empathic support.

The contributions to "Self Psychology and the Concept of Health" confront us with the question of whether, and if so how, self psychology can bring us to a better understanding of normal mental functioning than that provided by traditional psychoanalysis. There are two reasons, one general and one specific, why I consider this topic to be significant: (1) the investigation of the essence of mental health should to my mind occupy the center of *any* psychology of complex mental states; and (2) self psychology, in particular, especially in its therapeutic application, has indeed been characterized by an inclination to focus more strongly on the healthy aspects of mental functioning — in the clinical situation, for example, on inherent developmental potentialities whose presence within a web of seemingly pathological manifestations we often point out to our patients — than do other approaches, including that of traditional psychoanalysis. All the contributors to this section of the book were fully aware of these points; they emerged with particular clarity in Paul Ornstein's paper, which addressed itself directly to the task of defining mental health in self psychological terms.

It is indeed an important task to explore the meaning of mental health, and to ask, specifically, what self psychology can contribute to our understanding of the nature of this desirable state and of the means by which it can be attained. Let me, first of all, affirm again that self psychology, by viewing the infantile demands which emerge from repression not only as a source of disease and malfunction but also as a wellspring of health and productivity, is in a particularly good position to increase our comprehension of mental health. It is worth mentioning, furthermore, that, in its contributions to the understanding of mental health, self psychology has not restricted itself to offering descriptive criteria —Freud's disarmingly ingenuous definition (as cited by Erikson, 1950, p. 229) of psychological health as the capacity to work and love is a well-known example of such a limited approach—but sets itself the goal of explaining psychological health in structural and dynamic terms. As self psychology proceeded on this road, however, we came to recognize—leading us to significant insights, I believe, which I will discuss shortly—that, in its behavioral manifestations, psychological health cannot be described in terms that would have universal validity, that our statements regarding psychological health always apply only to the specific individual under scrutiny. What kind of mental health can Mrs. A. achieve, we will ask, or what can mental health mean with regard to Miss B.?[1]

Still, since we are not content to remain on the descriptive level and strive to define mental health in general terms, we must respond to the question of what all the individual forms of mental health have in common.

The self psychological answer is that we should speak of mental health when—via favorable life circumstances, especially in a person's childhood; through analysis; or, without therapeutic assistance, as the result of spontaneous effort—at least one sector in the personality has established itself in which ambitions, skills and talents, and idealized goals form an unbroken, functioning continuum (cf. the extensive discussion of the issue of mental health with regard to Mr. M. in *The Restoration of the Self* [1977a, pp. 6–54; especially pp. 53–54]). The ambitions, the skills and

---

[1]Up to this point our attitude vis-à-vis the problem of mental health is similar to the "multiple criterion approach" suggested by Jahoda (1958). As Hartmann pointed out (1960, especially p. 245), this is the approach that is most congenial to psychoanalysis.

talents, and the ideals of different people have, however, different aims and contents. Furthermore, the functional preponderance of the one or the other of these constituents of the self varies from person to person, both with regard to the choice of the leading constituent and with regard to the degree of dominance of any single constituent. It is easy to understand, therefore, that under these circumstances the behavioral manifestations of mental health vary widely in different individuals and that in the case of certain successfully functioning personality organizations — again we think of the playfully creative — it is not even possible always to ascertain the presence of the capacities to work and love, which were Freud's telltale indicators and baseline criteria of mental health. But Freud's powerfully simple statement was not a scientific definition. It was a moral pronouncement, the expression of his credo about the values that should guide each person throughout his existence. As the expression of his personal value judgment, however, it left no room for the possibility that others might have to invoke different means and follow different paths to the fulfillment of their particular nuclear aims and goals.

If the conclusions about mental health, as summarized in Ornstein's paper and emphasized in the preceding remarks, succeed in highlighting the hypothesis that it is the establishment of at least one functioning sector in the personality that provides each individual with *his* kind of mental health — a functional pattern to which, as I half-jokingly and half-seriously like to say, each person becomes addicted — then I believe that a good deal has been accomplished. Let me stress immediately, however, that our satisfaction must be tempered by the realization that the statements that have been made so far are incomplete since they focus only on the endopsychic substance of mental health. The claim that a person has achieved mental health when he has established a complete functional sector in his personality will surely be objected to, especially by the sociologically oriented psychologist, on the grounds that it disregards the social matrix in which we live. And yet, we can reply, although our definition may seem loose because it encompasses many variants of mental health and does not specify that the result of these various sectorial functional patterns must be useful to society or at least acceptable to it, we still believe that it constitutes a significant contribution to the psychological grasp of the nature of mental health. A psychologically healthy person, we may say, will live out the particular design that is laid down in the center of his self and achieve his particular nuclear productivity or creativity whatever the attitude of society to his actions may be, whether accepting or rejecting, approving or disapproving. To reassure those who might feel uncomfortable in view of the fact that our definition does not contain any reference to a specific moral code, I will add that I have become convinced—not as the result of abstract reflection but on the basis of clinical experience—that the creative-productive efforts brought about by the freeing of the nuclear patterns of a self will lead to socially beneficial results. I am convinced, in other words, that wholesome psychological development (via mirrored ambitions, alter-ego support for skills, and merger with idealized greatness)—whether successfully completed in childhood or, belatedly, in the course of analysis—lays down functional patterns (the nuclear self) which, in adulthood, lead to actions that benefit the social environment and will, sooner or later, be accepted by it. Immediate acceptance cannot be the criterion. In view of the fact that leading social values change, mere adaptation to a particular social environment can hardly be considered the most desirable result of a psychological cure. I think, in other words, and I know that most of my colleagues will agree with me here, that the capacity to go it alone, even for protracted periods, while one attempts to impress a hostile environment with the truths that one believes to have found or while one attempts to carry out the actions that one believes to be in the service of one's convictions, is not a sign of psychological imbalance but of inner strength.

Two other secondary but still important issues emerge from the contributions to the section on self psychology and health: (1) the question whether in our theorizing—in our theoretical formulations about the sectorial mode of functioning in mental health, for example—we should move away from and ultimately discard the traditional imagery of a psychological "space" (and of energic currents active within this space), i.e., whether we should cease to borrow our analogies from the field of classical mechanics, and (2) the question, raised by Robert Stolorow, whether the emergence and growth of psychoanalytic self psychology at this point in time is not an indication that the preeminence of science and its values has passed its peak and that we are witnessing a movement toward a renewed emphasis on humanism and humanistic values.

I admit right away that I am strongly inclined to accept the substance of the views that are implied by the first of the two above-mentioned questions. It seems that we might do well to replace the framework of Freudian metapsychology, whose imagery and thought patterns are derived from classical physics, with the new theoretical framework provided by 20th-century physics and its more advanced patterns of thought. What little I know about modern physics, in particular about the revolutionary conceptions with regard to the nature of matter and the behavior of small particles introduced by Planck, Bohr, and Heisenberg, does indeed seem much more closely akin to the findings and formulations of self psychology than the conceptions of classical mechanics with which Freud was familiar and which influenced the particular analogies he later invoked to formulate his depth-psychological findings in experience-distance terms.

But having expressed my agreement, I must now emphasize that, at least at this point in the development of self psychology, I do not believe that issues concerning fine points of theory formation should be allowed to occupy the forefront of our interest. I believe, in other words—and I admit that this opinion might well be unduly influenced by my personal predilections—that self psychology should at this time in its development emphasize observation and experience-near formulation, and not reflection and experience-distant theory. Since self psychology is still in an early phase of its development, it behooves us to devote our energies to the exploration of the new, or at any rate comparatively unexplored, psychological territory into which we are beginning to move. The task of refining our formulations should await the time when the flow of new discoveries, i.e., of new insights on the experience-near level, begins to ebb.

I am aware of the fact that there are many cogent arguments with which one could oppose the position that I am taking here. In particular, it could be argued that I underestimate the degree to which progress in science depends on the alternation between, or simultaneous progress in, observation and theory, and that we not only need observations in order to be able to form theories but also need theories in order to be able to observe. I am convinced of the truth of these statements and I have no doubt concerning the value of efforts to improve our theoretical formulations. Anyone who has studied the conception of the bipolar self should realize that I alternate between direct clinical observation in the transference (concerning the child's turning from a disappointing selfobject to a less disappointing one) and experience-distant theorizing (the dynamic-structural formulation of the clinical findings in terms of a shift from the functional preponderance of one pole of the self to that of the other one, a formulation in turn related to the concept of compensatory structures). But—and again I admit that I am expressing only a personal preference that can perhaps lay no claim to broader validity—the conceptual instruments I utilize when I attempt to lift my findings to the level of experience-distant theory has not been one of my primary concerns.

The reason for my comparative indifference to the selection of conceptual tools that I employ resides in the fact that I am at present interested in theory primarily as a means of communication. If the metaphor of an electrical tension arc from one pole of the self to the other serves the purpose of communicating my meaning about mental health on a more experience-distant level (i.e., beyond the description of this or that individual clinical instance), and if the image of a sectorial spatial continuum within the self in which the energic flow takes place achieves the same goal, then I am satisfied and do not ask myself whether analogies borrowed from the physics of Planck would be more adequate than the electrical analogies in a Newtonian space of which I am availing myself.

Still, I realize that good theory is not only an important means of communication, but that it can also serve a quite different purpose: it can be a powerful tool in the pursuit of research. Indeed, a valid mode of research does exist that proceeds in the opposite direction from the mode that I am describing. It begins with experience-distant reflection, leads secondarily to confirmatory discoveries via observation, and ends on the level of experience-near thought, e.g., with insights in the clinical field. Some of the great discoveries in physics have been made via this route. Biology and psychology, however, and especially the psychology of complex mental states, do not seem to me to lend themselves readily to this approach. Be this as it may, however, I would not contradict the claim that my mode of investigation in which the clinical situation remains the *fons et origo* of my theories might be inappropriate for those whose predominant style of thinking is different from mine. Indeed, I myself very occasionally make a forward move by reversing the direction of my activity, i.e., by allowing experience-distant speculation to guide the focus of my observations. There are certainly many depth-psychological researchers for whom this latter procedure is the dominant one.[2] Which is the better of the two roads? Although my personal preference is not in doubt here, we will probably do well to leave this question unanswered. Even though I have almost always taken the road that leads from observation to theory, my choice was not made in deference to some methodological dogma; it was pragmatic. If, to return specifically to the earlier suggestion, anyone who now works in the field of self psychology should in his investigations be influenced by the discoveries and methodology of modern physics; if he obtains specific leads for his research aims from modern physics; and if — and this is the crucial point — this stimulation and the correlated mode of investigative procedure enable him to make discoveries or to enlarge our knowledge within the new territory of self psychology, then I will unhesitatingly discard my bias and welcome his approach. Until this happens, however, until, in other words, there is

[2]Hartmann's conclusion (1950, p. 134), for example, that the analysand's angry response to an attack on his resistances demonstrates that internal drive control is maintained by countercathexes that are derived from aggressive energies may be taken as a specimen of this reverse-order procedure. It challenges the clinician to test a theory-based hypothesis whenever he observes the phenomenon that the hypothesis claims to have explained.

evidence that theoretical reflection does in fact lead the self psychologist to new clinical findings or that it enables him to perceive in a nonclinical area psychological configurations that had formerly been overlooked, I think that we should remain faithful to the approach that has been so rewarding to us up to now: prolonged empathic immersion into psychological material; the apperception—analogous to the various images we "see" in clouds or in Rorschach inkblots—of as many alternative configurations as we can derive from the data that our empathic immersion has provided for us; further observation to determine which of the closures, if any, will stand the test of time (e.g., which of the alternative clinical hypotheses is supported by subsequent clinical material); and ultimately the formulation in theoretical terms of that particular product of empathic understanding which has proved to be the most correct and accurate for the purpose of communication and with the aim of fitting the single experience-near finding into a preexisting, broader, experience-distant context.[3]

I will demonstrate the procedure most of us follow by giving you a more or less concrete account of a specific instance. My specimen concerns the investigation of the experience of a drop in self-esteem. How does the self psychologist investigate this crucial event in man's inner life? He will try to grasp its essence by immersing himself, over and over again, introspectively, via empathic participation in the inner life of his patients, and through

---

[3]In looking for comparisons with the observational attitudes and problems of other disciplines, it might well be maintained that it would be more fruitful for us, with particular reference to our research in the nonclinical areas, to familiarize ourselves with the observational attitudes and problems addressed by the protagonists of philosophical historicism (such as Vico, Herder, Ranke, and Dilthey) than with those of modern physics. It must be stated, however, that although the psychoanalyst in general and the psychoanalytic self psychologist in particular would agree with the historicist premise that every moment in life is unique and that we must cherish every one of the innumerable forms and nuances of human experience, it remains the specific task of science—and self psychology, as I will explain further shortly, is a branch of science, not of the humanities—to establish specific recurrent relationships between the data derived from observation, such as the discovery of self psychology that certain thwarted developmental needs of childhood are regularly revived in the psychoanalytic situation in the specific, definable form of the various selfobject transferences.

thought experiments, in the experience under scrutiny—par excellence, of course, in the clinical situation since this is the field of his greatest expertise. He will, in particular, survey the transference antecedents and, having determined the cause of the analysand's reaction, will try to think himself into analogous experiences of early life that were the prototypes of the current events and established the patient's specific sensitivity. The patient had felt secure in the belief that the analyst would always respond to him with reliable understanding—but then, all of a sudden, the analyst gives him an interpretation which shows that he is quite out of tune with the patient. The child was carried empathically by the omnipotent selfobject and felt safe in its merger with it, felt itself a part of this powerful figure and suffused by its calmness and strength, but suddenly was dropped by the selfobject. Whether the sensation of being dropped by the selfobject was caused by an actual physical "dropping" of the child (instead of the child's being put down with empathic gentleness) or by an experience only more or less distantly related to the sensation of being dropped and to the emotions that follow such an occurrence, the child experienced serious disappointment at the time. Oscillating between efforts to grasp the essence of the patient's reactions in the clinical situation and efforts to grasp the defect in the parental personality that created the patient's intensified vulnerability in this area, the analyst tries to define the experiential core of the devastating emotional event we refer to as a severe drop in self-esteem. It is only after he has done this many times—concerning himself (via introspection) and concerning a great variety of patients (via empathy) —that he tries to formulate the data of introspective-empathic observation in experience-distant terms, employing any suitable analogy that (a) will ease communication, (b) can be fitted into the broader framework of theories that have been established previously by workers who share his basic observational stance, and (c) promises to provide him with clues for further creative observation and discovery.

In view of the fact that, as I said before, I consider the formal aspects of our theories to be of only secondary importance at this point in the development of self psychology, it does not bother me to see that our metaphoric images will sometimes show traces of the experience-near understanding that preceded them. It is not the creation of an internally consistent system of purified abstractions that we are trying to achieve; we devise theories that are helpful to us as we continue to pursue our research.

But to return to Stolorow's point that I mentioned earlier. Can we, to paraphrase him, consider self psychology as a participant in a specific trend discernible in our time; does the self psychologist subscribe to a doctrine that supports modern man's attempt to move away from the predominance of science, and toward a new emphasis on humanism and humanistic values?

Let me say first that Stolorow's remark struck immediately a sympathetic chord in me; in view of my lifelong interest in and commitment to humanistic pursuits, I felt instinctively attracted by it. Still, on second thought, I have to admit that it would be very difficult to judge whether such a movement from science toward humanism is actually taking place and, if so, whether self psychology should be seen as part of this newly patterned cultural weave. We are too much the children of our own time to come to a reliable judgment concerning our generation, too closely involved to assess its basic condition and the direction of its development. But the issue raised by Stolorow can, and should, be approached from a different side. Since we are not simply the dispassionate observers of distant cultural changes but are deeply affected by such changes in the present, we will choose sides and try to influence the course of events. Seen in this light, the question becomes: do we want self psychology to assist modern man in abandoning his near-total commitment to the preeminence of science? Do we want self psychology to help him regain humanistic meanings and to provide him with a broader basis than that provided by the scientific view of the world whose ultimate value and command is that we not falsify our perception of reality, even if the result is painful to us?

In responding to Stolorow's moving assessment of the role of self psychology within the framework of the foregoing questions, I will say that I, personally, do indeed believe that, however important the goals of science are — let us call them unclouded vision and knowledge expansion—I do not think that they deserve to be placed at the very top of the hierarchy of values that are to guide modern man. We should strive to establish realism and the capacity to see truth undisguisedly as ego functions; we should not consider them primarily as values anymore. Moreover, knowledge in general, and knowledge concerning our psychological functions in particular, should be considered by us as tools in the service of our overriding goal—the goal of achieving a productive-creative, fulfilling life and of assisting others to do likewise. Still, while I am personally in sympathy with the shift in value-dominance that I outlined here, I am reluctant to commit self psychology to the service of such a move from science to humanism, and I do not wish its functions to be seen in this light.

Self psychology, to my mind, is science—a valid branch of science. While, when viewed in a broader context, all sciences should be regarded as tools in the service of man's goal of attaining a fulfilling life, and while, as I said before, I am convinced of the fact that psychoanalytic self psychology can serve this end with great effectiveness, it does so as a science, not as a branch of the humanities. True, it is interested in the psychological significance of man's activities and commitments in certain areas whose investigation, before the advent of self psychology, had been the prerogative of religious, philosophic, and humanistic thinkers and scholars. It bears repeating, however, that in its investigations of man's religious and philosophical preoccupations and of his artistic pursuits, self psychology does not abandon the essential stance of science; its methods and aims remain the methods and aims of science.

I have two, to a certain extent contradictory, reactions to Evelyne Schwaber's case presentation. On the one hand, I am filled with admiration for the way in which Schwaber succeeded in giving a fine portrait not only of the complex personality of her gifted patient but also—an achievement which I consider even more remarkable—of the friendly, development-enhancing atmosphere, which, in contrast to the guilt-producing ambience that would have been created by a rejection of the analysand's sensitivity and demandingness (conceptualized as a retreat from conflictual object love rather than as a stunting of mature forms of narcissism), characterizes the clinical situation in an analysis that is conducted along self psychological lines. On the other hand, however, I realize that even some well-meaning listeners to Schwaber's report who, on the whole, feel in sympathy with self psychology, would not be able to grasp her message, and would, in particular, come away with the conclusion that, although the therapist was undoubtedly a warm-hearted, friendly individual, the patient had not been confronted with his problems, had fled into health, had not been analyzed or, at the least, that his analysis had been badly incomplete.

I must admit that I am not able to arrive at a definitive judgment about the outcome of this analysis: my single hearing of the case material and of the analytic process does not allow me to come to a solid conclusion concerning the question of whether a good analytic result was achieved or whether the analysis remained incomplete. But I can say that the impressions I obtained do not rule out the possibility of a good analytic result, and, moreover, I am inclined to believe that a good result was indeed achieved.

With these statements, however, I have gone as far as I can go with regard to my judgment concerning the analysis under scrutiny. I know that it is very difficult to form a reliable picture of the personality of a patient and of an analytic process from a case presentation, even if one is fully familiar with the analyst's theoretical point of view and his basic clinical stance. And the difficulties are compounded when the analyst who reports his impressions has been working within a clinical and conceptual framework with which the listeners have familiarized themselves exclusively through reading, however conscientiously they may have studied the new outlook. Only prolonged and regular consultations concerning an ongoing analysis with someone who has worked with the new self psychological viewpoint for many years will allow the great majority of analysts to put the new theories and their clinical application to a fair test. That there are exceptions to this rule, that there are colleagues who, despite the fact that they have been used to seeing things in the classical, conflict-oriented way, respond positively to the study of self psychological writings with the feeling that they have always known preconsciously what self psychologists have to say, is a not altogether infrequent phenomenon whose explanation it would be interesting to pursue some day.

All these reflections are small consolation. We all wish that we knew a way to present clinical material so unambiguously that the reader's conclusions would be inescapable. But since, unfortunately, such a way does not seem to exist, I will now, at least temporarily, abandon the attempt to demonstrate the clinical effectiveness of self psychology by proving beyond doubt that the analysis conducted by Schwaber indeed focused on the patient's basic pathology and achieved a cure via structural change. Instead I will do the next best thing in order to be of assistance to those analytic colleagues who are seriously trying to evaluate our therapeutic approach by commenting on certain obstacles that make it difficult for us—and I use the world "us" advisedly since even those who have been working with the self psychological outlook for years experience these difficulties—to set aside preconceived notions and thus put the new viewpoint to a valid test.

I am approaching my task with a good deal of initial hesitation because I know that, in making my first point, I will not be able to avoid giving offense to some of my colleagues, however much I might try to enlist their friendly cooperation. Still, since I do not see another way, I will take the bull by the horns and state that for many of my colleagues, in fact for some of the very best of them, for whom I have the greatest respect and admiration, there arises at times a conflict between, on the one hand, their emotional commitment to analysis and to the image of Freud, i.e., to the body of knowledge and morality that psychoanalysis and the image of Freud represent for them, and, on the other hand, their emotional commitment to being healers and therapists.

Having made this rough-hewn statement, I will add that no analyst, however strong the pressure exerted on him by his commitment to Freud and to the tenets of analysis might be, would ever allow any harm to befall a patient who cannot conform to the demands of classical analysis. Such an analyst would under certain circumstances simply say that a patient cannot be analyzed, that he needs other means of assistance, and would then either provide the appropriate form of therapy himself or send the patient to someone else able to provide it. Furthermore, and more importantly, these colleagues would surely reply that it is artificial and misleading to create the impression that such a conflict between loyalty to analysis and loyalty to analysands could ever exist. We are loyal to the tenets of classical analysis, they would say, because via this loyalty we protect ourselves against the temptation of straying from the only path that will ultimately lead the analysand to the best resolution of his ills, as we show him the way, however great his resistances, toward the painful acceptance of reality concerning both his own limitations and the extent to which he can expect others to fulfill his wishes and comply with his demands. Still, while I recognize the inner consistency of these arguments, and while I respect the loyalty to analytic ideals that lies behind them, my original judgment remains unaltered. I thus affirm again that the classical analyst, despite the loosening of the theoretical constraints achieved by ego psychology (see, e.g., Hartmann, 1960), leans in general more strongly on the tenets spelled out or implied by Freud's teachings (in particular as concerns that amalgam of scientific theory and morality that is evoked by such terms as "knowledge expansion," "ego dominance," "facing reality," etc.),[4] while the self psychologist, though he, too, tends to subscribe to a specific hierarchy of values (cf. Kohut, 1973a), is more inclined to consider a specific patient's personality structure and his kind of health potential as providing the yardstick by which to measure the success or the failure of a psychoanalytic treatment.

I must stress that my impression that the self psychologist pays greater heed to variations in individual potentialities than does the classical analyst would not imply per se that the classical analyst is more theory-oriented while the self psychologist puts his empathic contact with the patient first. The self psychologist, too,

---

[4]See in this context the later discussion (pp. 528–530) of the role which the training analysis may play in mobilizing irrational layers of Freud-idealization in the analyst and in keeping them active after the termination of the analysis.

tries to formulate his findings in experience-distant terms, just like the classical analyst; and the classical analyst, too, however strong his commitment to the teachings of Freud, must be in empathic contact with his patient during therapy, just like the self psychological analyst. While the intensity with which theories are defended and applied is influenced by emotional factors, the essential difference between the classical-analytic and the self psychological approach is determined by the differences in the basic outlook that guides the investigators, by the particular data that each holds to be of paramount significance, and by the kind of theory that each ultimately derives from them. An outlook that puts the drives in the center of the personality will use a model in which the quality of drive processing becomes the yardstick with which to measure therapeutic success; an outlook that puts the self in the center of the personality will use a model in which the degree of fulfillment of the basic program of the self (the nuclear self) becomes this yardstick. To be more specific, the latter model is that of the bipolar self, and in our assessment of health and cure we ask the question whether (and, if so, how broadly and firmly) at least one sector of the personality has been established in which an unbroken continuum (from one pole of the self to the other, i.e., from [1] ambitions, via [2] skills and talents, to [3] ideals) of functioning self structure enables the individual to carry out the basic program of his specific nuclear self.

I cannot, unfortunately, elaborate further the important topics to which I was led in commenting on Schwaber's case report. I will, however, consider two of the important discussions, one by Miles Shore, the other by Sheldon Bach, that followed her paper.

I have little to say with regard to Shore's modestly framed but significant remarks, except to express my great pleasure at hearing his objective, scholarly testimony concerning the applicability of our basic findings in the area that lies beyond the bounds of the basic rule. That he could show us the usefulness of the self psychological discoveries in the setting with which he is familiar in his daily work — administrative and organizational tasks performed in a large university — gave a concreteness to his descriptions that is often lacking when we examine the topics that are farther removed from the self psychological observer, those concerning history, social and political action, art, and literature.

I must respond more extensively to the issues introduced by Sheldon Bach, since he raised questions that have been asked, directly and indirectly, by many of our colleagues, though, unfortunately, not always in the objectively inquiring manner that characterized his approach.

Before attempting to identify the crucial general issues that Bach raised in his discussion concerning a specific, pivotal moment in the process of the analysis of Schwaber's patient, we will look at the concrete — or, rather, to show at once the cards of my argument, the *seemingly* concrete — data on which Bach focused and which he interpreted differently from Schwaber. I cannot claim with certainty that I have fully and accurately grasped Bach's meaning, but I believe I am not far off the mark when I say that Bach felt that we may be sensitive, responsive, and helpful therapists with valuable clinical insights while our general statements (Bach had in mind our experience-near clinical formulations) are in error.

I must confess that, after pondering Bach's remarks, I feel that his reinterpretations of the clinical material in classical terms were open to the very reproach that he, unjustifiably, I believe, directed at Schwaber's self psychological interpretations, and that I feel this way not because of any contentious desire to turn the tables on him but because I am convinced that the facts justify my opinion. Bach presented us with a superb, and for me unexpected, clinical insight. His critique of our clinical theory, however, is, to me, ill-founded; it is an outgrowth of the fact that he has not sufficiently reevaluated the limits of the applicability of the traditional belief in the universal clinical relevance of the oedipal configurations in the light of the significant new clinical data self psychology has furnished over the past decade.

The powerful clinical insight to which I thought Bach's remarks led us was that Mr. R.'s personality had suddenly jelled in a significant way during his preadolescence and that a repetition of this decisive developmental step had taken place at a crucial point in the analysis, this time accompanied by insight and thus more reliably established than had been the case originally. This developmental step moved the patient into a working-through process resulting in structural changes and thus promises to provide the basis for continued mental health in adult life. As I see it, Bach, led by the intuition of the seasoned and gifted clinician he obviously is, had correctly focused on the pivotal moment of development and analytic process. Instead of recognizing, however, that a crucial developmental need had been reactivated in the analysis, that a fragmented self had once more reached out for the opportunity to become cohesive with the aid of a guiding ideal, he was, in my view, misled by his inclination to order the data of his observation in accordance with oedipal patterns. He thus interpreted the patient's experiences at this decisive point in his analysis as being due to unresolved conflicts, as an outgrowth of the raising to consciousness of formerly unconscious *defensive* psychic structures rather than being due, as we would judge, to incompleted development, to be interpreted as conscious manifestations of the formerly unconscious hope that he would now achieve a firming of certain nuclear *compensatory* structures that would provide cohesion to his self and meaning to his life.

As I see it then, Bach drew our attention to a fact that had heretofore been overlooked, or, at the very least, insufficiently appreciated. He provided a splendid clinical contribution that deepens our understanding of the case in a most important way. I am convinced, however, that now, after Bach has pointed the way, a self psychological point of view focusing on developmental issues is likely to furnish a more relevant explanation of the data than the traditional point of view that focuses on oedipal drive conflicts. Like Mr. M. and Mr. X. (see Kohut, 1977a) and Mr. Z. (see Kohut, 1979), so Schwaber's Mr. R., too, turned finally toward the decisive developmental step with the aid of the father and established—tentatively in preadolescence with the aid of the real father, decisively, we hope, during analysis via the working through of an idealizing father transference—that continuum from ambitions (perhaps derived from maternal mirroring) via skills and talents (perhaps reinforced via a twinship relationship to the father) toward idealized goals (firmed by the decisive idealizing father transference) that should provide him with reliable self-cohesion. Stated in behavioral terms, the father ideal should serve as the organizer of a productive-creative self and thus allow the patient to lead a fulfilling and meaningful life, to achieve and maintain the condition we call mental health.

The question might be asked why those of us who are familiar with the self psychological configurations that, as I hope to have demonstrated, explain a central aspect of Schwaber's analysand's personality and of the analytic process, needed Bach's guidance to get us started on the right road. I do not know the answer to this question — in fact there may be different answers that fit different individuals. Certainly blind spots concerning developmental disturbances in preadolescence, due to our own partially unconfronted failures relating to this stage, are ubiquitous and may explain our cognitive obtuseness. But there is also another factor which, perhaps in combination with the aforementioned one, may account for it. That we saw the therapist in front of us, with all her warm femininity, may have interfered for some of us with the ability to recognize that, at a decisive moment in the analysis, a transference involving the *father* as a selfobject imago had been activated. It behooves us to remember — a fact we all know and yet often tend to disregard — that transferences, especially the deepest and most pivotal ones, are determined by the patient's reactivated needs and not by the actual personality of the analyst.

Analysts have been taught to understand their patient's communications, in particular their free associations, in terms of conflict and defense. When a patient reports that he has become interested in painting or photography, the analyst is likely to turn his own mind to the task of determining how these activities, and the fact of their emergence at this point, relate to the ongoing transference, in particular how they can be understood as defenses against, or sublimations of, conflict-arousing incestuous drive-wishes. And if the patient, after telling the analyst about recently intensified visual interests in the sphere of art, turns now to associations about an ugly breast, the material seems tailor-made for the interpretation that he is defending himself against the emergence of oedipal memories relating to his mother's beautiful body (in the transference against the emergence of fantasies about the analyst's wife if the analyst is a man or about the analyst herself if the analyst is a woman) and that he does so by, on the one hand, denying the beauty of the incestuous love object — a defense — while, on the other hand, escaping into pursuits that are many steps removed from the oedipal field — a sublimation.

How well this all fits together — and yet how wrong it may all be. After I had begun, more than 10 years ago, to experiment with alternatives to the classical psychoanalytic orientation, I learned that in many cases the patient's personality structure and psychopathology became understandable only when seen in light of the new insights of self psychology. To be sure, my actual practice, especially in recent years, does not provide me with a representative sample of current psychopathology, consisting as it does mainly of analysts who come to me for reanalysis. In fact these self-selected patients belong almost exclusively, although there are exceptions, to a group in which oedipal conflicts play at best a secondary role. But since, luckily, many colleagues have in recent years shared with me their intimate and protracted acquaintance with some of their analysands via frequent consultations, I am able to conclude, on the basis of this broader sample, that analyzable self disturbances are encountered with great frequency by many analysts.

But we are not primarily interested in numbers at this time but with the clarification of a point of view with the aid of actual case material. Those who have studied my case reports (I am again thinking especially of Mr. M., Mr. X., and Mr. Z., but there are several other examples not only in my work but among the cases presented in Goldberg [1978]), will realize what I intend to demonstrate. In a nutshell: such actions as a patient's espousing a new interest might not be at all defensive in any sense of the word but might in fact be a positive achievement. After working through the transference to a mirroring or an idealized selfobject, the patient's self is strengthened and the patient, sensing himself as a vigorous, cohesive center of initiative, can now employ his talents and skills in creative-productive pursuits. In the majority of my male cases it was the mother who was the major pathogenic selfobject in the patient's childhood (it so happens that *all* of the examples I have mentioned up to now, including Schwaber's analysand, are men who fall into this category; but we need only think of Senatspräsident Schreber in order to see that a father, too, can be the pathogenic selfobject for a child who, as an adult, develops severe self pathology) and it was, therefore, the father imago which was revived as the needed structure-providing selfobject and gradually internalized, pari passu with the consistent working through of the idealizing transference. This process results in a decisive strengthening of the ideal-carrying pole of the self. There is nothing defensive about this; and nothing that is based on the resolution of the Oedipus complex.

And the ugly breast? Why must a patient's imagery concerning an ugly breast be of necessity defensive? Why can it not be, like the imagery used by self-state dreams, a message, indirect, it is true, but nevertheless pointing positively toward important genetic constellations? I believe that in many if not most such instances the patient's crucial, and, if correctly understood, deeply moving, message is this: that the mother in fact had been ugly—ugly in terms of the small child's need for a responsive-empathic maternal selfobject, not physically repulsive as judged by the aesthetic sense of an adult. She had been a mother, in other words, who had been out of tune with the child, had not known how to feed it, hold it, carry it, or to smile happily in response to its presence. This may well be the patient's message to the analyst when he recalls the ugly breast, and nothing could be worse, it seems to me, than a reinstatement of the former lack of empathy—the revival of the ugly breast—in the form of the analyst's insistence that the patient is defending himself against incestuous sexual wishes.

But how, it will and should be asked, does one know whether such imagery is oedipal-defensive or whether it is the carrier of a more or less direct message regarding the decisive pathogenic childhood atmosphere? How does one know, to return to the earlier example, whether a newly activated skill is a flight into health (away from the crucial transference experience) or a significant first step toward health itself (an integral part of the crucial, positive selfobject transference)? All I can do in response to such questions is to point up again the primacy of clinical observation over theory. Psychoanalysis is not a theory-based system. Its theories, in Freud's words (1914), are not the foundation but only the coping of the building; it is observation that constitutes the basis on which it rests. True, as one is invariably obligated to spell out in order to forestall the inevitable counterargument, there is no observation without theory. But the theories which underlie our investigations must be tentative and changeable, and—a precept which is of special importance with regard to the investigator's and therapist's use of experience-near theory—we should observe with as many alternatives in mind as we can muster (for a specific example of an observational procedure conducted in accordance with the aforementioned rule, see Kohut [1973b, p. 711n]). I am not asking my colleagues to believe my words. I only ask them to accept my interpretations of the data as being possibly true and then, with an open mind, to follow the unfolding messages of their patients for a long time. Only the protracted unbiased attempt to understand analytic material with the aid of the guidance of self psychological insights will allow analysts to arrive at a meaningful evaluation of the relevance of the self psychological point of view. (For a more extensive discussion of the need "to put aside the traditional way of seeing the data...for sufficiently prolonged periods," see Kohut [1977a, Chapter 3].) My colleagues and I have become convinced that in many cases, indeed, in the majority of instances encountered in a metropolitan practice, it is at present the self psychological orientation that is the most relevant to understanding our patients and explaining their psychopathology. For myself I will emphasize here again that I came to this conclusion not only on the basis of my own clinical practice but also after witnessing many instances in which stalemated analyses, with analyst and patient locked in a seemingly hopeless battle, became remobilized when the analyst began, under my guidance, to apply self psychological insights.

I feel that the second half of the section of this book on "Self Psychology and Its Clinical Applications" might well have carried the subtitle "Continuity or Discontinuity," in acknowledgment of the two questions which, openly or by implication, were repeatedly raised by the contributors. There was, of course, the perennial question of whether psychoanalysis and psychotherapy form a continuum or whether they are distinct and separate enterprises. But there was also, at least by innuendo or implication, the new, significant, and, to me, deeply perturbing question of whether self psychology is a step in the development of psychoanalysis — forward, as we maintain; regressive, as others maintain — or whether it should be considered as discontinuous and separate.

I will react first to the last-mentioned issue and state without hesitation or delay that, as far as I am concerned, self psychology is analysis, a step in the development of analysis.

Developmental steps are always accompanied by a degree of turmoil — whether they are undertaken by an individual or by a group, such as a group of scientists. Yet, after the step has been completed and individual or group has made its adjustment to functioning on a new and, we trust, more advanced level, the turmoil recedes and is soon forgotten, or, at least, downplayed by our memory. It is, for example, difficult for us to grasp how great the change was that analysts were asked to consider as still within the confines of psychoanalysis when Freud moved from id psychology to ego psychology in the early twenties. A perhaps apocryphal story has it that Fenichel was so upset when he gave his report on Freud's new outlook (embodied in his new structural model) to the Vienna Psychoanalytic Society that he could not hold onto his manuscript and that his voice was trembling as he tried to read it. And, I dare say, if an analyst other than Freud had introduced these ideas, they would, in the absence of Freud's direct approval, have been considered heresies — as unscientific, regressive, and incompatible with analysis. But times have changed, at least somewhat. Freud cannot be the ultimate arbiter anymore and, to the best in our profession, Freud's writings are not a kind of Bible but great works belonging to a particular moment in the history of science — great not because of their unchanging relevance but, on the contrary, because they contain the seeds of endless possibilities for further growth.

Whether or not self psychology will be accepted by the analytic community as an intrinsic part of analysis is a question belonging to the sociology of science that I do not feel I can treat with the necessary detachment. I can only speak about the properties inherent in psychoanalytic self psychology that determine its character; and with regard to these properties, to our basic stance, to our essential methods, I can see nothing that would interfere with our sense of the broad contact and continuity between classical analysis and our work. We hope that we have contributed something new that will continue to prove valuable; we know that we could never have made our contributions without the benefits of the work of our predecessors, in particular the work of Freud and the great ego psychologists who followed him. I see, therefore, no break between psychoanalytic self psychology and the psychoanalytic past but only broad contact and continuity. Rather than sensing any discontinuity, I see a sequence of developmental steps, from id psychology to ego psychology to self psychology. Ego psychology was accepted by analysts because they recognized that it had not done away with id psychology but had enriched and complemented the earlier findings. Self psychology, too, we trust, will ultimately be accepted by the analytic community as an expansion that complements and enriches psychoanalysis, building on the work that has preceded it, but preserving the essence of psychoanalysis as it has been handed down to us.

I will end these introductory remarks by commenting that Palaci's survey, aiming to demonstrate the particular continuity between ego psychology and the psychoanalytic psychology of the self, is in full harmony with the thoughts and sentiments that I have just expressed.

In the context of the specific questions on which we are focusing, the most important issue raised in the papers on psychotherapy can be put in the form of the following question: is our clinical interest in the self and its disturbances an outgrowth of the fact that the leading psychopathology has changed in our time, that the predominance of hysteria and of the other transference neuroses has now been replaced by the predominance of the disorders of self, or is it not so much the essential structure of the illnesses that we see that has changed but rather our viewpoint? Is it not the new viewpoint that we have discovered which allows us now to see the diseased self, its distortions, fragmentations, enfeeblements, while from the old viewpoint we could see only the secondary manifestations of self psychology (in the form of hysterical dysfunctions, of phobias, or of obsessions and compulsions)?

I know that, concerning this important issue, some of my colleagues would put the weight of their judgment entirely to one side: it is the observer who has changed, they would say. Self disturbances have always been abundant, they would argue, but they were not recognized as such and, since the core of these disturbances remained unrecognized, they were seen as object-instinctual transference neuroses.

Although I am inclined to support the opposite opinion, I admit that it is difficult, if not impossible, to obtain certainty with regard to a decision. I agree with the assertion that we have been able to shift our point of view decisively. As we observe the transferences of our analysands we are now able to focus our attention not only on structural *conflicts* (on drives and defenses or anxiety and guilt), but also on structural *defects* (on the stunted self and its need for a selfobject in order to complete its development). This new ability is without doubt due to a change in the observer. On the other hand, I do not believe that we should discount the possibility that the change in the observer depends at least in part on the fact that the world in which he lives has changed. We, too, in other words, are children of our time, just as Breuer and Freud were children of theirs. Thus our sensitivity to certain aspects of the human condition that are characteristic of our era is sharpened and we respond to them, just as the attention of the pioneers of psychoanalysis was drawn to certain aspects of man's state that prevailed during the formative period of their lives and they responded to them.

There is, however, as I have repeatedly pointed out in the past, still another fact that supports the point of view that self disturbances have become more important since Freud's time. In an address given in 1973, I maintained, as in essence I still do, that man's leading psychological problems have shifted (see 1973a, especially p. 680). And I supported my assertion by calling attention to a feature I now refer to as the "anticipatory function of art." The artist, I said, is ahead of the scientist—sociologist, historian, psychologist—in his response to and description of man's leading psychological ills. And it is only after much delay that the scientist, too, begins to notice the newly dominant psychological constellations and begins to attempt to explain the phenomena that have already been identified and made available to our perception by the work of the pioneering artists of the time. Perhaps one could say that with regard to the investigation of the broader arena of cultural activities, this sequence—from artist to scientist—is only another example of the principle that I have frequently emphasized with regard to the restricted activities of the analyst in the therapeutic situation; the fact that when dealing with the psychological world, understanding is of necessity the precursor of explaining. But be that as it may, the preoccupations of the greatest among the modern artists and writers are clearly different from those of the artists and writers that impressed Freud in his formative years. Need I do more than remind you again of the musicians of disorganized sound, such as Schoenberg and Webern, and of the poets and writers of disorganized language, such as Pound and Joyce? And then there are the novelists and dramatists, such as Kafka and O'Neill, who, though retaining the traditional means of communication, used them in their stories and plays to describe the broken-up, distorted, and enfeebled self of man.

Does the contemplation of the form and content of the work of the greatest artists of our era supply us with sufficient reasons for the assumption that it is not only the scientific observer who has changed but the psychological field that he now observes as well? I do not know how others feel about the weight of an argument that adduces the work of a Picasso or Alban Berg—artists, I would like to stress again, who were active in depicting the broken-up self and its artistic re-creation long before there existed any scientific approach to the diseased self—in support of the thesis that the predominant psychological ills of man have changed. To me, at any rate, the work of such artists constitutes a weighty argument, more convincing in fact than most statistical studies in which insignificant data are given the royal treatment of mathematical exactness.

But there is still another argument in support of the view that the emergence of a scientific psychoanalytic self psychology was only the appropriate reaction to a psychological shift that had already taken place. It is based on the fact that the social environment, in particular as it affects the experiences of the small child, has changed. Since I have discussed these issues in greater detail in the past (see, in particular, 1977a, pp. 267–280), I will do no more than mention headlines referring to the growing child's surroundings in our day in terms of: "the small family," "the absent father," "the working mother," "the lack of servants who are part of the family." We may suspect, at least as concerns the middle class of present-day Western society, that these features of family life can be understood as reactions to the sociological problems created by overpopulation due to lowered mortality, especially dramatically lowered infant and child mortality. But these are hypotheses whose validity the depth psychologist is not competent to judge; they lie within the domain of the sociologist and anthropologist. The genetically oriented depth psychologist, however, does have access to data—in particular via the childhood memories of his analysands—which demonstrate that the emotional traumata to which the child is exposed in our time are different from those suffered by the children of the urban middle-class families from which most of Freud's patients came, and from whom he collected the data on which he built his theories. Put into a nutshell, one can say that formerly more children were exposed to overstimulation due to the closeness with which the adult world surrounded them (with the result that they later developed conflict neuroses), while nowadays more children are exposed to understimulation due to the absence or emotional distance of the significant adults from the child (with the result that they later develop narcissistic personality and behavior disorders).

Does all this mean that I oppose the view that narcissistic and behavior disorders have always been present, in Freud's time and even long before, and that they were just not recognized and appropriately identified? Decidedly not. When the statement is put in such general terms, I can agree with it. I disagree, however—and I believe that the available evidence supports me—if the statement is taken to imply that the narcissistic personality and behavior disorders were just as frequent in the last decades of the 19th century as they are now. In contrast, I believe that there were more conflict neuroses in Freud's time than there are now, and that they were as characteristic for the era in which Freud lived as narcissistic personality and behavior disorders are for our own. And just as Freud, like almost all of his contemporaries, was unable to grasp the power and the significance of modern art and even ridiculed it (see his remark to Karl Abraham, in H. Abraham & E. Freud, 1965, p. 332), while many of us are able to feel its depth and power and specific message, so also with his and his collaborators' responses to the psychological ills of their patients. Freud and his co-workers were more inclined to respond to the conflicts of the cohesive self and to assign a place of secondary importance to the disturbed self, while we are more inclined to see it the other way.

Let me, in order to supply an illustration of this change in focus, speak briefly about anxiety hysteria which, manifested in the form of agoraphobia, can be taken as the most characteristic example of the type of psychopathology that challenged the minds of the psychoanalytic pioneers. Its elucidation was the beginning, and remained the cornerstone, of all of Freud's contributions to the scientific grasp of psychopathology. Since we are familiar with the basic positions of classical analysis, I do not need to spell out the details of the psychopathology of anxiety hysteria as it was formulated by Freud. The agoraphobic woman, simply put, does not want to go out into the street because she is afraid of her wishes to prostitute herself. Beneath the prostitution fantasies lies the unconscious incestuous wish for intercourse with the father which energizes the less deeply buried (perhaps even preconscious) prostitution fantasies. Such fantasies are thus understood as being simultaneously the expression of, and the defense against, the underlying oedipal desires. The fact that the agoraphobic woman is able to leave the house and walk through the streets when she is accompanied by a woman, in particular by an older, maternal

woman, is interpreted by the classical school as a more or less successful defensive arrangement. The mother's presence makes the
oedipal wish impossible to fulfill — there is no anxiety. Being alone
with the father mobilizes the wish because it seems nearer the
possibility of fulfillment — anxiety occurs.

And how does the modern analyst, i.e., the psychoanalytic
self psychologist, react to these data? He responds with admiration
to the insights of which he is now the heir, but he makes a small yet
decisive step beyond the classical formulation. On the face of it, it
is no more than a shift in emphasis; on closer inspection, however,
it is of great significance. For the psychoanalytic self psychologist,
what had been the central part of the psychopathology in the
classical formulation, the incestuous fantasy, is relegated to a position of secondary importance, while what had been peripheral and
secondary to the pioneers, the relief experienced in the presence of
the mother imago, becomes central and primary.

I can hear the outcry of certain colleagues who will immediately protest that such formulations are a retreat from the
hard-won insights of drive-conflict psychology. By focusing on
conscious experiences and on manifest side issues, such colleagues
would claim, self psychologists are advocating an attitude that, in
clinical application, would foster the analysand's retreat from the
core of her illness and prevent her from ultimately braving the confrontation with her central conflicts that eventuates in cure.

I can do no more here than plead for a dispassionate hearing
of our view. Our contribution, I must emphasize, does not con-
note a lessened appreciation of the impact of the oedipal wishes
and conflicts on our part. We do believe, however, that we are
evaluating their significance in pathogenesis more correctly than
classical analysis. Oedipal wishes and conflicts are ubiquitous. We
assume, in other words, in harmony with the insights of Freud,
that they are experienced by every human child who has reached a
certain level of psychic maturation, in particular, a certain level of
self-cohesion and assertive strength. The essence of the agoraphobic illness, however, as we see it, is not the Oedipus complex
but a specific structural defect in the self. The self of the agoraphobic woman, we say, has not built up specific structures via

transmuting internalization in childhood, and it is therefore still dependent on an external selfobject (the presence of a maternal figure) in order to prevent an outbreak of paralyzing anxiety.

But have I not with my preceding remarks contradicted my earlier statements? Have I not now taken the earlier position I outlined to the effect that it is indeed our perception that has changed and not the form of the disease? Have I not, in particular, demonstrated my agreement with this position by saying that even agoraphobia, that paradigm of classical analysis, is in essence a disorder of the self and that the structural conflict over incestuous wishes is secondary to the disturbance of the self? Yes, insofar as our understanding of the psychopathology of the classical transference neuroses is concerned, I must admit that our stance has changed and that we see things in a new light. But the fact that our explanation of the phenomena that were prevalent in Freud's time has changed does not mean that these phenomena are still prevalent in our time. That we now approach even the classical transference neuroses with the conceptual tools of self psychology does not mean that the clinical entities which predominated in Freud's time are the same as those which predominate in ours. We cannot escape the fact, in other words, that, when we look at comparable settings, i.e., the urban middle class of Freud's time and the urban middle class of our time, hysterias, including, in particular, anxiety hysterias, were abundant in the last decades of the 19th century while they now are rare. What accounts for this change?

Before replying to this question we must first restate it. We will not ask anymore why the conflict neuroses of Freud's time are now superseded by self disturbances, but why the self disturbances Freud referred to as conversion hysterias, anxiety hysterias, and obsessional neuroses are now superseded by the self disturbances we refer to as narcissistic personality disorders. The self pathology, in other words, that accounts for the hysterias in general and for agoraphobia in particular is different from that which constitutes the basis of the type of self pathology—narcissistic personality and behavior disorders—that we see with such great frequency in our time, and we assume, furthermore, that the selfobject failures that account for these two classes of self disorder are different.

What were the pathogenic aspects of the selfobject milieu in Freud's time and what are the pathogenic aspects of the selfobject milieu in our time? (1) The preponderant and era-characteristic selfobject failure in Freud's time concerned faulty selfobject responses during the oedipal phase. The selfobjects had, in other words, provided appropriate mirroring for the child's display and adequate opportunities for his merger with idealized strength up to the oedipal period but then failed to provide appropriate responses, such as joyful pride in the child's assertiveness, during the oedipal phase. Instead they reacted inappropriately, for example, by becoming stimulated by the child's libidinal exuberance and responding to it, alternatingly, with poorly controlled excitement and disciplinary prohibitions, or by becoming alarmed at the child's assertiveness and reacting to it with annoyance and threats. (2) The preponderant and era-characteristic selfobject failure in our time, by contrast, concerns not seductiveness and rageful competitiveness with the already nearly consolidated self of the child during the oedipal period but, for example, a pervasive shallowness of responses during the child's earlier years, i.e., faulty or inadequate mirroring and unavailability of the requisite merger with a source of idealized strength and calmness throughout the formative years.

With regard to the specific features of the selfobject failures that were characteristic of Freud's time, I will mention first that they are in harmony with the social conditions — prevalence of large families, enlarged further by the presence of servants — of which I spoke earlier. And I will add, furthermore, that they unexpectedly lead us back to Freud's original claim, later completely abandoned, that his hysterical patients had actually been seduced by their parents during childhood. Are we then returning to Freud's original claim? Of course we are not. While actual parental seductions do occasionally occur, such events do not constitute the frequently present pathogenic factor that we have here in mind. (A parent's actual seduction of his children is almost always the manifestation of a much more serious form of psychopathology of a parent than that which brings about oedipal psychopathology.) What we are speaking of here is not manifestly deviant behavior of parents toward their oedipal child but subtle distortions in their attitude due to preconscious responses — distortions in general far removed from actual incest with the child and from competitive brutality toward it. We may say, in other words, that Freud's original impressions were correct except that his patients' memories referred not to gross pathogenic actions from the side of their parents but to much less tangible, yet specific and pervasive pathogenic parental attitudes. Due probably to their fixation on certain unconscious or preconscious fantasies, these parents were unable to function adequately as the child's oedipal selfobjects, i.e., they were unable to react with pride and joy toward the next generation now starting out on the long voyage that would eventually lead it to the central position on the stage of life while the parents, members of the older generation, moved inexorably toward that stage of the voyage of life that ultimately leads to decline and death.

Before I leave the important subject matter of the reevaluation of the oedipal neuroses, I feel it would be useful to make a few remarks regarding the terminological and classificatory questions posed by our newly introduced hypothesis that in the oedipal neuroses, too, a self defect — though one that differs from those encountered in narcissistic personality and behavior disorders, borderline states, or psychoses — plays a significant role. Sound reasoning seems to require that, in view of the new hypothesis, we now abandon the distinction between (1) oedipal neuroses (structural neuroses; classical transference neuroses including hysterias, phobias, and obsessional neuroses) on the one hand, and (2) disorders of the self (narcissistic personality and behavior disorders, borderline states, psychoses) on the other hand. Instead, for the sake of taxonomic exactness, the new hypothesis would seem to make imperative the differentiation of oedipal from nonoedipal self pathology. I am reluctant to take this terminological step at the present time, however, because our hypotheses about what constitutes the central psychopathology of the oedipal neuroses are still tentative. Accordingly, I would rather live with a degree of terminological confusion at present than commit myself prematurely to the radical change in classification that such a terminological change would imply. For the time being, therefore, I will refer to the narcissistic personality and behavior disorders, borderline states, and the psychoses when I speak of self pathology or disturbances of the self; I will not subsume the oedipal (structural) neuroses under this term unless I so indicate.

There is a further reason for my reluctance to make changes in nomenclature. I am influenced by a degree of conservatism that —even at the price of terminological inexactness—leads me to maintain the sense of continuity of our science. That we will, for a time at least, generally refer only to the narcissistic personality and behavior disorders, borderline states, and psychoses when we speak of self disorders or disturbances of the self is, after all, no more inconsistent than continuing to refer to hysterias, phobias, and obsessional neuroses as transference neuroses after having demonstrated beyond a shadow of a doubt that the narcissistic personality and behavior disorders, too, eventuate in transferences—however different the transferences that typify the analyzable disorders of the self may be from those that typify the classical transference neuroses.

But now we must leave the fascinating inquiry into the relationship between the oedipal neuroses and the narcissistic personality disorders, and turn to Nathaniel London's interesting contribution to the present volume. London deals with the time honored topic of differentiating psychoanalysis from other forms of psychotherapy, in particular, from psychoanalytically informed intensive psychotherapy.

I believe that London's carefully thought out remarks are especially important because they deal with two interrelated issues that are a serious test of the clarity and solidity of our thinking: (1) the question of whether psychoanalysis can lay claim to a special and unique status among the psychotherapies and, if so, (2) the problem of defining this status. Strange as it may seem, I am less interested in the answer at which the discussant arrives—the answer to the question, that is, of whether or not psychoanalysis and psychoanalytically informed psychotherapy could, or should, be separated conceptually from one another—than in the way in which he develops his argument. And thus, even though my own conclusions differ from those reached by London, this fact does not lessen my appreciation of his discriminating and serious argumentation.

In a way, unless one has an extrascientific axe to grind, one can reasonably espouse either position with regard to the issue at hand. But then it must be admitted that there is hardly an analyst who is free of preexisting emotional commitments which force his reasoning powers into the service of foregone conclusions. Surely, a book could and should be written about a peculiar phenomenon that has a decisive bearing on the issue at hand, namely, the phenomenon of "the psychoanalytic movement." But will there ever be an analyst who has the objectivity, the knowledge, and the sensitivity to write it decently? Here, indeed, is an aspect of psychoanalysis that distinguishes it from other sciences, at least in degree. Insofar as the analyst, whether he is a clinician or an investigator, feels that he belongs to a movement, he is inclined to see disagreement as potential dissidence and to react to it with an emotional fervor that reminds one of the attitudes displayed by those members of religious or political groups who feel themselves fighting heresy or revisionism, respectively. And yet, despite this characteristic, psychoanalysis is true science. It is based on observation and it is open to change even though, at times, it seems that new views are accepted only on the condition that no specific author's name be attached to them; under the condition, in other words, that the new views infiltrate the body of analytic knowledge imperceptibly.

What accounts for the fact — the largely regrettable fact, I believe — that psychoanalysis displays some of the features of a "movement"? There are a number of explanations that may be adduced to explain the fact that many analysts experience themselves not only as clinicians and investigators but also as members of a movement. In what follows I will enumerate some of the factors that may account for this phenomenon, including one that has not been sufficiently considered up to now because, I believe, its full significance can be appreciated only when it is examined from the viewpoint of the psychology of the self.

Among the explanations of why psychoanalysis occupies a

special position among the sciences there are some which will be easily accepted by most psychoanalysts. There is first of all the fact that the complexity of the subject matter which psychoanalysis investigates has so far prevented us from obtaining the degree of consensus concerning either the data we gather or the explanatory hypotheses we offer that can be obtained in the physical and biological sciences. This difficulty we share with the social sciences and the humanities. Secondly, and this is a problem that does not plague the social sciences and the humanities, the intimacy of the analytic situation — our principal source of primary data — makes it difficult to provide others with the opportunity to validate our findings firsthand (e.g., via the recording or videotaping of analyses) without serious distortion of the field.

There are two further, interrelated factors that contribute to the idea that psychoanalysis is a "movement," led, like all religious and almost all political movements, by a single, ever-present dominant father imago. (1) There is the authority of a single leader, Freud, who, even in death, is not only experienced as the symbol of an abstract ideal but also — his picture hangs in many an analyst's office, his words are invoked with great frequency — as a concrete and actual presence. (2) Closely related to the foregoing factor, there is the effect of the training analysis in which the psychological configurations that psychoanalysis has delineated are not learned and discussed dispassionately but internalized against resistances, in a one-to-one regressive relationship with a parental imago, that, to some extent, is always experienced as a representative of Freud. (For a more detailed discussion of these processes, and of their effect on the nature of group solidarity among psychoanalysts, see my essay "Creativeness, Charisma, Group Psychology" [1976, especially pp. 793–804].)

But what is the special contribution that self psychology can make to the solution of the sociological (or rather psychosociological) puzzle concerning the in some ways unique position of psychoanalysis among the other sciences? The explanation that we can offer is not unrelated to the considerations I have just mentioned, but it orders the various factors and allows us to see them in a somewhat different light. Put in the most condensed fashion, the culprit that self psychology can discern is a specific flaw in our training analyses, namely, a neglect of the narcissistic sector of the psychopathology of the training analysand. If I am right in this view (and it is strongly supported by the lessons I have learned from reanalyzing analysts, especially during the last decade or so), then it follows that the training analysand's primary self disturbance is, in general, not confronted, the defect in his self not recognized, and its manifestations misinterpreted. Specifically, his idealizing transference is interpreted as a defense against a negative transference and his mirror transference as an evasive regression from oedipal conflicts and castration fears. In view of the fact that I believe the great majority of analytic candidates suffer not from classical transference neuroses but from self pathology, I consider these failures to be of far-reaching importance.

But how then, I will be asked, were our candidates helped in former years if they suffered from self disturbances and their central psychopathology was not systematically engaged in the analytic process? Our training analysands were feeling better, after all, when their analyses ended, and their work and interpersonal responsiveness improved. In replying to this important question I will first say that I agree with the assertion that the majority of our training candidates do indeed derive a good deal of benefit from their treatment. Still, having expressed my agreement, I must add that I have a very specific explanation for these successes. This explanation, simultaneously, helps us to answer the question we originally posed concerning why analysts have such a special, intense commitment and loyalty to their field, and, in particular, why their feelings of reverence toward Freud and Freud's teachings are so intense.[5] The answer, I believe (on the basis of the data that I have obtained from the reanalysis of analysts), is provided by the fact that, while the training analysand's self disturbance

[5]The question which I pose here and attempt to answer with regard to the curative effect of our training analyses can, and should, also be raised and answered with regard to the curative effect of analyses conducted in analogous instances outside our training system. Unsurprisingly, the explanation in these instances parallels, mutatis mutandis, that given with regard to the specific case of the training analysand. I cannot take up this issue in the present context, but hope to pursue it elsewhere before long.

remains unanalyzed because his selfobject transferences are mistaken for resistances, the deleterious consequences of this therapeutic shortcoming are to a certain extent ameliorated by the analysand's becoming an analyst. By becoming an analyst and feeling himself a member of a psychoanalytic movement, he assures himself more or less permanently of the presence of the selfobjects that he should have transmuted into self structure during his analysis. And we can say, therefore, that the intense commitment to analysis which analysts feel and display, the sensitivity with which they react to any criticism of their science and Freud, and the restricted availability of the free-roaming creativity that one would expect to find frequently among the members of a group that has enormous intelligence and psychological gifts at its disposal, are all to some extent manifestations of the fact that the individual analyst has, to repeat my joke, become addicted to his kind of health and will fight tooth and nail against any threat to his adjustment.

But how do these statements about the causal relationship between our candidates' unanalyzed selfobject transferences and their creativity-stifling and progress-hampering commitment to the analytic movement and the leader figure of Freud jibe with the points that I made earlier? I am thinking, in particular, of my assertion (1) that mental health may in certain instances be achieved via the establishment of the capacity to activate a single functional continuum within the self, and (2) that even the healthiest person remains in need of selfobjects throughout life, that, to put it even more strongly, the very healthiest among us are those who are most able to be sustained by the appropriate use of selfobjects.

It is not difficult to reconcile these two sets of ideas. They are not incompatible if we evaluate the difference between psychological disease and health, between desirable and undesirable solutions to an individual's psychological problems, in the light of the following formulation about what constitutes a cure in psychoanalysis. If, in the course of an analysis, we will say, the primary self defects are filled in subsequent to the mobilization and working through of the narcissistic transferences, then the restored self of the analysand will be able to fulfill its nuclear potentialities by establishing a creative-productive sectorial continuum between its ambitions and ideals. In order to maintain this sector of the self, and to safeguard its functioning, two conditions, one internal, one external, must be fulfilled. The internal precondition is the mobilization of adequate nuclear skills and talents that are able to operate successfully toward the realization of the individual's nuclear goals. The external precondition is the creation of a matrix of freely chosen selfobjects which — and this is the case with some of the most successful analyses that I have been able to evaluate — are often found only after a protracted and intensely pursued search.

Have I been led astray by the foregoing reflections? Have I forgotten that we are examining the question of whether psychoanalysis and psychotherapy are strictly separate or form a continuum? Am I failing to respond to the specific stimulus provided by London's discussion of these issues? I do not think so. However unrelated to the subject matter of his presentation the foregoing considerations may appear to be, they are in fact closely related to it. First, I wanted to explain why, in general, we are prone to claim a specific and separate status for psychoanalysis proper and why we are inclined to differentiate it sharply from psychoanalytically informed psychotherapy. We do so in order to extol the unique value of psychoanalysis proper and to assign a lesser position to psychoanalytically informed psychotherapy. The latter we consider only second best — a necessary compromise perhaps, but still, in terms of Freud's imagery, a downgrading of the pure gold of analysis by an admixture of baser metals. Second, and more importantly, I sought to describe certain aspects of the psychological forces that have up to now contributed to the cohesion of the psychoanalytic community in order to provide a background against which I can now, unfettered by the need to defend the separateness and uniqueness of psychoanalysis on emotional grounds, undertake the task of developing for you a view that differs from that presented so lucidly and convincingly by London.

In contrast to London I will argue that we should differentiate psychoanalysis proper from psychotherapy, even if the latter is carried on for a long time and is conducted by an analyst who is guided by his analytic knowledge in his therapeutic activities. I want to emphasize, however, that my argument is not in the service of the emotional needs that I just considered. It is not advanced, in other words, in order to protect the pure gold of analysis — protect analysis against the danger of losing its identity through being absorbed by psychiatry. Rather, I present my argument dispassionately, motivated only by the wish to point out certain specific factors that I believe define the essence of analytic treatment and its goals. In order to illuminate the factors that are specific to analysis I will focus on the two endpoints of the continuum between psychoanalytically informed psychotherapy and psychoanalysis proper and not, as London chose to do, on the intermediate area of the continuum. In this way, I will be able to sharpen the contrast between these two processes.

Before entering into specifics, I will propose that psychoanalysis proper aims at bringing about changes in a *sector* of the self of the patients who are seeking relief from the miseries of self pathology, while psychoanalytically oriented psychotherapy, even if carried on for a long time, aims at bringing about changes in a *segment* of the self. In this, I say no more than analysts have always been saying in prideful defense of their specific therapeutic enterprise, namely, that psychoanalysis affects the depth of the psyche while other forms of therapy only touch the surface. But perhaps the significance of my proposition will be more apparent when I phrase it differently and, turning it around, say that any form of psychotherapy that aims at bringing about sectorial rather than segmental changes in the self should be called psychoanalysis, without regard to the technical procedures that are employed.

But this general claim must be clarified. Restricting my remarks again to the treatment of self pathology, I will start with a feature that psychoanalysis and psychoanalytically informed psychotherapy have in common. In both instances the maturational forces striving to complete the structuralization of the self are mobilized at the beginning of therapy, i.e., the patient's intense childhood needs for the selfobject are reactivated. In both instances, in other words, a selfobject transference — or a number of them following each other in a genetically predetermined sequence —

will establish itself. And in both instances—a fact that cannot be stressed enough—a stage subsequently follows in which the analysand's transference image of the therapist fills in the defects in the patient's self because he has, more or less, been installed by the patient as the satisfactory selfobject that had been available to him in childhood, even though it had either been taken away from him prematurely, proved unreliable, or evidenced other flaws that prevented the full structuralization of the self via optimal frustration and transmuting internalization.

Among the forms in which a selfobject transference may establish itself, whether in psychoanalytically oriented therapy or in psychoanalysis proper, there is a specific one, the temporary gross identification with the therapist, on which I will now focus. I do so not because of the frequency or striking features of this particular form of selfobject transference, but primarily because I think the way the therapist responds to this manifestation of a selfobject transference indeed separates the wheat from the chaff—not the psychoanalyst from the psychotherapist, but the self psychologically informed psychoanalyst (or psychotherapist) from the one who is not. As I have been able to ascertain on several occasions, gross identifications with the analyst may constitute a crucial event during the analysis of certain patients with narcissistic personality disorders. The analysands who manifest the kind of behavior that indicates they have taken over the personality of the analyst are individuals who had formerly maintained strong defenses against their intense need for the selfobject whose disappearance or withdrawal or sudden unavailability had severely traumatized them in childhood. Fearing a repetition of the childhood trauma that threatened them with disintegration early in life, they cling to a brittle self-sufficiency and autonomy, at the price of a severe narrowing of their emotional mobility. After long periods of analytic work, however, sometimes after years of reconstructing the past and demonstrating to the patient his originally life-saving but now confining retreat from his need for a selfobject, the analyst, often to his great surprise, will be confronted by unmistakable manifestations of the patient's gross identification with him. The patient will suddenly dress like the therapist, will use the therapist's favorite expressions, or will buy pictures and furniture that resemble those in the therapist's office. Although these activities are in general not accompanied by insight, the self psychologically informed therapist will not reject them as resistances but, putting aside his often considerable discomfort at seeing his personality taken over by another, will quietly welcome them as a first step in the loosening of lifelong defenses. And, indeed, if these identifications are welcomed and interpreted correctly—as a forward move in analysis, as a first sign that the old needs from childhood are now being mobilized in the transference, as a first move toward the maturation of a sector in the personality that had been stunted in early life—then the shift from (a) the *enactment* of a selfobject transference (e.g., in the specific form of a need for merger with an omnipotent selfobject) to (b) the introspectively accessible *experience* of the need for such a selfobject will gradually take place.

How does the description of these events help us to differentiate psychoanalytically informed psychotherapy from psychoanalysis? It does so by allowing us to demonstrate the different responses of analyst and psychotherapist when they are confronted by this concrete and by no means infrequent occurrence. What the psychoanalytically informed psychotherapist and the psychoanalyst have in common is the understanding of the significance of the identification with the analyst; what separates them, in my view, is the fact that the working-through process that follows the stage of gross identification plays a greater role in analysis than in psychotherapy.

In analysis the stage of gross identification with the analyst is followed by an extended period of systematic working through, leading gradually to the relinquishment of the archaic selfobject and, pari passu, (a) to the strengthening of the pole of the self that is the carrier of the patient's nuclear goals and ideals and (b) to the patient's increasing ability to support these now strengthened inner structures via relationships to appropriate selfobjects in his real, present-day surroundings.

And what, continuing our comparison with the aid of the same example, are the goals of psychotherapy? Expressed most succinctly, and, insofar as our aim is taxonomic abstraction rather than clinical concreteness, disregarding nuances and grey areas, I would say that in psychotherapy the working-through process will play a less significant role and will, in particular, not be carried out as systematically in the transference as in psychoanalysis proper but will be activated — by transference interpretations — only to that minimal extent necessary to reach the psychotherapeutic goal. A minimum of transference interpretations may thus be necessary to enable the patient to make the shift from the selfobject analyst to other selfobject figures and to diminish his sensitivities sufficiently to enable him to make use of the selfobject support that he can obtain from appropriate people in his surroundings without immediate withdrawal from them when they disappoint him. And, furthermore, in keeping with the fact that, in contrast to psychoanalysis, our aim in psychotherapy is primarily the improvement of functioning and well-being and only secondarily the attainment of maximal structural change, it must be emphasized that that part of the transference involvement with the therapist that still remains at the conclusion of therapy must not be rejected by the psychotherapist. The patient, in other words, should feel free to return to avail himself of a temporary reactivation of the selfobject transference to the therapist when external circumstances have been especially taxing. Thus, the goal of psychotherapy is not the same as that of analysis, however much we may make use of analytic insights and techniques on the way to it; it is the replacement of defects in the patient's self structure by appropriate self-selfobject relationships. In psychoanalytically informed psychotherapy, the psychotherapist's aim is to help the patient shift from the selfobject support that was provided by the transference to the selfobject support that can be obtained from the patient's family, or friends, or from various societal institutions (such as religious organizations).

Having attempted in the foregoing discussion to delineate the borders between psychoanalysis proper and psychoanalytically informed psychotherapy, it behooves me to admit at the end that, in practice, these differentiating lines cannot always be drawn sharply. On the one hand there undoubtedly exist clinical instances in which, despite the fact that the analysis had been carried out systematically, i.e., that there had been prolonged, conscientiously pursued working through of the transference, the analysand may still need to return to the analyst for further analysis in order to bring about additional structure building via the renewed activation of a selfobject transference followed by working through. On the other hand, there are undoubtedly instances of psychotherapy which ended by an adjustment to the external world that could be maintained so successfully that the patient never needs to see the therapist again. Still, all in all, I remain convinced that it is useful to stress the difference between analysis and psychotherapy. Even if it is not always valid in practice, the differentiation is helpful in defining two different sets of goals and in clarifying the analyst's and the psychotherapist's principal tasks. Let me state my proposition one more time, and this time express it in the terminology of Freud's metapsychology, which, as I have stressed on numerous occasions, is not superseded but only complemented by the conceptual framework of self psychology. Expressed in the terms of classical metapsychology then, the difference between psychoanalytically informed psychotherapy and psychoanalysis is one of emphasis: the first is genetic-*dynamic,* the second dynamic-*genetic* in its ultimate aims.

Does the psychology of the self narrow the gap between psychoanalysis and the other sciences of man? In the section of the book devoted to this question, various contributors attempted to provide answers from the vantage point of their particular fields. Before reporting to you whether, in my opinion, the contributors did in fact lend support to an affirmative reply to our question, I will first say a word about the significance of the answer that we hoped to obtain. For those who are familiar with my views concerning these issues (cf. Kohut, 1970), it will come as no surprise to hear that, contrary to the belief of the great majority of my colleagues, I hold that unless psychoanalysis can sooner or later apply the lessons it learns in the laboratory of the clinical setting to the broader arena of human pursuits—to art, religion, philosophy, anthropology, and, above all, to history—it will not have made the contributions that society has a right to expect from it if it is to receive society's support, and it will become a sterile, esoteric enterprise which, in its increasing isolation, will either be an ineffectual enclave in our changing culture or at worst, will altogether cease to exist. I am deeply convinced, however, that, barring the ascendancy of overwhelming external circumstances, e.g., of certain forms of political totalitarianism, that are inimical to the survival of all insight-expanding introspective-empathic psychology, psychoanalysis can live up to its potentialities and become an important aid to mankind in its struggle for survival. We have no choice, I believe. However modest and sensible an attitude might seem that defines psychoanalysis narrowly as a branch of clinical psychiatry, as a specific form of psychotherapy, and the like, I am convinced that psychoanalysis, in the hands of some gifted and creative members of our profession, is capable of employing its research tools in the investigations of man's activities in the cultural and social fields, and that it will make contributions of great significance which will assist man in his attempt to gain control over his social and historical destiny.

I will resist the temptation to expand on my views and will give you instead a résumé of my reactions to the papers in this section of the book.

Two inferences impressed themselves with increasing force on me as I pondered the contributions by Gehrie, Kligerman, Mason, Scharfenberg, Strozier, and Zonis, namely (1) how significantly different in its essential emphasis the approach of psychoanalytic self psychology to man's thoughts and actions in the sociocultural and historical fields is from that of classical analysis; and (2) how great the potentialities of self psychology are in these areas, promising to surpass even its powerful leverage in the clinical setting.

Each of the participants contributed something special from his own field of expertise. But whether it was anthropology (Gehrie), art and literature (Kligerman), religion (Mason and Scharfenberg), history (Strozier), or political science (Zonis), certain themes appeared to me to repeat themselves. Whether a contributor, in other words, was dealing with artistic creativity or the position and significance of man's religious activities, whether he reviewed and assessed the contributions to psychohistory that have already been made by self psychology or whether he outlined the specific configuration of the self that characterizes a specific people or a nation, the overall conclusion that impressed itself upon me increasingly, beyond and above the specific knowledge that I gained from each of the presentations, was that new doors seemed to open in many directions, that new vistas were becoming discernible, and yet that progress was still slow, halting, and beset with difficulties.

I will not attempt to give you a detailed account of the impressive evidence for progress provided by the various contributions, but will restrict myself to mentioning that I consider the fact that our new findings and theories lend themselves so impressively to applications outside the confines of therapy, that they have stirred the imagination of workers in widely dispersed fields, to be, in itself, a reassuring testimony to the value and the validity of our ideas, one that augurs well for the future of self psychology.

Clearly, it is important that we take stock of our achievements to date in order to derive encouragement for our continuing efforts. It is still more important, however, to assess the difficulties that we are facing, to define the obstacles in our path and to face them squarely. What are these obstacles? I believe that they are of two kinds concerning, respectively, (1) the steepness of the road over which every investigator has to travel who confronts new sights with the aid of a new instrument of observation and is called upon to discern new configurations of meaning in the chaos of the phenomena he scrutinizes; and (2) the hard-to-overcome tendency of the investigator to return to the established, traditional point of view that he has formerly used and to drift away from the newly adopted vantage point which promises to provide him with new data and new meanings.

I will restrict my remarks to the last-mentioned set of difficulties. I know them well, have often experienced them in the past and, even now, still experience them from time to time. There is no better support when facing them than conceptual clarity—a full grasp of the differences between the old and the new, and a dispassionate evaluation of the relative shortcomings of each of the two methods of approach. What are the differences between classical analysis and psychoanalytic self psychology? If there is one major benefit of the present volume, in general, and of the contributions of self psychology to applied analysis, in particular, it is, at least for me, that it has clarified the difference between the new step in psychoanalysis which we call psychoanalytic self psychology and the steps that preceded it.

What then are the differences between psychoanalytic self psychology and the preceding stages of psychoanalysis as they emerged from the contributions to applied analysis contained in the section presently under discussion? I believe one aspect of the shift in emphasis that has been brought about by self psychology can be formulated as follows: up to now psychoanalysis has been a hope and a promise to some of those who study the experiences, thoughts, and actions of man outside the confines of the therapeutic setting. But it has also been a disappointment. The distance between, on the one hand, the level of explanation at the disposal of a psychology that examines man and his activities as a mental apparatus which deals successfully or unsuccessfully with the expression, the curbing, and the sublimation of drives and, on the other hand, the level of explanation required in the realm of the shared significance of the creative aspirations of man in his artistic, philosophical, religious, and historical and social activities was too great to be bridged. And how can self psychology now lay claim to having enabled psychoanalysis to narrow this distance, even though, as I must admit, it cannot yet bridge it completely? It does so not by discarding the valuable insights obtained by id psychology and ego psychology but by adding a new focus that allows us to investigate another aspect of man that is especially significant with regard to our scrutiny of man and his activities outside the clinical setting. Classical analysis, as I like to put it, focuses on Guilty Man while self psychology focuses, in addition, on Tragic Man. Classical analysis saw man as a precariously domesticated animal, as a bundle of insecurely tamed drives which are held back by external and internal threats, i.e., by the fear of punishment and by guilt. Self psychology does not deny the validity of this conception of man—how could it? It is not only Freud's conception but also that of such widely divergent viewpoints which jointly shaped the basic convictions of the Western world as Christianity (which teaches sin and redemption) and Darwinian evolutionism and its biological applications (which teaches development from the primitive to the progressively mature). But self psychology emphasizes that the basic outlook of classical analysis, that amalgam of Judeo-Christian ethics and Darwinian evolutionism which was the unquestioned guide of scientists in Breuer's and Freud's time, does not encompass all of man, that indeed it fails to investigate the aspect of man that is most characteristic of him, the dimension of his personality that is the most human.

The sum of parts may have a significance that cannot be derived from the scrutiny of the parts, however valuable the analysis of the details might be. Man's self, once it has been established, is, in its essence, an energized pattern for the future that, lying in the area of free will and initiative, has a significance all of its own, independent of the genetic factors that — in the area of cause-and-effect determinism — had originally laid down its contents and had given it its shape. It is this aspect of man, man's self struggling to fulfill its creative-productive destiny, failing or succeeding, hurt and raging or fulfilled and generous, which has been neglected by analysis heretofore. And it is the ability of self psychology to focus its investigative attention not only on the conflicts of Guilty Man but also on the struggles of Tragic Man that has already made it such a valuable tool for investigators outside analysis — a tool which, I trust, will become more valuable still in the future as we are able to refine it, increase our skills in handling it, and systematize the technique of its use.

I will conclude my comments concerning the significance of the papers on the application of self psychology outside the area of treatment in the narrow sense of the word — I am adding the qualifying phrase "in the narrow sense" because insights in the sociopolitical, religious, and historical fields, too, may exert a psychotherapeutic effect, first on the community and then, secondarily, on the individual members of the community — by returning briefly to a question that several contributors and discussants raised in the various sections of this volume, and that I considered earlier.

I am referring to whether we should try to bring about an integration of self psychology with, on the one hand, the work of such valuable contributors to modern depth psychology as Michael Balint, André Green, Béla Grunberger, Edith Jacobson, Otto Kernberg, Melanie Klein, Margaret Mahler, and D. W. Winnicott, and with, on the other hand, the body of classical analysis, which, despite the important contributions to ego psychology of Heinz Hartmann and his co-workers, must still be acknowledged as being essentially embodied in Freud's work.

With regard to the modern contributors that I named first, my answer, in a nutshell, is this: independent of any judgment regarding the comparative value and validity of the various contributions that relate to certain areas with which psychoanalytic self psychology has also been preoccupied, independent, in other words, of the question whether it is self psychology or any of these other schools which has achieved the more nearly accurate assessment of the psychological matter under investigation, it is difficult to see how we could comfortably bring about a workable partnership between their scientific projects and our own because the scope of their investigative goals is different from ours. To put it in the affirmative: the self psychological approach is not restricted to the clinical situation but is equally useful when applied to the complex activities of man in the social and historical arena. That self psychology can be as productive in its scrutiny of man in society as it is with regard to its investigations of man's individual development in health and in disease will not be doubted by anyone who read the contributions to "Self Psychology and the Sciences of Man"—I will remind you only of the fine use to which Kligerman put the theory of a transference of creativity in his contribution (and, I will add, in his recent work in general) and of Strozier's thorough and perceptive review of the self psychological insights that are already proving valuable to the psychohistorian. By contrast, I can see no way by which the findings of the aforementioned modern contributors, be they predominantly observers of normal development or investigators of psychopathology, can shed much light on, let us say, man in history—unless, by a tour de force, one claims that Klein and Kernberg, by stressing man's basic aggressive-

HEINZ KOHUT

destructive propensity, share Freud's outlook on the problem of
historical man (cf., in particular, *Civilization and Its Discontents*
[1930] and "Why War?" [1933]) or that Mahler's descriptions of
normal development point to a conception of man that is in harmony with the more optimistic outlook on civilization that is
generally identified as belonging to the world view of the political
liberal and the era of enlightenment.

And how about Freud and classical analysis? Despite the fact
that I consider psychoanalytic self psychology not only as being
part of analysis but indeed as lying in its very center, I do not see
how we could achieve an integration, in the usual sense of the
word, between this new step in psychoanalysis and the steps that
preceded it. Neither is it possible, to my mind, to achieve an integration of psychoanalytic id psychology and psychoanalytic ego
psychology, however great the yield of findings and explanations
provided by both approaches to the same field of investigation.
Certainly, the reasons I gave above with regard to our inability to
integrate the findings and theories of various other modern schools
with the findings and theories of psychoanalytic self psychology
cannot be adduced to explain our inability to integrate our findings
with those considered to constitute the mainstream of psychoanalysis out of which self psychology has evolved. Freud considered psychoanalysis as an encompassing psychology — just as we
do with regard to self psychology — and he thought that the therapeutic application of the science he had created was but a small
branch which, in his opinion, would retain its usefulness for only a
limited span of time. Although we do not share Freud's pessimism
with regard to the viability of depth-psychological therapy, we
completely agree with him that psychoanalysis, including, and par
excellence, self psychology, must also be employed outside the
clinical setting and that, potentially, it can make some of its most
important contributions in this area. The reason, therefore, why
self psychology and classical analysis are not suitable for simple integration with each other is not, as was true with regard to the
modern schools that I mentioned before, that the two enterprises
are of unequal breadth. Instead, even though self psychology and
classical analysis both move within broadly encompassing frame-

works, they aim at different aspects of man. Classical analysis sees man as conflict-ridden, struggling between submission to and rebellion against the pressures of civilization. Self psychology sees man *in addition* as a center of independent initiative, as a psychological organization held together by a self whose nuclear program (determining his potential destiny) he attempts to fulfill in the course of his life. As far as I can judge, these two approaches are not suitable for integration, at least not with the conceptual means that are at our disposal at this time. They are not mutually exclusive, however, but complementary, just as id psychology and ego psychology are complementary. Thus, both inside and outside the clinical setting, the analyst's outlook must shift from one viewpoint to the other — from focusing on the problems of Guilty Man to focusing on the problems of Tragic Man; and from focusing on the problems of Tragic Man back to those of Guilty Man — whenever the nature of the subject matter requires, as it normally does, that a choice be made.

Having said this much, it is important to acknowledge that the extensions introduced by modern ego psychology, in general, and by Hartmann's towering intellect, in particular, went a step in the direction in which self psychology is now moving. Hartmann's interest in problems of adaptation (1939a) which led him to the hypothesis of a conflict-free sphere in the ego and to the correlated hypotheses of the ego's primary and secondary autonomy — its innately determined growth, on the one hand, and its ability to disentangle itself from the inter- and intrasystemic conflicts that had interfered with its functions, on the other hand — contained the acknowledgment that, at least as concerned theory, a near-exclusive focus on conflict and disease stood in the way of fulfilling Freud's hope that psychoanalysis would ultimately become a comprehensive psychology. Still, even though ego psychology produced some beautiful general statements on mental health (Hartmann, 1939b) and even though Erikson, the most widely known among the modern psychoanalytic investigators of the psychological field outside the clinical setting, considered himself an ego psychologist, the actual influence of the conceptual framework of ego psychology in the applied field was severely limited by the fact that Hartmann's hypotheses still concerned an apparatus, i.e., the mental apparatus, and not a self. It is psychoanalytic self psychology which has hypothesized the existence of a core self consisting of nuclear ambitions, nuclear skills and talents, and nuclear idealized goals and has thus explained the fact that the human self is poised toward the future. The dynamic tension of the program laid down in our nuclear self strives toward realization and thus gives to each of us a specific destiny that we either fulfill, partially fulfill, or fail to fulfill in the course of our lives. It is this hypothesis of a central program that makes up the core of each person's self, an "action-poised programme arched in the field between his nuclear ambitions and ideals" (Kohut & Wolf, 1978), which also differentiates the self of analytic self psychology from Erikson's concept of "identity." The latter term, as I have discussed before (see Kohut, 1968, pp. 471n–472n), represents the point of convergence between the developed self and the sociocultural position of the individual. Its acquisition and firming (in adolescence and early adulthood) is but one of the series of leading psychosocial tasks that the individual confronts at various crucial developmental junctures during his life. Neither Erikson's "identity" nor the self of the ego psychologists of the New York school are, therefore, the self of analytic self psychology — they do not take into account the existence of a core program that points into the future and is responsible for the fact — the empirically ascertainable fact, I would add — that the personality of human beings has dimensions that are not only "beyond the pleasure principle" but also "beyond adaptation."

But let me now, after explaining some of the differences between the findings and theories of the modern ego psychologists and those obtained by the psychoanalytic self psychologists, tell you also that I feel that our work is a continuation of their work. And I want to stress in particular that I am grateful to Hartmann because his work gave me the courage to move further along the road that his acknowledgment of the legitimacy of analytic interest in healthy functions had opened. And even though I know from many personal discussions with him that he could not have accepted the "psychology of the self in the broad sense" with which we are now working, I am very happy that he still read the manuscript of my *Analysis of the Self* (1971) and gave it his approval.

There is, of course, a great deal of difference between the expression of a feeling of general kinship with the work of our predecessors and agreement with the details of their work. Advances in science are often motivated by dissatisfaction with previous findings and theories. Thus I must admit that, even before I began to move from mental-apparatus psychology toward an independent, complementary psychology of the self, I felt dissatisfied with certain deficiencies, as I then judged them, in Hartmann's conceptualizations. What I have in mind here — a feature, by the way, which I believe to be in part responsible for the lack of impact that Hartmann's work had outside of the area of theory itself — is the fact that his concept of a conflict-free sphere from which adaptive behavior emanates was too restricted, even within the confines of mental-apparatus psychology. To state my objection in terms that I have used when I discussed the question of the differentiation of psychoanalytically informed psychotherapy from psychoanalysis proper: the conflict-free sphere is a segmental, not a sectorial, concept. I tried, myself, in the past to remedy this deficiency by introducing the concept of an "area of progressive neutralization" (see Kohut, 1961, pp. 310n–311n; Kohut & Seitz, 1963, p. 368) and by adding the concept of "ego dominance" to that of "ego autonomy" (Kohut, 1971, p. 187; Kohut, 1972, pp. 620–621). Still, even with these emendations, the outlook of ego psychology differs decisively from that of self psychology. Even if, in other words, the former is enriched by the postulate of a conflict-free sphere in depth, it still continues to focus only on the problems of Guilty Man. And, furthermore, regardless of whether the conflict-free sphere is conceptualized as segmental or sectorial by ego psychology, mental health, to return to our specific example, will be evaluated by it against the background of the presence or absence of endopsychic conflict or of its location and extent. Whether or not conflicts interfere with adaptation is the question asked by modern ego psychology, and indeed this is the only yardstick that is at its disposal concerning this issue. The problems of Tragic Man — his inability to function even in the absence of conflicts; his

ability to fulfill his destiny even in the presence of conflicts — can
only be approached via the road opened by self psychology. As
was true for ego psychology up to 1926 when Freud made his last
major contribution to this new step in psychoanalysis, so also for
the modern editions of ego psychology: lacking the concept of a
self that has a nuclear program, they, too, cannot accommodate
Tragic Man and his successes and failures within their framework.

But now, despite the fascination which the application of
depth-psychological knowledge to the nonclinical areas has always
held for me, I must leave this discussion. In concluding, I would
only add that, however great my enthusiasm for the applied field
may be, and however great my expectations concerning the contribution that self psychology will make to the applied field in the
future, I have not forgotten that, at least for the present, there is
no more reliable test for the validity of the claim that self psychology enriches the psychoanalytic armamentarium by adding its
insights to those of classical analysis than the clinical situation. It
is the clinical situation that has in the past provided psychoanalysis
with the most reliable data concerning Guilty Man — and it is the
clinical situation that will now provide psychoanalysis, enriched by
the complementary viewpoint of self psychology, with the most
reliable data concerning Tragic Man.

I have now come to the end of my comments on the contributions to *Advances in Self Psychology*. Although the length of my
remarks, and the variety of topics they touched on, might seem to
call for a final synthesis, I will not attempt to summarize what I
have said. Instead, in closing, I will share with you some of my
thoughts and feelings about the position of the psychoanalytic psychology of the self at this point in time.

There can be no doubt that our findings and theories have
found many supporters who praise the usefulness of our ideas,
both in therapy and in the field "beyond the bounds of the basic
rule." And there can be equally no doubt that our findings and
theories have aroused a good deal of antagonism, directed not
only toward our experience-distant formulations but also at our
clinical approach.

Within certain limits I have no quarrel with either acceptance or rejection. Both attitudes stimulate thought and, via the back and forth of the debate, will help clarify the issues that are at stake. With particular reference to those who disagree with us, I can say no more than that my co-workers and I welcome their criticism and know that it is good for us to be exposed to it. Once the smoke raised by the exchange of arguments and counterarguments has cleared, all who had been involved in the dispute emerge as beneficiaries if the issues have been discussed in the truth-seeking spirit of science by sincere, serious-minded opponents.

But as psychologists with a bent for history, we cannot disregard the fact that both those who reject our outlook as well as those who accept it are under the influence of certain emotional forces. These forces emanate from specific psychological constellations which, when evaluated from a psychohistorical point of view, arise characteristically during the early stages of the dissemination of new sets of ideas.

It will hardly surprise you to hear from me now, as I attempt to assess the present situation and future prospects of self psychology, that among the emotional factors that fuel the controversies concerning our work and make them at times less useful and enjoyable than they should be, the narcissistic ones are the most powerful—in both friend and foe.

The friends, their imagination stimulated by the thought that they belong to a group of pioneers, are exhilarated by the apparent ease with which discoveries in previously unexplored territories are made. They may thus tend not only to be overly enthusiastic but also a bit arrogant and cliquish. The first attitude can be considered as a forgivable shortcoming. The second, however, is a much more weighty fault, not only because it may dissuade us from giving critical arguments the careful hearing they deserve, but also, and especially, because it diminishes our ability to think ourselves into the shoes of our adversaries, to recognize that most of them are not prompted by any base motives in their criticism of our ideas but by what they believe to be justifiable concern about the future of psychoanalysis, and to react to this group of opponents not by coldness and withdrawal but by continuing the debate with them.

And the foes? Again, whether they attack us via the distortion of what we have said and via the exaggeration of minor or peripheral flaws in our communications, or whether their opposition is transacted fairly, I have little doubt that their antagonism toward us is often intensified by narcissistic motivations, in particular by the wish to injure or debase us because they experience our ideas as a threat to their narcissistic equilibrium. Ever since they became psychoanalysts, many of them may have derived an important part of their self-esteem and inner security from their identification with the psychoanalytic professional community. And insofar as this community is still regarded as "a movement" by them, i.e., insofar as their identification with the group is maintained by a shared scientific ideology (including par excellence the uplifting sense of living up to the demands of a face-the-truth-courageously morality, as I pointed out earlier) and by a shared devotion to an idealized leader-figure, new ideas which question the unalterability of the basic scientific tenets or set limits to the validity or the relevance of the idealized teacher-figure's scientific formulations will be perceived instinctively as inimical because they seem to diminish the power of the group and thus secondarily to diminish the sense of strength that its members derive from it.

Although these are reactions that will be felt by the members of all sciences who are shaken by the introduction of a new point of view, it must be admitted that analysts may be especially susceptible to them. Still, I am aiming my remarks at a broad social phenomenon of which certain aspects of the opposition that we are encountering are only a specific example, and I would like to stress in particular that I am not focusing here on the antagonism toward us that is an outgrowth of individual envy or competitiveness. These latter motivations too are no doubt activated and they may lead to various forms of attacks on our work and us. (In a number of instances they appear, understandably enough, to arise in individuals who, in the past, had almost come to our findings and conclusions but had then shied away from them, unable to commit themselves clearly and openly to them as, I must confess, had been the case with me for all to many years). But, however temporarily upsetting to us the often dramatic manifestations of such individual attacks may be, they are not as important as the discomfort about our ideas that affects the responses of the psychoanalytic community as a whole.

What then can we expect from the future? Will our discoveries be accepted for the benefit of the patients who undergo treatment, whether in the form of psychotherapy or in the form of analysis? Will our ideas take hold?

Although I realize as I mentioned before that my personal bias, my personal hopes and fears, may interfere with my objectivity, I will give you my assessment of what the future holds in store for us. To begin with, I expect with a good deal of confidence that our discoveries and ideas will take hold. Whatever the present shortcomings of our theories, I have no doubt that, on the whole, they are not only valid but, of even greater importance, by comparison with the yield in insight derived from previous explanatory systems in depth psychology, they supply vastly more significant explanations of the phenomena that are actually encountered by the psychoanalyst, both inside and outside his office, i.e., as regards our patients in therapy and as regards man in vivo.

I am less certain that we will get credit for having made an important contribution to the progress of psychology, in particular to the progress of psychoanalysis. Two processes, going on at the same time, might obviate our receiving this recognition. I am referring to the fact that, while openly and by direct reference our work will be rejected, concurrently the ideas in our work will be accepted by infiltrating clinical practice and by bringing about a gradual shift in the point of view of those who work "beyond the bounds of the basic rule." Should this indeed be our fate, as it may well be, I admit, reluctantly, that it would be disappointing.

Of course this may not happen, especially in the long run. As I have noted, the forces that sustain the inner balance of the analytic profession at the present time may make it hard for the majority of my colleagues to accept the fact that new ideas and even a radical change in emphasis can be introduced into the psychology of complex mental states without endangering the important "sense of the historical continuity of the group self in the psycho-analytic community" (see Kohut, 1977b, p. 937). Future genera-tions, however, despite the conservative influence of the training-analysis system (which I consider irreplaceable but also im-provable), may feel more generous toward us. They will point out that some of our ideas have been around before us: in secretly car-ried out clinical application, in footnotes and innuendos in the professional literature, and in the work of the latter-day precursors of our work who, retrospectively reinterpreting their writings, make either open priority claims or imply, subtly or not so subtly, that they have been here before. Nonetheless, they will acknowl-edge that it was still our small group of psychoanalytic self psychologists that began to collect comprehensively the data on which self psychology is based, to formulate them systematically, and, last but not least, to bear the emotional hardship of pre-senting them openly and unmistakably. And this is, in fact, the stuff out of which discovery has, at all times, been made.

Let me come to the end on a note of confidence by making two comments concerning psychoanalytic self psychology: one ob-jective and scientific, the other personal and emotional but not less valid than the first.

The first remark concerns my observation that the very con-tents of our contributions, the lessons that we learned from them and applied to our own lives, have, in their effect on us, been of assistance in dealing with the criticisms of our work made by many of our colleagues in the psychoanalytic literature. If what we have discovered does indeed throw new light on the phenomena studied by psychoanalysis, then communicating it to our professional col-leagues and to the broader scientific and intellectually perceptive community will produce changes. However great the overt rejec-tion to which Freud's discoveries were exposed, they exerted, I think, some fundamental changes: witness the lessening of hypoc-risy vis-à-vis sex and aggression in human life, and witness fur-thermore (though here the influence of Freud's teachings is less ob-vious and the causal connection more open to doubt) the lessening of intergenerational distrust in consequence of our increased understanding of the oedipal tensions in childhood.

The early insights, however, did not help the pioneers to deal with some of the psychological maladies to which the professional relationships between analysts were exposed in the pioneering days — precisely in the areas where the insights supplied by self psychology are most effective. It is touching to see, for example, how Freud tried to handle the tensions between himself and some of his early followers, in particular those who ultimately broke away from him, by interpreting their oedipal conflicts to them. And it is even more touching to see how the very individuals who turned against Freud and ultimately broke away from him tried to stem the tide of antagonism that was welling up in them by confronting their negative father transference. What was missing, or what was only tangentially recognized at the time, were the narcissistic issues, with particular reference to those who, having temporarily filled the defects in their self via their idealization of Freud, subsequently tried to move away from him, attempting to fulfill the program that was embedded in their nuclear self. It would be a fascinating task to reexamine these heartbreaking early quarrels and dissensions that resulted in the loss to psychoanalysis of perhaps some of the most gifted of Freud's early students and friends. And it would be a fascinating task to examine whether, and if so how, the very unresolved narcissism of the dissidents became the topic they tried to investigate — whether, and if so how, they tried to master the tensions that they could not resolve endopsychically by dealing with them in their scientific work.

Are we still as helpless vis-à-vis group dissension as the pioneers? I do not believe so. True, we have our tensions and they have brought about phenomena that parallel those that appeared in the early days. But I also think that self psychology has given us an instrument that allows us to react with more equanimity and reasonableness and that the consequences of tensions and subsequent social rifts are therefore less deleterious. We believe, in other words, that, at least in the long run, we will be able to deal better with the narcissistic wounds that we suffer because we are supported by the insights provided to us by the psychoanalytic psychology of the self. In particular we should be able to escape from falling victim to chronic narcissistic rage with all its dele-

terious consequences and react instead with that appropriate mixture of accepting the inevitable, on the one hand, and of expressing healthy anger, on the other, which characterizes those
who have mastered their narcissistic vulnerability.

I have not forgotten that I promised an ultimate personal
statement concerning the problems confronting the self
psychologist as he contemplates the present state and the future
prospects of this new development in psychoanalysis. What I still
wanted to say is this: external acceptance, whether inside or outside of organized psychoanalysis, should not be considered our
primary goal. While we should, from our side, make every attempt
to communicate our findings and thoughts in such a way that they
have an optimal chance of being understood and ultimately, we
hope, welcomed by the community of scholars, our deepest
gratification must always come from the realization that we were
lucky enough to have participated in the growth of science, from
the realization that we have had the exhilarating experience, in all
its freshness, of seeing new territory and of taking a few steps into
it. The support that this experience has given us in the past will
also sustain us in the future. And the independence that we derive
from it is not an outgrowth of arrogance and contemptuous isolation, not what used to be called "narcissistic" in that pejorative
sense against which we have fought now for many years, but is
based on the inner security and sense of fulfillment that testify to
the presence of a healthy productive-creative self.

References

Abraham, H. & Freud, E., eds. (1965), *A Psycho-Analytic Dialogue: The Letters
of Sigmund Freud and Karl Abraham,* trans. B. Marsh & H. Abraham. New
York: Basic Books.
Erikson, E. (1950), *Childhood and Society,* rev. ed. New York: Norton, 1963.
Freud, S. (1914), On the History of the Psycho-Analytic Movement. *Standard
Edition,* 14:7–66. London: Hogarth Press, 1957.
_____ (1926), Inhibitions, Symptoms and Anxiety. *Standard Edition,*
20:87–174. London: Hogarth Press, 1959.
_____ (1930), Civilization and Its Discontents. *Standard Edition,* 21:64–145.
London: Hogarth Press, 1961.
_____ (1933), Why War? *Standard Edition,* 22:199–215. London: Hogarth
Press, 1964.
Goldberg, A., ed. (1978), *The Psychology of the Self: A Casebook.* New York:

International Universities Press.

Hartmann, H. (1939a), *Ego Psychology and the Problem of Adaptation.* New York: International Universities Press, 1958.

_____ (1939b), Psychoanalysis and the Concept of Health. In: *Essays on Ego Psychology:* New York: International Universities Press, 1964, pp. 3–18.

_____ (1950), Comments on the Psychoanalytic Theory of the Ego. In: *Essays on Ego Psychology.* New York: International Universities Press, 1964, pp. 113–141.

_____ (1960), Towards a Concept of Mental Health. *Brit. J. Med. Psychol.,* 33:243–248.

Jahoda, M. (1958), *Current Concepts of Positive Mental Health.* New York: Basic Books.

Kohut, H. (1959), Introspection, Empathy, and Psychoanalysis. In: *The Search for the Self,* vol. 1, ed. P. Ornstein. New York: International Universities Press, 1978, pp. 205–232.

_____ (1961), Discussion of "The Unconscious Fantasy" by David Beres. In: *The Search for the Self,* vol. 1, ed. P. Ornstein. New York: International Universities Press, 1978, pp. 309–318.

_____ (1968), The Evaluation of Applicants for Psychoanalytic Training. In: *The Search for the Self,* vol. 1, ed. P. Ornstein. New York: International Universities Press, 1978, pp. 461–475.

_____ (1970), Psychoanalysis in a Troubled World. In: *The Search for the Self,* vol. 2, ed. P. Ornstein. New York: International Universities Press, 1978, pp. 511–546.

_____ (1971), *The Analysis of the Self.* New York: International Universities Press.

_____ (1972), Thoughts on Narcissism and Narcissistic Rage. In: *The Search for the Self,* vol. 1, ed. P. Ornstein. New York: International Universities Press, 1978, pp. 615–658.

_____ (1973a), The Future of Psychoanalysis. In: *The Search for the Self,* vol. 2, ed. P. Ornstein. New York: International Universities Press, 1978, pp. 663–684.

_____ (1973b), The Psychoanalyst in the Community of Scholars. In: *The Search for the Self,* vol. 2, ed. P. Ornstein. New York: International Universities Press, 1978, pp. 685–724.

_____ (1976), Creativeness, Charisma, Group Psychology: Reflections on the Self-Analysis of Freud. In: *The Search for the Self,* vol. 2, ed. P. Ornstein. New York: International Universities Press, 1978, pp. 793–843.

_____ (1977a), *The Restoration of the Self.* New York: International Universities Press.

_____ (1977b), The Search for the Analyst's Self. In: *The Search for the Self,* vol. 2, ed. P. Ornstein. New York: International Universities Press, 1978, pp. 931–938.

_____ (1979), The Two Analyses of Mr. Z. *Internat. J. Psycho-Anal.,* 60:3–27.

_____ & Seitz, P. (1963), Concepts and Theories of Psychoanalysis. In: *The Search for the Self,* vol. 1, ed. P. Ornstein. New York: International Universities Press, 1978, pp. 337–374.

_____ & Wolf, E. (1978), The Disorders of the Self and Their Treatment: An Outline. *Internat. J. Psycho-Anal.,* 59:413–426.

Lynch, D. (1979), *Yeats — The Poetics of the Self.* Chicago: University of Chicago Press.

Matussek, P. (1971), *Die Konzentrationslagerhaft und ihre Folgen.* Berlin: Springer.

Sander, L. (1975), Infant and Caretaking Environment. In: *Explorations in Child Psychiatry,* ed. E. J. Anthony. New York: Plenum.

Index